"I am delighted at the collaborative ven
Two minds, thinking alike, bringing their
analysis of human culture has resulted in a fir.
Strohmer shake our complacency, challenge our philosophy, and transform our vision.
Their book offers a detailed investigation of how a biblical perspective can be developed
and applied in many areas of modern life, including the ones which Christians often
neglect. It is a thoughtful, probing work, but never dull. Those who like ideas but
dislike ostentatious erudition will feel completely at home. The illustrations are aptly
chosen and well developed, and its highly engaging style will make the most complex
analysis accessible to a wide audience. I wish the book every success."
Dr. Elaine Storkey
President of Tearfund, *author, BBC broadcaster*

"It is said that when Aldous Huxley read Jacques Ellul's *The Technological Society*,
he quickly started organizing house study groups to work through its contents and
plumb the depths of its implications. He would say that Ellul had said everything he
wanted to say in his *Brave New World*. Rarely had a book so riled and enthused. I
would posit that John Peck's and Charles Strohmer's *Uncommon Sense* warrants
matching enthusiasms. Thoughtful Christians and pagans would be served to
investigate its contents in similar study groups. This would be the best setting for
processing the carefully unfolded arguments of its authors, witnessing the possibility
of communal awakenings and joint commitments to faithfully integrate the wisdom
of God in our commitments to the world of human culture."
Paul Patton
Assistant Professor of Performing Arts, Hampton University

"This book will be an invaluable guide for anyone interested in thinking through
how Christian teachings might be applied to life in the world at the start of the 21st
century. Based on a careful analysis of contemporary culture, and rooted in a
sympathetic reading of key biblical texts, it explores issues as diverse as new physics,
corporate management, feminism, theology, pluralism, and much more, and proposes
radical solutions to many of today's significant issues. Not every reader will agree
with all the authors say, but no one will fail to be informed and challenged by their
arguments. Essential reading for anyone wrestling with how the Gospel can be applied
in sensitive and relevant ways to the concerns of everyday life and work."
John Drane
Head of Practical Theology, University of Aberdeen
Adjunct Professor, Fuller Seminary

"I remember John Peck leading communion at Greenbelt and reminding us that
in crisis times we should not be nostalgic and simply go back to the 'good old days' of
the 1950s. We should go back radically, to the roots of our being and our beliefs. This
book seeks to do just that. This thorough manual is more contentful than Tony
Campolo, more up to date than C.S. Lewis, and more disciplined and ordered than
John Smith! It recognizes that all wisdom is relational. It does not address the truth as

an abstract but as a living process of interaction with reality. The authors have taken culture, the Bible, the truth, God, you the reader seriously.

"Their contribution creates a tapestry whereby the threads of philosophy, theology, ethics, psychology, anthropology, and communication are woven together. We are shown the difference between mere knowledge and true wisdom, between assuming the right answers and asking the right questions. We are not so much told what to conclude but how to reach sane, human, godly conclusions. Basic questions and faulty assumptions are dealt with, such that we recognize that our relationship to truth is a responsible one whereby we do not simply know about something, but we are known by and embraced by the truth. The material will be useful to the expert and the amateur.

"These two brothers have given me a contemporary response to timeless issues. They have eminently shown us how to unpack wisdom and be changed by it. I think the book is utterly different to anything else on the market."

John Smith, Ph.D
author, culture observer, former "Bishop to the Counterculture"

"Few theologians grasp the complexity of issues pertaining to the arts, and their wider roots in contemporary culture. Seeing John Peck in action since 1986 at rock fests like Cornerstone and Greenbelt, and sharing panels with him at European arts conferences or academic settings at places like Cambridge University, I would have to celebrate this theologian's contribution to the entire conversation—the whole ball of wax, including the arts, philosophy, the sciences, law, and theology. Put his fifty years as an itinerant lecturer into quotation marks, mix in Charles Strohmer's finesse, and you have this book.

"Peck and Strohmer are uncommonly sensible, and they apply a level eye to concerns that often become distorted by doctrinal fealty rather than being creative wholistic responses to history in the making. Just as Jesus did, even on the Cross, they will choose a measured response to the culture rather than a screaming reaction to its many and varied ills. The response they proffer here will allow Christians, upon understanding it, to interact with the world rather than reject it from the safe, cosy corners.

"The fact that *Uncommon Sense* had to be self-published is a strike for freedom of thought and creative intellectual discourse, the likes of which have not been seen since Francis Schaeffer first opened L'Abri in the 1950s. Peck's been having a fifty year dialogue with the world in his attempt to love it; he deserves his disciples, and they in turn deserve a place at his feet—though the very notion of it would make him pale. This book is that place. It has every possibility of becoming a classic without losing its teeth in the face of current culture. This is because it is, fundamentally, an exercise in wisdom, and in love. It is not a book that one reads, absorbs, and then wears like yesterday's fashion. What is Christ-like about this book is its Christ-inspired vitality in everyday applications, and its relevance to every individual regardless of his or her station, profession, and age in life."

Karen L. Mulder
Arts editor, Christianity Today
Professor of Art and Art History, Union University

Uncommon Sense

By the Same Authors

What the Bible Teaches about the Holy Spirit (John Peck)
Wisdom in the Marketplace (John Peck)

What Your Horoscope Doesn't Tell You (Charles Strohmer)
Wise as a Serpent, Harmless as a Dove (Charles Strohmer)
Explaining the Grace of God (Charles Strohmer)
Building Bridges to the New Age World (Charles Strohmer)
The Gospel and the New Spirituality (Charles Strohmer)
America's Fascination with Astrology (Charles Strohmer)

Uncommon Sense

God's Wisdom for Our Complex and Changing World

John Peck & Charles Strohmer

Published in Great Britain in 2001 by
Society for Promoting Christian Knowledge
Holy Trinity Church
Marylebone Road
London NW1 4DU

First published in the United States of America in 2000 by The Wise Press, PO Box 4325, Sevierville, Tennessee 37864, USA.

Scripture quotations, unless otherwise noted in the text, are taken from the *Holy Bible, New International Version* (NIV), copyright © 1973 by International Bible Society. Other translations referenced are: the *New American Standard Bible* (NASB), copyright © 1960 by the Lockman Foundation; the *Revised Standard Version* (RSV), copyright © 1946 by the Division of Christian Education of the National Council of Churches of Christ in the U.S.A.; the *Authorized King James Version* (KJV, or AV); *Today's English Version* (TEV), copyright © 1966 American Bible Society; the *New English Bible* (NEB), copyright © 1961 Oxford University Press & Cambridge University Press; *J. B. Phillips Translation* (Phillips); *James Moffatt Translation* (Moffatt); the *Jerusalem Bible*; the *John Knox Bible* (Knox).

British Library Cataloguing-in-Publication Data

A catalogue record for this book is available from the British Library

ISBN 0-281-05428-2

Printed in Great Britain by
Antony Rowe Ltd, Chippenham, Wiltshire

The more I read the Bible
as a secular book, the more holy it becomes.
John Peck

Acknowledgments

Besides our colleagues, friends, and families, who have been especially supportive over the years, the authors wish to thank the many churches and organizations who have invited us in, and who, along with all the countless "anonymous" persons we have met in our travels, have sharpened our thinking. You're probably in this book somewhere!

In particular, John Peck would like to thank the Greenbelt people, who gave him practical encouragement, and Trinity Church in Livonia, Michigan, for giving him the time to get the writing done on the original manuscript during his year in-residence. Charles Strohmer would like to thank all those who provided ideas and insights over the phone when help was needed. And both authors send their grateful appreciation to those who endorsed the book.

We also want to acknowledge several persons who provided technical support or who gave a good deal of their time to sort out key phases of this book's five-year developmental process: Phil White, David Booker, Neil Silverberg, and Mitch Moore. And Chris Bourne. The last shall be first. What would we have done without *you*? You're wonderful.

Uncommon Sense:

God's Wisdom for Our Complex and Changing World

John Peck & Charles Strohmer

Book Abstract

Christians cannot faithfully meet the radical questions and crises that beset life today without an adequate understanding of how the world and human culture works. The only satisfactory framework of thought for this is the one which underlies the Gospel; that is, a biblical one. This is largely what the Bible means by "the wisdom of God." Since we have for generations neglected the wisdom of God in our commitments to the world of human culture, we are unwittingly working largely with sub-biblical frameworks of thought. So we need to catch up. For many of us, this is going to demand that we unlearn inadequate ways of thinking and living and relearn a biblical wisdom by means of a philosophy of which Jesus Christ is the Heart and Foundation. With this as the goal, this book offers a wide variety of illustrations from across the spectrum of biblical and present-day life.

Contents

Chapter 1. Transforming Our Vision

The issues of a new age have been forced upon us, and Christians are engaging the public like never before. But their views are not engaging. • A wisdom for "saving souls" is not enough. The Gospel must reach into the structures and systems themselves. • Several kinds of traditional christian wisdom and activism are failing to affect the structures. A new paradigm is needed, one that understands the structures and the *process* of wisdom development. • We must start thinking about the long-term goal of building up a biblical wisdom for public life that becomes instinctive.

Chapter 2. Healing a Generational Debility

Because the Bible slides past our eyes with a "stained glass window effect, " we have great difficulty believing that God is involved in "secular" life just as seriously as He is in "religious" life. • We have a wisdom that treats the Bible as a religious and moral book only. It does not see the Bible as instructive for areas such as technological advances, university campuses, economic developments, scientific debates, artistic expression, foreign policy, or welfare reform. • Much anecdotal evidence reveals that the issues of a new age continually expose the weaknesses of our privatized pietism. • The wisdom of the "separated life" has caused much mischief in our missions, politics, arts, work, and homes. It hamstrings our efforts to offer sensible and forcible solutions to society's "non-religious" problems. It cripples our response to Western culture's paradigm shift. • Two troublesome words: "religious" and "secular." • Jesus, and God's Old and New Testament people, were raised in a wisdom that saw life as a whole and God equally involved in all of its aspects.

Chapter 3. Present-day Life in the Old Testament

Secular life is important to the Lord, and Scripture is replete with instruction for it, even as it applies to non-Christians. Why have we missed this? • Entire books of the Old Testament are much more "secular" than "religious." • The Bible uses a "secular" word for "God," *elohim*, and it gives us wisdom for ecological concerns, courtroom testimony, business psychology, medical matters, social justice, diplomacy, and many other areas. • Such ideas in the Book do not seem relevant to the complexities of Western life because we: give them religious meanings, or look in them for moral lessons only, or allegorize them. • Determining what kind of biblical literature we are dealing with, and handling it accordingly.

Chapter 4. Interpreting the Bible's Secular Writings

God's creation is multi-aspected. It cannot be understood in religious and moral categories only. It includes many secular aspects. • Jesus and the early Church used the Old Testament for instruction in non-religious matters. • The Bible's wisdom literature can help us successfully even in today's complex secular life because: it has close associations with those outside God's covenant; it majors on creation and on human conditions shared by everyone; its stories usually surround public affairs; its ideas share the same basic logic with the Gospel, which is for all times and all places, as an anti-racist story in the New Testament reveals. • If we do not have a wisdom for secular life based on the fear of the Lord, then one based on the fear of another god takes over. This is largely our situation today, as an illustration from the world of christian business indicates.

Chapter 5. Wisdom and Communication Breakdowns

How the Bible sees "wisdom," and what it means by that word. • Why the authors emphasize "wisdom" rather than "worldview." • There are different kinds of wisdom, and God's wisdom has a different "starting point" from other wisdoms. • A working definition for "wisdom," and examples of how the term "wisdom" helps us see the link between theory and practice, ideas and actions, beliefs and behaviors. • A humorous cross-cultural example (American photographer and Japanese father) shows how different wisdoms can be mutually unintelligible, because their basic assumptions are different, and how this causes communication failures and affects people's behavior. • One's wisdom is not "a personal thing" but to a large degree a product of the culture in which one has been reared. • The Story of Naboth's Vineyard illustrates how different wisdoms are based on the fear of different gods and how this influences the political and the economic aspects of life.

Chapter 6. How Do We Get and Change Our Wisdom?

We normally get our wisdom like we pick up our mother tongue, from childhood, we simply absorb it from those around us as we go along, especially from authority figures. • One's culture affirms one's wisdom and subtly influences people with the culture's ideals, as the "hidden message" of any cereal box indicates. • Identifying the "gods" of a particular wisdom, and why we take so much of our culture's wisdom for granted. • We must learn a new wisdom if we have absorbed a faulty one. Changes are difficult and may be triggered by crises or by alternative lifestyles.

Chapter 7. Theories and the Bible's Strangeness

One's wisdom copes with new phenomena and circumstances by calling on the theories within it for help. A humorous illustration from the British game of "bowls" shows how wrong theories can cause great mischief. • Our theories help us cope with everyday life, as a story from South America indicates. An illustration from the world of Western science reveals how our theories relate to our wisdom. • We use theories all the time, and the wisdom of Scripture can help us develop better theories for the complexities of Western life. This becomes possible as we learn from the Bible's "basic ingredients," and from its styles and methods of communication, and by studying its "strangeness." • Discipleship of this sort means giving ourselves space and permission to experiment and to make mistakes.

Part Two: Getting the Lay of the Land

Chapter 8. Weaknesses in the Evangelical Attitude to Social Problems

Challenges faced when using scriptural resources to address issues in a mixed, pluralistic, society. • Shared moral standards can be used, especially in the West, where there are special opportunities for this. But there are problems with the approach through morality alone. • Numerous illustrations from the Ten Commandments, especially when thinking about politics, government, and lawmaking, reveal difficulties for societies that do not share our christian convictions. • The Ten Commandments were not originally about a personal moral ideal to be attained but a sample of social legislation. • Getting at the *intent* of a Commandment is a key for legislation today.

Chapter 9. The Help and Limitation of Traditional Resources

Besides the Ten Commandments, Christians have other methods of applying moral standards to law and social concerns. • Illustrations from ideas surrounding love, the family, equality, and justice show how contemporary non-Christian ideas can bedevil our wisdom. • Criteria other than morality, such as psychology and sociology, must be included when addressing everyday life. Education is a case in point, as is the evolution-creation debate. But, again, nonbiblical ideas abound. • We must ask basic questions about what our cultures and the Bible mean by love, or the family, or justice, or education, or _____.

Chapter 10. Cultural Conditioning: Interpretation Then and Now

Further problems that our pluralistic situations present to the "ancient" wisdom of Scripture and to christian convictions today. • Get your interpretation of the Bible's secular wisdom wrong, and everything that follows from it suffers, as a bit of comic relief demonstrates. • Correct interpretation is decisive for the practical side of our wisdom. • One must learn to distinguish a permanent principle from its cultural expression, then and now. The biblical reference to women illustrates this. • Jesus' philosophical method with marriage and divorce shows us a way to develop sensible and forcible approaches to today's pluralistic situations. He distinguishes between moral law and laws for social behavior.

Chapter 11. The Bible and Multiple Parallel Explanations

A visit to Flatland reveals the limits of our imaginations and why this hinders learning biblical wisdom (two diagrams included). • The mischief of the "one-explanation" syndrome. Why multi-dimensional thinking is biblical, and vital for our wisdom. • A multi-dimensional way of reasoning about life is surprisingly evident in the question, "Why did the Israelites not occupy all the Promised Land immediately?" • The answer shows five, not just one or two, biblical reasons why. Each represents a different aspect, or dimension, of life (in this case, the technological, the sociological, the educative, the ecological, the faith-religious). How can all five explanations be true at once?

Chapter 12. The Different Dimensions of Jesus and God's Creation

God has ordered the world according to secular laws and principles, e.g., aesthetic, social, economic, political, each in its own way. • Multiple parallel explanations are built into Scripture and even into the Gospel itself. • An illustration from the Incarnation, and a telling illustration from cartography, show that reality has more dimensions that human reason can work with at one time. • The "mineral, plant, animal," paradigm as a simple example of thinking multi-dimensionally about life. • All of life's dimensions, or aspects, are reconciled in Jesus Christ the Lord. He is the one authority for the laws of all the aspects, even today. In him alone will our thinking about everyday life be coherent. • Many benefits arise from this way of reasoning. It opens life up to us, and is of immense help in the process of developing biblical wisdom for the issues of everyday life today.

Chapter 13. The Unity and Diversity of Creation

Two more diagrams expand the idea of multi-dimensional thinking and point toward a more sophisticated biblical model (to be developed in later chapters) of the unity, complexity, and diversity of God's multi-aspected creation. • There are numerous "lower" and "higher" aspects for everyday life, each having God's laws governing their existence. Human beings are especially subject to the higher aspects. • This model, called modal theory, helps us develop a fuller understanding for the wisdom we will need in the complexities of daily life. • Analyses of a wedding ring and a church service indicate the relationship of the aspects to one another, and to Jesus Christ. • Modal theory and analysis provides distinctively christian ways to study the arts, politics, education, economics, family life, and so on, and to develop biblical theories for contemporary secular issues.

Part Three: Re-engaging the Culture

Chapter 14. Sources for Wisdom and the Importance of Words

Several Psalms and other Old Testament passages illustrate three sources for cultivating godly wisdom: creation, culture, and Scripture. • Looking at life before "the Fall" and why we today misunderstand "mastery," "dominion," "subduing," "cultivating," "conserving" (Gen. 1:28; 2:15). • "Naming" (Gen 2:19-20) as a process of separating and distinguishing. How we use words and names to control and manage our world. • Asking basic questions about things is essential. • Our contemporary notion of "the family" illustrates language and meaning problems, and challenges our notion of the "nuclear family." • Building up a meaning of "family" from the wisdom of Scripture.

Chapter 15. The Relation of Present-day Names to Biblical Names

Sifting through the highly compressed, complex, and technical language of Western culture reveals the "basic ingredients" of life to which that language refers. These basic ingredients are found in Scripture, and they are indispensable for responding with a godly wisdom in our complicated world today. • Illustrations from "the business corporation" and "the state" show ways to use the basic ingredients, or ABCs, of Scripture today. • The *hows* and *whys* of the biblical writers. • Why our experts need the intelligent amateurs. • Answering objections to using Scripture this way. • A fresh understanding of Romans 12:1-2 shows how our mental patterns must change under the influence of Scripture.

Chapter 16. Using Theology and Doctrine to Learn Wisdom, Part 1

Christian theology and doctrine have hidden possibilities for moving us beyond religious issues to help us speak forcibly and sensibly in secular life. Government and the democratic ideal are highlighted. • The Doctrine of Creation has implications for evolution. • How the Doctrine of God as Father includes motherhood. • These doctrines give us godly wisdom today for male-female relations, parenting, the nuclear family, and gender-equality issues.

Chapter 17. Using Theology and Doctrine to Learn Wisdom, Part 2

The Doctrine of the Incarnation helps heal the split between the spiritual and the material. • Two meanings of "spiritual" in Scripture. • The Incarnation spotlights the spiritual meaning of the material world. • Jesus' way of reasoning: every aspect of human life is intended to be spiritual. • The godly effect that the Doctrines of Sin and Redemption can have on racism and multiculturalism, justice and punishment, and lawmaking. • The godly effect that the Doctrine of Grace can have on educational theory and employment policy. • A truly godly wisdom continually refers to Scripture.

Chapter 18. The Wisdom of Words, Part 1

Another means of entering secular life with biblical wisdom is through words and language. Builds on chapters 9 and 14. Words are pivotal in any culture. • The wisdom of the Bible profoundly affects the way Scripture uses some quite basic words, whose meanings in culture may diverge from Scripture's. • An exercise in analysis, using the basic words "truth" and "knowledge," reveals how our Western understanding of these words is freighted with the powerful connotations of "science," and as a consequence ignores key biblical notions. • Wrapped around this discussion is an easy to understand explanation of how to use the Hebrew language to tease out hidden, yet vital, biblical meanings of Old Testament words.

Chapter 19. The Wisdom of Words, Part 2

Language is the chief means of communicating values, ideas, and insights, and of getting things done. • Our current understanding of many words may mean that things are not getting done quite right. • Correcting present-day notions of words like "love" and "relationships." • The word "justice," in particular as it relates to crime and punishment, shows how the flavor of the Bible's meaning of words can penetrate our societies. • What happens when less-than-biblical ideas inform basic words in our societies? • A further look into using the Hebrew language to gain insight about the meaning of basic words.

Chapter 20. Journeying Deeper into the Process

Ideas from previous chapters are pulled together in a more systematic effort to learn a godly wisdom for all of life. • How modal theory helps in the development of more biblically sophisticated approaches to complex secular affairs. • Numerous characteristics in some controversial areas of education and government highlight the practical expressions of this process. • Evangelistic value of this kind of thinking.

Chapter 21. A Special Case: Art, the Necessary Luxury

Is art beside the point of everyday life? • Christians have obediences to fulfill before God, for His glory, in the long-neglected aesthetic aspect of life. • A thumbnail sketch of the verbal art forms in Scripture, such as poetry, storytelling, and parables, brings an appreciation of the aesthetic aspect into our wisdom. • Characteristics of art done by Christians, and the implications of such art. • Art takes us into a "let's pretend" world to help us make discoveries. • The prophet

Amos shows why even some religious art by Christians may stand under God's condemnation. • The relationship of art to a culture's wisdom. • Art as grace to people. • Modal analysis and a controversial illustration from television entertainment explains how Christians can appreciate the strengths of art done by non-Christians. • The connection between art and evangelization.

Part Four: Building the Future

Chapter 22. New Discoveries Can Be Intoxicating

Brief cautions regarding several common pitfalls that come with the excitement of new discoveries. • Exhortations about personal reliability, self-discipline, private devotions, respecting the text of Scripture, having space for both reasoning and miracles, and learning from one another, both now and in the future.

Chapter 23. Toward a Biblical Philosophy of Life

As students and older adults, we don't have time to absorb our wisdom from scratch, so we must learn it deliberately and fairly quickly. • This extended chapter focuses on characteristics necessary for a more systematic and thorough study, for those wishing to make more concerted efforts at developing a biblical Christian wisdom that is effective in everyday life. • Another aim is to become more conversant with modal thinking. • The material is written so as to be used alongside Appendix 1.

This chapter unfolds in six parts. Part 1: Philosophy as the grammar of a wisdom. • Part 2: Begin by asking basic questions. • Part 3: The significance of a wisdom's *Logos*. • Part 4: Creation, Fall, Redemption. • Part 5: An adventure in analysis. • Part 6: The Source, Channel, and Goal of everything.

Appendix 1

A more developed visual aid of modal theory, with annotations surveying numerous characteristics of all the law-aspects and the relationship of the aspects to each other. Ways to use modal theory under God in Christ through Scripture. • For use alongside chapter 23. • Anecdotes, comments, and illustrations about business theory are included as a means for learning general principles by which to adopt modal analysis in other disciplines, such as art, law, education, or politics. • Questions at the end of each aspect survey are offered to stimulate further thinking in a discipline along the lines of exploration that have been developed in *Uncommon Sense*.

Appendix 2

Conversation with John Peck.

Bibliography
Subject & Name Index
Scripture References Index
About the Authors
Special Recognitions Page

Getting the Most from This Book

This book is about the *process* of wisdom development, and the chapter material and methodology serve that process. That being so, *Uncommon Sense* is not laid out in the often typical way that examines the broad spectrum of life via chapter divisions such as Education, the Family, Politics, Science, the Arts, and So On. The way of reasoning about life found in *Uncommon Sense* is quite different from that, largely because it tries to follow how God's Old and New Testament people reasoned about life and applied that way of reasoning in everyday situations. Although this may seem a bit different from what we in the West are accustomed to today, it is meant to help us recognize the ancient Hebrew imagination and how God's wisdom influenced the people's daily obediences, and what the challenges of that are as we seek to cultivate a biblical wisdom for today.

Readers will recognize, therefore, that this is an active not a passive book. It has been written in a way that will trigger ideas to coax readers along in the process of wisdom development right then and there. One way to facilitate that process when it presents itself, and so to get more from this book and from your time, is simply not to be in a hurry. Stop and play around with the ideas, work them up prayerfully and with Scripture, however you wish, even in the company of others. *Uncommon Sense*, therefore, does not do your thinking for you; it helps you to think, especially about everyday life under God. The book is not meant to be a quick read, but a context in which to play around with ideas. From the third chapter on, especially, many readers may discover themselves wanting to reach for pen and paper. If that happens, reach.

Further, this book is for people in all walks of life, to help them develop a more biblical wisdom for their particular work and interests. To facilitate readers who wish to make concerted efforts in that direction, the authors have included a fairly exhaustive Subject & Name Index to be used topically like a *Strong's Concordance* might be used with a Bible. There are at least a couple ways readers may take advantage of this.

One way is to peruse that Index, finding and listing the terms of a particular area of interest, including terms that are only indirectly related, and investigate those places in the text. For instance, a person seeking wisdom in the arts would find the words amusement, joke, metaphor, picture language, stage, and symbolic in that Index. A person looking for wisdom in science might be interested in terms such as measurements, natural world, objectivity, subjectivity, and unbiased. Someone in business might play around with words such as buying and selling, costing, inflation, prices, teamwork, and wealth. Teachers might note not just the obvious (classroom, teaching, schools) but also geography, illiteracy, and language. A reader interested in family matters would find entries like children's rights, nuclear family, parental authority, single parent, and submission among equals. Those interested in philosophy would find words like assumptions, basic questions, naming, and focal point. Many words will be found for a discipline or interest, and words will overlap disciplines and interests.

Another way (it adds a bit to the playfulness of the exercise!) is to peruse that Index and look up words that at first make you think *what in the world is that about, why have they included this?* Try: body-language, breast implants, golf, Hammer Azimuth, Marks & Spencer, Post Grape Nuts®, speed limit, stained glass.

By using the Subject & Name Index as just described, a person does not have to have read the entire book before being able to reap benefits. Further, consistent with the basic methodology of the book, the Subject & Name Index as a guide into the text is a good way to discover how the things of life form a unity within their diversity, in ways that may have gone previously unnoticed. Such discoveries are vital for building up a pool of God's wisdom not only for a particular area of interest but also for the rest of one's life, where we have, sadly, neglected so many obediences. This particular way of using the book is suited not only for one's individual endeavor but also for small group studies.

Note: just occasionally the designation "[JP]" or "[CS]" follows the personal pronoun "I." This is the way the authors indicate to readers which one is telling a particular personal story when it is not immediately clear who is telling it. Where it is clear, the initials are not used.

Foreword

In 1989 it was my privilege to write the forward to John Peck's book *Wisdom in the Marketplace*. It is an equal privilege to commend this substantially revised and enlarged version. *Uncommon Sense: God's Wisdom for Our Complex and Changing World* is in effect a summary of John Peck's life's work as a theological teacher. His collaboration with Charles Strohmer has enriched it greatly and the result of their combined efforts has been a volume equally applicable to Britain and North America.

Through most of the last century the temptation for many Christians was to accept a dualism which split off the "sacred" from the "secular" and confined the impact of the Gospel to personal salvation and personal morality. As we begin a new century that temptation still thrives in the church, but it is often accompanied by a consumer approach to life, where everything, whether "sacred" or "secular" is regarded as raw materials for a comfortable lifestyle. This is little more than a pick and mix philosophy where the only ultimate value is personal taste.

In both cases the result is to rob the world of the impact of the Bible through the church. The greatest loss is the loss of wisdom in public life. Neither the modern nor the postmodern world know where wisdom may be found. Our world loves intense experiences and all the latest technologies but it is starved of wisdom. These authors focus their attention on the Bible as wisdom for the whole of life.

The historian Paul Kennedy concludes his book *Preparing for the 21ˢᵗ Century* with these words: "We face not a 'new world order' but a troubled and fractured planet. The pace and complexity of the forces for change are enormous and daunting; yet it may still be possible for intelligent men and women to lead their societies through the complex task of preparing for the century ahead. If these challenges are not met humankind will have only itself to blame for the troubles, and the disasters that could be lying ahead."

It is time to bring the Bible out of the church and into the marketplace. I recommend this book wholeheartedly, for that is what it aims to do.

Graham Cray, Principal - Ridley Hall, Cambridge - January 2000

Part One

Crossing the Rubicon

~1~

Transforming Our Vision

In both Great Britain and the United States today, a lot of spirited debate about christian values and their place in public life is snapping around our ears like a crackin' good wind. The conversations are no mere tempest in a teapot. They have far-reaching ramifications and are at times controversial.

In America, from the corridors of power on Capitol Hill to the hallowed studios of talk radio, pent up ideas are being aired with worked up emotions. Social agendas are pouring into our mailboxes from organizations with leanings from infrared to ultraviolet. And the belligerent and polemical nature of much of the debate is dividing the nation rather than bringing consensus.

In Great Britain, the debate is generally not as publicly aggressive and polemical. Issues of values and their societal implications tend to be slightly below the surface, and in the media their debate is much more subtle than it is in the States. To a large degree, this is perhaps because, unlike in the States, Britain has no widely self-assertive, publicly combative, and tightly organized religious right pressing the debate. Yet much debate exists. For instance, all British political parties have recognized that discussion over humane values has been pushed into the background, and they are all, in their various ways, bringing it to the front. Not long ago, the Conservative Party trotted out John Major's "Back to Basics" campaign, a modest proposal emphasizing family values and personal morality, and during the 1998 Labor Party Conference, Tony Blair argued powerfully for a general sense of society and mutuality.

Of course campaigns like these lead quickly to everyone's reflections over values, and, on both sides of the Atlantic, the net result of the debate often merely reveals how many different pages everyone is on. Ask questions like "Where do we get our values from?", or raise voices of real conviction, and constituencies can be torn apart. It may be easier to square a circle than to reach a consensus.

Christian ideas are failing miserably in the public square. There does seem to be at least one solid conclusion. Conservative and liberal Christians would agree that their influence on society is not what they would like it to be, and the culture at large tends to say that it is being turned off by what christian influence there is. Both church and society come out losers here. As more and more people acknowledge the myth of progress and recognize that we have problems that education, government, and science cannot solve, a society's thirst for meaning and hope increases but the churches are not respected as a wellspring of answers. Especially troubling to the authors of this book is that in this milieu of despair and crisis, Christians are failing miserably in their task of offering sensible and forcible possibilities of meaning and hope to a culture that at least occasionally expects it from them. So, although this book is written largely to Christians, the authors have taken seriously readers who would not consider themselves Christian. We hope that they too will find rays of meaning and hope in the following pages.

This may not be easy for some readers because, taking a cue from the American scene, the general attitude of society toward Christianity is downright negative. Listen closely to the media debate and it appears as if Christianity is faced with a hopeless dilemma. After all, for more than thirty years American Christians have been addressing social issues like never before. So one would think that, by now, engaging the culture with christian ideas had become pretty sophisticated, worthy of applause. Yet, although blood veins in the temple are strong and throbbing, test results reveal that christian thought in public life is weak and failing. Instead of offering crackerjack arguments that get inside the contemporary imagination convincingly, we sound uninteresting, irrelevant, simplistic, bigoted, comical. A common American attitude toward Christianity reminds one of people dealing with their "inferiors," or of tourists who get a kick out of condescending to the "natives." That, or christian views are either lampooned or completely ignored. Take your pick. One need only watch television or chat with a neighbor to feel its bite.

We are engaging the public, but our views are not engaging. We are speaking out, but we are put in our place when we do. Whether the subject is technological advances, early childhood education, the entertainment industry, university campuses, government agencies, creation stewardship, judicial decisions, artistic expression, business management, or foreign policy we seem to be out-thought and outdone by those who would not consider themselves Christian. In the vital constructs and agendas of "secular" life, the incarnation of truly biblical christian thinking appears to be slight. Where it does appear, it doesn't seem to stand much of a chance against the complexities and sophistication of our age. In brief, the work that must be done to correct this is the thesis of this book.

Some Christians are detached, but "saving souls" is not enough.

There are a number of powerful christian attitudes toward everyday life. One is that of detachment. God calls us only to preach the Gospel, to "save souls," to win the lost, and after that we are to keep pretty much to ourselves. Any serious concern for society is an ungodly compromise. The authors of this book, however, disagree with the rolling up of christian thinking and activity to saving "souls" only.

One wit has remarked, only half-jokingly, that should the nation awake one day to find that all the politicians in Washington D.C. have suddenly espoused the Christian faith, the real miracle would be if politics actually changed. His point is that by default it would be politics as usual because the politicians would arrive at work that next morning, and what would they have to work with? The same political theories, platforms, and agendas that were in place the day before. "Saving souls"—as it is often said and understood these days—only deals with one's personal moral problem before God. Politics itself cannot be changed enough merely by filling Congress or Parliament with "saved souls." That is not what it is going to take to make political theory any wiser or political corruption any less (transformations in personal conduct aside).

Souls certainly have a bearing on politics, but even personal morality is no substitute for sound political theory. Take the abortion issue. Christians oppose abortion but still talk in terms of rights instead of duties (chapter 8, "The Sixth Commandment"), and they rarely take into account the socio-economic structures that, for example, weigh so heavily on a single mother. She may have no supporting community, a family scattered throughout the nation, and few if any employment opportunities. Bound to a pricey, highly mobile and industrial system, she faces problems fit for a hero! Hence, in shouting only for religious and moral answers to the abortion disaster, we seem to lack compassion; whereas we really lack intelligence.

Evangelization as it is currently understood may increase heaven's population one day, but it's politics as usual until the politicians—even if the lot of them are Christians, and that is the point—discover what the Bible means by law, justice, government, righteousness, and other matters of jurisprudence, and how to address socio-economic structures today thereby.

Other Christians are at war, but intensifying those efforts is futile.

In another camp—a large one— enthusiasm is unflagging as Christian activists take to the street in what they perceive as the progress of the past three decades. Plenty of work remains, they admit, and non-Christians will be upset about it, but we're at war, madam, and it's worth the fight to make this a christian nation. This tireless camp, however, is often working from sets of assumptions through which much of its activism hurts Christ's cause, leaving a bitter taste for Christianity in society. Despite its massive efforts not to, this group is in many ways turning society off (humanly speaking) to any help it may be able to receive from God through Christ and Scripture.

This large, established group is chiefly focused on issues, and on intensifying existing strategies and efforts to address those issues. They wish to involve more churches, recruit more activists, increase membership roles. But the situation is much more serious than the mere sigh, "For all of our efforts, not much results." This conclusion implies that we are pretty much headed in the right direction and that if we intensify our efforts and recruit more activists we can get the desired results. It is the contention of this book, however, that in significant areas we Christians may need to stop and rethink our direction—what we are doing and how we are doing it. Frankly, to our non-Christian contemporaries, we look a bit like Icarus flying toward the sun. Wood, feathers, and wax-glue seem a bit silly today, not the kind of approach that appeals to savvy Westerners. And the direction of our flight appears to be a little foolish as well!

Others stick to good works, but this leaves the structures untouched.

One area where Christians do excel is in good works. Open-hearted generosity and works of charity by Christians flourished like plants in a greenhouse during the 20th century. One only has to mention the Salvation Army to speak of the tip of a vast iceberg. Besides the big charitable organizations, countless Christians today are unsung heroes. They run hospices for AIDS victims and homes for the impoverished elderly. They establish crisis pregnancy centers, operate soup kitchens, and visit nursing homes. They create programs to help the urban poor, work in refugee camps, and run child care centers. These faceless Christians know that Jesus came into the world to reach the poor and needy, the outcast and lonely, the broken and despised.

As good and as necessary and as required as our good works are—woe to us if we neglect them—even our acts of charity may not be enough. That is, Christian aid can be like treating a cholera epidemic without investigating the water supply. A missionary to Bangladesh visited our church in Earl Soham, England, a few years back and explained that preaching wasn't enough because the people were starving. So he showed them how to improve their land's fertility, which was good, but it was not enough because their technology was inadequate. So he showed them how to make iron tools and implements, but that created economic problems because the people could not afford the initial outlay necessary to get the new system up and running. Finally he organized a simple credit plan, which solved that problem. Then he said, almost as an after-thought, "But they were not all that better off." Astonished, we asked why. The missionary explained that the rent which people paid to the government for their land was proportional to what they produced. Without a fixed rent, increased production meant more coins for the Realm. By the time the tenant farmers were done paying the higher rent *and* paying back on their loans for the new technology, they weren't much better off. When we asked the missionary why he did not petition the government, he answered with a shrug, "Missionaries could not get involved with politics."

Our compassion and good works, therefore, may be stymied or undermined by socio-economic or political circumstances. As difficult as it may be to admit, even our acts of charity may need rethinking. Again, we certainly must be compassionate, and our acts of charity are indispensable. But the situation today demands more than that. *The structures and systems themselves are frequently the problem.* Wherever the structures are at fault, we need to be aware and to be able to suggest ways ahead.

The way of thinking and reasoning explored by this book examines aspects of society's structures alongside issues and acts of charity to see where we may be able, through the Gospel and God's wisdom, to renew and redeem areas of the structures. This has been a greatly neglected part of our christian discipleship. We have obediences to fulfill to God here, obediences that will equip us with new, in the sense of fresh, ways of being public Christians who can articulate sensible and forcible ideas that cannot be gainsaid. We will be going into this as we go along. Let us just say here that God's method with Israel was systemic. At Israel's birth as a nation, she was given a Law that ordered the entire people as a systematic structure of justice and generosity, and the prophets continually called the nation back to that. If Christians do not enter the secular arenas with this kind of biblical vision, then others will enter, and have entered, in the service to other gods. And such is the nature of fallen life that others will commandeer our work, take credit for it, and then ruin it. And then blame us for it.

An increasing number desire a new paradigm. Another group of Christians is seeking fresh ways ahead. This group—small but slowly increasing— has strong desires to develop a new paradigm of God's wisdom by which to influence all aspects of society Christianly. It is aware of the need for structural change. Strides are being made here, on both sides of the Atlantic, yet these folk can often be found scratching their chins. They are usually pensive and you don't often get the expected answer out of them. Not because they want to be difficult or theologically slippery, but, as you might expect from people exploring a new universe, they are feeling their way. Here at the beginning of the 21st century, they see that the established christian strategies for influencing Western society don't have much clout, and they are seeking new biblical ways ahead. They are not traveling without a guide, however. Some of their thinking (the authors of this book would locate themselves here) comes from a neglected tradition of christian thought that has been gradually driven to become articulate in the face of radical cultural change. Much of it has an ancestry through Tertullian, Augustine, Calvin, Kuyper, van Prinsterer, and some medieval church-state theories. Trouble is, it has been swamped by a Hellenistic dualism. Other aspects of their thinking are the fruit of countless hours spent studying Scripture, consulting with colleagues, researching, teaching, writing, and interacting with their non-Christian contemporaries in an effort to find a transcendent wisdom (if we may put it like that) for all aspects of their societies' governance. These Christians understand that a new paradigm of God's wisdom is needed, and they believe that they have found some important clues, which can make the exploration, such as will be developed in this book, worthwhile and effective.[1]

Besides writing to develop this direction for a general audience, the authors find that Christians who are students at colleges and universities benefit greatly from the way of seeing that it makes possible. On campus, students who are Christians often feel sucker-punched by the pressures of pagan and other unbiblical ideologies in the curriculum and from their teachers, and they may despair because they see no biblically informed alternatives to take with them out into their fields after they get their degrees. They were not taught these alternatives in their churches, and even Christian fellowships on campus, although fulfilling necessary roles, such as for meeting new friends, having Bible studies, and sharing war stories(!), may not be of much help for the intellectual pain being faced day after day in the classrooms. These students suspect that Scripture must have at least some instruction about art, law, science, economics, education, sociology, and other kinds of curriculum, but that is not what they now find themselves studying in the schools. These students and the challenges they face have a special place in the heart of the

---

[1] We have been deliberately broad and brief in enclosing Western Christendom within the foregoing groups. Readers wishing breadth of analysis regarding at least seven different ways that Christians relate their faith to culture, especially to politics, could pick up a copy of Jim Skillen's *The Scattered Voice: Christians at Odds in the Public Square.*

authors of *Uncommon Sense*. We hope that the material in the following chapters will be to them a feast of ideas.

One paradox of our calling as Christians is that while we are commanded to come out of the world we are equally commanded to go into the world. When only one of these commands becomes the governing principle, our lives by default follow one of two paths. If the former holds our allegiance, we reduce the reach of Gospel of Jesus Christ to "saving souls" only. If the latter command holds our allegiance, we distort the Gospel by adopting the world's way of reasoning about public life, however unwittingly. In the former, there is no rhyme or reason for thinking biblically about anything other than church-related activities; in the latter, there is no genuinely transcendent wisdom being offered in public life. So the trick is *how* to live the paradox: to be in the world *for* the glory of God. For it is a glory that, whether we see it yet or not, infiltrates all of life: its art, its law, its science, its politics, its employment, its recreation, and everything else. As Christians we have obediences to fulfil here, for God's glory, without being detached or worldly in our ways of reasoning and methods in public life.

The goal is learning a biblical wisdom for everyday life that becomes instinctive.

We are not talking about a fishing expedition. It is not about using the Book to hook a few, new clever principles that can then be fed into today's society. The goal is to learn a wisdom that more and more reflects a biblical way of seeing life as a whole and God's involvement in that whole as informed by Scripture. *Uncommon Sense* is about much more than building up ideas and making them work. It aims to assist the personal development of a biblical wisdom that will become instinctive and govern our actions in culture in a spontaneous, godly way. It is a wisdom not only about goals, standards, and ideals but also about methods and means. Direction. *Uncommon Sense* is therefore to a large degree about the formative *process* of such a wisdom.

The authors believe that this is a missing jewel in christian discipleship, and that an understanding of the process will help us immensely in our efforts to live more fully for God's glory in this life and to at times capture the secular imagination convincingly.

Without this, we may face a vengeful reaction from society.

We must not underestimate the importance of this. If we do, Christianity could become a handy scapegoat for our nations' problems. In 1978, I[JP] was thinking about the need for my country's spiritual awakening, and I wrote this about England: "Without the self-restraint derived from a common moral ideal, a nation becomes ungovernable except by tyranny. Unless our nation has a spiritual awakening soon, we will probably have little freedom at all to debate christian attitudes. The trouble is, there isn't that much time. Revival doesn't guarantee results that fulfil all its possibilities. An expanding church might still fuss about a few obvious moral problems in society but be unable to relate its faith to the basic problems. Indeed, it might not even be able to handle its own problems. If God's people propagate a christian faith without proliferating a christian mind—a christian philosophy of life, or way of looking at the world—then there may follow a vengeful reaction from a society deprived of truly christian insight into its problems; a society driven by spiritual ignorance into despair, despotism, and persecution."

The extension of this across the Atlantic to America is obvious. The picture not unimaginable, as some news stories are starting to indicate.

~2~

Healing a Generational Debility

In order to think, speak, and act Christianly with a transcendent wisdom that gets inside the contemporary imagination convincingly, the Bible must first become open to *us* in a way that we may not be used to. The approach of this book to Scripture may therefore be a bit different from what is considered customary. But for good reason.

Traditionally, for most of us, the Bible slides past our eyes with a "stained glass window effect." That is, we read the Bible as what we might call a "religious" book only—a source for instruction in prayer, worship, church activities, moral behavior, evangelization, and so on. Certainly religious instruction must not be downplayed. Yet religious instruction alone gives us a private faith with very limited public relevance. It leaves us unequipped to study and apply Scripture with reference to the many "nonreligious" issues and aspects of life.

True, many Christians can quote the Book of Proverbs for business principles or relationship taboos. But we are talking about a much wider horizon. For instance, when it comes to children's rights, health insurance, welfare reform, scientific debates, economic developments, government subsidies of the arts, or the U.N.'s handling of global hot spots, it usually does not occur to us to check out the Book, which we assume has little or no distinctive wisdom for such matters. This is not the way that Jesus, or the apostles, or God's Old and New Testament people saw Scripture. They had a God who was involved in the whole of life and they had a Bible to match. For them, the Bible was not relegated to religious affairs only; it had significant instruction for what we today would call secular life. Twentieth century christian history and teaching traditions, however, have done much to undermine that way of learning from Scripture.

We are caught in a generational debility. A particular amount of mischief here surrounds the words "religious" and "secular." So just before we dig right in to our approach to Scripture, which begins in the next chapter, we thought it would be helpful to clear the air regarding a few powerful attitudes toward these two words.

During the early to mid-twentieth century, Christians took seriously the words, "Go into all the world and preach the Gospel." They also took seriously, "Come out from among them and be separate." As a result, while trying to live as Christians, they made considerable sacrifices for what they considered to be "the separated life." It is easy to satirize such a way of life, but the people who lived it will tell you that it had its strengths. It was not gloomy or dull, and many Christians thoroughly enjoyed it. It provided a great deal of leisure for getting to know the Bible and for enjoying close fellowship with others of like mind. Giving up things for the Gospel had its own satisfactions and joys. What is more, such renunciations created a certain strength of character, which equipped many young people of that day for lives of patient sacrifice and courageous service. (This tends to arouse amused cynicism today, rather than the admiration one would have thought it deserved.) And people knew what those Christians stood for. Between them and the world was a clear-cut division between light and darkness. They may have often been over-dogmatic, condescending, and even insulting, but at least people knew that becoming a Christian meant some kind of devastating reorientation of lifestyle.

The "separated life" and "split thinking" put a false guilt on Christians. The real criticism of that kind of Christianity was not that it cramped the personality or even that it was, necessarily, legalistic. After all, every lifestyle has its own rules and restrictions, even if they remain largely unacknowledged. Its weakness was that the restrictions were arbitrary and excessively inconsistent. For example, when Billy Graham's wife, Ruth, came over to England from America to "win souls," and was doing so with marked success, Christians in Great Britain were appalled: she was wearing lipstick!

As a way of seeing, "the separated life" was preached from pulpits and passed on from parents to children and a split in thinking between "the religious" and "the secular" began taking shape in practice. Take the choice of a career. The highest calling was getting people converted. So the evangelist became like the rock group's dream of getting to the top of the charts. Missionary work was right up there also. After all, missions involved the special spirituality associated with big sacrifices, not to mention the romance of going to a foreign land. Plus, you did not need to get a theology degree.

This was an important consideration because it meant that you could get into "spiritual service" without getting exposed to "modern scholarship." (Anyone in seminary had to be especially careful!) Then after you got people converted, you had to nurture them in the faith; so a pastor had a calling almost as high as that of the evangelist and missionary.

All this became "full-time work for the Lord," and the people doing it were thought to be fully dedicated Christians indeed, the really spiritual ones. They were "in the ministry." Work in "the world" was just work, a regrettable necessity. This way of seeing left most Christians feeling guilty about the way they lived and earned their livings. But there were ways around the guilt. You could funnel any extra cash you had toward "the work of the ministry," and you were free to do "part-time work for the Lord," which usually meant volunteering around the church or for a charitable organization. Or you might become an elder or a deacon, or teach Sunday school, or run the youth group. And there were any number of church committees that needed warm bodies. Your conscience rested a little easier if you jumped in like this, for you were then "more spiritual" than those who did not volunteer, albeit still "less spiritual" than your pastor, the evangelist, and the missionary. This was the assumption, even if people did not see it.

In such a milieu, Christians elevated "religious" concerns to an extremely high plane, as being "spiritual," and then they split the rest of life off from those concerns as having little if any importance in the long run. Everything associated with church-related activities became "spiritual," the only things worth fighting for. Whatever was happening outside church from Monday through Saturday—the exceptions being prayer meetings, Bible studies, and witnessing—was hardly worth the effort, unless it became a means by which to pay expenses "for the Kingdom." Religious life gravitated around itself to become the only thing that really mattered, and ordinary experience in "the world" drifted off until it was disconnected from God and merely to be endured until one reached heaven. God was busy in church-related activities, but throughout the week God must be resting—an interesting take on the Sabbath, indeed.

It made choosing a job a tricky business. The widespread assumption was that God had little, if anything, to do with the ordinary experiences of everyday life, even though, if God looked, that is where He would find me most of the time! This made choosing a "worldly job" tricky. It meant sorting through a range of hierarchies, and you had to be careful. It was best to go into one of the caring professions, such as medicine, nursing, or teaching. Although you had to be alert because biology was laced with evolution, and by the early 1960s, the public schools in the States were removing "religion" from the classroom to emphasize their so-called secular nature. Still, the caring professions were acceptable enough in most churches. Just below these careers, one could enter numerous occupations that were considered neutral: farming, accounting, factory work, auto mechanics, the construction trade, secretarial jobs, and many kinds of self-employment. Though you had to be careful in the factories because that usually meant unions. Areas such as law, politics, and the entertainment industry were definitely *out*. Those called your spirituality into question. Such careers really contaminated you with "the world."

It hamstrung christian service and evangelization. This way of seeing tended to produce christian lifestyles most appropriate to small businesses and professionals. It was also strongly individualistic, since staying clear of contamination meant confining oneself to one's own group and keeping to oneself in the world at large, rather than getting involved in its problems.

The split view of life also inhibited evangelization and christian service, producing a powerful attitude that still lingers with us. Evangelization degenerated into "soul-winning" only, and christian service became affiliated with church-related activities only. Honing one's witness so as to win others to the same lifestyle was the goal. The christian mind was narrowed down to winning souls so as to win souls so as to win souls . . . . If you did not do much of that, you were probably unspiritual. All you could be expected to do was to earn a living, to maintain quiet times, to be kind, nice, and honest, and to keep attending the church meetings and paying tithes.

It cost us our artists. Another form of the problem appeared in the arts. Music was an especially noticeable example. Religious music, such as hymns, choruses, and *The Messiah*, was all right of course, and when the more contemporary christian music came along, it was acceptable as long as it had "Jesus" in the lyrics. At the least, the music had to include overt religious messages or christian jargon words. The words were all-important: they had to be clear. The worst condemnation that could be pronounced on music was: "You couldn't hear the words." Instrumental music played by Christians was questionable, unless it was so conventionally religious in form as to be unmistakable. Without any words, Christians had no criteria for determining its suitability. So most instrumental music was suspect. This, of course, created acute problems for relating to any music that was not obviously religious. For example, when rock 'n' roll appeared it had to be evil because the young people were tearing up the concert hall seats and "going crazy." If not that, then it was worldly because it was "modern." For lack of any other standards, Christians turned the job over to history. Berlioz and Bach were okay (they had survived christian assessment); the Beatles were out, at least until ten years later. This attitude toward music is still so powerful today that many Christians simply cannot fathom, for instance, why Amy Grant has gone "secular." To them she has "sold out" more than just in concert.

This attitude also determined how Christians approached other forms of art. They put up with bawdiness in Shakespeare that they would not tolerate in Beckett. Ruben's nudes were acceptable but Andy Warhol's were not. It was the best they could do, and for many Christians it still is (chapter 21 offers a way out). One only has to browse christian book stores and gift shops to see how this attitude controls what is being passed off as *christian* art. Car license plate frames? Night lights with butterfly wings? Refrigerator magnets? Jelly bean prayer jars? These and a thousand other weird plastics are considered Christian because they are found in a christian store, or because Bible verses are stamped on them. Part of the scandal here is that this kind of consumerism and marketing has cost us a great deal: our artists. With rare exceptions today, no room within our churches is created for Christians to have their gifts and talents *as artists* nurtured. And since these artists will not sanctify the merchandisers, or because they become quite misunderstood by the churches, they often drop out of sight. This has been a terrible loss both to the churches and to the artists.

Just as tragically, this happens in other secular aspects as well. Many Christians today who recognize their gifts for politics, law, and other "taboo" areas may not use them because the split way of seeing life still affects them too much. "God can't be in it." Or if they do use such gifts, it is with a bad conscience and an inadequate guidance from their faith. One illustration of inadequate guidance often appears in churches that are beginning to appreciate the arts but accept them only if they support religious activities. Drama, music, entertainment, and other presentations must therefore be restricted to church services, evangelization projects, or youth activities.

The "separated life" was not able to keep the world out. Then came the late 20th century and it was no longer possible to keep "the world" out of our homes, churches, and experiences. In America, political decisions such as the removal of prayer from public classrooms and the *Roe v Wade* abortion decision, began to hit us where we lived. And on both sides of the Atlantic everyone watched more television and saw more movies, both of which brought not only the world's delights and glories before our eyes but also its tragedies, follies, and sins. It was all thrust before us. No family could keep the world out. There is the story of one Christian in England who ordered a television set, and as it was being delivered to his home, he saw this claim on the carton: "Bringing the World into Your Home." He promptly sent it back!

Even relatively safe areas like health care began giving Christians trouble that was both unpreventable and seemingly unanswerable. Problems surrounding abortion, contraception, genetic engineering, and life-support to the aged and the terminally ill all posed dilemmas from which there was no escape whereby "separated Christians" might serve the Lord and keep their noses clean.

It crippled our response to the culture's paradigm shift.

And then we began hearing about this strange creature called a "paradigm shift." That is, as Westerners began cautiously steering away from enlightenment rationalism and philosophical materialism, and a fundamental shift in the way they thought and reasoned began. A dominant assumption for life had been: "All that is seen can explain all that is," and on this foundation secular Western culture arose. God, religion, and the supernatural were quarantined, were for a bygone age, said those professing themselves wise. But this way of seeing left a tremendous spiritual vacuum in the Western worldview, and the pendulum inevitably began its swing the other way. The attitude arose: "Hang on a minute. All that is seen cannot explain all there is. There must be more to life than meets the eye." As this way of seeing began to gain ground, an increasing number of people who would not consider themselves Christian began to look at life through what we might call a "holistic spirituality" derived chiefly from a constellation of Eastern metaphysics and occult philosophies. This has evolved to become more defined, and so to acquire the identity "pantheistic monism," which is a fair enough description, although it is much more involved than our brief point here notes.

Most Christians attribute this paradigm shift to "New Agers," but historically that is quite simplistic, considering some of their quite ancient pagan associations. Closer to our time, this spiritual pioneering had clear roots in the 1950s with "the Beats"—poets and philosophers like Alan Watts, Gary Snyder, Jack Kerouac, and Allen Ginsberg—who threw down the gauntlet and, by fits and starts, challenged materialistic and rationalistic assumptions with Buddhism and hashish. In answer to the question: "What are you rebelling against?", Ginsberg read his poem *Howl* to a San Francisco audience in 1955. It included the following lines against a society whose "mind is pure machinery / whose love is endless oil and stone / whose soul is electricity and banks!" These powerful words, and many others, echoed throughout the spiritual vacuum and influenced what would become some of the 1960s leading counter-cultural voices, such as Jim Morrison and Bob

Dylan. *Then* came the look to the stars and the promise of the Age of Aquarius, a 2,000 year era of peace and harmony. Well, that age hasn't dawned, but an increasing number of people are discovering that life is a whole and that spirituality is related to that whole. Many of these folk have a sharp native intelligence and have become influential and well known for developing "spiritual" ways to look at the arts, law, music, science, business, medicine, and education.

Meanwhile, back in the fortress of pietism, Christians were generally anesthetized to what was really occurring. God was leading the *Zeitgeist* into the 21st century; an historic metaphysical and epistemological paradigm shift was taking place, such as happened during the transitions from the Renaissance to the Reformation and from the Reformation to the Enlightenment. But Christians did not realize they were part of the history. They were watching history in the making instead of making it. They stood as bystanders rather than jump in as participators. And when some brave souls did get involved, it was usually with a split view of life, which caused all sorts of headaches for them because the New Age folk they met no longer held to a split view. The Christians seemed behind the times, out of touch with reality. Part of the culture was beginning to see life as a whole, with spirituality informing that whole, and another part, the Christians, was still seeing life as split in two. For the Christian, religious and spiritual things went on inside the church walls and had little or no bearing on the things "outside." For the New Age folk, there were no walls.

We are not in the least suggesting that pantheistic monism is a way of seeing life that we would endorse. We are saying that it awakened secularist Westerners to the fact that there is more to everyday life than meets the eye. At the very least, it gets people thinking that maybe "God" and "spirituality" have a bearing on everyday life. A christian view might put it this way: God has created all of life and He is equally involved in all of its parts, not just in the religious ones.

> *We have a lot of catching up to do.*

Clearly we have much catching up to do. We may say, "If He's not Lord of all, He's not Lord at all," but living as if we meant it . . . . That is another matter entirely. Our lives, as Christians, are unavoidably becoming more and more bound up with the world around us—with its culture, its thought, its science, its art, its politics, its industry, its social structures—and with its evolving new paradigm. To learn how to address this as the Bible would is the homework before us, and a key to this approach will be to take off the stained glass lenses through which we read the Bible and then learn from what we might call the Bible's "secular wisdom."

Recovering two troublesome words: "religious" and "secular."
This brings us to a problem that has been waiting restlessly in the wings. Before we start in earnest in chapter 3 to discuss how we might learn from the Bible as a secular book, it is necessary to clear further ground regarding the troublesome words "religious" and "secular." The authors are fully aware of the emotions that the use of these two words can ignite within several popular viewpoints. For instance, briefly, a phrase like "learning to use the Bible as a secular book," which could be used to describe, in part, the thesis of *Uncommon Sense*, will at first drive some readers up the wall, for they would say, "There is no such thing as 'secular' life. All of life is religious (or spiritual)." Fair enough. All of life does proceed in the direction of the ultimate faith commitments that individuals and cultures hold. To put it another way, one's faith (even atheists have a faith) gives direction and meaning not only to one's religious, moral, and ethical behavior but also to the character of the person's art, music, politics, business interests, family situation, and so on.

For another group, "religious" will be the offensive term, one filled with connotations of an arid ritualism of which they want no part. A Christian with this way of seeing has a great distaste for the word "religion." Such a person would proudly say, "My church isn't religious." For other Christians, the word "secular" will be the boogieman term, chiefly because of a mentality that has been absorbed from decades of christian books and conferences that have decried "secular humanism." And yet another attitude would suggest that it is "dualistic" to say that the Bible has both religious and secular dimensions. "This is to remain trapped again in the split thinking," they would say. Beyond that, at a technical level in this sort of debate, one encounters the arguments of "structure" and "direction." This is but the tip of a vast iceberg, and we are asking that every reader try to be patient with our use of the words "religious" and "secular" wherever they appear in this book, whatever mindset you are bringing from your circle of discourse to our presentation.

We mean these words in their ordinary usage.
To clarify our use of the two words, we mean them as purely descriptive. We mean them as they are found on the lips of common usage, in which "secular" is used as distinct from "religious." This is what we might call their normal rather than their technical sense.

When we use the word "religious" in this book, that is a reference to the way in which people express the commitment they have to God symbolically. That is, it is about the aspect of life in which people explicitly express what gods (or God) they believe in, and how they approach these gods, and the moral claims these gods make on them. This is about rituals, sacred books, theology, explicit witness, devotional activities, such as prayer and worship, and the community that revolves around such things. Most people use the word "religion" to describe them, and unless it is otherwise indicated in this book that is what we mean by our use of the word. So it will be about what Christians do in their churches or what Buddhists do in their temples.

In its normal sense, "secular" is simply used as a word for that which does not pertain to religious matters. We are therefore using the word to describe that which belongs to those aspects of our life in the world: art, music, law, business, culture, science, government, legal processes, social relationships, the way we rationalize, and so on. "Secular," unless otherwise indicated by us, is being used purely as a synonym for one or more aspects of everyday, or daily, life. In this sense, no one escapes having a secular life. Only insofar as we accept the values of the fallen world do we become "worldly" in our secular lives. The degree to which we accept the values of the Bible in secular life makes us godly. (If you prefer, you can substitute the words "everyday" or "daily" for our use of "secular.")

Please note: in no way does our use of "religious" and "secular" in this book stand for the popular but misleading dualistic view of life that pits one against the other in a dichotomy. This will become more evident as we move through the chapters.

We are simply trying to use language that everyone can understand. In ordinary thinking, which is what this book seeks to be deliberately about, we don't want to use technical language where we do not need to. We appreciate technical jargon, but in this book that is not necessary. We don't want readers to have to learn a new language here, but to grapple with things and explanations in ordinary terms. After all, if you cannot explain it that way, you have not really understood it. Let's not lose these two words, like some Christians nearly did with words like "paradigm," "transformation," and "unity-in-diversity" in the 1970s and 1980s, just because they were on the lips of New Age people.

We would also like to make a further distinction: between "religion" (in the above sense) and "faith." People—Christians, Moslems, Hindus, Buddhists—may be intensely religious and yet they may base their secular lives, usually unwittingly, on values and notions that belong to "another god," a god other than the one on which their religious faith is based. When this has become habitual, it can be quite difficult to help people to see what has happened. Israel's and Judah's kings during the Old Testament period often fell prey to this. They would keep their religious duties to Yahweh at the temple but base other aspects of their lives and their policies on other gods. And for this they were soundly rebuked by the prophets. Whenever people begin to see this, it usually comes as quite a surprise, Christians included. For instance, even a devout Christian may discover that in climbing the ladder of success she has derived much more direction from a love of the gods of silver and gold, in the way she ran her company, than from the love of the God whose faith she professed every Sunday. In other words, a person who is a devout Christian may have faith (albeit, unwittingly) in the values of "another god" in some area of his or her secular life. We are not talking about ungodly *religious* values here, but ungodly *secular* values.

This book contends that no area of life is neutral, that the secular aspects of life (art, law, politics, education, science, and so on) can be judged either as godly or ungodly regardless of whether they are associated with prayer, worship, religious witness, or an obvious moral issue. Many of the analyses in the following chapters examine this in that light—matters close to the heart, too, such as maintaining a nuclear family, schooling our children, running our businesses, entering politics, creating art, and much more. We do concede that strides are being made here, and we will look at many in due course. Here we will just note that these strides probably are not what most people think.

Saving the soul for the Day of the Lord is therefore not the end of the story for those of us whom God has left in the world. Learning the Bible as a strictly religious book will not make our conversations with our neighbors, or our children's teachers, or our fellow employees, or our employers very interesting or appealing. But learning and building on God's wisdom for everyday life will. That will come to us when we hear the Bible speak to us in a secular way, a way in which its nonreligious instruction opens to us.

Jesus was raised in God's wisdom for everyday life. Many of the illustrations throughout this book have come from our struggles at College House[1] (Cambridge, England), where more than twenty years ago the Bible began speaking to many of us afresh, especially of Jesus Christ himself as a person intimately characterized by the culture of his day. We began to see Jesus vividly as a real man, a Jew, who, reared in the Old Testament tradition, knew how to speak out of a wisdom that addressed the secular life of his day. Old Testament studies began to make us more aware

---

[1] College House was co-founded by John Peck in 1977, somewhat like a Francis Schaeffer L'Abri center, where students could explore ways to make christian philosophy relevant to everyday life. Today, College House provides various settings such as weekend courses, evening classes, "hothouses" at the Greenbelt Arts Festival, and material in print. In its formal setting, College House offers courses leading to the Cambridge University Diploma in Religious Studies. Query: College House, 55 Sturton Street, Cambridge, CB1 2QT, England.

of a world of thought and life that showed, even after two and a half millennia, a strange vitality and relevance for our own age. We began to feel more and more that we shared the humanity of these Old Testament people, not just as believers but also as traders, workers, teachers, pupils, rulers, and subjects— people in need of God's wisdom in the marketplace. And we were discovering that we could find such wisdom by the bundle in the Bible.

Much of our work at College House has been in theology, in connection with the university, and our exam results have earned us a good reputation. Our approach, however, has been to draw students' attention not only to the Bible's religious message but also to its particular underlying *wisdom*. This enables us to give full weight to its humanly secular dimensions without undermining its divine authority; indeed, it makes that authority more meaningful and relevant.

This has had quite practical results, such as the phone call we had from a man who had attended our classes. He now organizes events in the performing arts. "These are not specifically religious events," he said. "But always in my mind, the christian faith is directing the form that these secular events should take. It is your teaching at College House that has made me think like this."

At one time, before a recession hit many businesses, we ran conferences on a christian way of doing business management. We were not without practical expertise; two of us at College House had been executives on what was then the largest christian arts festival in the world.[2] At one of these conferences, a man said to us at the outset, "I know about all these christian seminars. They're hot on honesty and prayer, but on the practical side they're no different from any other fairly good program. I'm not a Christian. You'll have to persuade me that there's any *real* difference." During a final talk-back after the conference the next afternoon, he said, "I've not been to anything like this before! You have persuaded me." It was also gratifying to learn from a friend that this man subsequently became a Christian.

So we Christians are beginning to awaken, even though rather belatedly, to this new, "modern," world. And we have a multitude of new decisions to make. We have got to think fast and radically right in the midst of God's world and in the face of God's Word. Prayers and religious convictions will not be enough. We must take seriously the command to "love the Lord your God with all your mind" in this new age, and we must do it through an acquaintance with the pages of Scripture that resonates with a wisdom that

---

[2] The Greenbelt Arts Festival, which reinvents itself every summer in England. Query: Greenbelt Festivals, St. Luke's Church, Penn Road, London, N7 9RE, England.

sees life as a whole and a God who is equally involved in all of its parts. When we learn to do this it will make all the difference in the world. It is going to be difficult, however, because many of us have been reared to believe that our faith should have nothing to do with the sort of thinking required. But in the next chapter we shall find some disturbing hints in Scripture itself. We may even find that, at the beginning of the 21st century, our societies may decide that they too could stand a good dose of this.

~3~

Present-day Life in the Old Testament

So here we are, so many of us, taught to regard the secular world as a sinking ship (you could only save souls out of it) and now we are being told to use the Bible as a secular book! This puts stress on the system, certainly, and we are entitled to feel a bit groggy and unclear about it. Quite naturally, then, we have to "search the Scriptures" to see whether it's true.

Does the Bible concern itself with secular matters? Does it address aspects of life that are not noticeably religious or moral? Does it deal with socio-economic and geo-political questions? What about issues surrounding art, law, business, science, linguistics, ecology, and communications? Or how about contemporary hot-button issues like justice, welfare, racism, and abortion? In other words, does the Bible have any secular literature? The strange thing is, once we start looking for it, there is so much, and it is so obvious, it is a wonder we ever missed it.

Present-day secular interests appear throughout the Old Testament. If our Lord could be said to have had a favorite biblical book it would be Deuteronomy. Here one finds the Ten Commandments and the famous declaration of faith made by Jews everywhere in worship, the *Shema*: "Hear, O Israel: the LORD our God, the LORD is one. Love the LORD your God with all your heart and with all your soul and with all your strength" (6:4). And Deuteronomy chapters 10–11 carry a higher concentration of language specifically about love between God and people than possibly anywhere else in the Old Testament. It was also one of the great basic texts for the teaching of the prophets. Most Christians who are familiar with the Bible will be acquainted with the first dozen or so chapters, but then their knowledge of Deuteronomy probably tails off until possibly the last few chapters. The middle chapters, which carry instructions about sacrifices, festivals, and the priesthood, seem less interesting. These chapters, however, include provisions about everyday life ranging from nesting birds to digging toilets. They also address war, finance, politics, eating habits, jurisprudence, and public health and safety, not to mention the treatment of criminals, children, wives, slaves, and the poor.

Why have we missed these secular interests? These areas lie outside our interests when we read the Bible because we do not usually associate these areas of life with religion. But more than that, such passages can seem non-germane to the complexities of Western life. So why bother to learn from them? Our complex and specialized societies produce technical jargon such as: socio-economic indicators, environmental catastrophes, geo-political structures, complementary medicine, regulation of credit, fiscal control of inflation, market-based economy, outcome-based education, semantic distortion, and green issues. Even the person who comes in to get rid of our mice and termites is now a "certified pest control technician." Everything seems to be getting more complex.

We have grown so accustomed to our culture's highly technical language that we cannot see how it could possibly relate to the many secular matters dealt with in Deuteronomy. We should not, however, let today's technical jargon confuse us. It is frequently about the same basic elements of everyday life as are dealt with in Deuteronomy. The Jubilee, for instance, was an institution whose significance was chiefly socio-economic. The laws against cutting down fruit trees in war (20:19), or taking a mother bird (22:6), or mixing seeds (22:9), as well as a reason given for the delay in conquering Palestine (7:22), are plainly ecological in nature. The laws about body fluids, quarantines, and sanitation (23:1–14) address practical health care concerns. All of these have little to do with religion. The extent to which we usually concern ourselves with such passages today is merely to "modernize" them, often by trying to find scientific reasons for those sorts of laws, which gives them some value for us today and some rhyme and reason for their inclusion in the text. (The relation of the Bible's "basic ingredients" to life's complexities today is crucial to developing a biblical wisdom and will be more fully developed throughout this book.)

Secular matters are important to God. What begins to come through such scriptures time and time again is that secular life is important to "the LORD." Further, to assume that such laws relate only to that time—as irrational taboos among primitive peoples—is to miss an essential point of their nature. Certainly the laws were laid down in a fairly primitive society, but that is not how they were given. They were given with an appeal to *reason*, and this is quite significant. Obviously they have authority because they come as a revelation from God; that is, they have a religious authority. And normally what comes by revelation comes simply as based on

God's judgment. This is God speaking—don't expect reasons, *just do it*. But many of the commands that involve secular instructions are not like that, for they call upon the recipients to use their reason and to act on that basis (as well as its being revelation). This means that God makes not only the command but also the rational principle behind it binding on His people. It is God saying, "Think for yourself, people!"

The Bible's secular instruction has a rational authority.

Now this rational authority and the appeal to reason is not time-bound but for *all* time. The wonder of this is that such biblical instructions can be so up-to-date. For instance, bribery is offensive because it makes it difficult even for a wise person to think straight (16:19). Contempt of court brings punishment because it is a deterrent to others (17:13). Polygamy is a special threat even to a king because it will ruin his personal integrity (17:17). And these are true for all times.

Notice the appeal to reason: do this *because* . . . . Such rational explanations are easily overlooked even though they are inspired. Yes, they address everyday affairs such as marriage, contracts, law courts, the family, and the environment, but our point here is not the subject matter; it is the *rationale:* reason rather than religion. They say, "Obey this not only because the LORD commands it but also because it is reasonable." For example, a Hebrew slave is to be freed ungrudgingly after six years *because* the master has done well out of his service (15:18). Trees should not be cut down indiscriminately *because* they are not enemies (20:19; especially RSV). And notice how well the rationale behind appointing cities of refuge is spelled out (19:3–7). The Law of Sinai was the only known law code of the Middle East in that period which contained such rational justifications.

Even a ritualistic book like Leviticus addresses secular life.

Deuteronomy is obviously a key Old Testament book, and it might be argued that this is precisely because it carries rational ideas about everyday life. Leviticus, however, is largely concerned with Israel's cultus; that is, the rites and ceremonies whereby Israel was to acknowledge its religious allegiance to the LORD. Yet here too we find the same rational authority in the laws about certain aspects of daily life. A case in point are the regulations about skin diseases in chapter 13, which have what we today would call a technical quality, for they carefully distinguish between a swelling, a rash, and a bright spot on the skin. These are not the arbitrary directions of religious taboos, to be blindly observed by the superstitious. Nor are they merely early scientific lessons. They require what we would now call medical skills. The medical examination is also quite technical, dealing with potentially contaminated clothing and with treatment based even on type of clothing: wool, linen, cloth, knitted. This kind of interest sounds remarkably current.

Entire Old Testament books are much more secular than religious.

Far more noticeable Old Testament examples address everyday life. The Book of Proverbs is a gold mine of secular nuggets, giving instruction about the aesthetics of communication (16:24; 20:15; 25:11, 25), courtroom testimony (17:8, 15; 19:5, 9), business psychology (20:14), social justice (19:17; 21:13; 24:11–12), diplomacy (19:12; 23:1–3; 25:6–10), a work ethic (19:3; 24:33–34), and much more. The Song of Songs, read as it stands, is a passionate love ode, with hardly a mention of God and no mention of faith, prayer, worship, or moral exhortation. Yet it is not profane or immoral. Just secular. Ecclesiastes begins by expounding an attitude to life—it's just one darn thing after another going round in circles—that no Jew or Christian would accept without qualification. It runs on in that vein with a depressingly earth-bound cynicism.

The Book of Esther does not mention God at all, and it contains no references to any of the chief ways of expressing one's religious faith that anyone (let alone a Jew) would have regarded as proper everyday practice. Esther does not mention worship, sacrifice, or dietary laws. There is no Law of the Lord, no synagogue, no priesthood, no scripture, no prayer, no temple, no altar. The only religious practice mentioned is fasting, which was a comparatively minor element in Israel's religion, and never referred to in it elsewhere as a means of influencing the Deity. In some passages, the writer of Esther appears to go out of the way to avoid mentioning God, even where it would have been quite normal and natural to bring God into the story (4:14–16; 6:1, 13; 8:17; 9:16–26). Another book in this respect is Ruth, which, interestingly, is powerfully devotional even though it has few religious references.

The Bible even uses secular words for "God."

Listen carefully to the conversation of committed Christians and you will notice that they tend to use a language for "God" that is different from the words used by the world at large. Christians speak of "the Lord," or "our Lord," or "our Savior," or "our Father," and suchlike. People who would not consider themselves Christians tend to use words like "the Almighty," or "the Supreme Being," or "the Creator," or "the Man upstairs," or "the Big Guy," or, often rather nervously, "God." (They don't want to use language that would commit them too heavily!)

There are, then, two kinds of God-language. One sort is natural within the believing group; the other sort is, so to speak, common property. We could call the words used within the believing group "religious" because they usually carry a special notion of God's salvation, loving care, and personal commitment, and they imply a profession of one's loyalty to God. They refer more to God's character as God comes to be known in personal spiritual experience. The other terms we could call non-religious, or secular, because they concentrate on the ideas of power, authority, and creatorhood in God—attributes held in common by all people who think about "God." This phenomenon is not unique to our age or culture. It is found within the Bible itself, which regularly uses words for "God" that are much more secular in nature than they are religious. In other words, in Scripture we find both a religious and a secular God-language.

By far, the significant religious word for "God" is translated in most English versions of the Bible as "Lord" (usually in small capitals, as in the AV, NAS, NIV, RSV, TEV). Knox, Phillips, and the New English Bible have it "Lord," and Moffatt, "the Eternal." This word in Hebrew represents the sacred name of the God of Israel. It was so special to ancient Israel that its people became afraid to utter it. And, partly because formal written Hebrew has no vowels, the pronunciation was forgotten. The word has four consonants, *yhwh* (or *jhvh*). The traditional way of saying this is "Jehovah," and most modern scholars are fairly confident that it was originally a word like "Yahweh" (the Jerusalem Bible has this). Those who used that name were marked off as belonging to a distinct community that worshiped "the Lord" as their God, for it designated the covenant name for God (non-Israelites would recognize the name merely as that of Israel's tribal deity). In the Old Testament that covenant community was, of course, Israel. In the New Testament, it is seen also as the Church, who called Jesus "Lord."

The recurring secular word throughout the Old Testament is the Hebrew word *elohim* (pronounced "el-low-heem"), or the even more widely used *el* (as in the last syllable of "Israel"), simply translated as "God" or "god." *El* had equivalents in most languages of the ancient Middle East (such as in Babylon: *bab-ilu*, "the gate of God"). There was also a slightly antiquated form, *eloah*.

When being spoken of by people outside the covenant community, *elohim* is occasionally used in the Bible for Israel's "god," appearing frequently as "the God." The word is also used for any beings of exalted authority and power. It is used of angels, apparently, in Psalm 8:5, and for spirits of the dead in 1 Samuel 28:13, and for magistrates, as in Psalm 82:6 (compare John 10:34). And it was often used of heathen gods. The *elohim* of the Moabites was Chemosh, and of Zidon it was Ashtoreth (1 Kings 11:33). The word is also found on the lips of non-Israelites talking rather ignorantly about Israel's "god" as being an *elohim* of the hills and not of the valleys (1 Kings 20:28). (This is uncomfortably like saying that Jesus is Lord in the Church and the home but not in art, law, business, physics, politics, or entertainment.) As people outside the covenant today use words for "God" as a reference to a vague Supreme Being, so people used *elohim* in the Old Testament as a word that did not imply any knowledge of quite who God was, or that God made Himself known, or that He made promises to people, or claimed their allegiance, or heard their prayers, or cared for them. Like "the Man upstairs," it was often barely a personal name at all, more like a description or a category.

Christians try to "sanctify" the secular passages by inserting religious meanings,

To feel the full force of the Bible's secular words for God, imagine reading a devotional book that does not mention Jesus (except possibly as a historical figure), or God's love and promises, or the call of grace to sinners; in other words, a book without any of the ideas of God that are distinctively Christian or even Jewish. We would feel dissatisfied. It would be like a holiday at the beach without sunshine. If the author had taken the Book of Ruth for her model, we might suspect her of an old fashioned romantic liberalism that confused beauty and holiness. If she had used Esther or the Song of Songs for her model, we might not recommend the book to anyone. Although we doubt it would come to that, for the author probably would not have had any success finding a christian publisher!

Many of the secular books and passages of Scripture pose serious difficulties to their expositors. The explicitness of the Song of Songs, for instance, troubles translators, and the lack of moral uplift in Esther is a particular embarrassment to one scholar who remarked, "There is not one noble character in the book." "I am so hostile to this book," Luther said, "I wish it did not exist!" To get around the difficulties, people usually attempt to "sanctify" such passages and books in one of three ways, such as by smuggling something religious or "spiritual" into the text by hook or by crook. So "additions" to the Book of Esther are found in the Old Testament *Apocrypha*, and Jewish scholastic ingenuity "discovered" the name *yhwh* four times in the text—twice forwards, twice backwards—as an acronym from four successive words.

... or by discovering examples of moral behavior or spiritual experience,

Another method of easing the secular problem is to concentrate on examples of moral behavior or spiritual experience in the books and passages. This is easy enough in Daniel or Ruth, but in the Book of Job this method actually undermines its message. The search for a moral lesson there explains Job's protestations of innocence as being a kind of pride which, though it did not exactly merit punishment, still needed to be dealt with through suffering. The point of the book, however, is that its protagonist suffered not because of his faults but because he was righteous (Job 1:1; 42:7). In the Book of Esther, the moral approach tends to elevate Esther into an ideal heroine delivering her people. Passages showing her in a less satisfactory light (4:4, 11) become obscured, and the whole story is then romanticized, its unpleasant realities ignored.

... or by the most
popular method: allegorizing.

Up to this century, by far the most popular means of expounding the Bible's secular material has been to spiritualize, or, more correctly, to allegorize, it. Its themes are then treated as an elaborate piece of symbolism, like Bunyan's *Pilgrim's Progress* or Spenser's *Faerie Queen*. So the Song of Songs becomes a poem about sinners being wooed to complete trust in the Lord and Savior, the husband of the Church or of the believing soul. Or it becomes an allegory of the believer's mystical union with Christ. Most allegorizing of this sort is justified by evoking the fact that the Old Testament is pre-Christian, and therefore that its relevance this side of Calvary is only that of a "type," a prophetic illustration. The Letter to the Hebrews somewhat supports this method in its interpretation of Old Testament ceremonies as "copies of the heavenly originals" (Hebrews 9:23, TEV). Though this has been known to revitalize the devotional life of God's people, it tends to reinforce the "religious only" way of knowing Scripture and therefore withhold biblical nourishment from secular life.

We have to question an indiscriminate use of allegorizing the Bible's secular passages and books for at least three reasons. One is that the Book of Hebrews aims its message especially to Jews and it expounds from the Books of Moses—the Law, or Torah, of the Old Testament. The Book of Hebrews, therefore, is a unique piece of literature and was used in a special way by the early christian teaching tradition. Second, it is only the ceremonial law of the Old Testament that Hebrews expounds this way, to show that the copies are now being replaced by a revelation of the Heavenly Original, and that respect for the copies necessitates going on from them to the real thing in Jesus Christ. (It is, of course, quite proper to treat symbols and copies allegorically.) Third, Jesus himself was born under the Law, and New Testament teaching never taught even Christian Jews to repudiate it. Remember, Jesus and they lived within a social environment that looked back to the Old Testament Law as God's will not only for the religious but also for the secular life of the nation. It would have been unthinkable for them to treat the Law's secular instructions merely allegorically. Further, Jesus never repudiated the Law as being the basis for the social legislation and the customary lifestyle of his own people, the Jews (though like most rabbis he often reinterpreted it). Even Paul, although an apostle to the Gentiles, did not hesitate to appeal literally to its principles. What Jesus did repudiate, and Paul after him, was the Judaizer's practice of reducing personal godliness and fellowship to a legislative program, which would mean, if one were a Gentile, becoming a Jew to become accepted by God.

The allegorical method is only appropriate to particular kinds of Scripture. The spiritualizing, or allegorizing, method in the Book of Hebrews is apparently a case of interpreting one particular kind of biblical literature according to its kind and function, or purpose, which is concerned largely with the ceremonial of the Old Testament. And ceremonial is by nature symbolic. That is the only way to expound its relevance, whether before or after the time of Jesus. The writer of Hebrews is also addressing Jewish converts and therefore adopts a style of exposition specially authoritative to them, such as in the references to Melchizedek and to the earthly sanctuary. Yet even though Hebrews is a unique piece of literature, in the sense that parts of the book lend itself to allegory, the writer does not hesitate to apply the face value of Old Testament passages literally where it is appropriate, especially in chapters 12 and 13.

Clearly, then, we are not meant to apply the allegorical method indiscriminately. So our first task is to determine what kind of biblical literature we are dealing with, and if it has a secular relevance to handle it accordingly. The Old Testament as a whole, then, does not require interpretation and application for our age because it is outdated but because its relevance has been transformed. Its principles, such as the rational authority, extend far beyond the cultural limitations of one elect ethnic group. They are just as relevant today.

From all of this we can see that our secular histories (if we can be allowed to put it like that) are quite important to the Kingdom of God. We see time and time again in the Old Testament that these histories can be quite pivotal indeed, such as when Abraham went to war against the four kings, or when Joseph served in prison or as Prime Minister of Egypt, or when Esther was chosen queen by a pagan monarch, or when Daniel rose to political power in Babylon. Today, with worldly thinking and powers still militating against God's rule in everyday life, our secular histories are no less important to the Kingdom, for, as we shall see, they can serve the purposes that God intends, and for His glory.

~4~

Interpreting the Bible's Secular Writings

With apologies to Forrest Gump, life is not so much like a box of chocolates as it is like those superhighways that roam our major cities. Some are eight or ten lanes wide running in one direction. The lanes of life, too, are headed somewhere. Each lane serves a different function, or purpose, and we are all on the road, traveling in those different functions at different times.

In chapter 13, we are going to explore this metaphor more fully, suggesting that there are fourteen or fifteen lanes of life—the religious (in the sense of ultimate faith commitments), the ethical-moral, the economic, the societal, the aesthetic, the biological, and others. We will then explore how the Bible sees their purpose and direction, and what methods and means we might use in those lanes to bring glory to God. Here we simply want to note that Christians, like everyone else, travel in different lanes at different times depending on what one is doing. A simple illustration would be that when a person is paying bills or investing, he or she is in the economic lane; when throwing a party, in the social lane. Christians, however, because of a split view of life (chapter 2), are accustomed to using Scripture as a map only for what we could call the religious and the ethical-moral lanes. That is, we are pretty sure of the purpose of those two lanes and the direction we need to be going in them, for we know how to use the Bible as the ultimate authority to back us up there. But life is such that we travel in all the lanes, depending on whether we are at church, at home, at work, at play. So the question becomes: where is the ultimate authority to back up the way we think, reason, and act in the other lanes? Are we driving in those lanes with biblical methods and means? Let's not be too quick to answer "yes" to this. For if we are not sure how the Bible addresses those aspects of life, we are probably headed in some wrong directions. If so, we are going to arrive at wrong destinations—no doubt being quite surprised when we do, as some of us have at times discovered! If our ultimate authority in those lanes is not Scripture, it will be some other source by default.

How then should we interpret the secular writings?

In the previous chapter we noted that our first task is to ferret out the Bible's instructions for what we are here calling life's secular lanes. Next comes interpreting that map for today, lest we find ourselves in a pileup along the highway. At this point, a significant question arises: if most of the Old Testament is to be taken as it stands, without allegorizing it, or looking for strained moral lessons or esoteric spiritual experiences in it, shouldn't those of us who are Gentile Christians be keeping things like the Sabbath, the food laws, and circumcision? If not, how then should we interpret the Bible's wisdom for everyday affairs?

The first century Church's response to a small but noisy contingent of high-profile religious leaders provides a clue. The "Judaizers," as they were known, believed that it was not enough for a Gentile just to become a Christian in order to be accepted by God. They argued that a Gentile also had to fully adopt Jewish law in order to become acceptable to God and able to participate in fellowship with their Jewish fellow-believers. So vigorously did the Judaizers press this point that for a while several apostles and other church leaders were swayed by it. This necessitated the "Council of Jerusalem" (Acts 15), which settled the matter only after much soul-searching.

The early Church provides an important clue.

The way the early Church addressed this idea and movement helps us understand how we can interpret Old Testament passages for today. Acts 15 records the apostolic Church's recognition that Gentiles do not have to become Jews in order to become accepted by God or to gain admission to the same full christian fellowship as enjoyed by Jewish fellow-believers. The Council of Jerusalem recognized that God saved and accepted Gentiles just as he did Jews: by grace through faith. Once the principle of "salvation by grace through faith" had been established, the practical question of social intercourse could be addressed. The conclusion was that Christian believers ought to respect certain scruples of their fellow Jewish believers. The conditions are laid down in verses 15 and 29 and deal with the main food laws and chastity. The principle here (see also Acts 21:25), according to some scholars, is a kind of negative form of the golden rule: "They should not do to others what they do not wish to have done to themselves." Christ's apostles, therefore, do not reject or allegorize Old Testament law on this occasion, nor do they apply it literally; rather, they show us that *through the Gospel* Old Testament ideas and principles could be universalized and set to work outside the Jewish nation and culture.

The New Testament largely takes the Old for granted as its foundation. Yes, it is concerned chiefly with one particular theme, which might be summed up as how Jesus the Messiah came to reconcile us to God by His death and resurrection. But like the Old Testament, the New cannot leave temporal issues alone. It details the organizational structure for the relief of widows in Acts 6 and 1 Timothy 5. It expounds the nature of civil government in Romans 13. Marriage and divorce, in its social as well as its personal contexts, are topics for Jesus, who also makes authoritative statements about taxes, children, inheritances, settling accounts, and many other non-religious matters.

The New Testament is about salvation, but it takes everyday life seriously.

Occasionally, Jesus diverts people out of the religious lane into a secular one even when they want the religious map. In one curious circumstance, the Gospel of Luke seems to go out of its way to indicate Jesus' deliberate answering of a religious question with a secular story. Jesus had stopped in Jericho to stay with a tax-man, which stirred up quite a controversy in itself, but, "While they were listening [to Jesus], he went on to tell them a parable *because he was near to Jerusalem and the people thought that the kingdom of God was going to appear at once*" (19:11). Now you can allegorize this parable as a religious "kingdom story," as people do, for the imagery lends itself to that. Yet the fact remains that the parable is a long story about people earning money. In other words, at the center of Jewish religious activity (Jerusalem) and in answer to a religious question (when and how the Kingdom of God will appear), Jesus tells a *secular* story, a parable about trustworthiness in the economic lane. This is probably not the way most of us would have answered a question about the appearance of the Kingdom! Yet this way of reasoning is normal for Jesus, for he sees life as a whole and God as equally involved in all of its parts. Here our Lord is showing in a quite pointed way how much the economic lane matters to God. Again we are reminded of the importance of our secular histories (chapter 3), and perhaps the most frightening aspect of the parable is that the judged are those who did not fulfill obediences to the king here.

The apostle Paul does not make many explicit references to Old Testament law, but when he does he takes its provisions seriously. In 1 Corinthians 9:9, when he cites Deuteronomy 25:4 in the context of paying preachers, "Do not muzzle an ox while it is treading out the grain," and he adds, "Is it only for oxen that God cares?", obviously he is expecting the answer, "Certainly not! This applies to us as well." Paul is not arguing that oxen do not matter. Just the opposite. His interpretation is applicable because oxen are valuable. His argument is what logicians would call *a fortiori*; that is, its reasoning goes: if oxen are important, then all the more so are human workers. He is not ignoring a law because he cannot apply it literally. Neither is he spiritualizing, nor allegorizing, a law that would be otherwise obsolete and therefore not binding. Nor is he reading it through stained glass, bending a religious meaning into it. His argument is forceful because the rational authority (chapter 3) of the law relating to oxen is binding, and his first conclusion is that its principle applies to any worker. Only on that basis does he then apply it to the Christian worker.

The Corinthian church was predominantly a Gentile church, yet Paul is here expounding the Jewish Torah and applying one of its principles *outside* the Jewish nation and culture and *into* a Gentile church's organizational life. (One application today may result from an honest examination of how ministers and workers ought to be paid by churches and parachurch organizations, who frequently assume that skills and services ought to be rendered at a greatly reduced fee, or even provided gratis, simply because those serving are Christians.) In 2 Corinthians 13:1, Paul does the same thing, applying the ancient Jewish provisions regarding testimony in court (Deuteronomy 19:15) to regulate investigations into the everyday activities of a largely Gentile Christian church. The practice also appears in 1 Timothy 5:19.

It is significant that Paul sees no reason to justify this type of exposition with an explanation (although in 1 Corinthians 10:6 he does solemnly remind his readers that the Old Testament narratives, as well as the Law, are applicable to them). It appears as if he and his readers took it for granted that the Old Testament addressed everyday life in their—more modern—times. The challenge they faced, to interpret this "ancient" material for their times, is also the challenge for us today. Again, through the Gospel Old Testament ideas and principles can be universalized and set to work for us in the present age.

Several features help us interpret the Bible's everyday material for our contemporary life.

Generally speaking, today's commentators are governed by historical, or even by chronological, interests in their scholarship. So they tend to regard the peculiarities of much of the Bible's secular passages and books as signs of late authorship, when Israel's religious life had lost its momentum. They point out that most passages and books of this kind belong to the last division of the Old Testament canon known as "the Writings" (the first two divisions being "the Law" and "the Prophets"). But some of the Writings, such as Chronicles, use the religious name "Yahweh" frequently, as do later books, such as Zechariah, in the two other divisions. On the other hand, some sections of Genesis do not use the religious name at all. (This might have an explanation in Exodus 6:3, but the subject is complex and involves considering other matters, such as the affinity of Genesis with the Book of Job.) So the historical and the chronological explanations do not help us much with the task we are seeking to accomplish through this book.

The secular writings have close associations with the non-Jewish world.

Several other features, however, will help us learn how to drive with the Bible in the secular lanes today, even in our pluralistic society. One feature is that these writings have close associations with the world outside of Palestine. The last twelve chapters of Genesis have an Egyptian setting, and most of Daniel takes place in Babylon. Proverbs, Ecclesiastes, and the Song of Songs are all connected with Solomon, who, far more than any other king, helped Israel become a leading nation geo-politically. And several of the Proverbs (22:20–21, for example) seem to have affinities with the wisdom literature of Egypt. In Solomon's reign the Israelite empire included many small neighboring nations, and, farther afield, non-Israelite political and commercial representatives from foreign lands were common at Solomon's court. As one scholar remarks, "Solomon was unmistakably the most secular of Israel's kings."

Of other books, Ruth is closely connected with Moab; Esther, like Daniel, is set in exile in a heathen court; and Job is the richest man "in the East," apparently in the Arabian Desert somewhere. These scriptural books, then, show that God's wisdom has a significance outside of the covenant community, outside of those who share faith in the LORD as their God.

They are connected with public affairs and are known as "wisdom literature."

Another feature is that most of these writings belong to a class known as "Wisdom Literature" (this is true even of one of the Psalms, 49, and probably more). Normally we think of "wisdom" as being possessed by people who have exceptional common sense or outstanding good judgment when conducting their affairs with people. Solomon in particular comes to mind, especially that cliffhanger with the two prostitutes and the baby. "When all Israel heard the verdict the king had given, they held the king in awe, because they saw that he had wisdom from God to administer justice" (1 Kings 3:28).

But to the ancient world, especially that of the Bible, "wisdom" also had a special meaning. It was connected with people in authority in public affairs, especially statecraft, commerce, and the law courts. "The Wise" in any nation were an elite who acted as counselors to the king. Like Daniel and his three friends, they were responsible and exceptional men attached to the king's court. The Magi who came to worship Jesus were such people. The Bible's wisdom literature is therefore connected with public affairs, with life outside of the Temple and the synagogue, outside of our church-related activities.

They major on the creation, which everyone shares, and on conditions shared by the whole human family.

A third helpful feature for today is that in Scripture the instructions for everyday life concentrate on God's work in the creation, such as with seed-time and harvest. That is, they deal with what we all have in common because we all share the same creation. Some of these instructions even have what we today might call science's interest in predictable things. Thus Solomon, who is renowned as a counselor and a musician and for his jurisprudence, is also noted as having expertise in botany and zoology (1 Kings 4:33).

Another feature is that they address human conditions that are shared by everyone: work and wealth, family and neighbors, economics and politics, and so on. For instance, the king in Israel, unlike many of the surrounding kings, was excluded from exercising the religious leadership of the nation (that is, its cultus, or acts of public worship). The task of his government was to concentrate on political and economic issues. This meant that in dealing with foreigners—people who owed no allegiance to the Covenant of Yahweh—they worshiped other gods—international negotiations and agreements could not be based on a common religious faith or law. They had to rest on whatever principles people had in common simply as human beings.

In these geo-political situations, of course, standards of right and wrong never developed to the heights found in the prophets, who continually called Israel's monarch and people back to the ideals of Deuteronomy for their nation's corporate life. Rather, a sort of minimum morality was required in global economics and in geo-political alignments for people to work together satisfactorily. This may seem strange to Christians today, but it was not strange, never mind "unbiblical," to God's covenant people of old. It did not make them feel guilty of "ungodly compromise," as it might (unnecessarily) do to us. Here is a paradox for our time. Applying this insight today would give us a way to lower our sights in the public square without lowering God's standards. In turn, we might just find ourselves becoming more listened to as Christians than ever before.

Such a standard appeals most frequently to prudence and common sense, with little reference to such demanding ideals like generous loyalty and covenant mercy. It takes account of shared, basic human conditions: people tend to overprice when they sell and underprice when they buy; fools won't listen to reason; people's nerves are precarious first thing in the morning, so it's wisdom to remember that when blessing (praising, congratulating) a neighbor. Again, such a standard addresses conditions shared by the whole human family. Romance is another, which, as the Song of Songs suggests, has its ups and downs for the godly as well as for the ungodly. Two others are cruelty and injustice, which people of all kinds suffer. And religious exhortations, the book also explains, are not always much help—Job discovers that wise men who don't realize this make miserable counselors.

The secular writings say: this is for humanity as a whole.

We may say, then, and this is quite significant, that the Bible's secular writings are about how people are, rather than what by the grace of the Lord they may become. They have the typical person's interest in everyday life, rather than in the way that God makes Himself known in special events to a special people. A likely translation of the concluding phrase of Ecclesiastes 12:13 sums up the foregoing features and epitomizes the concern of this wisdom literature: "This is the sum of man's duty." Literally it reads: "This is all mankind," or, "This is [for] humanity as a whole." It pertains to what all people have in common, created and fallen as they are, before considering the division between those within God's covenant and those who are not.

The Bible's wisdom literature therefore looks at the world as a whole, regardless of divisions of race or religious allegiance. And it does not look at the world in a disengaged way, as a mere spectator. It is always concerned with effective and consistent *action* within the world. It is precisely this wisdom, as will be shown in the next chapter, which we need in order to function faithfully under God in every aspect (lane) of life, to speak and act with relevance even in a culturally and religiously mixed society.

They share the same basic logic with the Gospel.

We mentioned that it is "through the Gospel" that the Old Testament's secular material can be set to work for us. This is another significant point. The Bible's wisdom literature can succeed today because it shares the same basic logical framework with the Gospel. Let us think again for a moment about the traditional approaches of many commentators (chapter 3). Such work has had outstanding value throughout the Church's history. Depths of devotion have been nourished by allegorical interpretations of the Song of Songs. Evangelists have used appeals from Job's comforters effectively and savingly. I[JP] personally have found the cynicism of Ecclesiastes invaluable for talking about the Gospel in English pubs. And, even stretching a point, we might say that the thought of God's name encoded in the Book of Esther is at least suggestive that the LORD is secretly present in situations from which persons have deliberately sought to exclude Him. We cannot imagine anyone doing this so well with Shakespeare's *Twelfth Night*, or D. H. Lawrence's *Sons and Lovers*, or Hawthorne's *Scarlet Letter*. So how is it that these approaches work so well with particular books and passages of Scripture?

It is because they share same basic logic with the Gospel. A certain framework of thought is found in them—a certain perspective—in the way their ideas are presented. Now this mindset "fits" the Gospel, which has its own inner logic; that is, it works with its own assumptions about the nature of God, the world, and people, although these are assumptions that the world at large does not necessarily hold at all.

How an anti-racist story from the Wisdom style shows relevance today. In the larger and more complex secular writings of Scripture it may be difficult to see their resonance with the Gospel at first. We can get acquainted with it in a more familiar and simple example from the New Testament "Parable of the Good Samaritan," which is presented in a literary form that is entirely characteristic of the Wisdom style. The Hebrew word for this style of writing is *mashal* (pronounced "maw-shawl"; the plural is *meshalim*). The word is translated as "proverb" in the book we have with that name.

We usually think of proverbs as pithy little sayings. Honesty is the best policy. A stitch in time saves nine. More haste, less speed. But there is much more to it. Basically the word meant "a comparison," and its impact depends on the principle that the rules which govern one aspect of life have parallels, comparisons, in other aspects. So, "faint heart never won fair maiden," we immediately know, is not about a weak cardiovascular pump! Anyway, a *mashal* could be a pithy saying, but also much more. The *meshalim* of the Wise might be quite extended passages like those found in Proverbs 1–8, where wisdom and folly are compared to two different kinds of women. Or they could be stories, what we call parables (the Greek word from which this comes, *parabole*, was the normal translation for *mashal*). Jesus was, of course, a master of the Wisdom style; in fact, Paul calls Jesus "Christ . . . the wisdom of God" (1 Corinthians 1:24).

As it stands, the Parable of the Good Samaritan challenges us to a thoroughgoing good neighborliness. Some of its sting, however, is in its bald secularity, is in, we might even say, its anti-religious nature. Jesus implies by it that devotees of religion do not have a monopoly on kindness. What's more, being religious might even hinder showing kindness and compassion (handling bodies and wounds could disqualify a Jewish priest from serving in the Temple). In using the Wisdom style, Jesus is echoing those words from Ecclesiastes: "This is [for] all mankind." No exceptions.

Jesus has a "Cross-shaped" conception
of neighborliness in his everyday wisdom.

The parable works for today because it has a conception of good neighbor-liness that "fits"

the Gospel *even though the parable is not itself religious in form*. That is, good neighborliness for Jesus is not just about lending the lawn mower to someone who is one day going to lend you an electric drill, or watching your friend's children after school because she is going to babysit your daughter on the weekend. It's not just about chatting over coffee, or even caring about local amenities. It is about putting oneself out, taking risks for a person in distress. It may even mean making sacrifices for your enemy. It is caring about people rather than about their race or religious allegiance, or your own taboos. It means giving in a special way: not just expending effort or contributing money, but making an open-ended self-commitment that may even involve others in the task. In this parable, therefore, Jesus uses the Wisdom style to give us a look at an everyday situation through the same set of values and attitudes that took him to the Cross. By this we see that the Gospel extends outside religious life.

All Jesus' parables, being part of the Wisdom style, disclose this same way of looking at common, everyday life. Thus we run across wisdom for folk who are managing estates, doing accounts, losing things, making bread, waging war. It is not that Jesus went around looking for religious lessons, jotting down useful sermon illustrations. No. For him the illustrations came naturally. They came out of his way of seeing the world's life as being shared by the whole of humanity *and being informed by the Gospel in the process*. This is why the Bible's secular passages and books can succeed today. It is why we can learn to interpret and apply them anytime, anywhere, for the Gospel has a relevance to all ages and cultures.

Again, merely to allegorize the Bible's secular literature is to lose its possible practical application for today's world. This is true even with "the best" allegories, such as Augustine's interpretation of the Parable of the Good Samaritan. Augustine, the great fourth-fifth century North African scholar, expounded the parable like this. The robbers were evil angels. The victim was Man lost in sin, going down from the City of Peace to Jericho, the City of the Curse. Jesus was the Good Samaritan. The inn was the Church. The two pence were the two sacraments of Baptism and Communion.

Well... Even granted that Augustine had a theological purpose in mind here, many of us feel an unnaturalness in that last one, an application rather different from what Jesus intended. But Augustine was, to put it mildly, no fool. Many of his ideas are astoundingly current. And one has to admit that his other images fit beautifully. In its day the allegory spoke powerfully, as it has for many highly intelligent and godly people since. What is the reason for its success? The allegory "fits" the Gospel. Nevertheless, his approach here, being allegorical, is different from the approach to the Bible's wisdom literature that we are presenting in this book.

The Bible's secular literature is based on the fear of the LORD. The view of the universe as being a reflection of the shared world of temptations and priorities, of choices and motives, of service and loyalty, of hating and loving, and so on colors all the biblical writings of "the Wise." It is largely what they meant by "wisdom," and it has a Gospel-way of looking at life. It is therefore much more than pithy sayings. It is always an intensely practical way of looking at things. And at its base is the all-pervasive significance of the spiritual dimension of faith, love, commitment, and, above all, an acknowledgment that the entire creation comes from the hand of "the LORD": the God who sustains all, who orders the destinies of people and nations, who has revealed Himself in the history of one, and who has pledged Himself specially to His chosen people. Thus "the fear of the LORD"—due regard for the absolute authority of Yahweh over *all* of life—is the foundation principle of biblical wisdom (Proverbs 1:7).

Please note: this is vital and fundamental, because it is the only starting point for any understanding of the secular world that has a hope of corresponding with the Gospel.

Jesus insists that this is the only way of interpreting Scripture. Our Lord makes this clear when explaining how Scripture itself can be misused. You could, he said, know what is in the Bible and interpret it wrongly if you did not have the right base, or starting point, for your "wisdom" in the matter. To the Jewish leaders who were in dispute with him, he declared, "You are in error because you do not know the Scriptures or the power of God." Now they certainly knew the text well enough, so what was wrong? Jesus later said, "You diligently study the Scriptures because you think that by them you possess eternal life. Yet these very Scriptures testify about me." It is not clear if Jesus is telling them to search, or if he is saying that they already do so. For our purpose here that is not important. His point is, "You can do what you like with Scripture; it will only speak truly to you if you read it in relation to me." Thus "the fear of the LORD"—the Lord Jesus Christ—is the basis of wisdom even in understanding Scripture itself.

The rest of the New Testament bears the same message. Paul is beset by people who preach a "gospel" that turns out not to be the Gospel (Galatians 1:6–9). In Colossians he also condemns the teaching of a "hollow and deceptive philosophy," one founded on "human tradition and the basic principles of this world," in place of one that is founded on Jesus Christ (2:8), and he says that we should see things from the viewpoint of heaven (3:2). James likewise talks about the wisdom that comes from below or from above (3:15–17). And Peter refers to Paul as writing with the wisdom that God gave him, explaining that some people who have not received instruction in the Gospel distort Scripture and what Paul says (2 Peter 3:15–16). These are all ways in which the New Testament reminds us that all of Scripture is based on the fear of the LORD, and that if we do not interpret it on that basis, life will go wrong.

Without the fear of the LORD, a God-less wisdom takes over.

Many distortions thus exist today, even within Christendom. For instance, if, instead of seeing life as based on the fear of the LORD, we see life as primarily a matter of morality, or of personal fulfillment, or even of meeting human needs, it may lead us to think of sin simply as a moral misdemeanor between human beings, or of salvation as gaining an integrated personality, or of love as a response to the demands of any situation. Then Jesus Christ himself gets to be regarded as a means to some other end, like solving personal disputes, or making people happy, or providing things.

Further, if our view of life is not based on the fear of the LORD it will subtly deviate from the biblical meanings of familiar concepts. "Truth" may become pictures recorded by television cameras. "Faith" may become, as someone said, "A yearn in soft focus," or working through a decision, or merely having a gut feeling or confessing a Bible verse. "Love" may become what two consenting adults make. "Impartiality" may become a refusal to make moral decisions at all. "Tolerance" may become complete indifference, a capitulation to the most intolerable situations. "Freedom" and "liberty" may become a license to do anything "as long as I'm not hurting anyone." Words like these have profound connotations and implications (chapters 14, 18, 19), and yet they get tossed about in the media with little meaning-reflection. Many listeners would find it difficult, if asked, to say what they mean by words like "justice" and "mercy." And few people would know their biblical meanings.

All of this is to say that the fear of the LORD must have a power even over the way we *think* about our secular ideas and beliefs and over *the language* we use to express them. That is, we must have the same source of wisdom, one based on the fear of the LORD, for the secular lanes as we have for the religious one. The mind abhors a vacuum. If our wisdom for life from Monday through Saturday is not based on the fear of the LORD and instructed from Scripture, a "secular secular" mindset, rather than a "biblical secular" one (to coin a couple phrases), takes over and gives meaning and direction to much that we understand and do in everyday life. Whether we are talking about crime prevention, or teachers' unions, or artistic expression, or education standards, or government spending, or retirement security, or any other non-religious area, we will by default develop an analytical process based on a "secular secular" mindset if we do not have one that is based on the fear of the LORD; that is, a "biblical secular" one.

*This is largely
the situation today.*

This is largely our situation today *as Christians*. Our loss of secular discourse with Scripture has meant that we have incarnated the basic assumptions, attitudes, ideas, means, and methods of the world's thinking about secular life. This has quite serious practical ramifications, for it means that we Christians are not usually saying anything fundamentally different from what the world already hears from within its own way of seeing life, from its own prophets. As a result, the world does not see anything really different from us at all. Like the car license plate frames and refrigerator magnets (chapter 2), we replicate how the world does life, stamp it with the name "Jesus" or with a Bible verse, sell it, and assume that that is all it takes for our efforts to be based on the fear of the LORD.

Harry Blamires got many Christians thinking about this vital piece of the puzzle in the early 1960s, with his perceptive diagnosis: "There is no longer a Christian mind." Blamires was not arguing that Christians no longer think. His contention was that they think about culture from a frame of reference and a set of criteria and evaluations that they had absorbed over the years from the "secular secular" way of seeing everyday life. Thus their whole analytical process for reflecting about their contemporary situations excluded truly christian thought about it. By Blamires' time, this was happening to believers by default, because not only had the mind of modern man been secularized, the modern christian mind had succumbed to the secularization process as well. Thus there was no longer a pool of thought in which to think christianly about modern culture, no uniquely christian theory of life to throw its weight around in the public square. There was no established christian teaching tradition—no packed contemporary field of discourse, to use Blamires' phrase—to tap into for thinking and writing about, for critiquing and solving the problems of, everyday life.

Forty years before Blamires' *The Christian Mind*, an astute British clergyman, G.A. Studdert Kennedy, already had his finger on the modern christian pulse. "A very large number of [Christians]," he wrote, "are dissociated personalities. They are one person on Sunday and another on Monday. They have one mind for the sanctuary and another for the street. They have one conscience for the church and another for the cotton factory. But they will not acknowledge the conflict" (Kenneth Leech in *The Eye of the Storm*, Harper San Francisco, quoting

Kennedy, p. 2).

What is said about history? It repeats itself because no one's listening? As Blamires himself said, it is difficult to do justice in words to the gravity of our loss, the loss of secular discourse with the Bible. One cannot characterize it without having recourse to language that sounds hysterical and melodramatic. Yet we would do well to ask ourselves why most of the acclaimed thinkers and prophets of our time are non-Christians. Christians may simply brush this off, saying, "Well, what do you expect? The world applauds its own." Maybe. But in not a few cases, the popularity and wide influence of the secular prophets is due to their being incisive and penetrating. That is, they reason more clearly and consistently within their way of seeing than we do about their way of seeing. As a result, our christian voice on social problems or political issues or international matters often pales before theirs. After all, our Lord himself said that the children of this generation are wiser than the children of light.

One may object, "Hold on. I don't think like that. I don't take my cues from the world. I attend christian conferences and read christian books." Unfortunately, in our time that does not guarantee one a "biblical secular" perspective. Blamires' point is that our loss of reasoning with the secular literature of Scripture is so thoroughgoing and longstanding that, as difficult as it may be to accept, the arguments, analyses, and "plans for action" promoted in our christian books and conferences are most likely carried out within a "secular secular" frame of reference, quite without our knowledge, or even the knowledge of those who developed the material. Not even our leaders, thinkers, and conference speakers, nor our pastors, escape this. Not even those of us who write books trying to address it! This is what we are up against as Christians influenced by the inveterate and ubiquitous presence of the secular worldview alongside our loss of secular discourse with Scripture.

A case in point: the world of christian business.

The force of the argument can be felt in the overheard wry comment that the only difference between a Christian businessman and his secular counterpart is that the former is in church on Sunday. The implication being that during the week there is little difference between the two in the way they run their businesses. Quite a reason for this is found in the "stained glass window" effect. Sunday after Sunday the businessman receives a steady diet of instruction that touches on religious and moral matters only. That is, there is little or no instruction from the pulpit, or from Sunday school, or from his Bible study group, that unpacks the wisdom of Scripture for the forty-to-fifty percent of the waking hours where his mind is on his work. To the degree that this is so, he will by default grapple with a big percentage of his life solely from within "secular secular" discourse about it.

This usually becomes quite irritating, for he knows that some aspects of work should be different from how they are, and yet he can't quite figure what direction to go. Sometimes he becomes intuitively restless for biblical wisdom here. He may even talk to his minister about it. And one Sunday morning, a message might resound from the pulpit about honesty and ethics in business dealings or about morality in the workforce. And if he dialed up a radio station, he might find a christian program about money management, or advice on employer-employee relations. But by and large, such instruction derives from the Bible's religious and moral teaching. And that's not scratching him where he is itching.

As much as one hates to admit it, this leaves that Christian without much that is uniquely biblical about business theory. So good business practices for that Christian become reduced to not telling lies, not breaking contracts, not flirting with secretaries. Fair enough. We need moral people doing business. But even non-Christians can drive fairly well in the ethical-moral lane. Our point is that the Bible's religious and moral instruction, as vital as it is, is not enough to make christian business theory much different from the world's. For instance, I[JP] find that when I start talking to Christian business people about making contracts that are generous in nature, they do not understand. This is because they are not thinking of business as a liberating process, which is how the Bible sees it, in part, because business by the Book is Gospel-shaped. This means that it is partly a rescue, a saving, operation.

Further, doing business by the wisdom of the Book would instruct people in such matters, believe it or not, as building design and advertising, workers' rights versus duties, and the use of natural resources. That is, such wisdom would help business people in the aesthetic, social, and biological lanes, respectively. Yet most Christian business people are not accustomed to digging into Scripture this way, nor are those who teach them. (Sections throughout this book offer ideas for theorizing in these areas.)

All of us are stuck in this condition. This is not to pick on Christian business people or our instructors in the faith. It merely highlights the business world to identify a condition all of us are stuck with, whether we are artists, pastors, teachers, nurses, journalists, designers, shop managers, economic analysts, you name it. We used the world of business merely to show that all who follow Jesus Christ are called to think different and to act differently *outside the sanctuary* from those who have another object of faith. Monday through Saturday is not a Sabbath rest for Christians from thinking and acting differently from those who do not follow Jesus Christ. When Philippians 2:1–8 calls us to have the mind of Christ, surely this does not mean for religious activities only. When the Bible calls us to know the will of God and to do it, surely that includes Monday through Saturday.

We are not in the least suggesting that the Bible can be used for answering all business questions. We cannot expect it to answer questions about what computer software to use, or what health care benefits to choose, or what new products to develop. Neither are we suggesting that the Bible can be used to answer all questions about psychology, technology, ecology, education, politics, or art. But the Bible does concern itself with secular life. More than we may have thought. And we are suggesting that every Christian can have recourse to the Bible's marketplace wisdom in ways never dreamed of.

If the Savior God made this world, it is surely ridiculous to have one mindset for understanding religious life and the Gospel and a different one for understanding everything else. What makes this so serious is that we live in this world alongside other human beings. We cannot prevent our thinking and our lives, or that of our children's, from interacting with others. Further, God has ordained that, willy nilly, we have at this point in time to be dependent on non-Christians and their inter-social arrangements for our daily needs. We vote from the same list on election day, rely on the same police, service our cars at the same garages. Christian schools still use many of the same textbooks as other schools, and christian supermarkets will not be all that different from others, even if the employees say "God bless you!" at the checkouts.

But there is a way out. In both Great Britain and the United States we find ourselves in societies that, because they are still living off of christian capital, are in crisis between biblical and secular ideals. In this ethos, one thing is absolutely certain: if we do not have a wisdom based on the fear of the LORD, if we do not choose and cultivate an understanding of the world that fits the Gospel and the Word of God, we shall by default find our thinking at the mercy of one that does not. As the next chapter will show, this will make many aspects of God's will and revelation for everyday life today both unintelligible to us as Christians and inaccessible to our societies.

~5~

Wisdom and Communication Breakdowns

*O*nce a dutiful and thrifty peasant's wife wrapped her shawl about her shoulders, took up her basket, and said to her husband, "Otto, I'm leaving now to go over the hill to nurse my sister, Anna. She's down with the fever, and her children need lookin' after. I won't be returnin' for several days. Look after yourself. And remember, when the cattle dealer comes to buy our three cows, make sure you do not strike a bargain with him unless you can get two hundred thalers for them. Nothing less. Do you hear?"

"For 'eaven's sake, woman, go. Just go 'n peace. I will manage that!"

"You, 'ndeed," said the woman. "You who are wont to do the most foolish things. I'm tellin' you now, we ourselves will be very lean cows this winter without that money." And having said that, she went on her way.

Two mornings later the cattle dealer came. When he had seen the cows and heard the price, he said, "I am quite willing to pay two hundred thalers. They are worth that. I will take the beasts away with me at once." He unfastened their ropes and drove them out of the cowhouse, but just as the cattle dealer was leaving the husband said, "You must give me the two hundred thalers now, or I cannot let the cows go."

"True," answered the cattle dealer, "but I have forgotten to buckle on my money belt this morning. Have no fear, however, you shall have security for my paying."

"And what shall that be," asked the man, "as you have nothing with you?"

"But I have these three cows with me," said the cattle dealer. "I will take two cows with me and leave one, and then you will have a good pledge."

The man saw the force of this and let the cattle dealer go away with two cows, thinking, "How pleased my wife will be when she finds how cleverly I have managed it!"

> **Wisdom is supreme;
> therefore get wisdom.**

The tale makes us smile. *We* know better. *We're* wiser than that. A fool and his money are soon parted. And other sayings spring to mind, especially about the virtues of wisdom. Some folks are wise and some are otherwise. Wise men make proverbs and fools repeat them. Through wisdom a house is built. Wisdom is more profitable than silver and yields better returns than gold. She is more precious than rubies. Nothing you desire can compare with her. Wisdom is supreme; therefore get wisdom. Sayings like these are instructive precisely because of tales about people like Otto, which came from early 19th century European folklore. How easily he got rooked, we tell ourselves. But let us thank the fool, for from him one may learn wisdom.

Certainly, "wisdom" is one of the great objects of human search throughout the history of our race, tracing back even to one of Eve's desires in the Garden. We may think that wisdom is reserved for old age, or that it is only about pithy sayings, or that it has a touch of cunning about it which gives certain people a clever understanding of situations that others would not have in a million years. The Bible's view of "wisdom" would include ideas like these, but there is much more to it.

How does the
Bible see "wisdom"?

Simply put, the Bible sees "wisdom" as the way in which the world works. That is, "In wisdom," says the Psalmist when speaking about the works of creation, "you [God] made them all" (Psalm 104:24). Jeremiah states that "God . . . founded the world by his wisdom" (10:12). In other words, the whole universe functions by the wisdom of God. We see this emphasized in a quite peculiar passage in Proverbs 8, which, incidentally, has produced a whole body of fruitful thought in christian theology. It sees "wisdom" as the very secret of the universe (8:22–36). Wisdom is personified there as "the craftsman at [God's] side . . . filled with delight . . . rejoicing always in [God's] presence. . . . [So] listen to me; blessed are those who keep my ways. Listen to my instruction and be wise."

This passage indicates that when God created the universe—with all its multifarious facets, with all the complex intricacies of its workings—first of all there was a concept, or vision, that dominated and controlled, or made effective, the process of creation, so that it "stands up" as it were. It doesn't exist like a cat and a dog fighting, which you can barely keep apart. It doesn't exist like nitroglycerin, which, if you gave it a jar, might suddenly blow up, and you would never know when. Rather, the creation has stability, and this stability is orderly. There are rules on which it works. There's a consistency to it, so that the same rules govern this earth which govern the farthest reaches of the galaxy. *That* was in God's mind as His wisdom. And through *that* He brought the world into being. This means that when you look out on the world and touch it and use it, you are touching God's own heart and mind. All the way through it you are touching a product of *God's* character.

But we're getting slightly ahead of ourselves.

This notion of how the Bible sees "wisdom"—the way in which the world works—may seem foreign to many of us. Science fiction writer Arthur C. Clarke can help us here. In his book *The City in the Stars*, Clarke visualizes a tremendous city millions of years in the future. This city is governed by a central computer. Everyone has their own free life and character, and all the rest of it, but the parameters in which everyone lives (billions of people) are determined by this amazing central computer. Their lives are ordered by the wisdom of this vast entity, to which they may refer for help. This might give us an insight into the fact that as a world, as a universe, we are governed by the patterns of thought, if we could put it like that, of Him who is our Creator. But our *real* universe is not ordered by the "wisdom" of some machine, however sophisticated. It is ordered by a Creator who loves His creation and wants us to be free to enjoy that love to the full.

The Son of God is the clue. Now the important thing about all this is that it is possible to know what those patterns of thought are. And we will know them in Christ. We may look on the Son of God (on his life, his character, his death, his resurrection), and we may look on what he knew that death to be (a death for human sin), and we may say, "This universe runs and works by those patterns of thought that we see in Jesus Christ." And everywhere, but everywhere, even in the fall of a grain of wheat into the ground, so that it can die and bring forth fruit, the patterns of thought and action that we see in Jesus Christ are stamped upon the structure of this world and universe, everywhere. This is what we mean when we talk about Jesus Christ as God.

That's a bit of a foretaste of where we are headed in this book, to learn how those patterns—the wisdom of Christ—are revealed in Scripture for everyday life. First we have more groundwork to cover. In this chapter we want to lay a good foundation for the idea of "wisdom" as the Bible speaks of it. We have said that it is about the way the world works. But there are different kinds of wisdom about that. In this chapter, we will begin to look at these, noting that their driving forces are largely accepted and held unconsciously and are often the cause of communication breakdowns between people who hold different wisdoms. We will also discover that it is difficult to detect our assumptions and to change them when they are faulty, and that wisdom is not strictly "a personal thing." And we build a working definition for "wisdom," which we will use throughout this book.

Why not use the term "worldview"? Just before digging into this, we would like to say a word about the use of the term "worldview" as it relates to "wisdom." When some of us in England were first exploring this subject in the early 1970s, the term we regularly used was the now familiar "worldview." In those days it had a fairly technical meaning as an English translation of a German word often found in theological texts, *weltanschauung*. It meant something profoundly radical and potentially revolutionary: that which dealt with fundamentals and roots: a way of looking at life that we normally absorb from our cultural environment from childhood and which functions chiefly unconsciously to give shape, meaning, and direction to everything we do. So it had quite a practical side to its meaning. By the time the ideas for this book were taking shape, however, "worldview" had become a popular buzz word and was losing its original meaning. People were using it mainly for ideas like "mindset," "social prejudice," or "passionately held convictions." That is, the term was losing its practical dimension, and today it is pretty much understood as relating to the world of ideas only. So I[JP] found myself vowing to write a book that did not use the word at all, because I needed a word that included "the practical." That forced me to search for an alternative, and my evangelical instinct took me to Scripture, where I found a term, wisdom, that said far more than the one I had discarded.

The trouble with the term "worldview" is that it now implies that we are somehow spectators before we are actors. "Wisdom," on the other hand, as the Bible denotes it, carries a profoundly practical as well as a theoretical meaning. It shows that one's way of *seeing* life has a direct bearing on how one *does* life; that is, how our ideas and actions are related. What's more, it carries connotations of "value." "Worldview" has come to suggest that we might survey life neutrally, like movie goers, virtually uninvolved. That is never, but never, the case. "Wisdom" shows the connection between thinking and acting, theory and practice, seeing and behaving. "Worldview" now tends to relate to the mind only. "Wisdom" shows the relationship between what goes on in our minds and what we do in the world. The word is so good that I hope it never suffers the same process of verbal inflation.

There are different kinds of "wisdom." In writing to the Corinthian church, the apostle Paul defends the authenticity of his ministry several times. He does this on one occasion by contrasting his ministry to that of others, and to show the dissimilarity he refers to the idea of "wisdom." In 1 Corinthians 1, he insists that he refuses to use, as he puts it, "words of human wisdom," and he points to a verse in Isaiah: "I will destroy the wisdom of the wise . . .". Then with the effects of the Gospel in mind, Paul asks, "Has not God made foolish the wisdom of the wise?" Here he is not referring, for example, to the wisdom of the Book of Proverbs, a wisdom, incidentally, in which he would have been trained to be a rabbi. Nor does he mean pithy sayings or the secular wisdom literature of the Bible. Uppermost in Paul's mind is the wisdom of the pagan world around him, which he sees as reduced to folly by God. (This world was predominantly Greek. So much so that for the Jews "Greek" and "Gentile" were practically synonymous.) Thus the entire chapter of 1 Corinthians is an exercise in contrasts between two wisdoms: God's and the world's. "Has not God made foolish the wisdom of the world? For . . . in the wisdom of God the world through its wisdom did not know him" (1:20–21). "The foolishness of God is wiser than man's wisdom, and the weakness of God is stronger than man's strength" (1:25). By his use of "wisdom" here, the apostle is explaining that the way in which the world really works (through God) is quite different from the way in which people may think, and that the different wisdoms seem like "foolishness" to each other.

In chapter 2 he develops this further, saying that his message was not one of "eloquence or superior wisdom" (2:1). Some people interpret this to mean that Paul regarded the Gospel as a message which demanded little intellectual activity and no serious effort at communication. But anyone who has grappled with his thinking in Romans, or felt the power of his language in Philippians 2:1–11 and 1 Corinthians 13, knows that this cannot be right.

God's wisdom has a different starting point from other wisdoms.

A key word here is "superior." By using it, Paul meant that he was not fighting with intellectual weapons chosen by and similar to, but somehow superior than, his opponents. Greek wisdom set so high a value on beauty of literary form, logical analysis, and sophisticated vocabulary that these qualities alone became the authenticators of truth. If it was skilled rhetoric it was true. Here was an idolatry of mind and speech that produced a style of communication which had lost interest in truth for its own sake. Words alone and the way they were used held the keys to truth. (This is not unlike the way in which "pictures" are seen as the keys to truth today: television.) All that mattered was refined argument couched in elegant rhetoric. Paul was not identifying the Gospel with that, with superior rhetoric or keener debating skills, because convictions founded on skillful apologetic or moving language are not sufficiently radical to be secure when the life-and-death issues of the Gospel are at stake (2:4–5). So it's not that he believed in mindless emotion or intuition, for he stated how radical and comprehensively significant his message was (2:6–8). *We certainly do speak a message of wisdom to those who are mature,* Paul said, virtually screaming. *But it is a different wisdom. It is a different way of looking at life, and it generates a different form of effective and consistent behavior. It is God's wisdom in Christ, the wisdom of the Cross. A wisdom that the world does not know.*

One of the more valuable benefits of the Bible's understanding of wisdom is therefore to help us see the integration of theory and practice. This is especially significant in our time because during the past few decades evangelicalism has approached secular life in two ways, broadly speaking. One way has emphasized "the Christian mind," the other what we might call "radical discipleship." These are both valuable movements, and the world benefits from both. But the former tends to concentrate on theory, often to the neglect of adequate practical outworkings, while the latter, although it has a fine record of sacrificial practice, has at times been captive to nonchristian ideologies and philosophies. We will cover this in some depth in chapter 7. Here we just note that the biblical theme of wisdom emphasizes the link between theory and practice, ideas and beliefs, thinking and behaving.

We now have a working definition for "wisdom."

Paul (remember, he is steeped in the Old Testament tradition) has this biblical meaning of "wisdom" in mind throughout this long passage in 1 Corinthians. And this brings us to our working definition. "Wisdom," according to the Bible, is a word about the sort of sense you make of creation in order to live in it effectively (it will affect what you think is effective living, too). Or you could put it like this: "wisdom" is about how you see life and act in it (according to how you see it). The apostle, then, means that people who have the wisdom of God think, see and act differently from those holding the world's wisdom.

The Corinthians were immersed in the Hellenistic way of looking at life, which controlled how one might reason, debate, persuade. (Again, not unlike the way people today are immersed in and influenced by television.) When Paul confronted the Corinthians about life-and-death issues, he first of all attacked that fundamental way of viewing life and the wisdom that flourished within it. For Paul, the beginning of true wisdom, and therefore of all true reasoning and all meaningful speech, was "the fear of the Lord" revealed in Jesus Christ (1:18, 24, 30). Consistent with that starting point, he explains, we teach a different kind of wisdom, a different view of life as a whole, and that results in a different kind of communication, which is why we reason and seek to inform and to persuade in a different way.

Different wisdoms will laugh at or be averse to each other.

The implications of this are crucial in the area of communication, and they come to light in Paul's reasoning. If we hope to make progress with our non-Christian contemporaries, communication must not be underestimated. So, Paul says, understand this first: one person's wisdom is another's foolishness. "We preach," says Paul, "Christ crucified: a stumbling block to the Jews and foolishness to the Gentiles, but to those whom God has called, . . . Christ . . . the wisdom of God" (1:23-24). This is the wisdom of the Cross, he says, and therefore my words and the ideas behind them will seem silly to those who have a different way of seeing how the world works. For instance, when Christians today are criticized or pilloried for their evangelistic zeal, they often imagine that this reaction comes from people who know what the Gospel is all about, and having understood it, are rejecting it knowing full well what they are doing. More often than not, however, people simply do not understand, for the wisdom may seem like nonsense (foolishness, to use Paul's term) to them. And the most troublesome opposition often comes from people who are desperately sincere. They may easily regard the Gospel not as a threat to their pride or conscience, or that it is too costly, but as a message that is simply wrongheaded. They may not imagine it could be true, for *their* way of seeing life may predispose them against the Gospel. So it does not seem right. It does not make sense within their way of making sense of things. It's unthinkable. Unimaginable. Improbable. As Paul said of his pre-christian experience, "I . . . was convinced that I ought to do all that was possible to oppose the name of Jesus" (Acts 26:9).

Many of us who are now Christians can recall our own former aversions to God's wisdom. In Detroit, where I[CS] was a teenager during the 1960s, one of the counter-culture's most revered underground rock music stations, WABX, vied for listeners on the radio dial right next to the nation's oldest christian stereo station, WBFG. I listened to ABX, as we affectionately called her, exclusively. Now in those days there was no digital lock on a radio signal, so it was not unusual for ABX to drift into "that preachy christian station." (A sign of the Aquarian times, no doubt—Mars struggling to align with Jupiter!) Whenever this drift occurred, I'd shudder. I couldn't reach for the dial fast enough, to re-align the signal. The wisdom I held could not stomach the wisdom of the other.

Yes, there may be other reasons for aversion or opposition. We can turn people off because we are rude, arrogant, or indiscreet. But that is not under consideration here. The reaction we are noting arises from fundamental conflicts between different ways of seeing life and living in it, different ways of understanding how the world works; that is, different wisdoms. The distasteful results (foolishness, aversion, pillory, criticism) arise because the hidden, conflicting assumptions about life are not being talked through by the two parties. This is true whether the Gospel is being preached or issues of secular life are being discussed by the parties.

Communication between wisdoms generally breaks down. Different wisdoms, therefore, affect communication. When people comment, as they frequently do, that other people's attitudes and actions are silly or ridiculous, they often forget that they are poking fun at people who probably take their lifestyles quite seriously. For example, not a few Christians in the 1980s ridiculed actress Shirley MacLaine, saying, "That crazy redhead with her wacky New Age ideas!" This completely missed the point. MacLaine has a sharp native intelligence, which she was putting to use during a serious spiritual search. Christians who missed that never got a hearing with MacLaine.

Cross-cultural experiences are often strikingly illustrative of communication breakdowns between different wisdoms. When comparing the Japanese and American cultures, Eugene Nida, a missionary anthropologist and linguist, remarked in his book *Customs and Cultures*, that in the United States photographers "have learned to appeal to the vanity of their customers by accentuating the attractive features of their [individual] appearance, so as to give them 'personality' . . . . In Japan . . . the photographers touch up a picture so that the person will correspond more closely to the proper Japanese type. Accordingly, when a Japanese exclaims over the picture of a Japanese girl, 'How lovely, she looks just like anyone', this is not an insult, it is quite a compliment, a perfectly natural one." Nida attributes the two dissimilar responses to American emphasis on individualism in contrast with Japanese attitudes of conformism.

A cross-cultural example: a Japanese father and an American photographer. With this in mind, let's imagine a Japanese man who has recently come with his family to live in the United States. He has had his daughter's photograph taken by a professional photographer, an American, and in due course he goes to pick up the photographs.

Photographer (proudly): "Here they are, sir. I'm sure you'll like them. They turned out great."

Father (appalled after gazing at the photos): "What is this? My daughter does not smile as broadly as that. And I know that she looks at people more boldly than I should like, but you have made her look quite shameless! I certainly do not like them!"

Photog: "What do you mean? I'm proud of these pictures. Your daughter's smile is striking. It's the most engaging feature about her face, especially when taken along with her frankness of manner. No one seeing these pictures will ever fail to recognize her anywhere."

Father: "But that is dreadful! How dare you make my daughter look like such an oddity? How would anyone invite her to a social occasion after seeing how she looks? Besides, these photographs would make her too embarrassed to be in company. She would know that everyone was noticing her!"

Photog: "But that's just the point! Think of how all the guys at the parties will be looking at her. She'll be able to take her pick of them."

Father: "That is appalling! Think how difficult it will be for me to choose a good husband for her with that going on!"

Photog: "Choose a good husband? What in the world . . . . Look, I worked really hard on these pictures. You asked me to take a special interest in them just for you, and I did. I can't understand you at all. Are you telling me you don't want people to admire her?"

Father: "Of course I do. That is exactly the point. How will people admire her if she looks like a shameless hussy?"

Photog: "Don't be ridiculous. That's not shamelessness. That's openness, friendliness. People will see her as she is. As an individual. As a real person. Isn't that what you want?"

Father: "Ridiculous? You are the one who is ridiculous! What kind of 'individual' would offend her family? What kind of 'real person' would show off like that, instead of presenting herself quietly among her people? I have no intention of buying photographs like these."

Photog: "Oh, come on. You're just being foolish. You're being possessive and unreasonable. You're turning down one of my best pieces of work. With pictures like that she could win a beauty contest. You're just being silly."

Father (almost speechless): "Beauty conte . . . ! You must be out of your mind! I bid you good day, sir!"

Hidden and conflicting basic assumptions cause communication breakdowns.

In their judgments about the photographs, both men are being completely consistent within their own wisdoms. Yet neither of them can begin to understand the other; hence their little word war. Neither person can see the other's line of reasoning because hidden and conflicting starting points (assumptions) in each man's wisdom determine the direction that each one's reasoning should go. For the Japanese, personal identity is essentially social. For the American, that notion is unacceptable; for him everyone is unique and social identity pales into insignificance before individuality. The American thinks, "How can the girl really be herself if she is identical with everyone else?" The Japanese thinks, "How can my daughter have her identity apart from the group?" It is impossible for either person to imagine any other alternative (without undergoing some kind of mental "conversion," that is).

Please note: this example is not about beliefs, opinions, or even convictions. It is about assumptions that are unquestioned and so deeply embedded that their truth is taken so for granted that we do not even know we are acting on them. We're just doing our thing, living as we normally do. We had not imagined, could not imagine, that things could, or perhaps should, be any other way.

Different basic assumptions produce different kinds of behavior.

Keeping in mind that "wisdom" is about a way of seeing *and* behaving, and the relationship between the two, let's look at how "Mick the meditator" and "Christine the praying Christian" approach healing. Mick the meditator is typical of many folk who, ten or fifteen years ago, would never even have dreamed of practicing "the laying on of stones." Today, however, he is among the increasing number of Westerners whose wisdom has been experiencing some quite fundamental changes. He is shaking off a Western wisdom that, for a couple hundred years, has been dominated by modernism. In its place he is gradually absorbing a wisdom that is based on what we might call a "holistic spirituality" derived from Eastern metaphysics. So once a week, in an effort to reduce his headaches, Mick now visits a healer who works with crystals. During each healing session, Mick enters a deep state of Eastern religious-type meditation while lying face up on the therapy table. He's got his eyes closed and his arms outstretched at his sides, palms turned up. The healer places small colorful crystals on Mick's forehead, along his arms, on his palms and chest, and in a straight line running from his navel to his neck. Mick lays there quietly meditating for twenty minutes and then the procedure ends. Dealing with headaches like that is unthinkable to Christine. She privately prays to God for relief from the headaches. Failing that, she might go to the elders of her church to have them pray for her, and the elders may practice "the laying on of hands." (This is not to say that both persons would not visit a doctor.)

In each person's wisdom, hidden and dissimilar starting points (assumptions) about the way the universe works influence how each will act. For Christine, the starting point is a personal, infinite, and all-powerful God who hears and answers prayer and who can be prayed to through Jesus Christ. Prayer might reveal why the headaches occur, or she may receive a grace from God through prayer that lessens or completely removes the headaches. For Mick, there is no God like that at home in the universe, one who can be prayed to. Within his wisdom lies an assumption that the source of reality is an impersonal and universal "cosmic energy," a kind of spiritual electricity that flows through the physical world like countless radio waves but is not material reality of any sort. According to this assumption, this subtle "life energy" can be tapped into for healing if you know the techniques for tuning into its frequencies. Also in his wisdom, sickness (headaches included) is "dis-ease," a condition in which a particular area of one's health is said to be out of sync with the harmonious frequencies of the universe. Crystals are thought to carry subtle nonmaterial wavelengths for tapping into the universal spiritual current, and meditation is thought to be the technique for making the crystals work like this. Thus Mick seeks to harmonize his personal energies with the universal energies to bring some relief. To pray to a personal God would be as unthinkable for him as meditating with stones laid on would be for Christine, for their fundamental assumptions about how life works are different. These assumptions go unquestioned; their truth being taken for granted. Neither person gets up in the morning thinking about them. Their actions just stem naturally from their assumptions. Neither person imagines things could, or should, be any other way. We'll leave it to your own felicity to imagine a conversation between them!

Our assumptions are not just a private matter but are shared communally. Another feature of an individual's wisdom is that it is not strictly "a personal thing." A person does not hold wisdom in isolation but communally. The foregoing personal judgments are not dissimilar merely because they are matters of individual likes and dislikes. These attitudes have come to be shared with the entire community to which each person belongs. Different wisdoms, therefore, represent corporate frames of mind, or collective mindsets, by which people live reasonably effectively with others in their particular community. Thus personal differences, such as between the Japanese father and the American photographer, are not merely between individuals but between different kinds of wisdom as each is shared with others within a particular culture or subculture.

To follow up one of our examples, traditional Japanese religion is socialized to an extent that even extreme forms of Western Catholicism would find difficult to handle; and within nations that assume the separation of church and state, it would seem unthinkable. Japanese education and industry also take on forms that reflect the same basic view of life: a strong commitment to group loyalty and self-denial that most Americans, with their rugged individualism, find unimaginable. And Japanese wisdom is effective, as anyone in American electronics or automotive fields will tell you!

The hidden assumptions of our wisdom control the way we see and live *all* of everyday life.

Their influence is all-pervading and taken for granted. The example of the Japanese father and the American photographer is not about the larger issues of moral decisions or religious convictions. It is about areas such as everyday expectations and attitudes: how we like our photos taken, forms of socializing, ways of arguing, styles of speaking, views of marriage. It is not that our hidden assumptions govern us in a deterministic manner; rather, they restrict the range of our options. The Japanese father would have accepted quite a wide variety of poses for his daughter, but certain facial expressions were impossible for him to accept. Surely it is not difficult to see that something that penetrates down to such details will also affect everything else in our lives.

The thing to remember is that we are noticing different kinds of *wisdom*, different ways of thinking about how the world works, different ways of making sense of life and living (acting) in it accordingly. However odd a particular wisdom may seem to an "outsider," it has its own consistency to the one living it, and its foundational assumptions are taken for granted by that person; that is, they are beyond question to the one who lives by them. Further, they are unprovable in the scientific sense, and so they are taken by faith. This is normal. In the ordinary way of things, to question the assumptions would be regarded as an eccentricity, like examining one's own eyeballs, if not a sort of insanity. This is why, when two wisdoms are at variance, a breakdown of communication occurs that no common language can overcome. The breakdown is so radical that what is to one party "obvious," "reasonable," "entirely right," "common sense," and "our duty" is to the other person "bizarre," "ridiculous," "unthinkable," "outrageous," or even "immoral." For example, it is reasonable for Mick the meditator to have stones laid on, but ridiculous to him to pray to God. Christine, however, returns the favor! It is bizarre to think about having stones laid on and entirely right to pray to God.[1]

These hidden foundation stones or driving forces of a wisdom have an unquestioned and almost sovereign authority in our lives. They are what the Old Testament would call "gods," dictating even the feelings

This is what the Old Testament means by "gods."

of conscience. It is not just that people will appear silly. It can be very serious. If anything is terribly wrong with the basic assumptions, people who live by the resultant wisdom may do things that are actually morally evil. Worse still, they may not think that what they are doing is wrong. This confronts us with a strange paradox: the more conscientious and consistent a person is, the worse the behavior might be. Extreme examples from history, like Adolf Hitler, Charles Manson, and Jim Jones, reveal the dreadful possibilities.

---

[1] In the book *The Gospel and the New Spirituality: Communicating the Truth in a World of Spiritual Seekers* (Thomas Nelson), I[CS] have tried to show ways to relieve the communication headaches that develop between Christians and non-Christian spiritual seekers. It really is a matter of wisdoms at variance and the problems that poses for the imagination. In the U.K., the book is titled *Wise as a Serpent, Harmless as a Dove* (Word Books).

Naboth's vineyard: our wisdom also directs our religious and moral values.

We have seen that our wisdom controls the way we see everyday life and act in it, and we have discovered that fundamental assumptions about life lay buried in our wisdom as hidden motivators. To illustrate these ideas, we have chiefly emphasized secular matters. Let us now see how wisdom affects our system of values, our sense of right and wrong, good and bad; that is, what we think and how we act on the issues of moral decisions and religious convictions. For instance, the headachy Mick and Christine, in their notions of ultimate reality, reveal that wisdom affects the religious aspect of life (Mick: pantheistic monism; Christine: monotheism). But there is more to it. A fascinating example is recorded in 1 Kings 21, in the Story of Naboth's Vineyard. Here we get insight about the Phoenicians, who were worshipers of a "Baal," a nature god who presided over the nation's fruitfulness and whose divine nature was thought to be shared by the Phoenician king. We also encounter Jezebel. She was from the Phoenician court of Sidon and had therefore been reared in a wisdom based on the "fear of the Baal of Sidon." Now Jezebel was consort to Ahab, the king of Israel.

At the time of the story, Ahab wants to expand his private royal gardens, and for this purpose he covets the family land of Naboth adjacent to the palace. He approaches Naboth with what, for a king in the Fertile Crescent at the time, is a generous offer: he will buy Naboth's land for the full price. Naboth's reply is illuminating. He does not say, "I'm not interested," or, "The price is too low," like a property owner today might say. He replies, "The LORD forbid!" Now we might think that is just the Bible's strong way of saying, "Not on your life!" (although it seems unlikely that a commoner would respond in that way to his king). Naboth's response is much more serious. He has no choice in the matter. He cannot sell the land. It is his ancestral inheritance, and a covenantal provision in Israel prevents him from selling it. That is what is behind his strong remark. Quite naturally, religious convictions in Naboth's wisdom instinctively shaped his view and response about the land.

Israel's faith in the Lord was bound up not only with God's deliverance of the people from Egypt but also with the land that God had promised to them and had given to them. Israel's land, therefore, was not theirs. It was the Lord's. (The Book of Joshua describes God's instruction to Moses to divide the land among the tribes of Israel and how Joshua handled its distribution.) Further, the Law of the Lord through Moses also established, by a variety of provisions, that nothing, not even utter destitution, was to alienate a family permanently from its God-appointed land inheritance. These elaborate provisions were made not only to keep the inheritance in the family but also to try to keep the family going for the inheritance. So Naboth was saying that he had an obligation to *the Lord* not to sell the land.

<u>*Ahab and Jezebel*
have conflicting wisdoms.</u>
Like a spoilt child, Ahab gets upset and Jezebel finds him sulking. When she finds out what has happened she is shocked: "Aren't you the king in Israel? What sort of king cannot enforce his divine will upon his subjects?" The wisdom in which she has been reared finds Israelite property laws outrageous, irksome, absurd. They are unthinkable. And in her wisdom she sees a way around them. Quite simple, really: if Naboth is secured by the law, put him outside the law and it will no longer apply to him. So first she turns a media spotlight on Naboth, hoping to rally public support for what is about to happen, because then the community will clearly see "justice" being done. So she frames him on a charge of treason (given her views, she may have half-believed that Naboth's response to Ahab was blasphemous and treasonable language). Naboth is thus made not only a criminal but also traitorous.

Jezebel's wisdom reasons irrefutably: the land is the property of the god of the land; the king is the divine representative of the god of the land; the king is also the divine promulgator of the law; his subjects hold their land as his tenants; therefore, with Naboth outside the law his patrimony is forfeit and must revert to the Crown. Where else can it go? With Naboth dead, the king will be rightfully in possession. Long live the king.

Ahab, poor fool, after Naboth's public execution, takes the land. But there he comes face to face with Elijah the prophet in a mood of biting condemnation: "So, you have not only murdered but usurped as well!"

<u>*Jezebel's religious assumptions*
shape her politics and notions of justice.</u>
Jezebel's wisdom is based on "the fear of the Baal," and this gives a certain shape and direction to her religious (faith) assumptions, her morality, her politics, her view of the land, and her notions of justice. All of this, of course, is disastrous for Naboth and grievous in the eyes of God. So along comes Elijah, whose wisdom, because it is based on "the fear of the Lord," is completely outside Jezebel's comprehension. She cannot conceive of a king who is not a semi-divine lawmaker but merely an administrator who himself is subject to the law. She cannot imagine how an ancestral heritage, especially if Naboth were a traitor, could never be the king's. Nevertheless, the king was but a man and the land belonged to the Lord God and did not revert to the Crown, ever. The land went to the "kinsman-redeemer," the *go'el*, the nearest of kin, who would hold it in trust for the family line, even if marrying the widow was necessary and possible for renewing it.

Undoubtedly Jezebel was villainous and unscrupulous. But she was also clever. She clearly intended this affair to appear as a proper act of government. Yet she made serious errors of judgment because her politics were the product of a wisdom based on a pagan conception of life. She was unable to comprehend an idea of justice that we in the West, reared in a wisdom strongly affected by the Bible, still take largely for granted.

Wisdom shapes all of our reasoning.

To review: wisdom is a way of seeing life and behaving in it according to how you see it. It is about the sort of sense you make of creation in order to live in it effectively (it will affect what you think is effective living, too). In every lane of life, all our reasoning and sense of values and priorities will be shaped by our wisdom, which in turn affects the way we think about, relate to, and behave among others. How we vote. Where and how our children are schooled. What we think about cultural hot-potato issues. The kind of entertainment we permit ourselves. Who we turn to for counseling in crises. Our views on spending and saving. What we think about environmental stewardship. The kind of church we attend, or why we may not have religious affiliations. What we drive and where we live. Who our friends are. And everything else that has to do with the lives we live. And this will affect communicating with those who hold to a different wisdom.

Naturally, any individual's view of life will have its own peculiarities arising from personal idiosyncrasies and interests, family tradition, and peer group attitudes. Yet for the most part we share the basic assumptions of our community and culture, and these control our spontaneous reactions to life's problems and circumstances. Think again of the Japanese father and the American photographer. People who have different hidden assumptions from ours may not merely disagree with us. They may think and act so differently that they may seem, at least at first, naive or eccentric to us, if not perverse or insane.

~6~

How Do We Get and Change Our Wisdom?

Besides understanding what wisdom is and how it affects people's communication with one another, a third part of the puzzle is how we get our wisdom. The way we get our wisdom is as simple as it is profound. For the most part, our wisdom simply grows up with us and in us. That is, we don't manufacture it or study it as a school subject, and we don't spend much time thinking about it. We absorb it throughout childhood. It develops in us, and we in it, as a singular part of its development in the history of the family, community, and culture in which we live.

We normally get wisdom the way we pick up language. Perhaps the best analogy for the way we get wisdom is found in the way we come to speak our mother tongue. We "pick it up" as we go along, by hearing, by imitating, by others correcting us. Long before we go to school to "learn English" from textbooks we are already using it with considerable fluency. By the time we begin to study it from books it is such a second nature to us that the way it comes across as a subject to be learned makes it seem strange, like algebra. We develop in our wisdom in exactly the same way. We pick it up, we absorb it, as we go along. Yet the analogy goes further. When we come across products of other wisdoms—Indian music, African medicine, Chinese architecture—our initial response is commonly like hearing a foreign language for the first time. We say, "How peculiar!" We take it for granted that our products are the normal ones and that the others are odd or even abnormal. This feeling can persist long after we know that the other people naturally regard *their* products as normal and ours as peculiar or abnormal.

So in the normal course of life, we do not formally learn our wisdom; we absorb it, more or less uncritically, as we go along. Early on, it develops in us largely within our homes, through various significant others and authority figures with whom we interact, such as fathers, mothers, aunts, uncles, grandparents, older siblings, and baby sitters. Then it comes from our schooling and from friends and neighbors, rivals and enemies, sports and religion. Radio, television, newspapers, and magazines are also big influences. Cultural heroes, advertising, and the art and architecture around us are other sources. Yet even though it has its spokespersons and expositors, each of us gives it a particular imprint from our own individual circumstances and personalities, just as we all have our own handwriting. Slowly it becomes a part of us. The eyes of our minds are continually and imperceptibly gathering additional tints to their lenses, and a way of seeing life and living in it effectively develops. The process also gives us highly developed instincts for responding selectively to the world around us, such as in determining what is important or unimportant. It is *our* wisdom.

By the time we are confronted with the wisdom of a different culture, much of it may seem so alien that we cannot imagine how any reasonable person would think and act like *that*. Some of it—especially if it's a biblical wisdom, and this is true even for Christians—simply gets explained away as being archaic or special, or it is ignored or overlooked because there is no place in our minds to put it.

The surprising wisdom of a cereal box.
So wisdom is a way of making sense of the world and living in it according to the sense we make of it. It is a way of seeing life and acting in it according to how we see it. It is about ideas and actions and their relationships. Examples like the Japanese father and the American photographer and the story of Naboth's Vineyard (chapter 5) reveal pretty clear-cut assumptions and their linkage with particular kinds of everyday human behavior. A culture's wisdom, however, also influences people and helps them cope by infiltrating, affirming, and guiding their lives in subtle ways as well.

An enlightening example (it's also a bit of fun) is to study the aesthetics and language of a cereal box. A surprisingly large number of people give these a quick once-over several times a week, because while they're eating breakfast there may be little else to look at! In the States, the front panel of the box typically showcases an immaculate bowl of cereal resplendent with bright berries into which a white silky stream is spilling like Angel Falls. Another popular motif displays any number of colorful cartoon characters. Side panels tell other stories. On one side, often labeled "nutrition facts," an impressive list of vitamins and minerals, largely in scientific language, greets the discerning eye. The opposite panel most often describes the cereal's natural goodness and wholesomeness. The back panel usually captures a glowing, suburban parent and child ready to enjoy some combination of entertainment and amusement leading to bliss. A Post Grape-Nuts® back panel once shouted: "Taste it, hear it, feel it, enjoy it!" Want fun and games? A General

Mills Cocoa Puffs® back panel once promised the children a game called: A Million and One Fun Facts.

The package says: conform to this. The whole package implies an ideal or norm to which you should seek to conform. In our day, however, many people already conform to it, so the package simply serves as an affirmation. Now that ideal has many aspects. It often includes, on the back panel for instance, the single parent nuclear family (you probably won't see a wedding ring on the parent's finger). Other aspects are found on the other panels. The message of the vitamin and mineral panel is that the scientist has been at work on this food—a strong attraction in an age when "science" has the status of a god over Western thinking. If a thing is "scientific," people are convinced. No questions need be asked. Never mind that most consumers don't know the real value of the ingredients, most of which they will receive from an ample diet. Science is the dispenser of health and the good life; it has been at work on this cereal, so it must be good for us. But since everything today needs to be "balanced," that's the task of the other side panel, which claims that the food is full of natural goodness. This panel comforts those for whom science might not be enough. And for those who have qualms about our technical prowess, or who feel unsettled by the culture's artificiality, here is security rooted in nature. This may be expressed overtly through health-nature words or covertly through natural-food recipes, with the cereal in hand, of course, as the main ingredient! The apparently contradictory message of the two side panels is necessary to capture the imaginations of two large groups of consumers, those with misgivings about the omniscience of science or the unpredictability of nature. The back panel, of course, is often about fun. Link that with a front panel of cartoon characters and a side panel with a recipe, and the children can have a real party with this cereal. As for the adults, they can rest assured that their children's health will not be harmed in the process.

So there it is: the nuclear family, back-to-nature, entertainment, science, health, and fun. It is a high ideal or norm within current American wisdom all neatly packaged and persuasively presented to give us peace of mind and to send us and our children off to a good start each day. No one questions it. It's just a normal part of the day.

The message reaches us unconsciously. Once you see through this kind of advertising it is easy enough to laugh at it. Quaker Oats®, for instance, once added the poetic phrase, "Yes, it's cold. But it warms the soul," in bold letters to the front panel of its Toasted Oats® cereal box. Want to venture a guess as to what that was all about? It ran at a time when an increasing number of adults in the States were becoming interested in "spirituality." Really. The formula, however, that demonstrates the metaphysical osmosis between cold cereal and a warm soul is no doubt going to remain within the hermetic confines of the Quaker Oats' alchemists! But make no mistake. The people who produce and market cereal make a lot of money. They know what they are doing. Their fingers are on the American pulse: the Family rules our morality; Science ensures our efficiency; Entertainment draws a crowd; Health matters to everybody; Nature grants both security and spontaneity; Spirituality gives people a way out. And Fun we must have when doing it.

So a culture's wisdom can be presented in quite sophisticated ways. Assumptions can be deeply imbedded and hidden, and yet very influential, helping people to cope by infiltrating, affirming, and guiding their lives in subtle ways. The message reaches us because most of the time we never reflect on our attitudes, or what makes us feel as we do, or how we process information. We simply see the images and accept them unconsciously because we grew up absorbing them. We are individuals, yes, but we are also part of a family, a group, a community, and a culture that endorses a wisdom. And these environments, which include such seemingly innocuous products as cereal boxes, strengthen its authority in our minds. (Perhaps this will give us a different view on the thousands of advertisements our children take in every week.) On this basis, in these environments, we build relationships with supporting notions, institutions, customs, and even with controversies, which in turn develop and confirm that particular view of life to us still further. Take, for instance, a difference between American and British cultures. In America, "truth" is authenticated by measurable results, while the British idea is that truth is authenticated by accumulated evidence. The former offers the certainty of mathematical statistics; the latter is conscious of the complex and conflicting nature of evidence. The American style aims at immediate effect; the British style aims at hedging one's bets, covering possible problems. And each style is an essential part of each culture's communication.

All of this is to say that things like these help to authenticate a family, a community, or a nation. An entire culture, then, becomes self-authenticating ("right") to those within it. As an example, take pragmatism in advertising. You have an idea. You market it. You get millions to buy it and then say that it's okay because millions have bought it! And this can be true even if the culture is grotesquely wrongheaded.

We must learn true wisdom where we have absorbed a faulty one. If we have picked up the wrong wisdom during the course of our lives and grown accustomed to using it, then the right one will have to be learned. If this sounds slightly odd, it is because we don't easily speak of "learning wisdom" but of "being wise." But we may be "wise" in a faulty wisdom. If so, the right wisdom has to take its place, and for adults, the process will be a tough learning curve. But it is the only way ahead. This is quite different from the "absorption process" through which we acquired wisdom from childhood. As adults seeking to change our wisdom we will have to *learn* wisdom.

One problem, here, is that only with great difficulty do people start understanding the hidden assumptions of their wisdom. This is because assumptions are normally beyond question. After all, people grow accustomed to using them, and, let's face it, the discovery that they are faulty might be embarrassing. But more than that, like land that has lain fallow for decades, it takes a determined effort to get below the surface of things, for the effort requires reflection such as most of us are not accustomed to. It's like trying to examine your own eyeballs. Jezebel (chapter 5) probably would not have been able to explain why she assumed that Ahab could take over Naboth's land. We could imagine her snorting, "Isn't it obvious? Who else could get the land? Who else could have any right to it?" The American photographer and Japanese father would probably have had a similar difficulty saying why they felt as strongly as they did. The Japanese is used to living by a cultural wisdom in which "the group" gets top priority, and that just gets taken for granted. At the least, he probably would not have the answer on the tip of his tongue but would need to think about it. So, too, with the American. He is immersed in a cultural wisdom in which "individualism" has been for so long so imperative that he is not conscious of the influence. And he may never have been. The same with Mick the meditator and Christine the praying Christian. Mick does not awake in the morning and remind himself, "Ultimate reality for me is impersonal, so I need to live consistent with that." He just goes to the crystal healer. Christine does not think, "Let's see, I'll talk to God because ultimate reality is personal." She just assumes that, and prays.

People who are intensely logically minded, of course, would rear an enormous edifice of reasoning to support their basic attitudes. But such edifices themselves are built on notions that have to be accepted (concluded) to start with—what geometry books call axioms. They are not regarded as needing proof but are, as we say, obvious. (They can be as apparently simple as "a straight line is the shortest distance between two points," or as strange as "a point has position but no size.") So religious people may rear edifices to the challenge, "Prove there's a God," but for most of them it will make little difference to their own beliefs if their arguments turn out to be unconvincing. An atheist, on the other hand, will quite happily commit himself to an edifice which in the end means that all he is saying is meaningless, while feeling that his opponent's criticism is hair-splitting and perverse. Each is starting from different "conclusions."

Identifying many assumptions and influences will be challenging.

It must also be understood that the process of absorbing wisdom from childhood is not just about being taught obvious facts (don't touch a hot stove; stay away from the road) or overt moral values (don't lie; say you're sorry). The process is also more subtle. In fact, the subtle influences and attitudes can be the most powerful in the long run, and most difficult to identify and change if they are wrong, because they come in unnoticed. An illuminating illustration, and a quite fundamental one with far-reaching ramifications across the spectrum of everyday life, is how children get wisdom from their parents unconsciously; that is, the parents don't realize what values they are imparting and the children don't recognize what they are picking up.

For instance, are the children raised in a home where they get to see their parents fighting, or do the parents hide their fights from the children? Is an atmosphere of honest questioning fostered, or do the children see in the parents an unapproachableness here? What topics are discussed at the dinner table, or does the family even eat together? What do the children see their parents regularly spending money on? Is there any pattern of activities in which the children actually get involved with the poor, the needy, the aged? What kind of entertainment do the children see the parents enjoying? What is the parental attitude toward the children's friends or school teachers? How are people of different races treated? Do mom and dad ever admit their mistakes to the children? Such questions are just the tip of a vast iceberg, and they are loaded with powerful implications for shaping a child's wisdom.

Changes are difficult and often triggered by crisis,

So, how do we go about examining our own eyeballs anyway? Normally we do not inquire into the basic assumptions on which our wisdom is built. Life is too short and too hurried, and things may be going well enough that there's no point in rocking the boat. Nevertheless, change is necessary. Since we can be resistant to change, even when we know it's necessary, situations arise that may force us to it. Life itself may present us with problems so revolutionary or so intractable that everything we take for granted may be called into question and there is a shaking of the foundations, a radical crisis. For individuals, it may be precipitated by divorce, bereavement, bankruptcy, approaching death, or having committed a previously unthinkable evil. It is not unlike moving—things that have been part of the furniture for so long that they have been overlooked now take on new significance.

The same principle holds true for communal and national life. Things may be going along fine for a long period, and then suddenly life is no longer normal. Events such as war, new technology, sudden prosperity, or natural disaster may force communities or nations to negotiate through periods of deep crises, and the upheavals are strong catalysts for change. During such times, a community or a nation faces problems before which its wisdom seems to stand helpless. And while this is happening it may interface with another culture that has a different wisdom which is pretty successful. If so, fundamental notions in the former wisdom are brought into the open and questioned, perhaps for the first time. But even then most people in the community are largely unaware of what is happening to them. As in our day, they may hear a peculiar term like "culture wars" and wonder what all the fuss is about. They may agree that something is terribly wrong but not understand that the wisdom of their culture is not coping with a deep crisis, that its basic assumptions are being weighed in the balance and found wanting.

... or by the alternative ways people live around us,

When the influence of new cultures or alternative ways of living establish their presence around us with noticeable degrees of success, our own cultures can become fundamentally challenged. Some time ago, for instance, people living in the U.K. saw people from India or Africa rather, I'm[JP] afraid, as one might see animals at the zoo: interesting, even exciting, but not to be taken home. Now they are loose on our streets, and some of them even tell us what to do! Besides the presence of Eastern and Third World cultures, the demands of international trade, the increase in overseas travel, and the vividness of television, which brings the global village right into our homes, have all been traumatic to us Westerners. And exacerbating all of this is the scientific ideal of "objectivity," which is such a powerful assumption within Western wisdom. That is, we must never let personal feelings, interests, or prejudices make us biased against the possibilities of the new.

Radical crisis, then, from any of a number of sources, and alternative ways of living, can reveal flaws in our wisdom. If our hidden assumptions are not what they ought to be, they cannot carry the weight of the crisis and they will fail to cope with the new situations. This can be deeply disturbing, especially for an older generation not raised in an age of such rapid change and therefore not prepared for it by their rearing. Yet if it forces us back to a new self-examination in the light of the biblical Gospel, the gains could be enormous.

... *or by unraveling the thread of a hunch.* A change in one's wisdom can also begin by following a hunch that you unravel like a thread to the end. To examine an assumption like that, especially if it is a long-standing one, can take you on quite a wisdom learning "curve." This process often begins when some practical situation no longer sits well. I[CS] remember when this happened to me concerning economic boycotts. I watched people stop shopping at K-mart because it owned Waldenbooks, which distributed pornographic magazines. I watched them stop eating at the Olive Garden restaurants, which supported pro-choice causes. They switched from AT&T phone service because it was sympathetic to gay lifestyles. Women switched doctors if theirs performed abortions. I went along with some of this kind of activism for a while. It seemed pretty good, and it gave you things to *do*, rather than just issues to complain about. The assumption was: don't spend your money in ways that support values and causes that you disagree with; be a better steward over "God's money" than that. Fair enough. I need to watch where I spend my money.

Then one day it hit me. In order to be consistently careful about who gets my money, then I can't be selective, can't boycott only what others had suggested. Besides those, I'm probably "supporting" any number of God-displeasing causes, however unwittingly. So if I want to live consistent with the assumption behind boycotting, I'm going to have to boycott many other corporations and businesses. When it occurred to me what that kind of research and eventual lifestyle change would entail, I realized that I would end up living as a hermit in the woods!

Of course, some things are not merely wrong but scandalously so, and righteous indignation, such as a boycott, is an appropriate response. So the boycott principle is not without merit. But I had placed too much in it. It is based on an assumption that truth lies in measurable results, and its success drives you logically to a situation that forces skepticism on a deeper level; hence my eventual insight. (Another piece of mischief is that, in sniping at issues, the boycott principle may divert people from tackling the fundamental problems of the structures and systems.)

Our assumptions, therefore, may not be all that they are cracked up to be, and if a crisis or an alternative lifestyle does not reveal it, thinking may.

~7~

Theories and the Bible's Strangeness

We have noted that any wisdom is put to the test by its ability to cope with new information and situations, and if it fails, all sorts of things go wrong. Here is where theories come into play, for our wisdom copes with new phenomena and new circumstances by calling on the theories within it for help. These theories, like our wisdom, are largely based on unexamined assumptions. Also like our wisdom itself, when our theories are inadequate and do not master the situation, usually the first thing to break down is communication.

Wrong theories in our wisdom cause much mischief.

Here is a playful illustration. It took place around a British game called "bowls," a leisurely sport most Americans will find unfamiliar. Bowls is usually played outdoors on a long rectangular patch of well cut lawn called a "green." A player—a bowler—starts the game by standing at one end of the green and rolling a small but fairly heavy and solid white ball, the "jack," down the green to the other end. The jack is not rolled again during that game. Players then take turns rolling their much larger and heavier black balls to see who can get closest to the jack. These larger balls are biased with interior weights and thus they follow various arcs when they are bowled toward the jack, not unlike American fingertip bowling balls en route to the pocket. A lot of sportsmanship ensues as bowlers roll their large black balls down the long green trying to knock opponents' balls out of the way while leaving their balls as close to the jack as possible.

Once as we were driving through a park, one of the younger members of our Peck family amused us by looking out of the back of the car and shouting, "Look, Dad, cannonball races!" Everyone looked around and saw a green with a leisurely game of bowls in play.

As my young son did, we all interpret any new phenomenon in terms of what we already know. So let's pull the car into a parking space, watch the game closely, and imagine a discussion between me and my son. I remark on the skill of a player who has rolled his ball just short of his opponent's ball and so got nearer the jack. My son is quite puzzled by my statement, but that doesn't stop him! He naturally responds, "What sort of a race is it where people only try to get even and not ahead?" So I explain the concept of "getting close rather than getting ahead." Rather dubiously he accepts the notion, but then he suggests that the players start aiming better. "After all, Dad, the cannonballs are going all over the place. One almost went round in a semi-circle." So I try again. But by the time I get through explaining the concept that these balls have a bias in them, he's now impatient with me and explodes, "Well, no self-respecting gunner would use ammunition that wouldn't go straight!" So I reply (fully assured and ever the expert!) that the bias is deliberately put into the balls during their manufacture. At this point my son gives up and mutters, "I can understand them using unbalanced ammunition if they have no choice, but actually making cannonballs like that… They must be mad!"

Communication breaks down intractably until the faulty theory is exposed.

You could hardly blame him. I failed to address his basic assumption that these were cannonballs, and that this mistake resulted in a different theory about the game and its rules. Because I had a different theory and failed to acknowledge that, he could not understand the game or my explanations of it.

What is more, and this is profoundly important, in his attempt to make sense of what he was seeing, his faulty theory meant that he asked the wrong questions. My answers, therefore, even though they were from the correct theory, were not helping him in the least, for they were not answering the questions that formed in his mind using the faulty theory. Like the Japanese father and the American photographer, we were talking past each other. My son's faulty assumption about this new experience that had come his way made progress impossible. It produced an erroneous theory in his mind about that new experience. My neglect, or ignorance, of that made communication impossible.

It is of course a parable. And the problem in that situation is a trivial one, easily resolved in terms of our common culture, unlike that of the Japanese father and the American photographer or Jezebel and Naboth (chapter 5). Yet the form of the problem is similar for all of us, even regarding the bigger issues, such as between an ethnic minority and the dominant culture, between liberal Christians and conservative ones, between labor and management in industry, between left wing and right wing politicians, and even, on a much larger scale, between Christians and non-Christians. As a culture increasingly fragments, conflicts become more wide-ranging and more common, until, if they are not corrected, a culture ends like the Tower of Babel. And along the way, the battle of ideas, tagged these days as "culture wars," often reduces to sniping at issues through hard line polemics rather than humble discussion between parties to discover ways to stop the fragmentation.

Theories enable us to cope with everyday life. Obviously, then, we need a wisdom that makes sound theories possible for coping with and communicating about life's problems effectively and consistently. And it must be a wisdom for understanding not only our own theories and their basic underpinnings but also the theories and assumptions of opposing viewpoints. Thinking again of St. Paul, when he speaks of opposing wisdoms he has in mind a bridge that must be crossed between the two "foolishnesses" in order for effective understanding and communication to take place[1].

People, however, can be terrified by the word "theory." But there is no need to be put off by it. "Theory" is not just a word for the intellectual. Besides, who is not intellectual? Anyone using the mind is intellectual. Our word "theory" comes from the Greek word *theoreo*, which means "to view." It did not originally mean viewing as a disinterested spectator or as a mere intellectual exercise; it meant viewing with an interest or purpose in mind, looking at a thing or an event for some practical purpose, such as, "The police have a theory that . . .". Thus *theoreo* gives us an appropriate concept to run alongside what the Bible means by "wisdom," which, as we have noted, includes both the theoretical and the practical and the relationship between them.

An illustration from everyday life in South America. Here is a fairly simple look at how a theory enables ordinary people to cope with practical, everyday life. In the Andes, numerous Indian tribes live high up in the mountains, and they have found a secret for tackling the most arduous feats of travel. They chew the leaves of the coca plant, and this acts as a surface anesthetic. It makes them immune to much of the muscular pain that comes from such exacting activity, and, apparently, it banishes fatigue. Obviously this is quite useful to them when climbing over that rugged terrain. Yet it can produce nasty side effects. It is not easy to determine how much an individual could safely use at a time, and it is ultimately disastrous to health. Also, the sheer bulk of the leaves limits the amount an individual can carry. If the person remains long in a region where no coca grows and runs out of leaves, he is out of luck.

---

[1] See footnote 1 in chapter 5.

One day, a chemist from the world of Western science appears. He observes the phenomenon and takes it for granted that it is not the whole coca leaf which dulls the pain. His wisdom gives him a theory which tells him that the effect is produced by chemicals in the leaf, for he has been reared and trained to think that way. He has, as we say, "a scientific background." It is not that the Indians are less intelligent. They have skills whereby they could completely outmaneuver the Westerner, from which the chemist might learn to the benefit of his own society. But in this business of using coca, the chemist's approach does not occur to the Indians. Their wisdom restricts the range of their options. It gives them a theory in which they see the efficacy as residing in the whole leaf, which, quite logically, they must make their own by eating it.

They have a theory about the coca leaf different from the scientist, and it produces a different way of analyzing and looking at that everyday occurrence. Due to that culture's animistic wisdom, it is more in terms of personal relationships than the chemist's, whose outlook, influenced as it is by naturalism and materialism, is less oriented to personal relationships and more interested in control of the environment. The chemist's wisdom enables him to theorize that it may not be the entire coca leaf which is needed. Further, he has a theory whereby he can identify a substance that can be extracted from the leaves and stored in bottles and used anywhere at any time with great accuracy of dosage: cocaine, which in its time has been an inestimable boon to the medical profession.

The chemist's theory is in certain respects more effective than the people of the Andes, in that it provides an ability to adapt the use of the drug to many changing conditions. This, incidentally, demonstrates (mind you, quite a long way down the road!) what Genesis 1:26 and 2:15 would call "cultivating and conserving" the earth. This is not about depleting the earth's resources or destroying the earth. It is about bringing the earth's resources under control for God's glory and everyone's benefit. This kind of control is of course not the only dimension of our existence on Earth, and in the West we tend to make a religion of it, but it is important nonetheless.

So we have the Andean Indian and the Western chemist. The wisdom of the former is as powerfully influenced by animism as the latter's is by naturalism and materialism, which in turn affects each person's theories. Our wisdom, therefore, becomes effective and expressive, and particularly revealing in new situations, by developing a model in our reason and imagination of how a thing works. This includes the cause and effect processes, the functions of the various elements in the thing under consideration, and the way the elements relate to each other, to ourselves, and to the environment. This model of how a thing works is what we mean by a theory. In science, of course, this takes a highly abstract form. For the rest of us, however, it is usually much less intellectually organized. The thing to keep in mind is that our wisdom gives us the parameters and possibilities of our theories—which explanations are feasible and which are not—whether one is a Japanese father, an American photographer, an Andean Indian, a Western chemist, a son in the car, or the reader of this sentence.

We all use theories all the time, and often need better ones.
The ability to form and use theories is a gift from God to us. It may be, and often is, misused, but it is still as much a gift from God as human affection or natural beauty, and to be used for His glory. It doesn't matter whether we realize it, or even whether we like it, we are using theories all the time. If we do not choose and use godly ones, and if we do not develop a means of finding out which are godly and which are not, we will be using whatever comes to mind. Since we have no right to presume on God for the things that He has left it our responsibility to do, and since sin influences the intellect often quite unknowingly, the likelihood is that any theory uncritically adopted will be ungodly.

Here's a quick illustration from law-making. Good laws, in part, liberate people to be loving (chapter 8). So what are we to think of a law that makes medical professionals, who happen upon the scene of an accident, afraid to help the injured person because they could get sued? This is not a law that liberates medical professionals (who could be quite loving in such a situation) to be loving. There is a bad theory behind such a law, which Christians working in the area of jurisprudence could seek to correct.

The way to better theories is through acquiring a wisdom that is becoming more and more biblical. Again, this means entering a process of change. Yes, on becoming a Christian a radical change is introduced into our outlook. We now say that we know God, and we are likely to take the supernatural more seriously. Personal religious experience, such as prayer, communion, and church attendance, takes on an entirely new meaning. The Bible, our moral obligations, and the religious attitudes of others also begin to have a different meaning, and we acquire sympathy with the causes that Christians identify with. Yet it would be unscriptural, besides being extraordinarily naive, to think that our entire wisdom on life changes completely straightaway. The Bible, after all, would not speak of the need for our mind's ongoing renewal if that were so (Romans 12:1–2), not to mention the apostle Paul's complaint that Christians fail to let the process keep working itself out (1 Corinthians 3:1–3; Galatians 3:1–3; Colossians 2:20–3:2).

Part of the difficulty in acquiring better theories through a more thorough biblical wisdom is the process itself, which stalls entirely too easily, often because we think we have arrived. The process, however, can be re-started by an increased humility of mind—an especially important admonition to those of us who have been Christians for quite a while! It is easy to fall into the trap of thinking that we are living quite consistent with biblical wisdom, that little in our thinking remains unscriptural. This may be true regarding the areas of religious convictions and moral decisions, but as we are seeing in this book, our thinking about secular life falls far short of how the wisdom of Scripture thinks about it. So let us be wise. Only one man ever lived totally consistent with biblical wisdom, and he got crucified for it! If we want to discover how consistent we are living according to the wisdom of the Bible, perhaps the answer is found in answering the question: how close are *we* to being sacrificed? Tough words, certainly. But we need to be tough on ourselves here, for the stakes are high.

The traditional Christian community can't always help us.

Another obstacle in the process is that we cannot do it on our own. As already noted, we absorb assumptions and develop attitudes to life in conjunction with our families and the community and culture around us. Unfortunately, what we have absorbed and developed from the christian community at large has considerably hindered the process of developing a wisdom that sees life as a whole with God equally involved in all of its parts. That is, we have been influenced for decades by a process of wisdom formation in which life is thought to be split into the spiritual and the material, the secular and the religious (or sacred). This means that those who desire to learn and develop biblical wisdom for secular life will find it hard to come by within the traditional christian community.

The situation today is such that Christians who awaken to their need for a truly coherent and thoroughgoing biblical wisdom, one that will penetrate the secular affairs of life consistently, are going to find that it is a desperate and daunting task, with few clues to follow and many vital signposts missing. It is, after all, a comparatively new enterprise for us, and we lack sophistication and expertise. Ministers raise bewildered, even disapproving, eyebrows at our questions. Christian friends struggle to understand what we are talking about and asking of them. Group discussions, even among those who do understand, may feel like a pooling of ignorance. Temptations arise to become impatient, to fall for easy and dogmatic answers, to wallow in self-pity ("Nobody understands me"), and to become simplistic. But the situation is improving. More resources are becoming available. Anyway, who said christian discipleship was going to be easy? When the Bible commands us not to be molded by the world but to have a renewed mind, surely this includes a change of thinking about secular life. Because of the obstacles, however, we will find it quite challenging, if not stimulating, to make the kind of changes that are needed.

We have got to get on with learning the wisdom of Scripture for secular life as best we can. Some fortunate persons may have a wisdom totally adequate for their needs and calling. They may be in a niche where conditions have even now not changed much, or where the demands of life are relatively simple and uncluttered. A person with a fairly basic task, such as looking after livestock on a remote ranch, might not need the range of wisdom required to be an effective politician or business director or architect. A sound instinct, drawn from a faithful devotional reading of Scripture, could make this person highly effective, especially where the work and environment is not far different from the Bible's. But nowadays television relates almost all of us to a vast world, and if nothing else, the children keep asking questions! So we need to wise up fast if only for their sakes. Most of us, therefore, need to learn how to do all that we can within our gifts and callings to bring biblical wisdom into the marketplace.

We can learn the Bible's secular wisdom from its "basic ingredients," We must find in Scripture a wisdom that enables us to cope with our complex and changing world in a consistently godly way. But the Bible does not often give us direct and explicit information about how to think and act regarding many of today's issues. It is not a handbook with a ready Index for that. This is because our era is, well, at least a couple of millennia and more down the road from when the Bible was written. Nevertheless, the Bible's wisdom can be interpreted for our time. Here is a brief introduction to several ways to kick-start the process both on your own and in study with others. (These ideas, all of which will take some time to develop in following chapters, are necessary to introduce here.)

One method is to dig around in the jargon of contemporary culture to see if the areas of life represented by those words is in any way addressed by the Bible. That is, the Bible "talks" in the language of what might be called "the basic ingredients" of today's complex issues and ideas. Our movers and shakers may use cryptic terms like "geo-political structures," "fiscal control of inflation," or "outcome-based education," and we may wonder what on earth the Bible can possibly have to say about them, if anything. Nevertheless, the most advanced mathematician once began by learning basic arithmetic; the concert pianist began with simple five-finger exercises. In the same way, the Bible introduces us to God's dealings with human beings in respect of the basic elements of human culture under conditions in which they can be perceived most clearly: in the simpler forms of human society. These "basic ingredients" have a direct relationship with the complexities of Western life. (We will discuss more of this way of learning wisdom from Scripture later, especially in chapters 15, 22, 23, where we will discover ways to analyze the complexities of Western life in their basic elements.)

... from its styles and methods of communication, When we can find no direct and explicit information, another approach is by studying the Bible's styles and methods of communication. Clues to the way we may do it were seen in the cereal box analogy (chapter 6). When we asked, "Why is the artwork and language on the box presented in that particular way?", we became aware of the underlying ideas and attitudes that were controlling the form of that particular communication, the principles behind it. The artists, designers, advertisers, and publicity consultants were all using their wisdom to prepare an effective message, and this, their wisdom, was as much concerned with styles and methods of communication—the choice of particular images and words, the way they were presented, who the audience was—as it was concerned with the information itself.

The Bible's wisdom, too, is concerned with styles and methods of communication. Thinking again of the apostle Paul, his (biblical) wisdom led him to adopt a particular style of speech and a method of communication: one that did not involve innuendo, euphemism, double-talk, or superior rhetoric. It was characterized by "plainness" of speech, as the Authorized Version puts it (this did not mean ugly or ungracious, but frank, honest, direct).

We live in a post-Christian era. Now that statement usually evokes a "woe-is-us" groan from Christians. But there is an upside. Not a few assumptions and ideas of Western culture's wisdom remain in place from biblical christian traditions. After all, the culture is still living off that capital. Wherever this is the case, these assumptions and ideas may not yet clash too noticeably with the Bible's way of putting things, and we may find ourselves having some common ground with our non-Christian contemporaries. Where the culture has only somewhat distorted the Bible's way of seeing life, it may not be too difficult to straighten out. People may ask us, "Where have we gone wrong?", and we may be able to reply, "We're not so far from getting it right as you may think."

... by appreciating and studying its strangeness, Of course, the question we are all asking is: where is our wisdom unbiblical? If only it were always easy to know! One way to become aware of that is to pause and consider, rather than to skip past, the places where the Bible's reasoning and ideas speak strangely to us. Let us become sensitive to the times when the Bible seems foreign indeed. It is easy to dismiss this

strangeness as being "Eastern" or "ancient," and maybe it is. But that in itself does not automatically mean it is outdated. Think again of the story of Naboth's Vineyard and what we learned by pausing to get inside the kind of reasoning going on in the minds of Jezebel, Elijah, Naboth, and Ahab.

Because of the different circumstances in which they develop, cultures other than our own always present us with the unusual and the unfamiliar. To people living in the tropics, igloos are an oddity, and that will make for distinctive customs, for instance, about how one enters a home and how the family sleeps. To people living in the large inland urban centers of America or England, the congested boat villages scattered around Hong Kong are peculiar; what would be an unconventional means of travel for the latter—cars—is a natural and everyday means for the former. But the kind of strangeness we are talking about here is different. Take the subject of "time," for example. I[CS] once knew a man who became livid whenever a plumber or an electrician arrived late at his house to make repairs. Like most Americans, he saw time like highly valued material. So time to him was earned, spent, or wasted. Further, he saw time as a duration between two events. So time for him was ordered. When the plumber was late, the man believed that his time had been wasted. If a repairman did not come on the scheduled day, the man in all likelihood would call another repairman, one who appreciated that time was valuable and who wanted to earn his fee by spending the man's time wisely! If the man would have been raised in Mexico or Spain, he would have been prepared for delays. You may arrive on the dot for an office appointment in Mexico but be kept "waiting" for an hour or more without it being considered discourteous. In fact, when making appointments, Mexicans may ask Americans, "Our time or your time?"

Another illustration comes from a tribal area in Asia, in which a group in the tribe was shown a picture of four objects: a hammer, a saw, a hatchet, and a log. They were then asked to say which did not fit together. We Westerners would generally put all the tools together, because we have been taught to analyze and classify things in abstract categories. So to us the log is the odd man out. Because oral societies, like this Asian tribe, tend to think in concrete-functional terms, this group placed the saw, the hatchet, and the log together, because you could make something with them. The hammer was not included because it was no good without a nail.

... by becoming sensitive to its perception of life.

So the strangeness we are noting here is deeper than outer cultural differences that appear, say, in the products. It is about the reasoning and the ideas that are taken for granted. Where the Bible speaks strangely like *that* to us, it must be treated as more than a mere curiosity.

Questions must be asked like, "Why is it given to us in that particular way, and does it have an interpretation for today?" (Again, following chapters will explore more of this in due course.)

This kind of strangeness in Scripture arises from its different perception of what life is all about, its *hows* and *whys*. The West, after all, has no monopoly on wisdom. We still learn from antiquity. We still study Plato and Aristotle without apology. If we can get under the skin of the Book of books, to look out on the world through the mind's eyes of its inspired writers, we can gain new ways of reasoning about the world at large, such as about its structures, its technologies, and its social relationships. We can make discoveries that are more than just "interesting." We can find subtle new meanings to concepts like "the family," "community," "freedom," "justice," "truth," "worth," and the spray of other basic ideas that gets splashed about like stardust in the media, but with little reflection. Having "biblical secular" insights in such areas would enable us to think more clearly, act more consistently, relate more effectively, and communicate more believably not only in today's world but also to future changes and challenges.

We may also learn from people's "sticking points."

Another way to learn from the Bible's wisdom literature is to discover and study in it where one of God's people dug his or her heels in and said, "This far will I go, and no farther." The prophet Daniel is enlightening here: a devoted Jew rises to great power in a pagan nation, under several administrations. He obviously has Yahweh's favor while doing it, and yet to get there he was put through a course of higher education that no card-carrying evangelical today would entertain. Talk about New Age! Nevertheless, he went through the education, took it on the nose, and at the end of it graduated *summa cum laude*. A lot of Jews would have said, "I'd rather die than go through that education," and this decision would be for them a matter of a godly conscience. But Daniel has a different sticking point about the matter. He will go through it. And along the way he has another sticking point. He will not use magic or divination to interpret dreams. He relies on the "God in heaven who reveals mysteries" (Daniel 2:28).

Daniel, too, will allow his name to be changed, but not his diet. Think about how odd this also must have seemed to other godly Jews at the time, for the threat of the Baals was for the Jews, all throughout their ancient history, a kind of religious bugbear. After all, "Baal" was the word you used for the god against whom Yahweh was implacably opposed. Ancient Hebrew antipathy toward the Baals so influenced the nation's psyche that it was not uncommon if, for instance, say through some lax of spirituality, a parent gave to a child a name which included the word "baal," that later writings, even in the Bible, would replace that word baal with one meaning "shame, disgrace." It is with this powerful connotation in his wisdom that Daniel accepts a new name, perhaps to match his new status. "God will judge" (Daniel) becomes "Baal is my prince" (Belteshazzar). Now he carried that name around in the Court. He had to respond to that name all the time. So, "What's your name, sir?" "'Baal is my prince' is my name." Just think what that meant to his soul as a devote Jew. But Daniel makes not a peep of protest. He does, however, dig his heels in elsewhere, such as regarding the food. Not a mountain most of us today might want to die on!

So here's a person who could go along with the heathen world he was in, at least over education and the sort of name he could carry, but not about food. Quite obviously, other Jews would have dug their heels in about the education, and certainly about accepting a name like Baal. But not this person. He has different sticking points, under God. Ask yourself, too, where was Daniel—more pointedly, *what was he doing?*—when his three friends, who were also in places of high government leadership, refused to bow down to Nebuchadnezzar's enormous gold image? Why wasn't Daniel facing the fiery furnace? Clearly, from Daniel 3:2, Nebuchadnezzar had summoned every official to the dedication. Further, where were Shadrach, Meshach, and Abednego when Daniel was facing the lions' den? Were their sticking points different?

This is not just fascinating. It's meant to be instructive for us today in our pluralistic situations. It will take some concerted unpacking of characters' lives in the wisdom literature to discover how, under God, Christians today can find their own godly sticking points. But the effort will be well worth it. Schools' workers, Christians involved with NGOs (non-government organizations), people making management decisions, and suchlike, report that this sort of approach has been indispensable to them in the complexities of today's world. Time and time again, what for one person is a godly compromise, for another may not be possible. And the different sticking points do not have to be causes for division. At the very least, this may help us all live together more peacefully, working together and appreciating others' decisions with less judgmentalism.

Apart from one man, people who never make mistakes…

A final word before we move on. When we begin comprehending how to apply biblical wisdom in everyday life and among non-Christians, we will be doing this work as disciples; that is, as learners, trainees. Now it is characteristic of learners that they do not always get things right the first time, and this we must keep in mind at all times. We are like amateur archers aiming from fixed points at moving targets;

to hit anything at all we must not only keep to our positions but also learn how to change our line of fire.

One of the tragic disabilities of Christianity, especially evangelicalism, is that we have never given permission to our thinkers and leaders to make mistakes. This has resulted in many bitter word wars and casualties from friendly fire. We have turned our commitment to an infallible Book and a knowable God into a mindset that makes it impossible for Christians to have room for experimenting, or even to be wrong at times, and still to retain their credibility and our confidence. We are not talking about gross moral lapses, here, such as occasionally scandalize Christianity. We mean the kind of tasks associated with this book. For example, in spite of the fact that not one of us spends an hour of our waking lives without ordering them according to theories, we treat theorizing with immediate contempt. This is because it smacks of intellectualism, certainly, but it is also because theories are by nature provisional and subject to correction and modification. Being corrected, however, is the very stuff of discipleship. We need to give ourselves, our leaders, and our thinkers permission to fail. We make no apology for saying that what follows is provisional and subject to correction, modification, or even rejection.

... never make anything.   In the next chapter, we will examine the problems of a wisdom that is based only on theology (religion) and morality. We will look at how Jesus dealt with the problem, and then offer a sketch-map for a journey whereby we may find other, better paths and landmarks.

Hopefully the rest of this book will introduce readers to a way of thinking for themselves, and thinking biblically when they do it. There is a further hope that those who benefit from it will learn to do the thinking far better than those of us who are doing it already. After all, what are we if no one can stand on our shoulders and, by so doing, see farther and better than we do?

Part Two

Getting the Lay of the Land

~8~

Weaknesses in the Evangelical Attitude to Social Problems

Besides the difficulties faced when using Scripture for instruction surrounding the complexities of today's life, also before us is the set of challenges when using Scripture to deal with issues in a mixed society. How do we as Christians deal with issues in a mixed, or pluralistic, society like ours? Certainly we have to find a way of saying how such a society might be run for everyone's best interests. But the classic problem is how we do that. For example, when that society is composed of Moslems, Hindus, humanists, and others, as well as Christians, how do we as Christians involve ourselves in a legislative process for people who believe in polygamy, animal sacrifice, and abortion? Do we have the right to impose one particular kind of conscience on other people? Questions like these have a particular bearing on legislation surrounding cultural hot button issues, such as the V-chip, censoring on the Internet, and cloning.

In this chapter we want to explore how we as Christians may respond to social issues in a mixed society in a way that is not an ungodly compromise to biblical truth. Because weaknesses in the evangelical attitude toward social problems are most obviously seen if we start thinking about politics, government, and lawmaking, that will be the approach of this chapter.

Problems arise when using religious and moral appeals to issues in a mixed society.

We Christians generally have a fairly restricted line of approach to social issues. We address them chiefly through the religious and moral teaching of Scripture. Further, we tend to assess people in terms of their religious and moral convictions. Now it is important to do so, but some Christians use this as an excuse not to have anything to do with non-Christians or to reject everything suggested by them. Nevertheless, we still have to live alongside of these other religionists in the same social units, and to do that we all have to share the same rules. Yet, as noted, in such a mix Christians tend to judge secular issues by the direct application of the moral and religious standards that apply to their consciences as individual christian believers. This is largely the way in which the Moral Majority practiced politics. It drew up shopping lists of policy questions on matters wherein moral judgments seemed to be decisive in christian terms. Candidates were to be assessed by their responses and Christians voted accordingly. This is still a popular approach with christian organizations, such as the Christian Coalition or the American Family Association. Though we may feel uneasy about the simplistic character of this, at least we can acknowledge from it that moral standards have a decisive place in the business of government. God's approval is never divorced from His moral law, and the Book does say that righteousness exalts a nation (Proverbs 14:34).

One time, a neighbor and I[CS] were talking, and within minutes he began venting about religious people being involved in politics. They should stay out of politics, he kept reminding me. The whole conversation caught me off-guard and I didn't know what to say. Some minutes later, it occurred to me that this neighbor did not realize that politics had to be anchored to some sort of moral standards. So I finally said, "I see what you're saying, but the problem is that you have to have some moral system informing your government. So which moral system do you want? A christian one or some other kind?" He saw the force of the argument and shrugged about wanting a christian one. But to answer, "I want the moral system of Scripture," is not enough of an answer. For how to accomplish this remains a puzzling social acrostic in our pluralistic lands today.

The moral approach is widely applicable, and the prophets used it.

Since it is obviously quite appealing, where, then, does the approach through morality take us? For one thing, a personal moral criterion is obviously widely applicable on a number of issues, even in a mixed society. There is a sense in which one can ask the question "Ought you to do that?" about any activity. It is particularly applicable to legislation, because everyone agrees that legislation ought not to encourage or enforce immoral or unethical behavior (though there is wide disagreement about how law and morality should relate to each other and what is immoral or unethical). Certainly throughout her history, the church of Christ has in one way or another called those around her to a social life that made the practice of christian notions of morality possible.

The best known Old Testament critic of his contemporary society, Amos, used the moral approach. Chapter 2:6 refers to people who sell the righteous for money and the needy for a pair of shoes. Amos is condemning the perversion of the law whereby a judge might condemn a man into slavery to his creditor over the debt incurred for the price of a pair of shoes, or essential clothing. (Malachi, in chapter 2 of his prophecy, makes a similar accusation against the priests, who were appointed in Israel to give legal instruction and advice, but who were practicing deception and partiality in this.) Elsewhere in those early chapters, Amos applies a moral standard even to non-Israelites, even to the non-Israelites' treatment of each other. So, in 1:6–10, he denounces Gaza "for three sins . . . even for four . . . because she took captive whole communities and sold them to Edom." Here we see that Amos is not just concerned about his own people. He is clearly condemning Gaza's heartlessness. In 2:1–3, he condemns Moab because they burned the bones of the king of Edom to lime. Amos makes this pronouncement even though Edom was no friend to Israel (1:11). This particular judgment is about two heathen nations and has nothing directly to do with Israel at all. Amos is criticizing cruelty, oppression, and aggressive brutal exploitation of other people. It is a moral problem, and the judgments are based on a morality common to all peoples. (This is similar in principle to the Bible's wisdom literature being for "all humanity"; chapter 4.)

In the West, there are special opportunities to use shared moral standards.

Amos' approach indicates that, though we may not expect others to act on our religious principles, we may appeal to a general sense of moral right and wrong. There is some sense of justice, for instance, that seems to be accessible to all human beings, and it has been used as evidence for the concept of "natural law." Spurgeon taught, as a basic evangelistic strategy, the maxim: "Preach to the conscience." Wesley used to say, "Preach law before you preach grace." People may not listen to christian dogma or acknowledge the authority of Scripture, but at least we may hope for their conscience to be on our side. This may turn out to be more difficult to utilize in a pluralistic society than we expect or imagine, but it is certainly worth taking account of. Indeed, such has been the influence of Christianity that non-Christians may have a greater sensitivity to its demands than many Christians. Remember, Abraham was rebuked by a Pharaoh!

The implications of the moral appeal to conscience are quite significant because considerable respect for biblical moral standards among ordinary people still exists in countries that have a fairly strong christian background history. Even if people are unaware that it largely comes from the Bible, they nevertheless probably will admit that they would not like living without that kind of law, order, and freedom, now that they are accustomed to it.

Trouble is, what respect there is for biblical moral standards has become pretty much inarticulate among ordinary people, and so its biblical basis goes unappreciated by them. Further, a loss of confidence in the authority of Scripture has resulted in an inability to spell out decisively what it teaches. In the West, law, at least on a national scale, is now largely established through debate without much, if any, reference to Scripture. In regional or local politics, however, especially in areas where there are large concentrations of Christians, it may not be unusual for Scripture still to have a voice in political discussions. This happened recently in the small town where I[CS] live. Hundreds of citizens met several times with city aldermen to cite passages from the Bible as their reasons for opposition to restaurants within city limits obtaining beer licenses. But as a rule, insofar as the media of communication are more controlled by a powerful and wealthy establishment, biblical viewpoints are likely to be at an initial disadvantage in a mixed society. This means that unless a biblical viewpoint is presented clearly, forcefully, and sensibly to ordinary people, its opponents will normally dominate the debate. This is surely what we see happening today.

Ordinary people need to hear well-reasoned, coherent arguments from us. When we Christians are confronted with violations of our moral ideals, it is not enough to express indignation, disgust, horror, or shock. Bald assertions of dogmatic assumptions will not do, still less angry vilification and character assassination of opponents. What is needed are well-reasoned statements of the moral issues involved, statements made by praying people who are prepared, as a part of their christian discipleship, to learn how to state the case coherently and effectively, so that it cannot be undermined by honest reasoning.

Christians are expected to speak out and take a moral stand. The power of the moral approach to social problems has the further attraction of offering society a readily accessible and often historically proven means of christian criticism. Christians do have, after all, a long and fairly honorable tradition of serious commitment to ethical thinking and action, and this is generally understood to be typically Christian. The world expects Christians to speak out against violations of justice, ethics, honesty, and integrity. And, of all Christians today, those who accept the fundamental authority of Scripture should be able to speak clearly and with some confidence on such matters. Among those who are not so committed to the Bible, widespread disarray exists, but even then at least the teaching of Scripture might be expected to provide focus for some discussion and perhaps for some consensus.

In our development of clear, forceful, and sensible explanations, it must also be admitted that moral judgments are not clear in some issues. And in other issues, if we knew the biblical text better we might have clearer answers.

Such situations do not have to be disheartening; they can pose a healthy tension for us, for certainly issues arise that need long years of research and debate before they come into true christian focus. But we cannot always wait. The world rushes on. We may need to speak now even about issues that are still unclear to us as Christians. At the very least, if we really care, we might find ways to hold back the flood, to stop the worst breaches in the dam. We might then get the time needed for the more subtle and complex questions. In the meantime, we can at least, even now, bear a good, clear, and relevant witness to moral ideals and standards, even if we have difficulties in showing how these might be achieved in society.

We may be able to appeal to an officially accepted standard. Those who live in countries where the Christian faith has some legal status in government have a peculiar opportunity. In the United Kingdom, for example, the law of the land is officially based on the teaching of Scripture. This is demonstrated symbolically at the coronation service by the presentation of a Bible to the Sovereign. The service is supposed to be, among other things, a formal public demonstration of the principles on which the state is to conduct the affairs of the nation. It ought not to be mere empty ceremony, and certainly no one in the U.K. should feel embarrassed defending a reference to biblical morals in public life. It is an appalling hypocrisy, however, to make this a solemn declaration of intent and then in practice to make no reference to such standards at all. It would be better, according to the Book, not to vow such allegiance to the Word of God, than to vow and not pay (Ecclesiastes 5:5). If Christian citizens do not speak fluently to condemn it, then surely they are guilty of condoning it by their silence.

In the United States, where there can be no official appeal to Scripture, and where the Separation of Church and State is a strong organizing principle, still, appeals can be made to where the law of the land was derived from biblical thought. It can then be shown how these ideas have been good for the nation and how their distortion or removal is bad for it. Many ordinary citizens are unaware of the influence that the Bible has had on some of the nation's founding principles. It is no small thing when a citizen's eyes are opened to how beneficial the moral truths of Scripture have been for developing the law and order of the nation and the freedom of its citizens.

But there are problems with the approach to issues through morality alone. As important and useful as the moral criteria are for social issues, their use involves us in considerable difficulties in mixed societies. One difficulty relates to the moral basis that we use for reference. Another relates to not being able to use moral criteria alone as a remedy for every issue. Both of these difficulties will be considered together now.

If asked to offer a summary of biblical moral standards, we would probably refer to the Ten Commandments. They obviously stand in a vital place in the Old Testament Law, and they also seem to have held this place in the New Testament (Matthew 5:17; Mark 10:9–11; Romans 13:9). For the purpose of dealing with social issues, they give us an apparently clear meaning to at least the minimum requirements for love to be properly expressed in social relationships. Throughout the past centuries it has been widely assumed in the Church that they can be used this way. It is not uncommon for people to misunderstand this and so to make the Ten Commandments into a moral ideal, which, if attained, is all that love requires.

Another common misunderstanding, here, can be found in one person's comment that he had trouble seeing how love could be properly expressed though a list of "thou shalt nots." This opens us to a brief comment on the nature of what might be called "negative law," which seems to be limiting people, and in a sense it is, but it is actually freeing people up to love in all kinds of ways. Negative law works like this. In the town where I[CS] live, the public library is located on Court Avenue, and from where I live, there are many different routes to get to that library. A person could take Hwy. 339 to the Parkway, turn left and take the Parkway to Court Avenue, and then turn left and take that road to the library. Or, you could take 339 to McMahan Road, turn left and take McMahan to Middle Creek Road, turn right to Eastgate Road, where you would turn left on . . . , and so on until you arrived at the library. You get the picture. There are a number of ways that you can get there from my house. If someone asked me how to get to the library, and I said, "You must go only this one way," then I have limited that person only to one way. The person is not free to take any of the other ways. But if I respond, "You must not go this way," then the person would be free to take any way of his choosing except the one forbidden. Negative law is like that. It precludes one way—thou shalt not commit murder; thou shalt not commit adultery—which frees people up to "get there" (express love in relationships) in many other ways. Negative law allows you to do what you like outside the prohibition. But back to the topic in hand.

Illustrations from the Ten Commandments reveal some of the difficulties.

Applying the Ten Commandments in a mixed society is challenging. They are more difficult to use socially than they appear. Certainly, it is increasingly difficult to apply them in the direct way in which it was done in Israel's day, when they were taken for granted by the nation. Today, a most valuable exercise would be to look carefully at their language and context and struggle afresh to get some notion of how they spoke to their original hearers. We also need to discover precisely what they were about. For example, are they about morality in general, or personal morality, or public morality, or what? Were they originally meant as a general summary of godly ethics? Or was some other aim in view?

Some may respond by saying that it is quite obvious what the Ten Commandments mean.

Others may say that the kind of study being proposed here is an attempt to twist or neutralize the Scriptures. Such a thing can be done of course. But we all agree that Scripture speaks afresh to every age and that it is our business to interpret it faithfully for our generation. The previous generation was reading Scripture to answer questions different from ours. We cannot be idly content with the weapons of a past warfare, when God's Word is for the present. We must in part, then, try to recapture some of the original significance of the Ten Commandments, and on that basis reassess their analogous use for today. We will, of course, not be able to succeed completely, but the effort will, under God, give us insights that we sorely need. This book will not have space for a full-scale effort, yet we can at least look at some features of the Commandments that present difficulties when approaching issues in a mixed society.

The First Two Commandments:
I am the LORD your God who brought you out of Egypt,
out of the land of slavery. You shall have no other gods
before me. You shall not make for yourself an idol in the
form of anything in heaven above or on the earth beneath
or in the waters below. You shall not bow down to them
or worship them.

We can't pass laws like the first two Commandments today!

The first two Commandments are about religious belief and worship. We find it generally impossible to believe (as many past ages believed) that they can be directly applied in any society where there is a wide variety of apparently sincerely held religious faiths. We may offer excuses for the Church's past history of religious intolerance, but we can no longer support it. However we may expound these two Commandments for Christians in our churches, there seems no way in which they can be applied as moral principles in a religiously mixed society with the same kind of direct constraint as, say, "You shall not steal." We know we cannot pass laws saying that everybody must attend christian worship.

Evangelicals would perhaps want to confine these two Commandments to the substance of their evangelistic call to the nation, telling it that any people who put hindrances in the way of worshiping the true God is in violation of God's Law. But most Christians would feel unhappy about enforcing such worship in the way that Old Testament laws did. So at the outset we seem forced to become selective about which Commandments we are going to use as legislative principles in our present age.

The Third Commandment:
You shall not misuse the Name of the LORD your
God, for the LORD will not hold anyone guiltless
who misuses His Name.

The Third Commandment is difficult to define for legal purposes.

This Commandment seems more promising. For example, Jesus, in Matthew 5:33, refers this to taking oaths as guarantees of truthfulness and honor (a principle echoed in James 5:12). Yet this raises problems for people to whom the Lord (the God of the Bible) is not God. Must we regard this Name as a socially accepted convention for guaranteeing truth in court? Even most Christians do not normally think of this Commandment in a forensic, or legal, context; they see it as a prohibition of "bad language." Further, because "blasphemy" in our law courts has now become not much more than "that which is offensive to religious people," it is difficult to apply this Commandment in any meaningful way as a moral standard for social action. Nevertheless, we are sure that it has a relevance, which needs to be discovered and applied. As we commonly understand the matter, however, we could not do so, especially in a multi-faith society, without an intolerance and an inconsistency that would bring the whole notion into disrepute. (On the whole, Christians sit strangely inconsistent to this Commandment. For example, obscenity, especially when it involves sex, is generally regarded with more horror than blasphemy.)

The Fourth Commandment:
Remember the Sabbath day by keeping it holy.
Six days shall you labor . . . but the seventh day
is a Sabbath to the LORD your God. On it you
shall not do any work.

The New Testament treats the Fourth Commandment strangely.

In the U.K., many Christians feel strongly that this Commandment is important for national life. Only in the early 1990s were Sunday shopping laws in the U.K. changed to permit stores to be legally open on that day, and this came about in the face of much strong christian opposition. It might also be said that a society which makes corporate worship difficult or almost impossible for Christians is hardly christian. Further, keeping one day separate is obviously an important means of cementing family life, we may argue, and it offers a bulwark against workaholism. That surely has relevance at a time when the family seems specially vulnerable. It might make sense, too, particularly when many people are unemployed.

The trouble is that all this does not naturally come out of a contemporary christian understanding of this text, which often spiritualizes it (chapter 3) using passages such as Hebrews chapters 3 and 4. Not to mention that many Christians work only five days a week—are they disobeying this Commandment? After all, it says six days shall, not may, you work! Further, even though "the Sabbath" is a subject used repeatedly by the Pharisees to accuse Jesus, the New Testament never cites this Commandment directly, and Jesus' teaching on the subject tends continuously towards a slackening of its stringency (Mark 2:23–27). And many early Christian converts were slaves who had no freedom to observe it.

In any case, the early Church seems quite deliberately to have adopted a different way of looking at this Commandment, as if to declare a break with the old order (John 20:19; Acts 20:7; Hebrews 4:8–9). Even the Commandment itself defines the expression "keeping holy" in terms of "rest" and "cessation from work" rather than as worship, which is the characteristic concern of Christians today when thinking about this Commandment. The worship pattern of early Israel was more on a monthly cycle. There is little stress on a weekly day of worship until the Exile, when it became focused on the synagogue. Even then, to a people for whom public worship was heavily liturgical and sacramental, the synagogue worship had more of the atmosphere of a school than it did of a church as we think of it.

Technology and industry today make its application tortuous.

The enormous cultural changes brought about by the new technologies of the last two centuries have challenged the traditional applications of this Commandment as a moral principle in a way that is unprecedented. The lifestyles of earlier ages were manifestly dominated by agriculture, much as the biblical world was. While agriculture is still vital to our survival, our lifestyle is not dominated by it. The demands of machinery for round-the-clock, round-the-week maintenance present a far more serious problem for the fourth Commandment than the need to milk cows or rescue bullocks from ditches. Cows are, after all, works of nature (and so, of God); factories are works of man, a sinner. Yet it is difficult in an age of scientific blessings to refute the argument that if the former requires Sunday work, why not the latter? If we use electricity for warmth and lighting for our Sunday services, then surely...

**Some groups want
different Sabbath days.**

On top of all this is the complexity of a society with powerful subgroups: Jews that keep Saturday, Moslems that keep Friday, and sects that keep other days. No doubt we can have apparently straightforward answers for ourselves as private individuals, but answers are not so straightforward in the maelstrom of legislative debate in pluralistic societies.

The Sabbath Commandment, with its protest against the idolatry of success and material achievement, surely speaks to our age. Although it is difficult to say just how the Commandment could apply socially today, we are sure that ways can be discovered, especially for employers and employees, who, after all, are those most concerned with work and most often in need of rest! And then there is the reality that in many periods many people are desperately overworked while millions cannot find employment. So unless we apply the Sabbath Commandment in a way that is consistent with the rest of our faith and faithful to its biblical use, then we will be drawing on it with a rope of sand. If we are not biblically consistent, we shall be inconsistent.

The Fifth Commandment:
Honor your father and your mother.

***Our culture makes it virtually impossible to
express the Fifth Commandment in legislative terms.***

This is another Commandment whose social imp-lications we do not seem to be aware of. Most of the talk about it revolves around the problems of rebellious teenagers resenting parental authority. But this is possibly as much a symptom as a disorder. Our culture has virtually disenfranchised its parental generation, a generation whose advice and influence we desperately need because their expertise is in the area of human values. It takes a long time to develop a perspective on life and character, which means that it is really only available at first hand to the older generation.

At least three characteristics of our age contribute to this attitude. To begin with, technological change occurs so rapidly that older people cannot learn the skills of the new society quickly enough. Second, the materialism of our society reduces our concern for values and character and increases our interest in personality manipulation: "How to improve your relationships," "How to have a better self-image," "How to have self-esteem," "How to . . . ." Third, the process of making the parental generation irrelevant reduces their ability to express themselves and to maintain their self-respect. This makes them even more irrelevant, and a vicious circle is well on its way. Look at what is left for them toward the end of their lives. A gold watch at retirement, the token honor of "senior citizen," the condescending adulation, "He was a great guy," and housing in a community of other ageing people who usually present little or no challenge to their abilities. No wonder their mental vision atrophies (from isolation and loss of use). No wonder we call them "vague," "difficult," and "helpless." What else can they become? Until we slow up our headlong pursuit of material sophistication and personal self-satisfaction and learn of life from their stories, what else can they become?

Now our adolescents are not stupid. It is certainly within the realm of possibilities that they do not honor their parents because they see that their parents' lifestyle does not honor the grandparents, with whom, interestingly, the young often have a better relationship.

The Sixth Commandment:
You shall not commit murder.

The Sixth Commandment does not mean all human life is sacred. This Commandment seems plain enough, socially. Most societies have recognized the principle with laws in one form or another. There is, however, a growing confusion whereby all killing gets spoken of as murder. This usually appears in present-day debates on capital punishment. The fundamental difference between the two in biblical thought, and in most cultures, is found in public law. Killing done as a deliberate personal act is murder. Killing done under the constraints and limits of public law is not. Only when the sense of obligation to public law is weakened can the confusion arise.

This Commandment is not much help with the case against abortion. This Commandment is also used in the abortion debate, though often in a simplistic and question-begging fashion. One thing to be realized is that this Commandment is not about the "sacredness of human life." That is, there is a sacredness about human beings, made in God's image, but their earthly life is another matter. To be a human being is to have an eternal dimension in which only God may correct our failures, and which alone gives meaning to the present. But our earthly life is only "sacred" insofar as God endorses it. When God says a murderer should be put to death, God regards the murderer's earthly life as no longer sacred. Clearly, this Commandment does not imply an absolute sacredness to human life. Therefore its use in the abortion debate would be quite limited, such as to the murderer of a baby in the womb. That is why when it is used in the abortion debate the way it is today, about the sanctity of human life, this

Commandment doesn't really get us anywhere, for the argument involves us in an elaborate casuistry about when the fetus becomes a person.

There are far better ways of arguing the case against abortion. One quite biblical way would be an argument from duty. This is a fundamentally different approach, and it may be worth a brief mention here to highlight how it may help us make a coherent, well-reasoned, and effective argument that ordinary persons can follow. Take, for instance, one area of ethics in its relation to the unborn baby: when a fetus becomes a person. Evangelicals generally discuss this in categories of "the rights of the fetus" as against the mother's "right to choose." The trouble with this kind of thinking (American evangelicals have been to a large degree forced to use it by the Constitution) is that it is not the way the Bible thinks about ethics. In Scripture, rights, insofar as they are spoken of at all (there is no special word for them), are defined by duties. For the primary concern in the Bible is duties, not rights. Thus, you have a right to any particular thing in so far as you have a duty toward it.

The problem with using "rights" as a core for ethical discussion of the unborn is that it makes duty a self-centered affair. That is, if I claim my rights I am imposing duties on others. That's the problem. And others' duties depend on whether I want to waive my rights. If I want to waive my rights, they don't have any duties. The Bible, however, doesn't work that way round. It says we have duties. This opens up a fundamentally new approach to the abortion debate. For one thing, it takes the pressure off having to know and to argue only from the category of a "person with an inalienable right to life." It also means that even if we cannot know when or if the fetus becomes a person, we can still know that we have a duty to the fetus, whatever it is at whatever point of its development. Further, if someday the ground were shot out from under the "rights" argument—if it were someday shown by biologists, for instance, that the fetus was not a person (thus not having a right in terms of the Constitution)—it would not mean that we therefore no longer had to respect the fetus. We still could not do with it as we liked, for we would still have a duty to it. We would still have strong ground for arguing for the baby's birth. This principle can be highlighted by taking the whole discussion back a step; that is, every young man before he is married has a duty even toward his sperm.

Our categories of reasoning may not be all that biblical. From this, we see that the categories of reasoning used in pro-life debate may not be all that biblical. They may be American, but that is another story. The biblical category of "duty" is much more to the point because everything, then, does not hinge on "the person" of the fetus.

Whether it is a person or not, the duty we have to a fetus can give life to the unborn. You see, if it isn't a person, then we can't talk about rights. And if it is a person, we're currently stalled by the elaborate casuistry as to when the fetus becomes a person. But if we start talking about duties, then the question becomes what is the mother's duty to the fetus? What is the father's duty to it? What is the doctor's duty, the community's duty, the government's duty? My duty? This by-passes the question of whether the fetus is a person; maybe not entirely, but largely. At least it means that we can take the ethical argument to a point where people have to do something about it and cannot just disengage themselves. All of this is to say that if our moral and ethical thinking works the way the Bible's does, it never lets us off the hook in the abortion debate just because we cannot say for certain when the fetus is a person. We're never in a place where we can say, "I can't do anything about it." We have duties. All of us. Legislation that headed in this direction would liberate the love of those already born to protect the life of those as yet unborn.

Here we see then that, even in an apparently obvious case, unless we penetrate the force of the Commandment in a biblical way, we shall be shown up as inconsistent and obscurantist. There is little evidence for regarding our earthly physical survival as sacred. Indeed, by the time of Moses, the principle of Genesis 9:5 was self-evident: no murderer's life was "sacred," and to treat it as such was to be an accessory to the murder.

The Seventh Commandment:
You shall not commit adultery.

The Seventh Commandment deals with only a small area of sexual wrongdoing. If we are thinking of the Ten Commandments as a summary of the moral law, then this one is strangely inadequate for sexual morality. As it stands, it ignores a whole range of sexual behavior, from common fornication to rape, let alone pederasty or incest. When we come to apply this to social life, we have little to say to the world beyond the fact that people shouldn't commit adultery. In the Old Testament, however, adultery was not only a moral wrong but also a crime, capable of carrying the death penalty (Leviticus 20:10; Deuteronomy 22:22). When we see the effects of adultery on the innocent spouse, the children, and the co-respondent, we may well appreciate what this Commandment offers. But there are other sexual distortions, even within marriage, that it does not touch. Not only, then, is the seventh Commandment inadequate as a summary of sex ethics. The aspect of sexual relations that it does focus on makes it difficult to interpret and apply today as public law.

The Eighth Commandment:
You shall not steal.

The Eighth Commandment seems to be the clearest, but...

Of all the Ten Commandments, the one against theft seems to be the clearest, and it is easily applied socially in the form of public laws even in a mixed society. It is about so-called private property. But property is not quite private. Thus the biblical idea behind "stealing" is not so much about private property as it is about private responsibility. People have a responsibility as stewards for what they "own" (we're back to "duty" again). Theft from this perspective is about interfering with our ability to carry out our proper duties toward what is "owned." Such laws belong to a race that has received a command, at its beginning, to cultivate and conserve the created world. Further, the notion of "privateness" is itself profoundly modified in Scripture by relationships in the extended family. (We saw implications of this in the story of Naboth's vineyard; chapter 5.)

The Ninth Commandment:
You shall not give false testimony against your neighbor.

The Ninth Commandment is another strangely limited prohibition.

As a summary of the moral law about telling the truth, this would be extraordinary. The style of its language is forensic: it forbids anyone who is giving testimony in a court of law from stating falsehoods that might lead to a neighbor's conviction. All sorts of falsehoods are not covered by this prohibition. So, for instance, is it okay to give false testimony in favor of one's neighbor? Of course, we would not expect it to be read that way! But it does point out how careful we must be in interpreting and applying Scripture. In short, this Commandment is merely forbidding perjury in court.

The Tenth Commandment:
You shall not covet your neighbor's house; you shall not covet your neighbor's wife or his manservant . . . or anything that is your neighbor's.

Can you imagine a government passing laws against coveting?

Many of us feel more at ease with this last Commandment, simply because the New Testament has directed our attention to the idea that morality is not so much about acts as it is about desires, motives, intentions, attitudes. And so we are fairly happy inveighing against the society around us as being greedy and exploitative, and therefore covetous. It is with this Commandment that the christian social conscience, especially when combined with pleas for justice, has felt at home. But we are forced to admit, surely, that when politicians respond with a question like, "What sort of legislation do you Christians ask for, in order to reflect this?", we are pretty vague.

The Decalogue was not intended to cover all morality.

So we see that the Ten Commandments do not always speak in the way that we take for granted. We also see that as a summary of the moral law, they are not nearly so wide-ranging or so easy to use in a mixed society as they may seem. There is considerable debate about all this, of course, but that only shows more clearly that applying the teaching of what seems to be even basic biblical texts needs far more stringent thinking than it has occurred to many of us to do.

That formal, forensic characteristic in them suggests that their original purpose was somewhat different from what we usually think. That is, the Ten Commandments make what we might call a "constitutional" statement about what lawyers would call the intent of the laws. This forensic characteristic is the special character of the Decalogue, and it indicates the spirit in which future legislation, even in cultural conditions different from Israel's, might be consistently developed beyond the sample legislation which we know as the Law of Moses. If that is so, then the Ten Commandments can indeed help us in our own lawmaking today, albeit not in quite the way we have been expecting.

A common reason why this is difficult to understand or different from what we were expecting relates to the "stained glass window" through which we read Scripture (chapter 2). I[CS] remember a discussion I had with a pastor who had just finished preaching a 10-week series on the Ten Commandments. The series had been an exposition of various personal moral applications surrounding each Commandment. I asked why he did not include some messages which showed that the Ten Commandments were a model for social law (at the time, political discussions were in full swing due to up-coming national elections, and such an approach would have been most welcome). He replied that this approach had not occurred to him. It probably could not have, for he was reared in a wisdom, again, as most of us were, that is bound to a religious-secular dualism, and his seminary training had not healed that split. So the Ten Commandments were merely an ideal to aim at for personal moral obedience.

~9~

The Help and Limitation of Traditional Resources

B esides the Ten Commandments, Christians have other methods of applying moral standards to law and social concerns, and these are often felt to be less literalistic or legalistic. One particular method is in alliance with post-christian humanism. It is a style of thought that appeals to the notion of "love" as a social-moral standard and ideal, and it employs many christian motifs and ideals. Nevertheless, just as problems arise when using the Ten Commandments in social law, greater difficulties arise from using "love" as a moral-social ideal, for it has too many possible meanings.

"Love" as a source for social law is bedeviled with pitfalls. For instance, non-Christians who use "love" as a style of thought for law often claim to outstrip Christianity in compassion, but they do so in a way that produces subtly different notions of justice and caring, and even of law, from the ones found in Scripture. And often they are supported by Christians who sit loose to the authority of the text of Scripture, who may adopt a relativistic ethic that regards biblical law as at best a rough guideline, to be ignored at one's discretion. The results of this approach certainly will not do for evangelicals. In practice, those who use this style to implement their moral ideals in any sort of legislative form are forced to work with ideas and ways of reasoning that are not typically biblical.

The bad fruit of this frequently appears in the criminal justice system. For example, a universal compassion that includes the wrongdoer equally with the victim cannot be made the subject of direct legislation without confusing the deserts of the criminal with the rights of his victim. Another of its problems arises in the divorce courts. For example, when legislation involves sex, marriage, and children the result is inevitably a profound uncertainty about the sort of clear moral standard needed in child custody battles for consistency and decisiveness. Judges and juries can be at a great loss here, and true justice and caring can go out the window, all for the sake of "compassion."

*For one thing, law
is enforced, love isn't.*

A problem that continually besets the whole moral approach is that when you are applying morality to legislation you have to work out the implications and results of your application in a special way. Legislation is never simply about enforcing moral standards or ideals for people who want to obey the law. If that were so, the task would be fairly easy and there would be few lawbreakers and little rebellion. The problem is that law has to deal with people whose consciences may not only be insensitive but also positively distorted. They may consider a given moral standard, say in sexual matters, as an utterly impracticable pipe dream, like imposing a speed limit on a race track. In other words, the law has to cope with people who want to evade its force, or, if they are prepared to obey the letter of the law, have no desire to observe its spirit. Further, it has to regulate people who lives are in such a tangle that too strict a law might make life impossible for them. (How many ministers have felt despair counseling a convert whose life has been a tangle of inappropriate emotional involvements, inadvisable commitments, and broken marriages?) In short, as the Bible succinctly puts it, the law is for the unrighteous (1 Timothy 1:9) and must therefore be enforced. To confuse this with the nature of "love" distorts what the Book teaches about it.

*We have to see the
principles behind morality.*

This means that we have to get behind whatever moral ideals we want to use for legislation and work out the considerations and principles that make up their meanings and the reasons why they are significant. Questions must be asked like: what is fidelity, chastity, truth, property, religious commitment? Then we have to refashion the answers we get in a form appropriate for legislation in a mixed society.

We are not concerned here with proving the validity or the absolute demand of a moral law (anything ultimately true is notoriously impossible to prove). Our task is to express its imperatives in a quite different form: we must produce laws that people at least think should command their respect. A law that people cannot think is somehow reasonable to obey easily becomes a dead letter and tends to undermine the authority of law as a whole. This is significant because widespread rebellion, rather than submission, can be fostered through fiats that impose legislation on people who are set in their ways to resist such laws. This is, in part, how totalitarian regimes arise.

*Disciplines and criteria other than
morality must be included in the process.*

But this is not the end of the story. Analyzing the meaning and function of moral ideals, like love, forces us into other areas of study, such as psychology and sociology. Now there are profoundly different ways of studying these subjects, and the danger is that some ways produce results that would make nonsense of a moral law altogether. An extreme example would be a penal system based on a sociology that regards criminality as no more than the lifestyle option of an alternative social subgroup. A little less far-out would be a penal system based on a psychology that attributes all criminality to deterministic factors in the personality that are beyond the wrongdoer's control. Some years ago, a young man named John Hinckley attempted to assassinate then President Ronald Reagan. During Hinckley's trial, the defense trotted out a psychological litany of so-called deterministic elements in Hinckley's past, hoping to sway the jury into thinking Hinckley had no choice. It didn't work. The prosecution made mincemeat out of the deterministic line of defense by citing all the "choices" Hinckley had to make in order to get into position over a period of several weeks to plan what he was going to do, such as when, where, and how. (See C. S. Lewis's *The Abolition of Man* for a trenchant analysis of this kind of reasoning.)

Education is a case in point. Criteria other than morality must be included when addressing social life because there are so many areas over which morality does not function as a criterion, at least not directly. Look at education. At first sight, one would imagine that there is little to worry about as long as christian moral standards are being taught and exemplified by the staff. Yet it is now widely understood that every school has its "hidden curriculum," which is implied in its pattern of discipline, in its numbers, and even in its architecture. For example, since overcrowding creates aggressive emotions, a basic thing like the size of a classroom could actually militate against christian virtues like longsuffering or turning the other cheek, which the teachers were trying to instill. Or, when biology is taught with an unspoken assumption that human beings are only sophisticated animals in an advanced phase of evolution, then christian virtues like patience, forgiveness, and self-control begin to sound slightly quaint.

In using the term "hidden curriculum," we are not talking about oily men with cigars sitting around in smoke-filled rooms plotting social engineering through the latest set of textbooks. We mean subtle influences like those just mentioned, which can even militate against what is formally taught, often in ways completely unknown to the staff. Even in christian schools a christian ideal, let us say of self-sacrifice, may be formally taught but subtly undermined by another part of school's composition. An ostentatious athletic program or the latest high-tech computers in the classrooms might easily "communicate" values of one-upmanship or pride.

What about the extreme emphasis that is often placed on academic achievement and test results? Christians need to ask why even their own schools may place this as the highest value offered to students and parents. This must surely strike us as strange, given the fact that the Bible places an extremely high value on servanthood and not so much on academic achievement. And if Jesus' teaching methods are a model, then the goal will be developing insight rather than just accumulating factual knowledge. Again, this kind of influence is usually "hidden"; although it can often be "seen" quite noticeably as the highest value when, for instance, analyzing a school's brochure as we did the cereal box (chapter 6).

Many areas, then, will have to be addressed apart from any moral criteria. So the kind of studying that would be necessary for education alone will involve us in a wide range of other considerations, from community organization to curriculum content. And we must accomplish this in ways that do not make nonsense of biblical moral law.

Moral standards and ideals, then, are not enough for addressing our social-political life christianly. Can we find other material in Scripture to give us guidance? We certainly can. Discussion about school subjects, for instance, eventually involves us in the evolution debate. And we have sometimes felt that we could judge the value of biology or science classes by their stance in relation to the theory of evolution. Unfortunately this has proven to be something of a blunt instrument.

Creation material often produces more heat than light. Although the Creation Story is often our guiding light, when this is argued with secular educators and scientists it usually produces more heat than light. For it immediately involves us in the "science-faith" controversy, which is not only exhausting but also showing no sign of ending, in spite of so many attempts at reconciliation or conquest. The problem is that the biologist cannot abandon the evolutionary theory, for he has no other means, or model, of arranging evidence and experiments for a meaningful study of his subject. Asking him to give up the theory is like asking him to give up biology. Biologists are in a situation not unlike that in physics just before Einstein: Newtonian mechanics might be splitting at the seams, but it was all they had. Most serious biologists, if they are faced with it, will admit that their situation is like this.

If we had concerned ourselves to critique evolution as a philosophy of life, we might have done better, but we have been scared into silence by the very word "philosophy" applied to faith. It is one thing to use a theory for scientific study of one aspect of life (theories are always provisional anyway), and it is quite another thing to use it to explain our very existence; that is, life itself. In this respect, as a philosophy, evolution is seriously vulnerable and grossly misused as a theory. (This potential for misuse is true of theories in other disciplines as well, such in psychology or sociology.) More often than not, the creation-evolution issue goes little beyond an argument about the authority of a literal understanding of Genesis One and Two. But if those two chapters are not a scientific text, we have to stop treating them as one.

Here is where our theories (chapter 7) are again seen to be vital. Evolutionists, for instance, can rightly accuse creationists of having no alternative theory on offer. Creationists, therefore, are laboring to develop a theoretical alternative to Darwin's. The kind of approaches to the complexities of contemporary life being suggested throughout this book could open new windows to creationists for ideas that could assist them toward their goal of developing an alternative to the theory of evolution. Of course, there will be no room here for a full-blown discussion of what this might entail, but perhaps a sample of what could be discovered would be useful.

We can appeal to the personal substrata behind the Creation. We are thinking here of the Bible's metaphors for what are usually referred to as the "inanimate" parts of creation. For instance, Scripture speaks of having a "covenant" with the stones of the field, and it speaks of the trees of the field clapping their hands. Now these descriptions only work as metaphors if there is a basis for them. That is, they are not merely poetry. There is something behind them. Otherwise, there is no point to them. So, for instance, because a biblical christian wisdom instructs us that a personal God is behind all parts of creation, this means that in some way there is a personal dimension even to the "inanimate" parts (we do not mean in a pantheistic or animistic sense). This, it seems to us, gives the Bible its basis for the above metaphors about stones and trees. Some clever persons may find ways to use ideas like these as a uniquely christian contribution in an alternative for the theory of evolution.

Another illustration can be found in a desire of some theoreticians to discover "a fundamental unity underlying all forms of knowledge," even between the sciences and the humanities. This may seem esoteric, but debates surrounding this are increasingly in the media. Which in itself is quite revealing. A uniquely christian contribution would say, "The unity you're looking for is not going to be purely abstract and impersonal. There's going to be a personal substrata to it, because behind it all, what you are on the trail of, is that which is Personal. That's where you will find the 'explanation' for the unity in diversity that is characteristic of our experience of life."

We are suggesting ideas like these because the Creation Story is so essential to a biblical wisdom, and biblical wisdom so essential to educational life, which continues to make headlines in the States regarding legislation that permits or excludes classroom teaching of creationism or evolution. So we cannot afford to leave the Creation Story bogged down in primitive waters. Despite the predisposition of people to pooh-pooh that story, we need to learn how to articulate its implications in and for society today. Further, to jump momentarily to another topic, if people dismiss that story, for what ever reasons, they have no rhyme or reason for listening to the Gospel Story, for redemption of creation makes no sense without the Creation Story.

The Doctrine of Man is a useful criterion. One element in the evolution debate that has proved valuable is the discussion of the thoroughly biblical question, "What is man?" (Psalm 8:4). The biblical notion that people are in the image of God has been particularly important partly because it appeals to much that people need, such as dignity and a basis for developing a new sense of personal responsibility for their behavior. Assertions that man is merely the victim of a historical process, or a sophisticated computer, or an advanced kind of animal, ultimately destroy any meaning to life, including the meaning of the assertions themselves! The biblical Doctrine of Man offers a way past such dead ends through considerations such as human self-consciousness, the rational faculty, the moral sense, and the power of self-determination. We can understand these as functions of the Image of the Creator, in which human beings are made.

"The importance of persons" places the value of persons above things. The question "What is man?" makes us aware of other vital biblical themes. One is the importance of persons over against ideas, things, and institutions. Throughout Scripture it is obvious that people are more important than things. A comparison of the laws of Sinai with other law systems of that age shows that the latter gave slaves only equal status with "property," at best. This was never to be the case in Israel. It is true that slaves could be flogged and bought and sold. But in those days so could children. Centuries later, Paul could still remark that a child was in many respects no better than a slave (Galatians 4:1; compare Philippians 2:7). The point, however, is that because of being created in the image of God, the Law of the Lord see slaves (children, too!) as equally persons with the rest of the human family. Many of the ancients may not have, but the Law did.

This gives us a valuable principle for our own legislatory thinking, such as that crimes against the person must be seen to be more heavily punishable than crimes against property. It also gives us good reason for condemning any laws (they're usually archaic ones) still on the books which inflict the death penalty for crimes like stealing certain kinds of property. Such laws say to criminals: if you're about to be thwarted in your theft of certain items, then you might as well murder the person because if you get caught it's the death penalty anyway. This biblical emphasis on the importance of persons can also help us sort out what is happening to our own criminal justice system, such as when murderers can be out of prison after three or four years while thieves and extortionists may be in prison for a decade or more. What about the terrible injustices against victims who end up, for all practical purposes, with less rights and legal recourse than the criminals who injured and violated them? Enterprising Christians working in the area of jurisprudence ought to be discovering ways to end these injustices.

Warfare is another area where the importance of persons over things would be a useful guiding light. The development of weaponry designed to destroy people but leave property intact should ring loud alarm bells in the Christian's mind. It could be a starting point for a new awareness that this generation could be wrong in being the first to believe that methods of warfare can no longer be trammeled by questions of conscience. On the other hand, this principle does not offer much help in many issues about the non-human objects and their place in warfare, such as issues relating to ecology.

"The covenant" and "the family" are two more biblical sources. Another source of guidance from biblical material is the covenant, although this is a quite neglected idea for most Christians today. All of God's dealings with His people tend to take the form of agreements that are like what we today might call binding contracts with mutual obligations. This makes the principle of faithfulness to commitments vitally significant. So social structures or legislation that make it easy or even profitable to break contracts will always be suspect to Christians. Also, principles that we could derive from the Bible's notions of covenant might be applicable for creating more just bankruptcy laws, especially in situations when companies that declare bankruptcy are held virtually unaccountable for debts. The importance of keeping one's promise (a theme hardly referred to in the Decalogue, incidentally) needs to be reasserted in this present age.

As with all the foregoing principles, this one is fairly limited in its application. After all, in such a complex society as ours, it is easy to trap people in unfair contracts. And we need to remember that even under Mosaic law not even vows were, in law, unconditionally binding; although a broken vow, for whatever reason, required the Lord's forgiveness (Numbers 30:5–12).

In the Bible, family relationships are fundamental to society on every level, and the teaching of Scripture always points to the necessity of maintaining them. No less than three of the Ten Commandments relate in one way or another to this theme. So Christians naturally tend to object to legislation or even to a system of thought that regards family life as expendable. And they will tend to resist theories that suggest alternative social structures in which children are removed from the family environment for their rearing.

One problem that arises when we think about applying this is that the Old Testament notion of family, which spills over into the New Testament, is different from ours. We will look more at this in chapters 13 and 15, but for now we can say that today's insistence by Christians on the integrity of the nuclear family, not to mention its enjoyment of it, easily overlooks the fact that in Israel members of the extended family were not isolated from one another as they are in our society. One tremendously beneficial result of this was that many of a family's internal tensions were eased out among the circle of relatives who were close at hand.

As with the foregoing ideas (love, the creation, the covenant, and so on) in order to make use of this biblical idea, we have to ask ourselves questions like: "What do we mean by 'family'"? "How is it supposed to function?" "Where does our thinking deviate from that?"

"Equality" is a popular source, but tricky to handle.

"Equality" is popular, but tricky to handle. The principle of equality has particular attractions, similar to the way "love" does, because it seems to offer some common ground with many other reforming spirits of our time. But in practice this presents all sorts of problems for those who are committed to a truly biblical wisdom.

One of its more subtle intricacies was revealed in 1979 in the U.K., as the result of a statement made by some twenty Anglican bishops, which gained wide circulation under the title "Immigration and Social Justice: A Christian Statement." It seemed to many of us, on the face of it, to be a careful, well-thought-out document. It began with the assertion of the Fatherhood of God and the consequent equality of everyone, whether male or female, black or white, or whatever. Consequently, it maintained that "any discrimination against another human being on racial grounds is a blasphemy." This Anglican document aroused the curiosity of a christian parliamentarian, Mr. Enoch Powell, who was well-known for his pleas for controlled immigration and for other policies that have been condemned as racist. He was something of a scholar with keen powers of analytical logic, and he applied his talents to this document with devastating effect. Among other things, he tackled the notion of "equality." He pointed out that the great proof-text in Galatians 3:28, "there is neither Jew nor Gentile," is qualified by the phrase "in Christ Jesus." His point was that even if people are equal in some respects, there are many in which manifestly they are not.

One cannot just take the term "equality" and throw it about indiscriminately. Here we are not concerned with the rights and wrongs of the issue but the importance of the method and language of the reasoning involved. If your process of justification is faulty, then even a true proposition and correct reasoning become open to successful challenge. And that is even more serious than the collapse of a false proposition.

A word's connotation can have a powerful influence. A related point is that we cannot assume that a word means the same thing to everyone whose lips it is on. Of course we know this, but we can get caught off-guard regarding a word's connotation, especially when, like "love" or "equality," the connotation has a strong emotional appeal. Many common abstract terms, like equality, justice, fairness, truth, and love get tossed about, especially by the media, precisely because of their appealing connotations. It is a way of bringing people to the discussion because they feel good about what they are talking about. But mischief soon arises. You find that the people start talking at cross-purposes even though they are on the same topic, as is so often seen on television panels where the guests are debating a cultural hot-button issue. People watching in the audience may wonder what all the fuss is about. Further, because a word's connotation can be more powerful than its denotation, a word can be used manipulatively. In the much of the West, for example, the name "Jesus" still gives many non-Christians a warm cozy feeling of love and security, even though, if you asked them, they would define "Jesus" as nothing more than a "great teacher" or a "holy man."

So, in understanding the limitations of traditional resources for social policy, we must also be wise about words. A political leader who uses the term "equality" might mean something quite different from what the audience "hears." "Equality," then, is a concept of dubious value for our task. At the very least, it requires an answer to the question, "What kind of equality are we talking about?"

"Justice" is another popular but mischievous concept. Other motifs lead into similar difficulties. A classic example is "justice." Christians naturally want to take up the theme of justice for the poor and the dispossessed, with consequent curbs on the powerful. But what does justice mean under these circumstances and how would it work itself out in society? Does it mean positive discrimination? Does it mean that a poor man who steals a wallet containing $200.00 ought to receive a lighter sentence than a rich man who steals the same amount? At what point does taxing the rich to maintain the poor become a kind of Robin Hood theft? Questions like these are just the tip of a vast iceberg.

In order even to begin to influence society in this area, we Christians would first have to reach a reasonably clear notion of what we mean by justice. Next, we would find that we kept reaching points where further progress was only possible by facing up to some more quite radical questions, and these might even be concerning the answer we had just arrived at! Don't worry. This process is normal and happens repeatedly. If it does not, then we will remain at junctures where we simply do not know what we are talking about.

So we have to keep asking, "What does the Bible mean by _____?"

The foregoing resources, including the previous chapter on the Ten Commandments, can help us make progress in secular life. Yet, as we have seen, these resources have their limitations and will only take us so far in our task. Nevertheless, they do give us important areas where much homework by Christians is needed. This kind of task will not be without fruit, for it gives us layers of biblical material by which to engage our non-Christian friends and colleagues about issues of secular life that are important to them. In the next chapter we will try to learn more about this by seeing how our Lord dealt with a significant issue of his day.

~10~

Cultural Conditioning: Interpretation Then and Now

One of the hot topics that has spread throughout grassroots America the past few decades is how the Supreme Court interprets the Constitution for today. After all, its an ancient document (at least relative to America's history!), and if people are not doubting its relevance they are often questioning how that relevance can be applied today. Interpretation, then, becomes decisive.

Wrong interpretations affect everyday situations. The same holds true for that ancient book the Bible. Interpretation is decisive because it provides instruction and direction for the very practical things that we Christians do. Get your interpretation wrong and everything that follows it suffers.

You may have heard the following story, but it bears repeating. An English woman was going to teach school in Switzerland and so she wrote to the village schoolmaster inquiring about the house where she would be living. One of her questions concerned bathroom facilities, which in her English idiom was known as a "water closet," or simply a "WC." When she wrote with questions about these facilities, the schoolmaster was puzzled by the unexplained initials and sought the help of his friend, a parish priest, who decided that the woman was asking about a wayside chapel. The schoolmaster wrote back to the woman:

> *Dear Madam,*
> *. . . . There is a WC located 9 miles from the house, in the center of a beautiful grove of trees. It can seat up to 250 people at a time and is open Tuesdays, Thursdays, and Sundays. I admit it is quite a distance away if you are in the habit of going regularly, but many people take their lunches along and make a day of it. The last time my wife and I went was 6 years ago. It was so crowded we had to stand the whole time we were there. It may interest you to know that a supper is being planned to raise money to buy more seats.*

Likewise, it may interest you to know that my daughter first met her husband there, and they were later married in the WC. It pains me very much not to be able to go more regularly, but that is from no lack of desire on my part. As we grow older, it just becomes more of an effort, particularly in cold weather. When you arrive, I would be happy to go with you the first time, to show you just where it is and to introduce you to others who may be there. Remember, this is a friendly community.
Yours truly,
The Schoolmaster

This bit of comic relief identifies what is perhaps the central problem waiting in the wings throughout this whole discussion. It besets our entire enterprise, and it will probably have been niggling every reader to some degree. It is the problem of applying to present day conditions the ideas of a book written between two and (at least) four thousand years ago. We began to assess this in chapter 4, and here we will take it a few steps further.

Discerning permanent principles and cultural expressions, then and today.

Simply put, the Bible is an ancient book and a foreign one. God chose to reveal Himself to a particular culture during a particular period of history, and straightforward transference of its ideas and language soon becomes obviously unsatisfactory. For instance, a legal prohibition in the Law of Sinai was, in its day, important enough to be preserved on three separate occasions (Exodus 23:19; 34:26; Deuteronomy 14:21). In the King James Version it reads, "Thou shalt not seethe a kid in its mother's milk." On one occasion a typist reproduced this for me[JP] from a tape as "Thou shalt not see the kid . . . ." A natural enough mistake, certainly, for the King James language makes the original injunction barely intelligible today. But we are not talking about an understanding of the words as much as we are the cultural practice referred to in this text. And for the kind of thinking and engagement with the world that is under consideration in this book, there is a further problem: distinguishing a permanent principle from its particular cultural expression at the time. For the expression of the permanent principle might look different today. If so, and if we missed it and stuck only with its cultural expression in Israel's day, we would not be interpreting Scripture correctly.

A case in point: biblical reference to women.

An illuminating example is the Bible's attitude to women. How much of it is cultural expression, how much permanent principle? Scripture, for instance, has much to say about the virtue of submissiveness in women. But this is also required of children and slaves; and most men, at least in their more serious moments, would feel that such a comparison is going too far! And in the tenth Commandment, against coveting, wives are listed with slaves and animals as part (albeit the most significant part) of the total household in a way that embarrasses us if we think about it. That was very much a man's world, where even the word for "male" had the same root as the one for "memorial." How far are we to take this into account today? Is there some factor outside Scripture which decides that? If so, how does Scripture retain its authority over our thinking?

The issue is sharpened to a point if we consider Paul's notorious injunction about hat-wearing in church (1 Corinthians 11:3–16), which is a way of dressing, by the way, that has only recently been disregarded by many Christian women. Paul's instructions are apparently clear: a woman ought to have her head covered in public. So she should wear a hat. But in first century Corinth that could easily mean a "veil," meaning that Paul is calling for some kind of purdah or yashmak, which is a veil worn by Moslem women to cover their faces in public. On the other hand, a woman in that society in public with her head uncovered was considered a mark of easy virtue, sexually responsible to no one in particular. An equivalent today would be a dress that was too provocatively revealing. In that case, a woman might wear a hat but entirely violate the intent of Paul's instruction. Further, we have not begun to tackle the idea surrounding "authority on her head because of the angels" (1 Corinthians 11:10).

That our immediate understanding of the passage is colored by our own cultural conditioning is evident in the nervous reactions we have to the above passages, even though they come straight out of the Bible. Yet the irony is that the whole understanding of it that we need depends heavily on the extent to which we see the instructions themselves as culturally conditioned.

Cultural conditioning raises some radical questions.

We are faced, then, with a number of other questions. What remains as permanent principles in all the changes of human cultural history? What do the changes represent? Are they a progress that makes the past obsolete? Do cultures always change for the worse? Are the French right in saying, "Plus ça change, plus c'est la même chose"? (The more it changes, the more it doesn't.) What is change? What do we mean when we say that things are changing? What do we mean by "history"? By suggesting so many questions, and particularly these kinds, which we may not be used to, we are not trying to put readers off to interpreting the Bible for today. We are hoping to show what it will take to make us credible when attempting it. Whatever approach we make to the issues and challenges of our time, whatever resources we draw on from Scripture, these awkward radical questions, which often appear to be so remote to everyday life, actually keep confronting us in everyday life. We cannot escape them. If we shy off and say we haven't time for that, because we've got to do something practical, we will quite literally find ourselves in situations not knowing what we are doing.

But once we start asking questions like that, we move into another world. We are apparently landed in the perilously rarified atmosphere of philosophy. And this will trouble many of us who think that we have been warned by Paul not to fall prey to philosophy (never mind that this itself is a wrong interpretation of Colossians 2:8). So our instinct may be to go back to the Book for another route. Let us take a look, however, at an example of how Jesus applied the Old Testament to tackle philosophical-type questions to a problem in his own (more modern) day. In fact, it is learning from these kinds of questions that makes a forceful and sensible biblical approach to our complex and changing world possible.

Jesus' method with marriage and divorce.   Almost all of our Lord's personal teaching on marriage and divorce is found in Matthew 19 and Mark 10 (it's the same story). The Pharisees had tackled Jesus on the subject by asking him about possible legitimate grounds for divorce. This was a big issue among Jewish teachers at this period, for there is evidence that divorce was becoming increasingly common in Jewish life. The basic text in the Torah was in Deuteronomy 24:1, where instruction is given if a husband gives his wife a "certificate of divorce . . . and sends her from his house" because she "becomes displeasing to him because he finds something indecent about her." For legislators today, one of the obvious problems, here, is that the interpretation of the original injunction becomes less clear as circumstances change and history passes. In Jesus' time, there were two great schools of thought about what Moses meant by "something indecent." The strict Rabbi Shammai taught that divorce was only allowable on grounds of adultery. The more "humane" school of Rabbi Hillel believed that anything, even a badly cooked meal, could be grounds for divorce. (Possibly this was not so much about divorce itself as it was about the husband's absolute authority in the home. But the view was extremely liberal, nonetheless.)

He distinguishes between the Law of Moses and how man was made.   Jesus' response is profoundly significant. In the first place, he makes a sharp distinction between the Law of Moses and the implications of human nature as God created it "in the beginning." He is bringing his audience back to the ideal: let the married not separate. On this basis, Jesus establishes a principle about marriage and divorce that is far more strict than that of Shammai. Divorce is out of the question unless the bond has already been violated by adultery. Further, in Matthew 5:32, Jesus makes a husband who casually divorces his wife responsible for the adulterous situation that would arise from her remarriage. A woman without a husband in that social environment was highly vulnerable, which helps to explain why Jesus makes the divorcing man responsible.

Of course, both the Pharisees and Jesus' disciples have difficulties with this. When the Pharisees see it as a contradiction of Deuteronomy 24:1, Jesus replies that permission to divorce was granted "because of the hardness of your hearts." He is saying that Moses provided a lower standard for those who could not accept the ideal as the one to live by. When the disciples twig to the implications (having one of their better days; this one did not need to be explained later!), they respond in despair: "If that's really true, then it's better not marry at all!" Now Jesus' reply seems to affirm that: not everyone (even among his own followers) is able to take his teaching (a very different thing, he points out, from inability through birth or circumstance). But if they could take it, then they ought to.

Let's face it, this method of handling the question is a little embarrassing to us. Jesus appears to be suggesting different rules for different circumstances. He seems to be offering a double standard of morality—one for the spiritually elite and one for the rest of us, who can't rise to such heights. In chapter 7 we considered learning how to grapple with the "strangeness" of Scripture whenever we come across it, rather than letting that strangeness slide past. Matthew 19 is a good example. We can have second thoughts about a passage like this (in this case, what looks like Jesus' double standard) and decide to skip it rather than try to understand why it strikes us oddly. It is when we stop and ask questions like, "Why does it seem this way to us?" and, "How is Jesus reasoning here?", that we can break out of our cultural wisdom and let the strangeness of Scripture instruct us. When we ask questions like this of our case in point here, it opens another way of understanding Jesus' response, which our traditional wisdom precludes, and that in turn gives us help for the broader task before us, of communicating biblically to our present age.

He distinguishes between moral law and laws for social behavior. Jesus' handling of the question reveals the way he is reasoning about the situation. The Pharisees are obviously preoccupied with the meaning of the Law of Moses. This is largely because they see morality itself as a kind of divine governmental law, so they keep insisting that morality is about keeping the Law of Moses. But Jesus' concern is for the divine principles behind the Mosaic Law. He is insisting that morality is about motives and desires and the original intention of God.

This is his calling as the prophet Messiah proclaiming the Kingdom of God. (His sense of having a special calling also appears elsewhere, such as when he is asked to adjudicate in an inheritance dispute. He says, in effect, that he is not a magistrate and not, as a human being obeying his calling, authorized to act as one.)

Something quite significant to our discussion is coming into focus here. In this controversy over divorce, Jesus is making a sharp distinction between the Law of Moses and God's real intentions for mankind. He is saying, in effect, "You Pharisees keep thinking that the Law of Moses is what should determine your moral standards. But that's not what it's about. The Law of Moses is governmental law aimed at regulating the life of a nation that has many people in it who are unable to keep to God's standard, or original ideal. But morality is not that sort of thing. Morality is about the kind of person God intends you to be. If you are a disciple, then this is God's intention for you for marriage. If you can accept it, then act on it." Jesus is saying that the Mosaic Law is not in itself the moral law. Unlike the moral law, the Mosaic Law does not have an absolute claim regardless of those to whom it is addressed. It is a modification of the moral law relating to the "hardness of men's hearts."

This way of reasoning is often foreign to Christians. Those wishing to explore other biblical precedents for it could look at passages such as Acts 15, where a Jewish contingent in the Jerusalem church organized a campaign in Antioch to urge the wholesale adoption of Jewish law by all Christians as an indispensable condition of salvation. This, of course, was eventually opposed by the ensuing Jerusalem Council (chapter 4). What was at stake here was the potential dividing of the church into two bodies, Jewish and Christian, right at its outset. Just as the Pharisees were preoccupied with the meaning of the Law of Moses, so too were these Jewish Christians. The Council at Jerusalem resolved the controversy by working from the meaning of the divine principles behind the Mosaic Law, as Jesus had done, to discover what later cultural expressions of it might be. We also noted that this was Paul's approach, such as when he applied the "oxen-principle" to paying workers (1 Corinthians 9:9; chapter 4).

So the Decalogue is not simply morality. Our study of the Ten Commandments (chapter 8) showed that their treatment of moral questions was rather specialized. It was, we suggested, forensic: about the administration of governmental law. This means that the Law of Moses was originally a law code for the purposes of government. It is true that there is more religious exhortation and personal moralizing of its detailed provisions than we should expect today. This may be partly a matter of style, or possibly a symptom of the religious-secular split within Christianity. Or it may be a symptom of a different notion about how government is to be done. Nevertheless, none of this argues against the fact that the Ten Commandments were a code of jurisprudence. It is morality stated for legal purposes.

Jesus, then, using a philosophical way of reasoning, makes clear distinctions not only between a permanent principle and its cultural expressions but also between morality and jurisprudence. He sees morality and jurisprudence as two distinct, though related, aspects of our human existence, which must not be confused. Each aspect has its own value, its own way of functioning in our lives, which our Lord recognizes, approves, and seeks to regulate according to its own nature.

Governmental law treats morality in a special way. Sometimes you have to say a lot to say a little. We now come full circle to the beginning of chapter 8. Using the ideas of chapters 8, 9, and 10, we are now enabled to get help from Scripture about the function of governmental law in human life, and this means that we also have some idea of a biblical view of politics, since politics is largely about government. Jesus is basing his teaching on the view that governmental law must work in tension between two factors: the moral ideal and the degree of moral sensitivity and capacity on the part of those governed.

In our search for ways of judging how we may think as Christians about the society we live in, we have now moved beyond using the Bible's religious and moral criteria alone. In the first place, we have seen that there is at least one other dimension of life, that of jurisprudence, or government, and that it functions by its own God-approved, God-appointed principles. God is just as involved here as He is in the religious and moral aspects of life. And we have seen that we can ferret out some of these principles from Scripture and work toward their cultural applications today. (Latter chapters explore the Bible's way of extending this principle into other aspects of life.)

Also, we have seen that, by implication, Jesus calls his hearers to think about the nature of the things they are discussing. He is working with questions like, "What is law?", "What is its relationship to morality?" and, "What is the true nature of marriage?" We may be tempted to back away at this point, protesting that the whole matter has become too abstract, too rationalistic, too theoretical, too philosophical, too remote for practical life. But the Bible itself is frequently posing such questions. "What is Man?" "What is Truth?" "Man, where are you?" "What have you done?" "What is your life?" "Where is wisdom to be found?" Now these are radical, in the sense of root, or fundamental, questions; that is, they are philosophical ones. Neither Jesus nor the Bible is put off by them. And what we will discover is that the

Bible has its own way of answering them, and answering them in ways that are not remotely abstract but utterly practical, even in today's complex and changing world.

~11~

The Bible and Multiple Parallel Explanations

Can you imagine a world of two dimensions only? It is populated with two-dimensional (2D) beings of various geometrical shapes, such as squares, triangles, and circles. It's called Flatland, and it is pure "surface," possessing length and width but not thickness. (The original story, which is not our rendition here, is found in the Victorian fantasy *Flatland*.)

Now imagine what might occur if one of the Flatlanders, let us say Circle, came face to face with a three-dimensional (3D) ball called Sphere, who happened to be passing through Flatland, descending on it from above. Keep in mind that Circle's wisdom is based solely on the two-dimensional way he has been raised to think, reason, analyze, and act. The conversation opens with Sphere entering Flatland and being perceived by Circle as a point. Then the fun begins, as all sorts of possibilities arise.

> *Circle (to point): "I've never seen you around here before. Who are you?"*
>
> *Sphere: "I'm just passing through. Name's Sphere. I'm a ball."*
>
> *Circle: "A what? You're a point. Can't fool me."*
>
> *Sphere: "Pardon? I'm no point. Are you making fun of me? I'm four inches thick."*
>
> *Circle: "Thick? What do you mean thick?"*
>
> *Sphere: "Well, I've got three dimensions. You know."*
>
> *Circle: "Three dimensions? I don't understand."*

Suddenly Circle not only hears strange ideas but also sees unexpected things, for in passing through Flatland, Sphere is expanding right before Circle's eyes.

> *Circle: "Whoa! What's happening to you?"*
>
> *Sphere: "Nothing's happening to me. I'm the same as I've always been. Are you all right?"*
>
> *Circle: "But you're . . . . I don't know."* Circle doesn't know the right word, "expanding." *"Now you're a circle, just like me! But different. How can that be? It's not possible."*

Sphere: "You must be seeing things. I'm the same size and shape I've always been."

Just when Circle begins to suspect that he may need a good psychiatrist, things get even stranger.

Circle: "Now what's happening? You're... I don't know." He doesn't know the word "contracting." *"Oh, this is so frustrating! What's going on?"*

Sphere soon comes to a point again, which, for a brief moment, comforts Circle.

Circle (to point): "Now that's better. So, can you tell me what... No! Wait! Wait! Oh, no. Where have you gone? Come back! We need to talk."

But Sphere was just passing through and won't be returning.

"Even my friends won't believe this," Circle mutters as he walks home.

Illustrated,[1] this is what Circle saw:

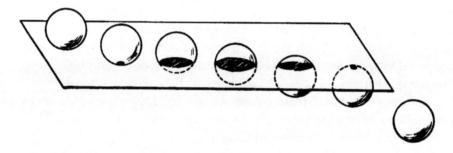

Fig. 1: A three-dimensional sphere passing through the two-dimensional world of Flatland starts out by looking like a point, then expands, then shrinks to a point, and eventually disappears—at least that's the way it looks to the Flatlanders!

You can play around with this and imagine a whole range of encounters and conversations between 2D Circle and various 3D beings passing through Flatland, such as a cube or a 14-sided object. Also, imagine the difficulty Circle will have when explaining to his 2D friends what happened, should he even want to!

One encounter, however, rocks Circle the most. Risking another stroll through Flatland Park, he sees five 3D phenomena all at once. These appear to be somewhat similar to Sphere, yet also different. The five phenomena are

---

[1] The authors wish to acknowledge their reliance on Figures 1 and 2 and their adaption for use here as inspiration coming from another context and meaning in the *Spiritual Counterfeits Project Journal*, Vol. 17:1-2, 1992, p. 12.

in fairly close proximity to one another and they seem to move in a group. Circle's immediate problem is not knowing which of the five to address first, so he speaks to them all.

    Circle: "Who are you all? What are your names?"

    Voice: "What do you mean? I'm the only one here."

Now the Voice terrifies Circle, for it's not coming from the five visible phenomena but from outside Flatland. After he calms downs, he recognizes another problem: how can the five be one?

    Circle: "I'm more confused now than ever. Last week... Well, never mind that. But now there are five of you."

    Voice: "Not five. One."

    Circle: "But I see five. And I don't even see who's talking to me. I must be going mad."

    Voice: "You're only seeing parts of me, instead of the whole."

    Circle: "Parts? Hey, can't you at least stop moving around? The same thing is happening as happened the other day when... You're... Oh, I don't know." Circle again lacks the words. Here he needs the word "changing," but it's not in his vocabulary.

    Voice: "I think I know what's bothering you. When I move about in your world, it appears as if I'm changing shape and size. But I'm not. I'm just three-dimensional."

    Circle (muttering to himself): "Where have I heard that before?"

    Voice: "I have many other parts, too."

    Circle: "I don't believe you. No one would. Anyone can see five separate things. You're lying. How can they be 'one' if they aren't connected? I'm having trouble enough lately, but I'm not going to fall for that. And what is 'change'? Who are you, anyway?"

    Voice: "The problem is simple, really. You can't see how the parts are connected. If you would..."

    Circle (running off): "I'm outta here. This is too much. First there was that appearing-disappearing act by Sphere, and now these five guys won't talk to me but a voice I can't see tells me it is one with the five. I've got to find someone I can talk to about these strange events."

We'll leave it to your own felicity to imagine the conversations between Circle and his 2D friends. We'll just say here that if you thought it was difficult for Circle to explain Sphere to his friends, it was harder for him to explain the human being, Circle's last encounter.

Illustrated, what Circle saw might look like:

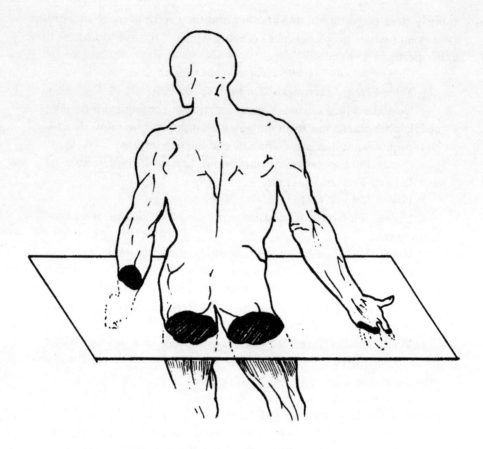

Fig. 2: A human being as perceivable by a two-dimensional wisdom. Note the five shaded areas that Circle saw. Every movement by the human will alter his two-dimensional configuration.

The Flatlanders, of course, have been raised in a particular kind of wisdom in which they have their own theories for explaining everything that happens in Flatland, both old and new experiences. Now their theories, like all theories, have their own ways of reasoning and are based on whatever can be imagined to be true, or at least possible, in that 2D world. So when the 3D Sphere tries to convince the 2D Circle that it, Sphere, has not only length and width but also thickness, Circle can't get his mind around that. It's unimaginable to him. Even though it's true. The difficulty is that only one explanation, the 2D one, is possible for Circle. Sphere's explanation lies outside of any theory that Circle in his wisdom can imagine to be possible.

Of course, it makes perfect sense to *us* why Sphere appears and disappears, or starts as a point and ends as a point. And we can also explain the "impossibility" of "five being one," and the "invisible" voice. These things are clear to us because we have a wisdom in which they make sense. For Circle, they produce a crisis. He has been raised with a wisdom that cannot understand what is happening. His imagination is therefore unable to grasp the kinds of explanations that would fill out the story more fully. (Circle's mystification is analogous to the bewilderment we face when trying to fathom God, such as when thinking about the Trinity and the Incarnation.)

Multiple explanations are vital for developing biblical wisdom.

Circle's dilemma is often our dilemma. We may get so locked into looking at things from a certain perspective that it can get terribly frustrating when someone suggests another view. It can't be, we say. We have our one explanation and can't seem to break out of it. Additional explanations remain outside of what we can imagine to be true, and yet they can be true, and necessary. This is significant. So here we need to explore this significance. Besides understanding the weaknesses in the appeal to moral ideals alone for addressing everyday life (chapters 8-10), we must gain a respect for multiple explanations of events and situations if we hope to further the process of wisdom development.

Too often we get caught in the "one-explanation syndrome." Here are a few simple illustrations. A broken marriage is explained with the statement: "That happened because the wife had an affair." A teenager's jail sentence is explained with the statement: "That happened because both parents work." A church splits and someone says, "I'll tell you why that happened. When that church's pastor resigned, it was all over for that church." One hears comments like these everyday, and the language usually implies that one reason is meant to explain what is a complex event. That is, when someone says, "I know why such and such happened," usually one explanation is running through the person's mind as the reason that "such and such" happened. The marriage failed because of an affair. The teenager became a criminal because the parents did not spend enough time with him. The church split because the pastor left.

"One explanation" analysis runs throughout much of christian wisdom today. Events and situations, however, are much more complex than pinning them down to one explanation can excuse. Things simply cannot be explained with any one reason. Just ask the parties involved! Yet we are so used to thinking in terms of "one explanation only" that additional reasons, should they be offered, and offered as a valid, can seem out-of-the-question. Frequently, the person offering additional reasons is looked on as a moral relativist. Events, however, are complex. Many reasons contribute to a divorce, or to a rebellious teenager, or to a church split. One explanation can seem plausible enough, but to fully understand what happened, more understanding is needed. Now, we may easily nod our heads to this, but in practice we may be closer to Circle's attitude that we are to the Bible's. So let's return to the Book. For the kind of multiple parallel reasoning we are suggesting is part of the warp and woof of biblical wisdom.

Why did the Israelites not occupy all the Promised Land immediately?

It is quite likely that if you were asked, "Why did it take so long for the Israelites to occupy all of the Promised Land," you would have one, possibly two, scriptural reasons for an answer. Yet the Bible provides no less than five! Four are in Judges; the other is in Deuteronomy. They are quite fascinating just for their sheer variety, and one does begin to wonder how they can all be true at once. As we look at them they will help us get to grips with how the Bible understands and reasons about the world we live in.

The first reason (Judges 1:19): they did not have sufficient armament.

This explanation is given quite simply: although the Lord was with the men of Judah, and although they took possession of the hill country, they were unable to drive the people from the plains because they had iron chariots. The chapter then refers to the failures of most of the other tribes, indicating that they too were unable to occupy the lowlands.

A Technological Reason

This is a straightforward technological reason, specifically concerning the military and armament. In the plains, the iron chariots would be free to attack *en masse* and to maneuver adequately. Israelite infantry might be able to evade them, but it could never keep rank or re-group for an effective counterattack.

It is clear in Scripture that the Lord God of Hosts always took war seriously as a fact of life. There were, of course, miraculous deliverances from time to time but, generally speaking, warfare was no easier for the Israelites than for anyone else. In Psalm 144, David is on record as praising the Lord who trained him for war, and by that means he had conquered subject nations in his empire. In Deuteronomy 20, laws are laid down for warfare, including rules for the treatment of prisoners of war. Some of those laws are remarkable even today, let alone then. Deuteronomy 17:16, for instance, tells the king, "Thou shall not multiply horses for thyself." Since horses were an important factor in war, this prohibition, in today's technical jargon, is about unilateral strategic arms limitation. We find nothing in the New Testament to show that this has changed in any significant way. Soldiers there are always spoken of with respect, even though people's experiences of them could have been unpleasant, to put it mildly. Yet this is only hinted at (Luke 3:14). So the Bible treats war as a reality in which the laws governing how victory is to be won are taken seriously.

The reason given in Judges 1:19, however, is not merely a matter of military strength. It is really one of superior technology. The chariots were made of iron rather than of wood, which made them formidable armament. The Israelites were late on the scene with iron technology. They had not mastered it even in Samuel's time, which was one reason why the Philistines were so much trouble to them. Even as late as the time of Elisha, the loss of an ax head was a serious matter. So, though there may have been occasions when God intervened in battle, in terms of military technology alone the Israelites had no chance of competing with the Canaanites. And Scripture recognizes this.

_____ In the remainder
The second reason (Judges 1:28–2:3):   of Judges chapter 1, it
Israelite treaty arrangements with their enemies.   is clear that the
_____

peoples whom Israel did defeat were taken into their social order, albeit as slaves. As a consequence, Judges 2 speaks of a judgment called down upon the Israelites for failure to obey the Lord's command to root out all their enemies.

A Sociological Reason

The reason given for this particular judgment is what today we would call a sociological one. The Israelites were forbidden to accept the Canaanites even as slaves because they would be a continuing threat to the integrity of Israelite social life. In Deuteronomy 7, the danger of intermarriage is stressed, as is the possibility that the attractiveness of Canaanite religious symbolism, in its cultus and architecture, might compromise Israelite worship of the Lord their God. In a world where nature worship was in the very air people breathed, the attraction of elaborate and highly emotional ritual—a facet of a far more developed and sophisticated culture than Israel's—would present an overwhelming threat and an unhealthy fascination. Even in the desert, having seen Egypt's gods decisively defeated, Israel still hankered after Egypt's cultural amenities. The generation invading Canaan had not seen that; they had only known the culture of the desert. History is full of examples of how a subject people have eventually radically modified the lifestyle and values of their conquerors, from the Greeks of the Roman Empire to the black slaves in North America. So, like technology, the societal aspect of life is taken seriously by Scripture.

We have already seen, in the case of Ahab and Jezebel (chapter 5), how persuasive and consistent (on its own terms) the logic of an apparently successful society can be when it tackles one with a different mindset. The Book of Proverbs, as we might expect, concerns itself quite extensively with many of the more practical aspects of societal life. In the New Testament, the same concerns are recognized. "Don't be misled," says Paul, "bad company corrupts good character" (1 Corinthians 15:33; see also: 2 Corinthians 6:14–18). First Peter, which seems to be a sort of follow-up letter for new converts, has some fascinating insights into the societal interaction between the Christian and the world outside (2:11–12; 3:3–4; 4:2–11). So the judgment pronounced by the Angel of the Lord in Judges 2 was not merely against Israel's disobedience to some arbitrary divine ruling. It was explicitly stated to be based upon Israel's failures to follow principles of social interaction.

These two foregoing explanations for failure of complete immediate conquest are different because they relate to different features of the situation. But though each one on its own is consistent and understandable, they stand side by side too. It can also be argued that the first (the technological) refers to the beginning of the conquest and the second (the sociological) to its later stages. But our point is that, rather than being applicable to different situations, they are naturally linked by a common relationship to Israel's struggles in the Promised Land. People today may find it difficult to understand how these two explanations can work together without being contradictory. But the Book of Judges sees this way of reasoning as normal. It sets the two reasons alongside each other without any sense that they need to be reconciled or related. There is no hint in the historian's mind that that way of reasoning is illogical or contradictory, or even that it needs explaining (to the original hearers). It is simply taken for granted in their wisdom.

The third reason (Judges 2:22–3:5): to teach battle experience.

The next reason is quite peculiar on the face of it. It argues that the Israelites failed to drive out the Canaanite nations, so the Lord did not drive them out either in order that the Israelites would learn how to fight them. But if the Lord had driven them out, they would not have needed to learn! Of course there is more to it than that.

An Educational-Psychological Reason

This is a different kind of reason again. It belongs to what we might now call educational psychology. Apparently, Israel's morale degenerated to that of the loser. The Israelites' initial compromise with the indigenous peoples first affected her social life and then her religious life, and her will to fight was undermined in the process. The determined attitude needed for struggle and resistance was lost and had to be relearned. If at that point God had given them the whole land by a succession of miracles, they would not have appreciated it enough to make good use of the resultant peace. Further, for the next three centuries the land was under threat from invasion, and Israel, in a continued state of loss of morale, would have been thoroughly defeated. They could not have survived in such a state except by a succession of miracles, which in the nature of the case would have to be unending. Without them, Israel would have fallen prey to other invaders, like the house "swept and garnished," to be possessed by devils seven times worse than the first. The unconquered peoples, therefore, were to remain in the land as a psychological device to spur the Israelites to learn the arts and skills of establishing a nation able to take care of itself against its enemies. Educational psychology employs methods that are familiar to those engaged in counseling where problems of motivation are involved. (The need for some children to meet a challenge as a stimulus to learn is commonplace.)

This is not an isolated biblical example of this reason. The Israelites wandered for forty years in the desert, not only as a punishment but also to learn obedience through testing, to toughen them up for the rigors of invading Palestine. In the same way, the Exile, centuries later, had an educative significance. In the New Testament, the educative ideas of training and learning become dominant notions in the one word "discipleship." The word carries the idea of learning under the discipline of a teacher or guide. Believers are regularly referred to as "disciples," and the idea is built into the Great Commission of Matthew 28:19: "Make disciples of all nations."

Learning, of whatever kind, has its own principles of operation. One such principle is the necessity of controlled experience: testing. People learn by being exposed to situations in which they may discover the limitations of their skill without the results being too irrevocably disastrous. In the case we are considering, the nations left in Canaan did not constitute the threat to Israel's existence that later invading armies might and often did. Indeed, the indigenous peoples would obviously have an interest in their own self-defense, not unlike the way today's Palestinians would say they do. But to Israel herself, they were to be as thorns in her side to force her to learn defense skills, like the goad that drove the donkey to keep moving. Under Samuel, Saul, and David, that education paid off against the Philistine expansion, which threatened Israel's survival as a nation. In christian discipleship, the lesson is clear enough too. The education is a character training process, and, like that of Israel's, it repeatedly confronts us with situations that challenge our weaknesses and force a flexing of our moral muscle to meet and defeat them.

We are dealing here with a different set of causes and reasons from technological or sociological ones. And we are seeing the same pattern. The psychological-educative reason may not seem to fit with the others, but, if so, that is only in our thinking. As far as the way the Bible sees life in the world, it is an understandable and valid reason, fitting with the others.

The fourth reason (Judges 3:7): the failure of faith. That the Israelites did not trust the Lord is of course the most frequently cited explanation for their failure to occupy all the Promise Land immediately. This reason is the one that usually comes quickly to mind (see also: Judges 10:10, 13). But, mind you, it was not a failure of faith in the miraculous. After all, immediately after the Israelites in the desert had accepted the discouraging report of the ten spies but then realized that they were losing their chance of conquest, they went ahead and attacked the Amalekites and Canaanites anyway. Clearly they were expecting divine help. The unbelief, the lack of faith, went deeper than that.

A Religious Reason

There was a shift of spiritual loyalties, a hankering after other gods. This occurred frequently throughout the history of ancient Israel. The insidious thing about it was that it was often disguised as a worship of the Lord while having the kind of devotion that was appropriate only for a heathen Baal. One God for the Temple or synagogue, another for daily life. That shift of religious loyalties resulted in a shift of commitment to a different kind of law, for different gods have different laws. For example, Paul, in Acts 27:21–26, has a faith for miracles too, but it is according to the Word of the Lord. The Psalmist, in Psalm 119, bases his wisdom and insight on knowing God in His Law. The Persians, wise in their generation, reckoned that their only hope of bringing down Daniel was by the law of his God (Daniel 6:5). Other gods, they knew, had other laws. When Israel switched allegiances, therefore, various kinds of judgments came from God, and these had the net result of delaying full conquest of the land. If the Israelites did not trust in the Lord to give them the whole land—by whatever means—then they would not get it.

In the Judges' account, this particular reason appears late on the scene. The chief limitations on the conquest of the land had already been laid down by then. This does seem more of an explanation of what happened afterwards. The overall picture so far, then, is of an initial military failure through lack of heavy armament and a carelessness in not rooting out the enemies that were conquered. This resulted in integration and intermarriage, with consequent loss or weakening of religious loyalty to the Lord. And the whole community was at times accordingly characterized by a lack of fighting morale.

The fifth reason (Deuteronomy 7:22): to preserve the balance of nature.

The previously listed reasons can be more or less harmonized as a pattern of causes and effects in which the operation of some may bring others into play. But this fifth reason (see also: Exodus 23:29–30) is a quite different animal.

An Ecological Reason

To begin with, it has no direct connection with the specific needs of just the Israelites. It is related to a different concern altogether. Namely, if the conquest were too rapidly decisive (if, in fact, the Israelites had been fully obedient to the Lord!), then there would have been more territory under their control than they had manpower to deal with, and the ecological balance of man, plant, and beast would have been upset to the detriment of all the inhabitants. (This is a typical concern of Deuteronomy.) And the writer does not envisage any miracles coming to deal with it. On the face of it, this explanation does not seem to fit in with the others. The chain of causes and effects that the others are working with does not seem to apply here; in fact, this one seems contradictory to them. Nevertheless, it "fits" with the others within a biblical wisdom.

How can all five explanations be true at once?

Here we meet the strangeness of Scripture again. Why do we have five answers for the same question, not to mention that one seems quite the odd man out? First of all, we must say that the writers were not stupid or naive, and we must give full weight to this. Those who wrote the Old Testament material, who copied it down throughout the centuries, who preserved it as literature, who developed from it a body of instruction, were not ignorant of what it contained. Indeed, in some respects, its language and reasoning must obviously have been more directly intelligible to them than it is to us. (To read some commentators, you would think that no one before the last two centuries had ever made an intelligent reading of the texts.)

Were the writers irrational or ignorant of logic? They were not modern-day scientists, but there is no reason to believe that they were any less sensitive to logical or factual inconsistencies than we are. It is true that the texts did become read liturgically, and thus they became susceptible to a stained glass window effect, which bathed the plain words in a mystical light. Long before that, however, they had been records and exhortations and proclamations and stories in ordinary use. And in the hands of the rabbis, they underwent the most minute inspection and expository comment. This is an important consideration for our approach to many parts of Scripture that appear to be inconsistent or contradictory.

Often, scholars and commentators explain such phenomena—as apparently inconsistent statements—as due to authorships, traditions, and schools of thought that were in conflict, or even as contributors to the same finished literary work. In doing this, they seem to assume that those same authors, compilers, and editors in those days either did not know or did not care whether they contradicted themselves. Or else they seem to assume that, if those ancients did know that the material was contradictory, they were so inept at their task (in spite of demonstrating superb literary skills in other respects) that their attempts to cope with the contradictions were a pathetic failure—so pathetic that scholars living two thousand years later, working in another culture and speaking an alien mother tongue, are clever enough to confidently pass such critical judgments upon their work.

Strained reconciliations don't remove problems like this.

Even among scholars who take Scripture as divinely authoritative, there arises the damaging tendency to seek to reconcile explanations at all costs. And it usually costs a great deal: credibility, because one frequently ends up with strained attempts to make religious or moral explanations final and comprehensive. This is done by trying to force explanations that are outside the religious and moral aspects (as some of the foregoing reasons are) into religious and moral explanations. In other words, we're in Flatland, living with an imagination in which other kinds of explanations are not possible. Worse still is the refusal to face such problems and to accuse those who raise them of being ipso facto skeptics and liberals. But the problems do not thereby go away. If they are not faced, they pass into the hands of the Enemy, who uses them as if they were insoluble examples of irrationality. Then they become the weapons of unbelief.

~12~

The Different Dimensions of Jesus and God's Creation

The phenomenon of multiple parallel explanations, though not always so extensive and obvious as in the Conquest example, is not uncommon in the Old Testament. It is found in the first two chapters of Genesis, where apparently different accounts of the Creation appear, and there are points at which they are not easily reconcilable. For example, in Genesis 2, trees apparently appear after the creation of Adam. Later, in Exodus, the dramatic parting of the Red Sea is explained as the direct action of the Lord and, on the other hand, as the result of a strong wind driving the water back throughout the night and falling at daybreak.

It is not impossible to reconcile many such passages of course, although we ought to be critical of attempts that are strained and unnatural. The important point is that the combination of a "natural" explanation and a "supernatural" one, or combinations of explanations, such as the five discussed in the previous chapter, offered no problems for the original narrators, as they so often do for us.

Multiple explanations are built into Scripture and even into the Gospel itself.

As with the Old Testament, multiple parallel explanations are not even a shadow of a problem for the New Testament. Perhaps the most obvious and controversial example is the way in which Scripture says that our salvation is applied. Some texts say that we are saved by faith, which means that God does it all. Other texts indicate that being saved by faith means that we have to do something: make our commitment. Problems intrinsic in these two forms of explanation have challenged the best intellects and split churches in two. Yet the New Testament writers were blissfully unaware of the problems! Ephesians 2, for instance, puts both ideas side by side, and Romans 9 contains the same apparent conflict in a negative form in relation to sin and condemnation. For centuries, commentators and theologians have been offering explanations. Yet so confidently does Paul expect his (mostly relatively uneducated) readers to find it completely straightforward that he does not even bother to make the slightest comment on his words. There is no suggestion that anyone back then might feel the need for any logically reconciling explanation whatever. (For Paul, the controversy does not rage around the doctrinal, theological problem but around the religious and moral issue of allegiance to the Lord.) Even when James deals with the issue of faith and works, with an awareness of possible misunderstanding and controversy, he shows no interest in the tension between "faith and human responsibility" that has so beset later generations. It is obviously not one that bothered his readers.

A way to ease into this kind of reasoning process is analogous to approaching an island from different directions. From the north, one finds the mountain; from the south, the beach. From the east, one finds the jungle; from the west, the city. It's a pretty poor explorer who, having been sent out to report back on the island, explains it all as a city or a mountain because that's been his only approach to it. And think of the conflict that would arise when he meets another explorer who says, "You're wrong. It's a jungle out there," because that is all he has seen. Neither person is completely right or completely wrong; they simply haven't got the full picture. Obviously, the two explorers need to pool their information. Events, situations, things, people; all of these can be approached from many different directions and then the different kinds of information can be added up to "make more sense" of whatever is under consideration. Further, the island approach helps us not only with the past and the present but also with the future. Think of the lost opportunities, for instance, if an explorer returned to his corporation and reported, "There's no business possibilities there. No people. It's all desert."

The people of the Bible take something for granted that we don't. Going back to the Book, we see that a different way of reasoning and perceiving life is at work there, a way in which the questions that have teased later generations do not arise with the writers of Scripture. Ancient Israel and the early church were involved in different questions because they started from different assumptions. Our difficulties today are rather like the problem of the "cannonball races" in chapter 7 or the "impossible" explanations that Circle heard in Flatland (chapter 11). But, though the writers of Scripture have a radically different perception of life, it is not an irrational or an obscurantist perception. It is not as if the biblical writers regarded the world as a mass of conflicting phenomena, which therefore had to be ruled by a pantheon of warring gods. They were quite clear that the world belonged to one God: the Lord, whom they in no way regarded as schizophrenic or capricious. That this one God had built into creation multiple parallel explanations was quite reasonable to the writers of Scripture. In fact, as we noted in chapter 3, one of the remarkable characteristics of the Bible's secular wisdom is the frequency of its appeals to reason, which is one of the characteristics of multiple parallel explanations. Jeremiah, for instance, is overwhelmed not merely by the wickedness of Israel's rebellion but also by the sheer irrationality of it. So we come again to the "reasonableness" of Scripture. Thus the Bible certainly gives us no example that would excuse us from using our reasoning. Rather, it insists that "by wisdom" God founded the world (Proverbs 3:19).

When we are faced with apparent contradictions within events or situations, our tendency today is naturally to look for *one* explanation, and then to use it to reconcile the others into some kind of unity. The obvious choices for us are religious, moral, or ethical explanations, and it is disappointing when they don't work. In the case of the Conquest explanations, it is evident that neither the religious or moral explanations fully reconcile all the assertions, the whole story. This is true of other examples as well. And if secular books like Esther are anything to go by, they were not expected to.

We have been suggesting throughout this book that Christians are influenced by the wisdom of their cultures, and the "one explanation tendency" of Christians today is a case in point, for it is characteristic of a Western wisdom in which, besides dualism, reductionism is a strong influence. In the Bible's way of reasoning, however, nothing in the universe can be fully understood by one explanation.

The Incarnation: reality has more dimensions than human reason can work with at one time.

The Bible has a special way of handling multiple parallel reasons that don't seem to "fit." The simplest, most basic form of the conflict is seen in a vital area of The Doctrine of the Person of Christ: how do we describe Jesus consistently as God and man at one and the same time? Donald Baillie, the Scots theologian, has quite a helpful approach to this dilemma. In his well-known book *God Was In Christ*, Baillie responds to the trouble that theologians who have tackled this problem usually get into: either they end up by subordinating one or other of the two descriptions or they picture Jesus Christ as a hybrid, neither truly God nor truly man.

Baillie argues that this "paradox of grace," as he calls it, is due to a fundamental but quite understandable difficulty like that of cartographers, who face an apparently impossible task: representing the surface of a globe—three dimensions—on a flat page—two dimensions. To cope with this they picture the contours of the map in different ways called "projections." Perhaps the most common of these is the "Mercator projection," in which the meridians are equally spaced, parallel vertical lines and the latitudes are parallel horizontal lines spaced farther and farther apart as their distance from the Equator increases. This means that the areas of the territories at the poles are shown as much larger than they actually are in relation to the size of the ones shown at the equator. So Greenland in comparison with India is much too big. The Mercator Projection is the one in which Africa looks almost as wide across its east-west stretch as it looks in length from north to south. In many of the later projections, such as the "Hammer Azimuth Equal Area Projection," the areas of some territories, such as South America and Africa, appear quite elongated. (If this is new to you, get to the nearest atlas and look at the small print in the margins.)

The Mercator projection is the one that most of us got accustomed to in school. I[CS] can still remember the strange feeling that came over me years later the first few times I saw the world mapped in those "odd-looking" elongated projections. The continents just did not look (seem) right. Yet neither projection is wrong. Each works on its own principles and within its own limits is true. But neither by itself supplies a full picture. So, Baillie argues, the "contours" of Jesus in human terms are complementary to those in terms of his divinity. Neither explanation can tell the whole story, and neither can be resolved in terms of the other. *What reconciles them is their relation to the same ultimate reality*: Jesus Christ.

Many "dimensions" are found in Jesus himself.
This is capable of further extension. As a human being, Jesus functioned in a considerable number of different dimensions, or aspects, of life. For instance, he was a historical person; that is, he was a Jew born at a particular date, given as Quirinius' first census, and dying at a particular date, "under Pontius Pilate" (as the Apostles' Creed states, using the contemporary method of dating). In contrast, he lived and taught a morality that was certainly not time-bound. We also see the aesthetic dimension, for his teaching method was profoundly aesthetic in character. His parables are acknowledged masterpieces of the storyteller's art. You could say that Jesus was, so to speak, "all artist," yet it is obvious that he was not merely an artist (chapter 21). He was, in addition, a controversialist, and here we have yet another dimension; he was a master in the strategies of verbal warfare. It would be ludicrous, however, to think that his unique influence could be exhaustively explained in such terms, just as much as it would be to rationalize his death merely in political terms, even though he lived as a citizen of a country under occupation—his life and teaching reflect that—and died under political accusation. Attempts to represent his mission only in political terms distort Scripture. Yet even this is not the end of the story, for Jesus was

obviously a religious figure; supremely so, one could say. Jesus, however, cannot be explained exclusively in religious terms, if only because the bulk of his teaching was cast in a secular form, and in other ways it was so at odds with even revealed religious devotion that he could be believably accused of attempting to overthrow it.

We have, therefore, a whole range of different accounts of this man Christ Jesus confronting us. One student might see his political significance and give an account of his life in those terms. Another might expatiate on his consummate artistry in storytelling: his economy of language, deftness in painting word pictures, skill in pinpointing for his hearers the crucial issues for decision. Others might study the way his life inspired the new literary genre we call "Gospels." Some people might concentrate on his family life, the way he behaved towards his parents and relatives. Study might also be made about his humanitarianism, including the tension he had between his love for his own people and his care for all he met.

Our attempts to reconcile all the explanations may not be very convincing. Problems would of course crop up in all this. We would wonder how so loving a man could at times be so harsh when his mother approached him. We would be puzzled that such an artist could be so crude in his language about blood in John 6. We would grapple with his refusal to be mixed up in politics even while teaching with unavoidable political implications. Such problems cannot be properly dealt with if we remain inside one dimension, one explanation, one projection and try to resolve the diversity. We often stick to our guns, however, to our lone explanation. Trouble is, when we try to "explain" Jesus to someone without our vested interest in the subject, our lone explanation sounds unconvincing. Non-Christians are apt to question our intellectual integrity, and often their intuition is telling them that what we are saying doesn't "add up," and so we leave them not just unanswered but sounding like we are contradictory.

If we are honest, we may admit to ourselves that what we are saying is more like guesses or rationalizations than proper explanations that illuminatingly reconcile these conflicts. Unfortunately, we can be so shielded from criticism by our circle of fellow believers that we no longer feel this and we end up resenting such criticisms. A common example are Christians who concentrate on the love and compassion of Jesus, which they largely derive exclusively from the Gospels. This can lead to an unhealthy tolerance of immoral lifestyles, forgetting that one day Jesus Himself will be quite "intolerant" of the ungodly, as he is seen in the Book of Revelation. For those who over-emphasize the loving Jesus, the judging Jesus is largely a non-entity.

They are reconciled in a quite different way: in Christ.

When you actually meet and then get to know a person, it is then that the puzzlingly varied comments which you have heard about the person take on a new significance. So we speak of a "many-sided personality" or a "complex person," in which we see differing, subtle facets. All the puzzling remarks and quirky descriptions are brought together, or reconciled, in the reality of the person himself, and they are brought together in a way that is likely to defy logical analysis only or even clear articulation. It is in the encounter with the actual person that puzzling discrepancies are overcome and reconciled in an experience that makes us content with provisional explanations for the time being, even when they are not wholly satisfactory.

Some may say that this is sheer obscurantism. Certainly, not all apparently contradictory statements can be dismissed in this way. But it is a fact of life, and students of logic are well able to make distinctions between a contradiction and a paradox. People are always paradoxical and more complex than any explanations, and the explanations simply cannot be reconciled apart from the person. If that is true of us ordinary mortals, obviously it is going to be true of Jesus.

This is true even for the creation.

The same principle applies to explanations of the creation. Simply put, just as it takes multi-explanations of Jesus for us to "make sense" of him, so too for his creation. That is, creation cannot be explained only materially, or only scientifically, or only religiously, and so on. The world functions in a great diversity of dimensions, or aspects, each having its own characteristic principles of explanation and a kind of kinship with the others (chapter 13). Thus any attempt to explain the world through one or two aspects only ends in disaster. But we know this. It seems too obvious, so why bother mentioning it?

What we have to keep in mind is that the great diversity of creation itself, as the Bible says, is "reconciled" *in Christ* (Ephesians 1:10; Colossians 1:20). That is, there is nowhere else in the whole of creation, in all of its history, where all the aspects can be brought together and explained as a consistent, intelligible whole. This is why creation when explained by other gods ends up as a universe of irrationalities and irreconcilable contradictions. In other words, the Bible sees no one or few of the aspects, even the religious and moral ones, as being adequate to reconcile or fully expound the nature of the others or the whole. Jesus Christ himself, the God-man, the Agent of creation, is alone the One in whom such comprehensive explanation and reconciliation is possible. And we can push the argument further by saying that any attempt to explain the world using even *all* the aspects is insufficient. As the Bible puts it, Jesus Christ alone is the one in whom all creation holds together as a coherent unity (Colossians 1:17). And so far from this preventing us from creative thinking, we shall see that it actually generates it.

Ordinary thinking works with this idea constantly.

Although thinking about life as a complex unity of numerous aspects may appear unfamiliar here on paper as we make it conscious, it is not really strange in our thinking. We all use it unconsciously at some time or another, and people have articulated more formal models to describe it. E. F. Schumacher, the author of *Small is Beautiful*, uses it in another of his books, *Guide for the Perplexed*, in an elementary form based on the "animal, vegetable, mineral" model. Dr. Mackay, in his *Christianity in a Mechanistic Universe*, uses a multi-dimensional approach when he attacks materialism's "nothing buttery," which is his phrase for arguments that explain some spiritual experience as "nothing but" emotional, or psychological, or culturally deterministic, and so on. Mackay makes a distinction between a physical explanation of chalk marks on a blackboard and what the chalk marks mean. The former, he suggests, are like a scientific explanation; the latter, like a religious one. He is here using two dimensions, or aspects, of explanation. Loren Cunningham, founder of Youth With A Mission (YWAM), is credited with developing a model called "The Seven Mind Molders": church, government, family, education, business, arts and entertainment, the media. These models are used to help people appreciate life's complexities and to look multi-dimensionally at the world and human activities in it.

Now if all the aspects (we will look at a model with 15 in the next chapter) are only accounted for in Jesus, and if Jesus is Lord, the Image of God, God made man, then to look for a *comprehensive* explanation of everything anywhere in creation (it's all biological; it's all in the mind; it's all nature), or even to look for it in our religious convictions or in our theology, is a kind of idolatry. It gives to something created a place that properly belongs to Jesus Christ alone. Again, when this happens—it is going on around us all the time— it makes created things into what the Old Testament calls "gods," which end up competing or warring with one another.

With Christ as the reconciler, we can be confident that in him our thinking will be coherent.

So what does it mean to find all of life's "aspects," including its paradoxical facets, reconciled in Jesus Christ? First of all, it does not mean that we have discovered an answer that will enable us to put everybody right, but it does offer a secure approach to considering the problems of the world around us. It will not give us the right or ability to present, say, a political or economic program that must be accepted because it is true, whatever other people think, but it does mean that we can address the world around us with a consistency that will command respect.

In this kind of wisdom, we can pursue every line of inquiry and be confident that *in Jesus Christ* our thinking will be coherent. We shall not invoke the Bible one minute and science, or tradition, or conscience the next without any clear cohesion between them. We shall not pontificate about moral ideals without facing the other aspects of our human problems in a biblical christian way. In matters where dogmatism is inappropriate, we will be able to offer alternative ways of thinking about human issues, and we will be able to do it with the confidence that we shall not repel people for the wrong reasons through some irrationality. Further, we can do this knowing that whatever there is of truth in what we say, it may "speak for itself."

We have a resource for exposing non-christian attempts at coherence. This way of thinking also offers a way of penetrating non-christian systems of thought. Any human attempt to have a consistent body of thinking has to have a focal point—what the New Testament calls a *logos*—that does for it what Jesus Christ does for christian thinking. That focal point always has to be something in this created order, such as Mind, Matter, Progress, Life-Force, Humanity, Self, or Whatever, for there is nowhere else but in the created order to get it from. After all, where else can one look? One line of christian attack is to identify and expose such creational focal points to demonstrate their inadequacy. A recent example is in the proliferation of business management theories. Some are "scientific," convinced that the secret of success lies in accurate measurements. At the other extreme is "the Art of Japanese Management," the stress is on relationships. The former has its focal point in Reason, the latter in Intuition. Though you can get a lot of mileage out of these on their own merits, neither Reason nor Intuition is a sufficient *logos* for a business theory in the long run because sooner or later, as history reveals, the inconsistencies and contradictions within each become too much to bear, things begin to break down, and each starts drawing somewhat haphazardly on the other for help, or people drop the one and run to the other, thinking that have found the solution. (Eventually the process repeats itself.)

We can live with unresolved questions and learn from them. We should also be relieved of a certain kind of anxiety. Because all things are reconciled *in Christ* and no place else, the heat is now off any feeling that we simply have got to reconcile all the discrepancies in order to make Scripture believable. The heat is off because *we* can't do it. Jesus Christ does. This does not mean that we shall no longer be aware of any paradoxes and inconsistencies or that we will ignore them. It means that we won't be worried by them, because we know that one day they will be seen as they are: reconciled *in Christ*. For us, not everything that looks like an inconsistency, or even a contradiction, need actually be one. If our trust really is in Jesus and not in our systems of thought, we can investigate apparently incompatible statements in Scripture in a spirit of positive inquiry without some sneaking feeling that our faith or intellectual integrity is being threatened. In this context, the problems of Scripture, such as its "strangeness" (chapter 7), become growing points of our understanding. We can live with the paradoxes and learn from them.

We won't have to impose religious or moral lessons on the secular passages. Multi-dimensional thinking will also give us a way of going back to those secular books and passages of the Bible to read them for what they are without trying to squeeze out of them, or into them, a particular religious or moral lesson where there is none. This will gives us a way to gain vital insights into the way that Scripture sees commerce, or history, or erotic love, or the intricacies of bureaucracy and therefore, surely, the way that God wants us to see them.

In other words, we gain understanding of biblical wisdom for everyday life; we have a biblical way to face non-religious subjects without needing religious arguments. We are no longer restricted to the religious and the moral dimensions in our assessment of what is going on in secular life or in the church, and as a blessed consequence we stand some chance of developing theories (chapter 7) that have a distinctly biblical christian shape to them about the nature of aspects like social relations, economics, politics, business, and art. Clearer ideas of the God-ordained contours of life in terms of its differing aspects will become available to us. And this, for instance, will help us begin to assess the possible positive values that make socialism and monetarism so attractive, as well as to declare why we reject them. We can consider issues such as the "stream-of-consciousness" fiction in literature on its own terms as literature, or the latest economic theory, or a controversy in the arts. And we will be able to consider not only whether such issues promulgate atheism or immorality but also the extent to which their way of explaining and understanding life's problems corresponds to a biblical wisdom. Christian history, too, will no longer have to subordinate military, ecological, or sociological considerations to religious ones, any more than the Bible does.

This is just to mention several of the countless approaches that will open to us as Christians who desire to speak forcibly and sensibly in everyday life for the glory of God. We cannot impose our convictions on the world at large, but at least people have the right to know the kind of ideas that biblical Christianity generates for everyday life. If that wisdom is true wisdom, then we are giving the world the chance to respond to God's offer of earthly *shalom*. We have as much duty to minister *that* to the world as a christian doctor has to offer the best medicine he knows to a non-Christian patient.

We can talk christianly about the nonreligious things that interest non-Christians.

This way of thinking and reasoning will also serve our evangelistic efforts. Being able to develop a distinctively christian understanding about art (chapter 21), for instance, will help us understand what kinds of christian evangelism are damaging even when they are theologically and morally unexceptionable. For instance, art in Scripture—we are not necessarily meaning religious art here—works by suggestion and by association in its style; that is, it is not preachy, and deliberately so. Further, styles of art which suggest values that contradict what the Gospel stands for will not do. With this in mind, 1 Peter 3 now carries an aesthetic message: rather than asserting a strong, clear verbal witness, a zealous Christian wife may win her husband to the Lord through a lifestyle characterized by the aesthetic qualities of modesty and good taste. Further, we can study the Bible to understand art in terms of the laws or principles ordained by God for the proper functioning of that aspect. This is important for the Christian who is an artist because these laws and principles require their own kind of obedience from the artist, something more than simply creating a pleasurable enticement to listen to the message. This is not to suggest that a study of the Bible is all that this artist needs. The Bible is not an exhaustive or comprehensive source for understanding art. But for the Christian it is an authoritative one.

Bible studies take on whole new meanings with ideas like this in mind, not just for our artists but also for our lives as mothers and fathers, as business people, as politicians, as scientists, as self-employed, as teachers, as whatever. Whole new layers of Scripture will open to us, and through that all sorts of fresh possibilities will present themselves for the glory of God.

~13~

The Unity and Diversity of Creation

As a backdrop to this entire discussion is the way of thinking and reasoning that we, the authors, are using, and we have reached a point in this book where it will be helpful to say what a biblical model of this might look like. In seminars and workshops, we have found that a visual aid of this model can be quite helpful here. This model will help us recognize the numerous aspects of creation and understand their relationships to one another and to Jesus Christ. It will also assist us in exploring more thoroughly the multiple dimensions of God's creation as well as to see its unity. The model can become quite sophisticated, eventually helping us identify and work with 15 aspects. But we need to work toward that. So to get us going, we will begin with the rather rudimentary version mentioned earlier: "animal, vegetable, mineral," and to it let us add "human." This will provide us with some basic ideas and principles to apply later to the more developed model.

Diagramed it would look like:

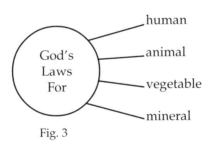

Fig. 3

There are lower and higher aspects, and everything has laws governing its existence.

Let's look at some basic ideas for making this work for us. Note that the aspects follow an ascending scale. By "mineral" we would mean anything that is not alive (in the way plants and animals are) at all. It can occupy space, it has weight and mass, and it can be pushed about, but it does not grow by itself in a way that interacts adaptively with its environment. By "vegetable" we would mean any living thing that does not have consciousness (as animals and humans have) or a mode of expression beyond showing symptoms. By "animal" we mean something living with a consciousness that can find expression in some deliberate way. By "human" we mean a physically living being having an animal-type life plus self-consciousness and self-determination. These, of course, are merely general characterizations and not comprehensive definitions, which are surprisingly difficult to arrive at considering we are all confident that we know what the terms refer to!

Also, and this is significant, within each aspect are God's laws for the existence of all the things within that aspect. In other words, everything is subject to laws that govern its particular kind of existence or being, and these are God's laws. For instance, stones do not need food but living things do; humans reason but plants do not.

Explaining "higher" things only in terms of a "lower" aspect is possible but insufficient.

Next, since "mineral existence" is basic to everything, it is possible to give an explanation of anything in mineral terms, even things above the mineral, and that explanation could have the appearance of a full explanation, even of a satisfying unity. For example, a human being could be explained in terms of chemical composition: so much water, so much carbon, so much sodium, so much potassium, and so on. Human "movements" could then be explained as being solely electro-chemical processes, and the statistics of the person's size, weight, and volume could be given. The full mineral explanation would be complicated, and we might not be able to complete it, but it would be enough to show that at least in principle one could develop it into a self-consistent explanation of everything that a human being is and does. The explanation would employ the same laws that govern rocks and clouds and all other "mineral" objects. And we could obviously, in principle, do the same for cats, cows, or gooseberry bushes.

Yet bushes, cats, cows, and people are clearly not the same sort of things as rocks or clouds. There are other possible explanations of their existence that are not applicable to rocks and clouds. Thus attempts to explain the human being, or anything "above" the mineral aspect, fully in mineral terms is insufficient; it leaves us with many gaps and unanswerable questions. The reason for this is that God has ordained laws for the upper aspects which the ones below them do not have. That is, there are laws that God has ordained for plants bearing seed after their kind, or for the way in which His word causes the hind to calve, or for the way in which human relationships should ensue. The laws of the human aspect, therefore, have no meaning for the way

God has separated the water from the dry land or "how the clouds hang poised."

The "higher" forms can give extra meaning and value to "lower" ones.

Another basic principle is that to some extent some forms of existence are capable of "taking over" and reorganizing other forms in such a way as to give them a new mode of being and significance. This has a bearing on the "relationships" among the aspects. For instance, the grass "takes up" into itself minerals from the soil to participate in plant life. The cow then eats (takes up into itself) the plant life and absorbs it to make animal life. The human being then uses cowhide to make a jacket or to cover a chair or a Bible, or part of the cow may be "taken up" in a meal to make human life. Another kind of this "extra meaning" is seen when the human being makes an animal into a beast of burden or a pet.

So there is a kind of ascending scale—mineral, vegetable, animal, human—where the "higher" can heighten the significance of those "below" it. Anyone whose pet has died has experienced this poignantly. I[CS] remember the tears and heartache that my wife and I experienced when our first parrot, a bright Red Lory named "Louie," died suddenly one morning. We were an emotional wreck for a week. I mean, we are talking here about a bird whom you could play "fetch" with on the kitchen floor like a puppy, and who could speak fifteen-to-twenty phrases as clear as a bell, some of which he said in context, such as "See ya later, catch ya later" when you were leaving the house. Several weeks after Louie died, I happened to be talking to a friend about how bad I felt about the loss. The friend listened and then said, "Well, it was just a bird." *Just a bird?* Birds are those things that fly around in the woods behind our house, can't say words, and won't let you get near them. When you find one of those dead, you don't give it much thought. Louie was more than that to us because we had invested "upper aspect" meanings (see figure 4, aspects above the psychical) into that animal. This heightened its value, and our pain and loss.

Higher beings exist subject to the laws of more aspects than things in the lower ones.

Further, things in the higher aspects are subject to their own, additional, laws for their existence, laws not found in aspects below them. For example, animal life, though subject to mineral laws, has its own animal laws. Drop an animal from a fifth story window and on landing it will cease to function properly as an animal, and after a while, if left to itself, it will be indistinguishable from something mineral, like dust to dust. In other words, it will no longer function like an animal because certain of its animal laws were broken. In contrast, drop an iron bar from that height and on landing it will remain an iron bar, bent maybe, but still fully functioning in the mineral realm.

The principle here is a quite significant one with far-reaching ramifications, opening to us another of the many possibilities of this model. For instance, if we treat plants or animals like stones or water, we violate laws that are special to their modes of existence and eventually they will lose their distinctive qualities. The same is true of human beings. Humans are subject to all the laws governing all the lower aspects, but in addition, the laws of self-consciousness and self-determination apply to them. If human beings, therefore, are treated for too long like animals, they tend to lose the qualities that make them characteristically human, and they will eventually begin to act like…

We must not explain and treat creatures solely in terms of one or two aspects.

This may help us to see more clearly the importance of today's battle of ideas over the question: "What is Man?" It is not a merely academic question. If people think that they are no more than highly complex mineral objects like robots or computers, then they will begin to think and act that way and their responses will become purely logical and passionless with little or no moral concern; eventually they will lose the ability to behave lovingly. If they see themselves as animals, they begin to succumb uncritically to their instinctual drives. Worse still, they will tend to treat others accordingly. Decision-makers will judge their problems in statistical terms appropriate to inanimate objects. Dictators will try to brainwash dissidents by psychological conditioning or by training their reflexes to obedience by the experience of pain. (Perhaps you would like to speculate now on the results of reversing the process. What happens when people treat an elephant-shaped rock as if it had the qualities of a real animal, or a computer as if it were a human being, or the earth, moon, and sun as if they were divine?)

We really have to deal with more than four aspects.

You will have observed in the foregoing that the principles or laws that govern these diverse aspects of our existence are not necessarily religious or moral. It is true that human beings are uniquely subject to moral and religious laws, but they are also subject to other kinds of laws (Fig. 4) as well as the laws governing other living and non-living objects. Now these "other laws" too are ordained by God, for that is the way He has ordered His creation. With that, we would now like to spring a more sophisticated model on you. But first, here is a summary of the principles noted so far, which are applicable to the model below:

1) Everything is subject to the laws that govern its particular kind of existence or being.

2) It is possible to explain anything in the most basic terms, but that will be unsatisfactory.

3) The aspects, or modes, range from "lower" to "higher."

4) In this ascending scale, the lower can get "taken up" into the higher, and the higher can give new meaning and significance to the lower.

5) Things in the higher aspects are subject to their own, additional, laws for their existence.

Those who work with this kind of thinking have identified at least fourteen aspects. There are fifteen in the model below.

Diagramed, it would look like:

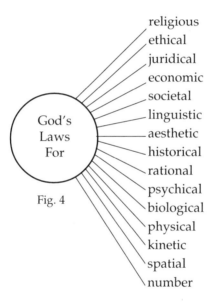

Fig. 4

This may look overwhelming, but only at first! This model simply teases out more aspects, especially the characteristics of human life and activity, providing categories for doing biblical thinking within them and among their relationships to one another. The five principles for the rudimentary model apply here; it's just that there are more aspects to work with. And, as we shall see, rather than stifle our thinking and creativity, it actually stimulates it tremendously.

Human beings are specially subject to the higher aspects, which form a structural unity.

In this model, often called "modal theory" ("modes" being a more technical name for the "aspects"), we immediately see that human beings are specially subject to the laws of higher aspects, or those above the "psychical," which do not apply to animals, plants, or stones. Note, too, that these include aspects that are not religious or ethical-moral. We discover, then, that God's laws exist for each of the aspects of human life "below" the religious and ethical-moral aspects. And, just as with the religious and ethical-moral aspects, the laws in the aspects below them cannot be violated if certain desired results are to be achieved. Take the aesthetic aspect, for instance, in which music would be included. However prayerful and loving a musician may be, if that person disobey's God's laws for harmony, pitch, or timing the result will be music that shows it in the discomfort of the hearers!

But there is more to it. A structural unity exists within the higher aspects just as we saw one in the "crude" animal, vegetable, mineral, human model. In this unity, the significance or meaning of the lower are "heightened" by the higher, just as in the crude model. For instance, staying with the subject of music, music has its own God-appointed laws, and using those laws, human beings can produce sound that is patterned in a way that gives pleasure. But the same pattern of sounds can be heightened in value, such as by being used to express and confirm solidarity when, for example, it is a means of fellowship in a community sing-song. Or it may be used in a specially significant form of commitment that expresses loyalty to a cause, such as singing an anthem for a school or nation. Or it may be used more significantly still in worship, as a means of declaring with others the love and greatness of God. Here we see that the aesthetic aspect may be heightened, as the patterned sounds we call music are used in different aspects of meaning or significance: from social to ethical to religious (notice that those levels themselves are built upon each other rather like animal, vegetable, mineral).

Now suppose we reverse the process and try to explain music that is used to praise God entirely in terms of some lower aspect of meaning, such as in the same way we thought of explaining man as an animal or a computer? If we believed that our enjoyment of hymn singing was merely the pleasure given by the patterned noise (some behavioral psychologists come close to saying that), then a whole segment of our religious experience in worship would be obliterated overnight. A similar distortion would occur if we said that the pleasure of hymn singing were merely that of enjoying a togetherness with other people. Also, distortions arise if we say that music is only "real" music, or "proper" music, or even "good" music when it is religious music. If that were true then a musician who is religious would be automatically a better musician than one who isn't.

They provide another way to appreciate multiple parallel explanations.

Modal theory also gives us a way to appreciate, at least a little more, multiple parallel explanations. Take the Conquest sample again, and our discovery of the five explanations why Israel did not conquer Palestine immediately (chapter 11). One of those, you will remember, was about the treatment of the environment (biological and other lower aspects). It makes very little difference whether a farmer is morally upright, a churchgoer, or a man of prayer if he does not obey God's laws for conserving the fertility of his land—he will eventually make a dust bowl out of it. So, too, ancient Israel. God's environmental laws had to be obeyed or the experiment would have been a disaster. Ecological laws (biological aspect, for one) are given by God (Isaiah 28:23–29), and people use them properly only by being duly subject to them. The Conquest sample also showed us, in the terms of modal theory, consequences of laws violated in societal and religious aspects, and how the historical aspect (sometime referred to as "cultural formative") had its role.

They help us to develop fuller understandings of things.

Modal theory, therefore, allows us to identify 15 aspects and to work up fuller understandings of the issues and events we may be considering. At the risk of getting a little ahead of ourselves, we want to offer a simple illustration here. As we proceed, if you are still struggling with this, think again of what it is like to approach an island for many different directions.

Let's ask a basic question about the gold wedding band I[JP] am wearing: "What is it?" The answer would depend on who we were asking. A <u>statistician</u> would tackle things like the ring's weight and dimension, and to do this he might employ a <u>physicist</u> and a <u>chemist</u>, who would explain the nature of the gold and its mixture with other metals. But is that all there is to the ring? Of course not. Others would have to be called in, possibly an <u>optometrist</u>, who, with the science of optics, would describe the ring's appearance. The <u>medical person</u> might also come along and say that there is more to it even than that, because gold can be used medically in injections.

So we would add all this to our understanding, but the question still arises: "Have these experts told us the whole story?" We have been considerably accurate so far, but is that all there is to the ring? Even all these explanations still leave me with an unsatisfactory understanding. So in comes the <u>historian</u> to date the ring and to say what culture it came from, and he would probably have the <u>craftsperson</u> with him to assess the engraving and style. So we get more understanding. Ahh, I see the <u>jeweler</u> arriving. He gives it the once-over and says he will give me $200 for it. Do you think I would take it? No way. I'd have to be desperately in need of money to do that. Why won't I take the money? Because its economic value does not represent its value to me. I would say to the jeweler, "You don't know what this ring means to me. It represents the commitments my wife and I made to each other." So it has a symbolic value for me, a high symbolic value. I'm now assessing the ring in moral terms. "But why is that so important to you," the jeweler may argue. "People today get divorced all the time." To that I would have to say, "Yes, but the commitment we made was not just to each other but to <u>God</u> in the presence of a <u>minister</u>." Now the ring also has a religious significance. All of that is involved in answering the question: "What is it?" The answers have come from many different perspectives, depending on who was asked.

This is an important way to use modal theory and analysis. Note that each person is working with the laws of different aspects and that, as we saw earlier, the higher give additional significance or meaning to the lower. If you want to try a little homework yourself, work out which aspect is represented by the underlined words in the foregoing. Hint: more than one are possible in some instances.

> *We now have a way to deal with the complexities of contemporary life.*

We want to stress that so far all of this is being illustrated in the simplest ways. There will be time enough in the following chapters, and in Appendix 1, to illustrate its use beyond introductory ideas. Our purpose here is first to introduce a way of thinking and reasoning that opens us to a new world of biblical ideas for fulfilling our obediences to God in everyday life. Actually, it is representative of the way we see and engage life anyway. We are just not used to it being mapped out to us. So it can seem a bit odd at first, like children feel when in school "learning language" from a textbook when they have already picked it up at home. Nevertheless, it is our normal way of knowing and engaging life. Life is happening around us like this all the time.

Take church services for instance. If asked "What's church all about?", many would respond, "Isn't that obvious? It's about our religious lives." Fair enough. Now answer the question referring to modal theory for your analysis. Certainly we see the religious aspect functioning, but what else? Most people would immediately see the moral mode too. But what else? In actual fact all the aspects are present and functioning. There's elders making announcements (juridical) and deacons taking the offering (economic). There's the minister's message (linguistic, rational) and the coffees and donuts after the service (social). There's the flower arrangements (aesthetic, biological) and the size, shape, and cornerstone of the building (physical, spatial, number, historical). And so on.

Modal analysis, therefore, equips us with a way to identify the many different aspects of life, and to deal with their complexities under God in a biblical way. It also helps us to see the relationships of the aspects to one another. Take architecture, for instance, and economics and mathematics. Mathematics and economics are important for architecture, but the laws that govern each activity are not identical, but they have relationships among them, and these need to be understood by the architect as well as the laws of each aspect. Further, we now have a way to go back to the Bible to explore not merely what it says but how it is said and why it is said like that; that is, its way of reasoning, which can introduce us to God's ideas and laws for love and work, friendship and government, history and art, and more. This will enlarge our understanding of God's wisdom, and this will in turn become vitally significant for us as Christians in our interactions with the society in which we find ourselves.

One application here is that it gives us a way out of one of our age's most fundamental dead ends: the penchant of non-christian theories of life to fasten on one or two aspects as keys for understanding the universe and human nature. So humanists fasten on reason, communists fastened on technology and economics, and Buddhists tend to fasten on psychology. And they do this as a way for understanding and judging *all* of life. This gets them into trouble in the long run because everything can't be explained only economically or only psychologically. Now Christians often judge the value of everything only in terms of religion and morals, and this gets them into trouble in the long run for the same reason. Modal theory helps us steer clear of this reductionism because it shows that no aspect is capable of fully explaining all of life, for each is but a part of life. That is, the aspects find their unity in Jesus Christ alone (see Appendix 1). The Bible can help us understand this in fresh and exciting ways, not only to help non-Christians see a problem but also to know where we as Christians may be violating God's laws for one of the aspects.

We have a way to develop biblical theories for secular matters.

But what we are suggesting will take us even further than that. Take the Christian and non-Christian business person. It is not merely a matter of the Christian being honest, or not flirting with the secretaries, or not breaking contracts. We all probably know non-Christian business people who could be described that way. So those characteristics in themselves do not necessarily mark the Christian off from the non-Christian. But a uniquely biblical theory of business certainly would.

That is what the Christian business person ought to be working to develop. Here we just want to note that by using modal analysis alongside Scripture, the business person will be greatly assisted in this. For one thing, a biblical theory of business would show the person ways of doing business that are Gospel-shaped: saving, redeeming, and liberating, rather than just profit-making. Not that it would reject the idea of profit. But it would define and discipline it. It would inevitably stop it from becoming an end in itself. And *that* would indeed mark us off from our non-Christian counterparts in business. Modal analysis, therefore, can help us tremendously toward developing distinctively biblical theories surrounding life's secular activities, such as in the arts, business, the family, economics.

To sum up: modal theory looks at the "whole" of life as being made up of different aspects of existence, such as religion, law, economics, social matters, and art, and it sees each of these aspects under God's law, functioning by their own God-ordained laws or principles. This helps us get to grips with the way God has ordained that the different aspects of everyday life should be conducted, and it shows that our obediences to God cannot be limited to the religious and moral modes of our being. It gives us a way to do distinctly christian studies of the arts, politics, economics, sociology, and so on, and it enables us to deal with the paradoxes of Scripture and to understand the disguised idolatries of current Western society more clearly. We now have a framework of thought that enables us to understand more consistently the manifold grace of God in His creation. Of course we still need information about that creation, and the next chapter is about getting that information and processing it faithfully.

Part Three

Re-engaging the Culture

~14~

Sources for Wisdom and the Importance of Words

So, then, if modal theory can help us develop our wisdom for everyday life, the next step is to find ways to make it work there, especially for areas common to everyone, such as art, law, business, science, politics, education, the family, entertainment, and so on. We will begin by building up a pool of information from three sources for wisdom: creation, culture, and Scripture.

It is a convenient aid to memory that Psalms 1, 19, and 119 are all about the Law of the Lord. Psalm 19 is particularly germane for our present purpose because it sets the Law of the Lord alongside of the rest of creation around us, to reveal that God is known not only in Christ through Scripture but also in His creation.

Psalm 19 falls into two distinct halves. The first half is about how God's glory (the impact of His presence and character) is "declared" by the heavens, and in particular by the sun. The general drift is that this revelation of the "glory of God" (note, *elohim;* chapter 3) is all-pervasive. Yet there is a secondary idea: this is not a verbal revelation of God's glory. A key to this part of the text is verse 3, although its exact meaning is not certain. Its ambiguity is preserved if we translate it literally as: "There is no speech, no word; their voice is not heard." This can mean either, "Wherever people talk, you can hear them [there's nowhere where you can't hear them] speak," or, "They don't talk, they don't use words; you don't hear them speak." (The authors prefer the latter because of the contrast in the Psalm between revelation in nature and revelation in Scripture.) This shows up clearly when the Psalm moves on, in verse 7, to the Law of Yahweh. What is meant here is quite obviously verbal and therefore able to change the thought-life of human beings, as well as their emotions, attitudes, self-awareness, moral character, and ability to cope with life properly. The Psalm ends, appropriately, with an appeal to the Lord that our words, and our heart as well, may be pleasing to him.

The first part of this Psalm is closely connected with Psalm 104, where a similar theme is developed in considerable detail and applied to our work in the world, such as cultivating plants, enjoying the produce, sailing off to sea, and going to work. This also appears in Psalm 8, where our task in the world receives the greater stress and has to be justified in the face of the overwhelming grandeur of God seen in His creation. With Job chapters 38 and 39, Psalms 8, 19, and 104 constitute outstanding scriptural descriptions of the glory of God in the natural world.

Three sources of wisdom: nature, culture, Scripture. These Psalms proclaim that God's will and work in the world can be understood by observing and studying: 1) the natural world, 2) our work in it, and 3) the Law of the Lord. Here, then, are three resources for information and insight in the process of learning true wisdom. One is the inarticulate, wordless world of nature, which nevertheless "speaks" to everyone about itself; for instance, in the discovery of natural laws. And over the world of nature we are called by God to exercise "dominion," in the sense of cultivating and conserving (see below). Another resource is the work of mankind, carrying out, albeit in degrees blindly and in a fashion spoiled by sin, the cultural task allotted to him in his beginnings. For it is not just untouched nature but also human work that reveals God's will. The third resource is the Law (Hebrew, Torah) of the Lord (Yahweh), which has the force of "direction" that reveals the true goals, aims, values, and meaning of life on earth. This means that developing a genuinely christian wisdom in the affairs of this world involves investigating three kinds of "raw material" for thinking: nature, culture, and Scripture.

Nature, the Universe

One source of wisdom comes from investigating and seeking to understand God's created order of things, what we call "nature." To be wise in our "dominion" over the fish of the sea and the fowl of the air, we must learn how they exist. If we think that sharks only like Arctic waters, there are parts of the world where our effectiveness in the sea may be uncomfortably brief! Understanding God's created order, however, entails discovering and working with laws related not just to obvious contexts like fish and fowl or farming and forestry. For instance, to develop the sort of wisdom required for building airplanes, we need to know how objects behave when they pass through air. No amount of Bible knowledge will substitute for that! If we don't know the way in which radioactive materials act on the human body, our control of nuclear power will break down disastrously. And so on.

In other words, there are God-ordained principles or laws that can be known only by investigating God's created order. Francis Bacon (1561–1626) almost single-handedly turned people's thoughts to this through developing and promoting his method of "induction," which gave Europeans a systematically new way (different from Aristotelianism and Scholasticism) of discovering how people could learn from nature. Bacon also said that we ought to use the laws of nature in a "holy" manner as we develop our sciences. By this, he meant that the created world must be approached with christian reverence and humility and that the works produced using the laws of nature ought to be motivated by christian charity. Knowledge gained, Bacon said, ought to be used to serve others by alleviating human suffering and increasing human well-being. His method, which is second nature to us today, involves examining multitudes of particular experiences with nature and developing general laws of nature from that. In this way we are studying and understanding what God has actually wrought in the creation. This is of course a big discussion, and Bacon had a lovely way of putting it: "Nature can only be commanded by being obeyed." Now, in the act of doing that, we inevitably use the next resource for wisdom.

Human Work, Cultural Activity

Knowing God's creation is not something any of us does in isolation from the activities of our race, past and present. "Plants for man to cultivate." "Man goes out to his work." "Labor until evening." "Ships go to and fro." These references from Psalm 104 (others like them are found elsewhere in Scripture) show that we hardly ever meet with God's creation except as it is affected by the activity of human beings. We don't even study the stars without locating them using patterns that were historically created by human understanding.

Wisdom, then, involves us in the study of creation as people have already been ordering it. This means, for example, knowing about how the fruits of the earth have been cultivated, fought over, hoarded, adorned, used, bought, sold, and legislated about, as well as how they have been fashioned into things of beauty, signs of power, and symbols of faith. These are what we could call cultural activities, and our study would involve learning how these various activities go on, such as learning the principles on which they produce certain effects and fail to produce others. There are laws, for instance, in the rational and the aesthetic aspects governing the way our use of language works, laws not just for grammar but also for the more subtle way language works. For example, use a word or phrase too often and too indiscriminately, in whatever the language, and it always loses the precision and influence of its meaning and passes into jargon or becomes a cliché. That is a law of language. If a commodity is greatly needed but hard to get, it becomes expensive to buy. That is a law of economics. If a person does not know how to arrange melodic sounds on the neck of a guitar, no amount of strumming will pack the concert hall. One must know where the notes are and how to play them. That is a law of music. A statement cannot be true and false about the same subject at the same time. That is a law of logic (more precisely, of analytical thought). True wisdom, therefore, involves us in discovering God's laws for such things and using them for God's glory. Now these laws are discovered and developed in human culture. Which brings us to the third resource.

Scripture, the Mind of God

Just as the activity of studying creation for wisdom involves us in understanding the way people have been ordering it, the study of Scripture relates both to nature and culture as our standard for discovering the mind of God concerning *the direction* by which both nature and culture are to be ordered. We want to spend some time with this now, and perhaps the best place to start is at the beginning of the process of mastery to which God appointed us. It is first described in Genesis 1:28 and 2:15.

We are called to a special kind of mastery. These two passages are about what is frequently called "taking dominion." Yet even "the devil," said Jonathan Edwards, "has souls under dominion." Genesis certainly is not talking about that kind of mastery—although from the way people have exploited the earth since time immemorial, you might never know it. Both Christians and non-Christians have grossly distorted this biblical idea of mastery, as if there existed for human beings an independent and absolute right of possession and lordship to exploit the earth. Let us think for a moment about how the Book sees it.

Adam is on the scene, and Genesis 1:28 and 2:15 explain that he is to "subdue" the earth and to "work" and to "take care of" the Garden of Eden. Now this is to be done by the use of force, as the Hebrew words here suggest. But it is to be a controlled force, which, incidentally, is especially important in regards to government. It is force, for instance, in the sense that force must be used to cut down trees and to shape the wood, and it is controlled in the sense that there is some end in mind, a product that could result from any number of choices. This means that "subduing" is about taking the raw materials and making them conform to what is going on in the mind. This is quite unlike animals using their instincts. A human being has some design, some product, some goal, some end in mind, and uses a controlled force to bring about that intention. So "subduing" is not about merely hewing with the ax. It is about controlling the ax (or the saw, or the wood chisel) to conform to certain ideas within one's thinking. It is hewing, sawing, and chiseling with a purpose. So at this point we could ask: is the subduing taking place according to righteousness or unrighteousness? Is it being done to the glory of God or to the glory of another god?

Further, Adam does not form or subdue alone. There is a community (two). Eve's assistance and suggestions—she is a kind of alter ego to Adam—are in the picture. So subduing is not done alone. It extends to the community and group. This means that the ideas of the community influence the type of subduing done. For instance, in the U.S., tables look different from tables, say, in Japan, which are just inches from the floor because you do not sit round them on chairs.

But there is more to it. The Genesis 2:15 passage adds the ideas of "cultivating" and "conserving" to the process. So you work the earth into a field, the seed into corn or fruit, the corn or fruit into bread or jam. A piece of gold is mined and "cultivated" to become a wedding ring. And so on. By this process, people are bringing "out of" the raw materials not only practical things but also sets of values. (Recall from the previous chapter that things in the lower aspects can get new meanings as they are "taken up" into the higher aspects.) Unless human beings develop such meaning and value, it remains latent in the raw materials. The creation, then, becomes valuable as people "subdue" it. And it becomes valuable not only economically but also aesthetically, socially, morally, and so on. So someone sees the potential in the raw materials, like the tarry stuff in the North Sea, and digs it out and processes it into oil. But because the Hebrew word has the basic meaning "to serve," this is not about exploitation. (Interestingly, the same word "serve" is used in the Decalogue: six days shall you serve.)

So after it is cultivated (worked), it's got to be "conserved" (looked after), which brings us to the other half of the Genesis 2:15 passage. The community is "to care for it"; that is, to guard it. This brings us back to the question of whom we are serving in everyday life. If it is God that ordains our rest, then it is God whom we serve the previous six days. So the community, set in the earth to fashion and maintain it, must keep before itself continually the question, "Are we working according to sin or righteousness? Are we serving for man's glory or God's?" All of our efforts and work, therefore, must be done with reference to obedience to God. Our will must be subject to our Creator's across the spectrum of life, in all of its aspects.

This gives a special meaning to the word "knowing," in a phrase like "knowing God's creation." For it is a "knowing" that carries with it personal responsibility (we will explore this in chapter 18). In other words, "knowing God's creation" is not just about having information and facts about creation;

it means that you just can't do with it anything you want. Ever.

We use words and names to control how we manage our world.

We get another clue to this process of mastery in Genesis 2:19–20, where God delegates authority to Adam to *name* the animals. "Naming" is a means of control and communication. In Genesis 2, it is the means whereby Adam makes explicit the nature of animals as something distinct from human nature. We therefore order the Creation by naming it. And this is still at the beginning of the process of mastery to which God appointed us. (Chapter 23, part 4, carries this discussion further.)

From this we see that we actually exercise our control over the world around us by the process of naming, and naming is a product of our ability to reason. We recognize, for instance, that certain animals have characteristics in common; black patchy markings, for instance, with a very long neck and funny ears. We put these characteristics into a particular "class" of animal, to which we give a name "giraffe." This activity of naming involves a quite complicated process of analysis (seeing a whole as capable of being described in terms of many parts), of abstraction (treating the distinct parts as separate entities), and of classification (grouping things together by the parts that they have in common). Think again of modal theory and analysis. In this way, we can refer to "giraffe" in our memory and imagination without having to see one. We can also recreate "giraffe" in someone else's imagination by using that name, that word. And, if we wanted to, we could find names that would group it with other creatures, names like horses, camels, or ostriches.

This process of mentally separating, or distinguishing, is so fundamental to proper thinking and reasoning that the normal word in biblical Hebrew for "to understand" in its widest sense is from the same root—*bîyn*—as the word for "between" (*Strong's Concordance*, #s 995–998). "To understand," then, essentially involves the activity of dividing or distinguishing *between* the parts of creation and the parts of the things that identify them.

Asking basic questions of things is another primary task.

"Naming," then, is a special use of words, a process of separating or distinguishing, so that in collaboration with others we can develop our control of the world around us. This use of words and names is vital (chapters 18–19). Virtually everything we do as human beings depends on it. If it goes wrong, then our work in the world goes wrong, as the Tower of Babel vividly illustrates in the extreme. Wisdom in this world, therefore, means being able to distinguish things and name them properly. It is not enough just to know how things behave in creation. We must be able to refer to them and to their characteristics in a way that people may know precisely what we are talking about.

Also, we must understand our human language in a way so that we know what other people are talking about. Many of the bitterest conflicts among human beings have arisen because of misunderstood language. The Church itself has never been a stranger to such conflict. In the early Church, for example, bitter disputes arose over the statement that Christ was "one substance with the Father." Friendships were broken over the word "substance," for it meant different things in different parts of the Church. For some Christians, "substance" meant what essentially distinguishes one thing from another. To them, the statement meant that Jesus Christ wasn't really a distinct Person, that God was not a Trinity. To others, "substance" meant the basic qualifications that Jesus and the Father and the Spirit had in common; that is, Deity. To them, the other folk had to be saying there were really two or three Gods.

One of our first tasks then, in a godly effort to understand our world, must be to ask basic questions like: "What is this (thing, activity, institution) called? What is meant by the word ____?" So we would be asking questions like: "What is education? What is psychology? What is government? What is science"? This would raise other questions, to be considered later.

Asking basic questions of things—even, perhaps especially, things we take for granted—is vital. It helps us arrive at clearer understandings of what things are, even common areas such as family, education, and work. Without this, we may start a discussion surrounding, for instance, what ought to be done about education by taking it for granted that everyone understands what education is. But that may be far from the case. Wisdom, then, involves us in knowing about God's creation and understanding clearly the meaning of our language when we talk about it.

The family: an illustration of language and meaning problems.

Knowing God's creation and understanding what we mean by our words about it is not a simple task, especially when we are going to check what we are doing by Scripture wherever we can. Let's look at an example close to home, the common word "family." Most people would agree that they have a pretty fair idea of what they mean by that word. But they would not be on the same page. In fact, it has become difficult nowadays to talk about the family with clarity and consensus because different groups have different view about what constitutes a family. So even with this most basic institution comes terrible misunderstandings, though we are all using the same word.

For most Christian readers here, the family probably means mother, father, and their children, often, and somewhat endearingly, termed "the nuclear family." There may be foster children, or an elderly relative may be, as we say, "living with us," but generally in our minds they are "extras," not really what we mean by "the family." There are many parts of the world, however, where there is no word in the language that refers exactly to such a group as "mother, father, and their children." In many cultures, the word that would be used in a way nearest to the way we use "family" would be a group of people living under one roof and including three or even four generations. It might include uncles, cousins, and others related by marriage. It might include persons connected by some other kind of institution for which we have no parallel, such as slavery. In such contexts, even our phrase "extended family" would not be an adequate equivalent. In other places, the children may not normally be brought up by the parents at all; in some African communities it is the customary responsibility of grandparents. Before dismissing such a custom as primitive and unsatisfactory, remember how Samuel was brought up!

Other difficulties also arise. The phrase "one parent family" is commonplace now, although to many people it still refers to a rather abnormal family, in which, for whatever reasons, something seems to be missing. Should anyone say so in public, however, many voices in our society declare accusingly that this implies discrimination against people who have lost their partner through no fault of their own. They insist that we must regard the one parent family as an alternative family equally valid with two parent families.

The discussion does not end there, though. Homosexuality is an increasingly open feature in our society and, with processes like artificial insemination and embryo transplant, a lesbian may have a child. So voices are arguing that the notion of the family must include groupings with two women, or two men, and children. Other voices argue that the concept of the family must be redefined as a social or a legal, rather than a biological, unit. For such people, the basis of analysis and classification is different from the one that evangelical Christians would use. But when faced with the challenge, "Why?", we might find it difficult to give a reasoned and coherent explanation of our attitude, say, if we were discussing issues in family planning. When we can't find clear reasons for our attitudes, non-Christians are quick to accuse us of dogmatic irrationalism, or to say that we have no right to impose our particular convictions on others. There are, they say, so many other viable conceptions of "the family," the members of which can be equally responsible and faithful to the claims of that kind of group relationship. We also hear the argument that cultures change with history, so why should one particular form of family be sacrosanct? Obviously, we soon lose control of our subject if we don't actually know what we are talking about.

Back to Scripture to determine word meanings. So a typical christian response might prove disastrous. After all, we have an instinctively negative response to the mention of change and variation, especially in so fundamental an area. So we say that we have a standard, and that standard is Scripture. And we know that we must go to Scripture for our meanings. And in this case, it is not uncommon to hear our speakers refer to the "biblical ideal of the family." But beyond this, we may have quite some trouble saying just what Scripture means by that.

Nevertheless, the Bible must determine the meanings of the words we study in it. Perhaps the biggest problem with the issue under the microscope here is that Scripture does not refer to family life in terms of the nuclear family, as we so casually assume. Even where that kind of arrangement could be said to be the subject under consideration, Scripture hardly ever imagines family life as being as isolated as it is in our experience. The "ideal of family life" in Scripture (insofar as it speaks of ideals at all) is one in which the so-called nuclear family is firmly set within the extended family, and set within the context of covenantal commitments such as the "kinsman-redeemer," which were taken seriously. You might want to take a deep breath, here. For the concept of family life that we today defend as Christian doesn't turn out to be all that biblical.

Notions of "family" are partly from creation and partly from culture. Because this discovery can come as something of a shock, it is worth pausing to ask ourselves how such a curious situation has arisen. Why have we assumed a notion of "family" as being biblically christian when it is at variance with the facts of Scripture?

Notions of what the word "family" means are a compound of two elements. One is from the creation as God has ordered it: that children are the product of two parents and that those children are taught to act out a role in the society within which they were born. The other is the particular way in which any given society believes what life is and how it should be organized; that is, its wisdom: its way of seeing life and living in it; its system of values; its notions of right and wrong, good and bad, true and false, real and unreal; what it thinks is ultimate and more important than even life itself, and what is only accidental and dependent for its meaning on something else.

In the wisdom of many cultures, the biological relationship is of overriding importance. In such societies, "family" will be a word for a biological unit. In our Western world, however, biological life is increasingly regarded as a matter for human manipulation. In such a society, "family" is a word to be understood in terms of social agreements and technological control. That these two areas are in a state of rapid change is largely responsible for the strident disputations that are going on surrounding the family. Further, stress today on the sacredness of the individual and, predominately in the U.S., "rugged individualism" has created a highly developed concern for personal privacy. This has shed its light over the family as an institution in which two individuals choose each other and produce other individuals. The present conventional view among Christians is powerfully indebted in some degree to all of these influences.

Earlier we mentioned that culture is a resource for wisdom and that some of that wisdom may be found to be in the service of God. But not all cultural ideas are good ones. Wherever a culture's ideas diverge from Scripture, we must be willing to change.

Understanding a word as its meaning is formed by the culture of Scripture.

Let's tackle just one of the above points. In the cultural tradition of Scripture, the individual, though certainly seen as the fundamental unit of decision making, is not the only unit of responsibility. Take the issue of sin. It is true that, as Ezekiel declared, every person must die for his own sin. Yet for Ezekiel, like the rest of the Scripture writers, sin and responsibility for sin were not simply matters of private wrongdoing and guilt. They were included in the disobedience and guilt of the sinning community. This becomes clear in the great intercessory prayers of Ezra 9, Nehemiah 9, and Daniel 9. The more godly that people are, the more they are aware that they cannot isolate their individual responsibility from that of the people to which they belong. So the community—it may be as small as a family—is another unit of responsibility for decision-making. In such a cultural wisdom, as in "ancient" Israel, it would have been next to impossible for Old Testament saints to imagine one of our current customs as normal, in which two people marry with only a token reference to the wishes and needs of the parents and the extended family as a whole, and in which the resultant new family has only tenuous links with the relatives, apart from the demands of legislation.

So it is not enough merely to study what is happening in our cultures to find out what is meant by "family life." The same is true of anything else, like politics, or economics, or work, or art. And the reverse is equally true. No amount of Bible study alone will do instead. Nor is it enough simply to study how human beings understand the meanings of the words they are using, though without that study no faithful communication will be possible. With the results of all our investigations into the world around us, we need to go to the Bible consistently to see how these things are understood there, and change wherever we must.

We must read Scripture on its own terms and "give in" to its thinking.

And we need to go to Scripture in a particular way. A countless number of those of us who are christian ministers have confidently referred to the "biblical notion of the family" as exclusively nuclear, and we have offered countless Bible studies on the basis of it, well-supported by a wide range of biblical texts. We have also been engaged in counseling and pastoral support, grappling with the explosive stresses that mount up, even in the best of small communities, where the intimate relationships develop and boil to the bursting point. Yet in all of this teaching and counseling, we have been largely unaware of the unbiblical conditions that have produced the problems we are trying to address. Unbiblical conditions even in our churches. We just have not noticed this, for the very reason that we have been working with a mindset too effectively conditioned by the culture around us. (It can be powerfully argued that much of the disruptive stress in marriages today is due to the explosive confinements of the nuclear grouping.) Frankly, that notion of "family" which was so normal to people of biblical times would not fit anywhere into our way of thinking about it, for we have seen one part of the story (the man-woman-child grouping as the normal minimum for what constitutes a family) without seeing the rest: the biblical "nuclear family" only functioned properly in close covenantal relationship with other "nuclear families." A society like that, of course, would be a quite different community from what we are used to. For one thing, we would probably regard it as primitive. Be that as it may. It is certainly more typical of Scripture. Our society, with its high divorce rate and large number of households comprising an unmarried person living alone, is surely outrageously primitive in a far more serious sense.

So we need to see as clearly as we can how far our minds are being wrongly molded by the world around us, not on the surface level of opinion, fashion, and behavior, but in the meanings we uncritically assume for the words we use, even when we are reading the text of Scripture. Wherever necessary, our thinking must give in to Scripture and be transformed by it.

~15~

The Relation of Present-day Names to Biblical Names

As noted earlier, the world today has developed some complicated notions that become expressed in highly compressed and often technical language that does not seem to have much contact with the text of Scripture as it stands at all. "The state" for instance, is not an obviously biblical term, and you won't find "industry" or "economics" in a Bible concordance. Even in church life, what is the biblical status of a "denomination"?

This language gap is not because the world has become so different that we just don't share the same humanity with the people of Scripture any more, or that the Bible is now irrelevant. Western culture is certainly more complex, but we are not the only pebbles on the beach. There are other cultures, too, some quite sophisticated, and they would also use language not found in Scripture. Does this mean that the Book is not for them? Of course not. It is for them, too, in spite of the language gaps.

All cultures have developed out of the same "basic ingredients." In fact, cultures do not develop unless their peoples learn mastery over the basic ingredients. As noted in chapter 7, the most advanced mathematician began by learning the simplest calculations, and the international concert pianist began with five-finger exercises. If the most elementary principles are not mastered, then a severe limit is set on how far one can cope with new demands. Further, when we are confronted with something new and unfamiliar, it is a sound instinct to see it in terms of its basic ingredients. Most adults read words and even phrases in whole units, but if they have to read out some unfamiliar word, they will revert to the childhood method of dealing with it syllable by syllable.

The Bible deals with the basic elements of human culture, the ABCs, its fundamentals. The Bible uses the same principle. It introduces us to God's dealings with people in respect of the basic elements of human culture, under conditions in which they can be perceived most clearly; that is, in the simpler forms of human society. Scripture deals with the issues of life, then, in its primary units. It shows us the beginnings of the historical process that leads on to the present day. In the previous chapter we saw that asking basic questions of a thing is vital to our task. Discovering a thing's basic ingredients is a way to gather answers to such questions. We'll explore some possibilities of this process here (chapter 23 also).

In the development of human history, the basic features of human life are seen most clearly in elementary types of society, and then they become combined and complicated in a way that makes the result as different as a cake is from the ingredients that make it up. If you don't like your cake, or if you want to improve it, you go back to the cookbook recipe, where the basic ingredients and original instructions are set out. No cook, however, would expect the book to describe in detail every possible variation and refinement of the recipe that there might ever be. Rather, enough information is given about "the raw materials" and "the process of cultivation" to be able to vary the recipe or to make intelligent experiments without losing the basic features.

In Scripture we are presented with the basic ingredients of cultural life in the history of Israel and her neighbors, and we are shown the way that some historical processes and responses led to certain results. It is for us to identify *faithfully* those basic ingredients, processes, and responses *and* the resultant product in our own culture. Sometimes cooking requires a thorough mixing of the ingredients (as in baking a cake). At other times, as in a meringue, it requires division of the ingredients ("Separate the yolk from the white..."). We can expect to see both processes in Scripture history and in the rest of human history, including our own.

An example of analysis: the "business corporation" and "the state."

The Bible, therefore, deals with the things implied in today's complex language. This means that we need not fret when we cannot find today's technical words in Scripture, for we will most likely find the basic ingredients. Let us consider the "business corporation" as an illustration. In order to really understand what we are talking about, we must begin by asking ourselves what this word actually means. "What is this thing? What is 'business corporation'?" To do this properly will involve asking other basic questions like, "What is its purpose? What is its basis? What special characteristics distinguish it from other human activities or institutions?" We will also need "to understand" it (*bîyn*, previous chapter) by breaking it up into its component parts, what we normally mean by "analysis." Some of its elements will be fairly obvious. "Work" is certainly one, and another would be "working with others." So it is, in part, about "relationships with other people within a social unit." It also involves the use of capital, that is, wealth that you're not relying on for your survival, so we also see the economic aspect. Now we would find quite a bit about these sorts of things in Scripture.

Therefore, although the Bible does not use the term, or even the concept of "business corporation" in our contemporary sense, it does carry instruction about its basic ingredients. It also gives us insight on the way the ingredients became combined in Israel's life; not much, mind you, but enough to give us highly suggestive, authoritative clues. These clues come into focus after we have answered questions about the ingredients themselves, such as: what does the Bible mean by "work"? How does it describe the way people relate to each other? How does it talk about wealth, especially "spare" wealth?

"The state" is another common example. If ever there was an influential institution today, the state is one. It is difficult to detect anything in Scripture that quite corresponds with it. But if we ask our fundamental questions, such as what it is and what goes to make it up, then things get a bit easier. So, for instance, one important element in the state is "governmental authority," which has a prominent place in Scripture. The state is also about "nationhood," which is a quite significant dimension to human life in the Bible. Of course, more is involved, for the state is not just a nation's body of government. It is about independent nationhood, and it carries the notion of being represented in the nation and in the world by a distinct body of people who act as its functionaries, some of whom are its appointed symbols, such as in England the Queen. In other words, some notion of "bureaucracy" is entailed, which is another element found in Scripture. For instance, the growth of bureaucracy under Solomon, and the way it functioned to quite a high pitch of sophistication in the Persia of Daniel's experience, are fascinating matters for study.

The foregoing illustrations of the business corporation and the state are introduced merely to start us thinking about the possibilities available to us from the ABCs of the Book. In no way must it be thought that that is all we need to know about what a business corporation or the state is. For that, thorough study must be made.

A basic rule: your analysis must discover counterparts in Scripture.

There is a great deal to be said and written about the nature and function of the business corporation and the modern state, and this is not the place for that. The Bible, however, does not release the christian community, especially through those gifted for the task, from the grind of studying and thinking about such matters. And in this exercise, it seems that one basic conviction must grip the Christian; namely, that any characterization or analysis of a subject must reduce it to categories or phenomena that have counterparts in Scripture. If it cannot or does not do that, then it is either wrong or inadequate, and will not be relevant.

For instance, if we are talking about cars on our roads, it is not wrong to say that they are machines of propulsion for transport. Transport is certainly seen in Scripture, but "machines" as a characterization for the exercise we are suggesting is inadequate. Instead, we will need to ask one of the basic questions, such as, "What are we really dealing with here?" Part of the answer will be in the notion of self-propulsion, which in Scripture finds representation in the horse or ox. Another element concerns a constructed device like a cart or chariot. Another would be about the responsibilities of the people involved. And so on. If in the course of this subject we are going to discuss traffic control, we will have to consider not just the way traffic lights work but how social and legislative authorities may act (societal and juridical aspects), for example, when making rules for passing a motorist who is stranded next to a car that has a flat tire or has been in an accident.

Another way is to discover the **hows** *and* **whys** *of the biblical writers.*

So far, the chief way in which we have been considering Scripture as a resource for understanding the world under God has been to go to it for direct information and instruction. This is the way that traditionally we have been accustomed to learn what it teaches about God, people, and christian doctrine. Only incidentally do we ask *how* it says it or *why* it says it that particular way. This, however, becomes important for developing the type of reasoning being offered by this book, for it helps us to get insight into the wisdom of the biblical writers, to tease out the hidden assumptions of Scripture.

In chapter 5 we considered an imaginary conversation between an American photographer and a Japanese father. What each person said was clear enough to the one speaking, yet the two utterances were completely in conflict. In order to understand what was going wrong, it was not enough simply to understand what each person said; we had to know why both persons said what they did—their hidden assumptions and logic. In that instance, fortunately, we had access to outside information, without which we would have had to tease it out as best we could from the dialogue itself.

In the case of Scripture, of course, we have far more than several meager lines of dialogue, and it is an important means of getting clues to the way the biblical writers thought about life. Although the Spirit of God spoke through them with greater meaning than they could ever imagine, especially in the Old Testament, what they wrote was hardly, if ever, meaningless to them as they wrote it. Even in giving laws, the Lord was concerned to give reasons, so that the laws made sense to the people (chapter 3). Now a thing only makes sense, has a meaning, in terms of one's own particular wisdom. So the wisdom of the Cross, for instance, was an outrage both to Jews and Greeks, who were working with different kinds of wisdom.

If we can understand *how* something that makes little sense to us could made a great deal of sense to a biblical writer, and if we can understand *why* it was said as it was, then we stand a good chance of getting insight into where that person's wisdom differs from ours. This will not always be the case, because sometimes other factors make for obscurity. Occasionally it most certainly will be the case, and important discoveries are possible. (Examples in following chapters.) The method whereby this is done is akin to the way in which the message of the cereal box was teased out (chapter 6). It is an exercise in examining what is being implied, suggested, and indicated by the rather intangible thing we call style. The ability to do this is stronger in some people than it is in others, but it improves with practice in all of us, and most of us can at least recognize when it is being done faithfully.

"Seeking wisdom" as the church's task, and ours in it. Clearly this task of investigating, naming, understanding, and analyzing the inner logic of Scripture—studying its hows and whys, teasing out its hidden assumptions—can be a tricky exercise, and to the activists among us, some of it will appear to be fussy nitpicking. No doubt that will occasionally be justified! Nevertheless, if we hope to witness christianly to this age in the Name of the Lord and in the interests of a more obedient culture, it is essential that as a christian community we do good work in this area. A doctor will tell you that half her task is about good diagnosis, and half of that is about good observation and analysis. Careless work or arrogantly superficial efforts are going to be disastrous on the part of people who think that they are automatically experts because they know the Bible text or have a degree in sociology.

It would be easy to give up at this point. We may not be experts, and we may not have the time or the talents to embark on such taxing programs of study. We may not be used to such demands being required of our intellectual life, and maybe our background has taught us to believe that our answers must always be simple, so that "he who runs may read" the message. Certainly there is a simplicity in the Gospel. To meet Jesus and trust him is the most natural thing in the world for a child. But living faithfully as an adult in a complex world is not simple. We are not expected to think like geniuses (unless we are one), but each of us is expected to think as hard as we can and to make what contributions we can to the ministry of the whole body of Christ in its witness, teaching, preaching, healing, and persuading. We must all do our part in this, as service to God in the world according to our particular gifts and callings. And we may need to be prepared to double up for others who have stopped functioning.

We need both our experts and our intelligent amateurs.

For the task we are dealing with here—developing an authentic biblical wisdom among the People of God in this generation—we need in particular two kinds of Christians in our churches. One kind will be what rather hesitantly we might call the experts, those called to work in a particular area of life. It may be what they do for a livelihood, and often it is. But in this rather odd fallen world it may be a spare time activity. These people develop expertise by a certain degree of concentration and specialization. They are likely to be experts in only one field, and so in other respects they will be no better off than the rest of us. They tend either to become leaders and spokespersons in particular aspects of life or to provide resources for leaders and spokespersons.

Besides the experts, we need the intelligent amateurs. These people are ordinary, average Christians who pursue their own callings but who also seek to understand the world around them as far as God grants them resources, abilities, and opportunities. They won't be experts, but then they won't speak like that, either. Most of the time they won't be on platforms or in pulpits or writing authoritative books. This does not mean that they will be silently submissive or inert. They will do all sorts of study as their interests lead them, and they will be able to talk clearly, to listen intelligently, to make worthwhile contributions in discussions, and to have opinions worth accepting or disputing. Any of which may lead to discoveries. When they see a call to action, they soberly commit themselves to it. *Above all, they know how to ask good questions.* Such people are indispensable for creating a climate in which wise leadership can flourish. They may volunteer for community projects, or join education committees, or become precinct delegates, or even deacons and elders.

The experts need the intelligent amateurs.

This above all the expert needs. The worst possible thing is for the experts to go unchallenged. We suffer at present far too much from the tyranny of the expert. Not only does the expert tend to have an inadequately challenged authority in his own area of competence, but he also gets to be listened to with reverence in areas in which he is not competent. So rock stars are interviewed to pronounce on social ethics, physicists pontificate on the meaning of history, and politicians seem expert about everything! The only people who are expected not to address the world (though within the church the situation is different) outside their competence are religious leaders! (We wonder why?)

Further, constant work within one's own discipline easily leads the expert to become unaware of significant questions from outside that are vital for that work. Any teacher worth her salt knows, possibly more than she cares to admit, that her thinking and understanding has developed best in response to intelligent questioning, especially the sort that rocks her on her heels and makes her rethink some position.

The non-expert, particularly the intelligent amateur, has a special power of discrimination. This is invaluable. Paul prays for those engagingly loving Christians at Philippi that their love would abound in thorough knowledge and insight, so as to discriminate the best from the rest (Philippians 1:9–10). Experts, curiously enough, are not the best endowed with this ability—maybe they are too busy studying the trees to appreciate the forest and the surrounding countryside. None of us can fulfil our callings as well as we might without a supporting community, and the experts are no exception. Other things being equal, a community like the church is going to have teachers and leaders whose quality is chiefly determined by the acumen of its general membership. If the members are suckers, they will be led by fools or rogues and hardly suspect it.

To sum up the thoughts of this and the previous chapter so far, we can say that to learn biblical wisdom we must investigate the natural world (nature), the world (culture) of mankind, and the text of Scripture. We shall be studying creation, though, in a special way: letting the way Scripture speaks determine the kind of language we use to describe creation. We shall also allow it to indicate the way we are to go about analyzing it for the purposes of effective understanding. We shall seek to get behind the surface statements of Scripture to understand its particular kind of wisdom, which we can then use to apply its truth to our present age. And none of us will do this in isolation. We must contribute as best we can to this task in the Church, each according to his gifts and calling.

Answering some current objections. All this is placing considerable weight upon Scripture. Yet the results from the more simplistic efforts to apply the Bible to the complexities of Western life have often been discouraging, if not disastrous. Non-Christians have picked up this discouragement from Christians and have written off Scripture as a book for reference for anything except information about the origins of Christianity and Judaism. After all, they say, the texts are ancient and Israel was only a small tin-pot nation living in a tiny area of the globe and lacking the tremendous resources and sophistication of the great empires. As a source of insight and information, not promising. Others might say that the only reason anyone bothers with the Bible is because so many people have regarded it with religious, even superstitious, reverence.

Our initial response to such opinions must be twofold. First, we ought to emphasis that the fact that the Bible is ancient is not to the point. Here on my desk I[JP] have a recently published book on warfare. The cover comment speaks of it as "a book to be read not only by every commander and officer, but by every one of us who is interested in peace." I understand that in some military academies it has the status of a standard textbook, even though it was written some 2,500 years ago (*The Art of War*, Sun Tzu). In the same way, political theorists today find it illuminating to study Plato's *Laws* for an understanding of their own task. However, nobody expects simply to transfer in some mindlessly verbal way material from either of these ancient works into a contemporary situation. That is not the way the texts are used. Why, then, merely because it is found in a collection of religious literature, should the Law of Moses or the Bible's wisdom literature be excluded from the same use at least?

Our second response is this. What happened to Israel in Scripture is not important because Israel was an exceptional community or an ideal society. Far from it. Israel was an elect nation, certainly. But all that means is that she was chosen for a specific purpose. The way that Israel actually responded to God just cannot be regarded as an absolute model for the rest of the world to imitate, as some authoritative ideal. Even a cursory view of the texts would show that. In Deuteronomy 7:7, Moses is cited as saying that God did not choose them because they were outstanding in numbers or in power or even in righteousness. In other words, they were in themselves no different from the rest of the world.

Israel, then, is a sample of how God deals with ordinary human beings in their personal and social lives. Her law is not a law for people with beautiful ideals willing to obey God's every word. This is not More's *Utopia*. The law given was for sinners, for ordinary, spiritually and morally disabled, people. It is a *sample* of how God's law functions in mercy, judgment, and deliverance as demonstrated in the cultural history of one nation picked out for that express purpose, picked not because of its outstanding qualities but because it was so typically ordinary.

Other nations also had their ideals, their faith, their visions, and their miracles, and they too failed and fell. Israel was put under the spotlight for others to see what elsewhere was ambiguously hidden in gloom. For example, Amos states that the Lord removed the Philistines from Crete just as much as he did the Israelites from Egypt. But the Philistines would not have seen it as "the Lord" any more than many Americans or English would be able to see the Lord at work and sovereign in their lands. Thus the Philistines could not see God's purpose in their being removed, or the value of it. They could not know if it showed God's grace or His judgment, for there were no prophets or a Moses to give a clear vision. Further, Amos proclaims startling divine judgments not only on Judah and Israel but also against Israel's neighbors. What was hidden in the gloom, therefore, is that God is Lord of *all* nations. But how God works is only clearly seen in the case of Israel. This, then, is how Christians have to read it, not as a blueprint or scale model but as a sample of God's ways in politics, economics, culture, art, and thought.

Scripture and life must be read with the new mind. But it devolves on Christians also to read it, and indeed to read everything in life, in a very special way. Paul, in Romans 12:1, winds up his exposition of the Gospel by exhorting us to a total dedication to Christ. This is to be followed by an ongoing transformation: do not be conformed to the fashion of the age you live in; undergo a structural change (12:2). The language here implies that what is needed is a nonconformity that is not merely a change in outward forms but also the adoption of a new way of thinking and reasoning about life; that is, change regarding fundamental motivations. For instance, nonconformity is not just about not wearing risqué clothing or not keeping up with the Joneses. You can do such things and still think like the world. After all, many non-Christians do not wear risque clothing or keep up with the Joneses. Rather, it means a *new way of thinking and reasoning* about how we should look and what our homes should be like, and so on.

"The world," in Paul's sense here, designates that which is sin-infected around us. "Wherever human sinfulness bends or twists or distorts God's good creation, there we find the 'world'," writes Albert Wolters in *Creation Regained. That* world, which includes the way people think and reason, is the one under consideration. Thus Paul, like Jesus before him, calls Christians not to something as superficial as mere outer forms and behaviors, for our problem lies deeper than that. He is therefore calling for a structural change, and it comes by the renewal of the mind.

He uses a word for renewal that is radical. The Greeks had two words for "new." One meant "new" in the sense of "fresh," "recent." If used today, it would apply, for instance, when the points in your car's ignition system were worn out and you bought a new set of points, a new version of the same thing. The word used in Romans 12:2, however, means radically new, because different. It could be used if you scrapped your car's gasoline engine and fuel system and replaced it with a diesel one. You would have the same car, but quite different. So the apostle is not just talking about a new set of ideas; he is talking about a new way of thinking and reasoning altogether.

The word for "mind" is interesting too. It is the most comprehensive word available. Vine's *Expository Dictionary of Old and New Testament Words* states that the word (Greek, *nous*) means: "The seat of reflective consciousness, comprising the faculties of perception and understanding, and those of feeling, judging, and determining." Combine this with Paul's meaning of renewal and he is speaking of a radically different way of being aware of the world, a radically new way of perceiving it, of using one's critical faculties, of feeling sad or glad, excited or depressed, confident or fearful, or pleased or angry— about everything that goes on around us and in us. An analogy might come from one particular way to get a new woollen sweater. We could go to a store and buy one of the same type and pattern as the one we were discarding. But if we were making the sort of change Paul is talking about, we would need to find someone who could take the old sweater and wash it, unpick the wool, dispose of the worn-out threads, and then knit the wool up into a different kind of garment in a different style, fit, and pattern. That would be not just a fresh sweater but one "transformed by the renewing of the sweater."

Our mental patterns must change under the influence of Scripture. In one sense we go on perceiving the world just as everybody else does; but when our mental patterns begin to change under the influence of Scripture, then the way we perceive things changes. Family life, for instance, would be seen in a new light and in a new context, and it would therefore become related to the rest of our experience in a new way. It would be a renewed way of understanding it, defining it, assessing it, and living it. And the process will go on and on, through our transformed perceptions of community solidarity, human responsibility, scientific investigation, educational theory, law making, business life, friendship, work, art, and more.

So if we are to let the process of scriptural wisdom develop in us, we must let God use Scripture to change the very framework of thought and way of reasoning through which we look at the world and act in it; that is, our wisdom. We must allow it to challenge, by contrast with, the ideas, things, and arguments we normally take for granted. We must give up the pointless struggle to make sense of the words of Scripture in terms of our own thinking. We must stop making up quick equations between the words and situations of Scripture and our contemporary situations, reinterpreting the peculiarities of Scripture to conform to our methods of reasoning, methods that we have unreflectingly drawn from the world in which we grew up (the wisdom we absorbed from childhood; chapter 6). We must surrender our own assumptions—the ideas we have always taken for granted as "normal" because we were reared in them—and accept the ideas and the ways of reasoning about life that the Bible takes for granted as "normal."

Curiously, but comfortingly, when we start to do this, we begin to feel a new kind of exciting security, as we sense the power of a logic that seems now and then to touch the rough bottom of reality in the stream of life, a logic that we felt must have been there all the time.

~16~

Using Theology and Doctrine to Learn Wisdom, Part 1

From the fourth century on, the Church became split over whether the Spirit "proceeded" from the Father only or from the Father and the Son. In the Middle Ages, a famous controversy arose about how many angels could dance on the head of a pin. It is tempting to regard such "petty" matters with a condescension we habitually reserve for the past, at least till we hear of a modern controversy, such as whether Adam had a navel! Petty details can turn out to be the tips of very large icebergs of thought, with implications going quite deep indeed, revealing enormous differences of attitude and experience.

Angels and pins involve the very nature of reality. For instance, is the world of spirits part of the same order of reality as the physical world? If not, then how does the human spirit exist in relation to a body? Can we cultivate our spiritual life and ignore our bodies? If so, then how do spirits occupy space? What happens if evil spirits are exorcized? The Procession of the Spirit also turns out to be quite important, for it fosters different types of devotion; one being rather lacking in content, the other being concerned expressly with the character and work of Jesus Christ. And the question of Adam's navel can lead to different ways of responding to the Bible's message and language. For instance, was Adam made fully grown, or did his body evolve and become human by God's divine action?

It is certainly a pity that Christians have had to quarrel so bitterly. Yet when it comes to doctrine they seldom quarrel over trivialities. Seemingly small details can act as symptoms and symbols of quite distinctive styles of faith, devotion, and religious practice. We should not be surprised, then, if the great themes of the Gospel have immense implications, far more wide-ranging than we had bargained for.

Theology and doctrine reach beyond religious beliefs into secular issues.

In this chapter we want to see how theology and christian doctrine can be an immense help in speaking forcibly and sensibly in secular life. Many people, however, assume that theology and doctrine are only about one's religious beliefs. Thus a general feeling exists throughout Christendom that wrong theology and doctrine are only going to affect church life, or how one prays and does evangelism, or what conversion and sanctification are, or moral questions like the extent of our obligations in matters of honesty or chastity. We tend to be impatient at squabbles over "lesser details of doctrine," as we call them, because they don't seem to affect the main (religious) aspect of life. Although they surely ought to be matters over which we can agree to differ, history tells a different story.

The earliest Christians were mostly quite private individuals, and not a few were slaves with little significance in public affairs. Paul says that not many wise or influential people received the Gospel call (1 Corinthians 1:26). Yet within days, it seems, these ordinary Christians found themselves at the heart of a political conflict. No less an issue than political sovereignty forced them into the public eye with their christian faith, as the Book of Acts clearly shows.

Romans 13 is another case in point. It has a body of teaching about government that is often said to relate to a period in which the Roman government was said to be relatively benign, at least in contrast with the picture of brutality painted in the Book of Revelation. Yet it was the very teaching represented in Romans 13 that forced Rome to show herself in such a brutal light. Paul states there that rulers are "servants of God." From the point of view of the citizens, that gives rulers the right to rule. But from the point of view of the rulers, it makes them responsible to Another. In the case of the Christians, the assertion made their Roman rulers responsible to the God of the Christians! This was implied in the question over which countless Christians struggled and suffered and died: "Do you call Caesar 'Lord'"? By insisting that Jesus alone was Lord, they denied divine honors to the emperor. But more than that, they asserted thereby that Caesar's government was to be judged by, what to Rome was, an alien standard: the moral standard of the Church. This strong conviction carried the People of God through persecution right to the throne of the Empire, even after and beyond Constantine. Church leaders in the Dark Ages often risked their lives to assert the same message to the barbarians who set up their petty kingdoms when the Empire fell. We may criticize the medieval Church in the light of the Reformation, but we ought to recognize the greatness of its achievement.

That achievement was initially based on the conviction that Jesus Christ was Lord; that is, that he had divine authority over the highest human secular authorities in history. And, as some Christians are arguing today, the medievals actually lived out a wisdom that applied the Bible to everyday life much better than we today do.

Theology and christian doctrine influenced the rise of the democratic ideal.

All of this is to say that theology and doctrine affect politics and government. For instance, we in the Western world value our democratic institutions with their concept of limited sovereignty. Have you ever asked yourself why it is that these institutions arose in Protestant countries initially and why they seem to have such a precarious existence anywhere else? No single reason, of course, is going to provide a full explanation, but among the multiple explanations is a theological one. It surrounds the rise, largely after the Reformation period, of the doctrine of the "priesthood of all believers." This is not the only force that was at work upon modern democratic ideals, but the doctrine did initially have a profound effect on church government, which did influence democratic political theory quite strongly. If all believers are priests, then the authority of the minister becomes representative rather than mediatorial. That is, the minister is no longer authorized merely from above, for his function also depends on the will of the ordinary church members. This attitude produced forms of church government in which even the lowliest members of the congregation could take part in discussion and decision making. Over time, this gave people an expertise in self-government that made democratic institutions workable at a basic level. The influence of the non-episcopal churches has been most effective in this respect, perhaps because these churches were more inclined to follow doctrines to their logical conclusions.

The democratic ideal has also been secured by christian doctrine in another highly significant way. Saying "Jesus is Lord" meant not only that rulers could not be absolute but also that the common people could not have absolute authority. That is, the deliberations and the actions of the people were not about what they thought was right but what they believed the will of God to be as it was shown to them through His law in Scripture, as interpreted in and for their ages. This feature of the democratic ideal has almost receded out of sight in our Western nations, with the result that democracy is being increasingly replaced by demagogy. Here is a failure to remember that it was, after all, the common people who called for Christ to be crucified. Theirs may not have been the greatest blame, but that people in bulk can be deceived and manipulated is undeniable. In Britain, this understanding that no human beings, even those with the greatest support, can be trusted with unchallenged power, lies behind the notion of "Her Majesty's Opposition." In America, it is found in the balance of powers among the legislative, judicial, and executive branches.

The Doctrine of Creation has implications for evolution.

So doctrine does not stop at religious convictions. It influences many other areas of life, significantly at times. For example, the Doctrine of Creation has implications that make a thoroughgoing evolutionary philosophy impossible for the Christian. It does not exclude some kinds of evolution—though we might prefer to call it "development," even in biological theory—but it severely limits it. For instance, it is impossible for the Christian to see human beings as "the state of the art" in the evolutionary process out of animal origins. The Doctrine of Creation means that human beings always have a foot outside the present order of things that we know with our five senses. So we are rightly wary of purely naturalistic explanations of human nature and of projects like eugenics and genetic engineering applied to man.

Regarding evolution as *theory*, we could say to our secular counterparts something like, "We can accept it if you talk about evolution from the dust, if you must, but only as a theory and not as dogma or philosophy. What we will resist is that evolutionary theory explains the whole person. We resist this because people are made in the image of God. So if you are going to say, in place of the Bible's statement 'made in the image of God,' that we are made in the image of an ape . . . . That sort of argument, that sort of idolatry, we will not accept. For, though there is a dimension of the human being that is formed out of what was already there, there is also a dimension that is not formed out of what is already there. That is, the 'breath of God' put us in a different context from being merely evolutionary, merely appearing out of only previous matter from on-going physical laws. The breath of God gave us our transcendent dimension."

So theology and doctrine can infiltrate society.

Theological teachings produce particular mindsets within christian communities, mindsets that are a manifestation of particular kinds of wisdom. These mindsets, in varying strengths, infiltrate and influence the societies in which the Christians live. By that means, a subtle but powerful change takes place in the way things are done in the world. The process is relatively slow but astonishingly pervasive and effective (think again of the democratic ideal in the West). In fact, it is much more effective in the long haul than the overt efforts of churches and their leaders to alter the course of events by the direct use of power or authority in the name of their religious convictions. At the same time, *it only takes place where Christians have an interface with the world at large with a wisdom that is exposed to the world with enough challenge to arouse possible opposition.* Third century hermits in the Egyptian deserts, whatever their calling was, were not effective in this respect. And as our present age has recently witnessed, communist governments were little concerned with people's *private* individual beliefs and worship. Humanists, too, tend to be rather amused by naive attempts to judge politics, education, or science directly by the light of religious beliefs or moral ideals alone, if only because they so obviously smack of a long discredited ecclesiastical tyranny. But they have no defense against the logic of a wisdom whose secular ideas have their hidden roots in biblical truth. For truth in the long run is invincible, and even more so when it cannot be identified with a particular interest group. Christian doctrine, then, as long as it is formed by Scripture, is deeply significant for issues of everyday life.

The Doctrine of God as Father affirms and influences the family.

As another illustration of everyday theological influence, let's take the family. One way to approach this through the Book, as we have noted in earlier chapters, is to ask basic questions of things. So let's ask: what is family? Part of the answer, certainly, is "parents and children." Now there is quite a lot in Scripture about this, which we could pursue in developing our wisdom. But that would mean quite a broad range of pursuit to start with, so let's narrow it down a bit more by asking another basic question: what is a parent? Since we know that the Book speaks of God the Father, let's look at a few features of that here.

One of the peculiarities of John's Gospel is the way that he continually speaks of God as "the Father" and Jesus as "the Son." In the Bible's way of thinking, they are not just any father and any son, or even the best of all fathers and sons. John's language is rather like the way people used to refer to the First World War before World War 2. It was simply referred to as "the War." There had been, and were still going on, other wars, but the War was something different. It was called "the war to end wars." When we speak of "the" thing in this way, we mean that it is unique and that all other things bearing the same name have to be judged in relationship to it. Thus we are not to think of God as being like earthly fathers, even the greatest and the best.

Likewise we are not to think of Jesus as simply the most perfect son there ever was. John is saying that if you want to know what fatherhood and sonship really are, then you have to start by looking at Jesus Christ and how God was Father to him. This is probably the idea in Paul's mind when he wrote in Ephesians 3:1–15 about "the Father" of our Lord Jesus Christ, "from whom his whole family . . . derives its name." The Greek word for "family," here, is *patria*, a derivative of *pater*, "father."

God, therefore, is not a father because He is like a human father; rather, the reverse is true. Human fathers can be regarded as fathers because in some limited way they are like the Father of Jesus Christ. They can be what they are in this respect because God created man in His own image. Man is a kind of limited, time-bound copy, and thus different in that fundamental respect from his Divine Original. Of course, in our human experience, differences arise due to sin, but that is not under discussion here.

Human beings are not copies of God in the way, for instance, that amateur painters might copy a masterpiece, with differences between the copies and the original due to the talents and styles of the artists. The difference between the Divine Original and the copies is more basic than this. One way of describing it is that they are copies rather in the way that a poster may be printed off from a plate: the illustrations and writing on the copies are like those on the printing surface of the plate because they have been created by the plate. But the copies are also different from the plate because the plate is not "just another product" of the same kind. The plate is unique in that it is not a copy. It has some fundamental qualities that the copies do not, such as that it produces the copies, which is something the copies cannot do. So human fatherhood is like God's Fatherhood because it is, as it were, printed off from the latter, but it is unlike God's Fatherhood because *that* is the source of all other fatherhoods in a way that human fatherhood can never be.

The archetype of Fatherhood influences our understanding of parenting.

There is a technical word for this, and it is so useful that, in spite of our general hesitation in using technical language, we think it worth knowing. It is the word "archetype." (It is different from "prototype," which is a smaller pattern which someone else copies to make "the real thing.") God's Fatherhood, then, is the archetype of all fatherhood, and Jesus Christ's Sonship is the archetype of all sonship.

All this talk about fatherhood, however, may have left some mothers feeling slighted! Where's some biblical help for us, they may be thinking. Interestingly, Divine Fatherhood is also different in that it includes motherhood and therefore is an archetype of "parenthood" as well, which can give us clues about motherhood. The most obvious passage is Psalm 91:4, which Jesus seems to echo in Matthew 23:37, when crying over Jerusalem: "How often I have longed to gather your children together as a hen gathers her chicks under her wings" (see also: Deuteronomy 32:11). Here are images of shelter, compassion, and refuge from trouble. Another is that, while the titles for God in the Old

Testament are masculine, one of the quite dominant attributes is decisively female, as in verses like Isaiah 66:13—"As a mother comforts her child, so will I comfort you"—and above all in speaking of God's tender mercies. The Hebrew term for "tender mercies" comes from a word meaning a womb. Language like this in a confusing environment of female fertility gods is truly remarkable.

A rather curious passage is James 1:18, where the word "birth" is the Greek word *apokueo*, "to give birth," or "to bring forth." *Kueo* is "to be pregnant." The KJV translates *apokueo* as "begot"; the RSV has "brought forth." It is remarkable because this literal and absolutely feminine quality is being used not only of "the new birth" but also by the apostle James, whom one usually thinks of as this great patriarchal character. All of the New Testament writers had images of salvation, of course. For instance, Paul spoke of "adoption," John of being "born again," and Peter of "new babes." But James—a definite man in a man's world—well . . . his idea is the quite literal, and painful(!), one of a mother giving birth to a child.

An early understanding of the Trinity may also be helpful. For instance, in the older Syriac literature, before Greek theology made itself felt, the Holy Spirit is feminine. An old Syriac translation of John 14:26 reads: "The Spirit, the Paraclete, she shall teach you everything." Now this kind of thinking was not an anomaly; it was part of the wisdom of everyday conversation. So Aphraates, writing in the fourth century AD about virginity, states, without any explanation whatsoever, "When a man hath not yet taken a wife, he loveth God his father and the Holy Spirit his mother." Here, then, is a Doctrine of the Holy Spirit with a strong feminine dimension.

Further, the personification of "wisdom" as a woman in Proverbs 1 may also be of some help. Though some people today have taken the Greek word for "wisdom," *sophia*, and deified it as a feminine god, we would not want to go so far as to say that Proverbs 1 gives wisdom an independent existence. But we can say that because wisdom is essentially God's and because it is characterized there as feminine, this gives us important clues when applied to our topic here, motherhood. For instance, it is an intensely practical virtue, which (only coincidentally?) is accorded to a virtuous wife and *mother* in Proverbs 31, where it is shown to exalt the honor and dignity of womanhood and the importance of a mother's teaching. Again, we would not want to say that wisdom has an independent existence. Yet as some wit has remarked, maybe we could say that Wisdom is God's favorite woman! Anyway, we can learn much from the fact that wisdom is at the heart of God's existence and is depicted in a feminine context in Scripture.

It gives a special significance to the family unit.

All this talk of archetypes in relation to fatherhood and motherhood may appear rather refined and academic, but the beauty of finding archetypal images in Scripture is that they have quite definite effects on any christian wisdom. The archetype of fatherhood is no exception. It has many practical ramifications for us in our lives as believers, and it gives us many transforming approaches for engaging concerns of secular life.

For one thing, it gives the lie to the humanist's gibe that God made man in His own image and religious people have merely returned the compliment. (It is the humanist himself who has really done that!) It is true that in practice we may actually develop our idea of God as the Father and Jesus as the Son out of our human experiences of parental upbringing, which lays a heavy responsibility upon all parents. But this is not the final word, for we may learn that our idea is mistaken. We cannot even develop an ideal of fatherhood or sonship from the best of the parenting that goes on around us, though it helps. After all, the ideal of "the best" varies from age to age and culture to culture, and we have no guarantee that our own age has any monopoly of understanding—"modern" is not necessarily synonymous with "better." Thus within human experience alone we lack an authoritative criterion. The Christian finds that criterion by considering the way in which God related to the Son, His Son Jesus. Obviously, people's views on the nature of fatherhood and sonship inevitably affect the ways in which they are going to behave within their family life. But one thing is for sure: God did not spoil His Son.

Further, the Bible sees the family as the basic unit of society. It is wisdom to realize that the stability of a society rests on the stability of its building-blocks. To believe that the family relationship is derived from an archetype in the very nature of God Himself is to give that relationship a unique place in the way we understand and assess community life. A society that violates such a relationship by casual disruption of family life is as doomed as surely as someone who tinkers with high explosives and neglects the rules governing its behavior. Many of our marital breakups, and much co-habiting and indiscriminate sex, is "casual" in the sense that it is informal (a temporary response to the immediate situation), having no interests in social roles or responsibilities. This is not to demand that anyone understanding society must declare a belief in God as "our Heavenly Father." It is simply to insist that true wisdom in social life gives this special importance to the family. It may be a wisdom that we have learned from our religious faith, but in the mercy of God, others may, up to a point, live on the accumulated capital of that wisdom without acknowledging whose account they are drawing on.

_____
**It also affects sociology
and psychology.**
_____

This wisdom must also inevitably play its part in whatever academic disciplines involve such matters. In the case of the family concept, sociology and psychology are obviously affected, and a christian wisdom here, as noted above, would strongly emphasize the fundamentalness of the family unit to a healthy society. Other kinds of wisdom will affect these subjects differently.

So some sociologies begin with the idea that society is based on individuals agreeing with one another for mutual protection against the more aggressive members. Others use the notion that man has a herd instinct against the rest of the animal world. Others, such as a Marxist sociology and a monetarist sociology, see human life in society as largely governed by the activity of producing, buying, and selling. All these imply that you could have a successful society without making the basic relationship of family life fundamental—it becomes a cultural option. If there is such a thing as a christian sociology, it could not possibly develop properly within the framework of thought that permitted such implications. Christian sociological thinking would admit that there might have to be substitutes for the family in exceptional situations, even perhaps alternative social arrangements, but it would be obliged to see them as no more than courageous attempts to fill an unhappy break in the whole structure.

_____
**It gives us submission
among equals.**
_____

If God's Fatherhood and Christ's Sonship are archetypal, then so is the relationship between them. Fatherhood and sonship cannot exist separately. There has to be relationship between the two. It is clear from the Gospels that Jesus saw himself as in some way dependent on his Father and subject to His authority. "I always do what pleases him," Jesus said (John 8:29). The Father took the initiative and Jesus followed suit. As he said, "The Son can do nothing by himself; he can do only what he sees his Father doing" (John 5:19; the whole section, verses 16–44, develops this theme). The Epistle to the Hebrews, intent on showing Jesus as God's last word to man yet says that Jesus "learned obedience . . ." (5:8).

At the same time, the Bible sees Jesus as having all the status of the Godhead. For that to be true, he must be God. Thus John says clearly, "The Word was God" (John.1:1), and Paul says baldly, "Christ . . . is God" (Romans 9:5). As our sacrifice for sin, Jesus Christ is the very heart of the Godhead: "The Lamb in the center of the throne" (Revelation 5:6, 13; 7:17; compare 3:21; 13; 22:1). Everywhere in the New Testament, Jesus is known as one who can claim worship, obedience, faith, and love such as cannot be given to any mere representative of God who was not God Himself. It was, therefore, as

Paul says, no robbery for Jesus Christ to be equal with God (Philippians 2:6, KJV). And yet the Son was subject to the Father (Matthew 26:39).

What confronts us in the Godhead itself, then, is a relationship between equals in which one has authority over the other. As noted, this is an archetypal relationship; that is, it is a pattern within the being of the Godhead that produces copies of itself in God's creation. To most of the pagan world this is outrageous. It is hardly conceivable that two beings can be equal while one has any authority over the other. How often do we hear the contemporary language of equality saying, "I'm as good as the next person. No one's going to tell me what to do!" As the influence of the christian wisdom erodes, in every area of life there is pressure to attack the notion of authority on the grounds that it is incompatible with real equality. This can be found in many schools and homes (especially as portrayed on television and in film), and it appears in industrial and sociological disputes. A classic example can be found where christian arguments about some aspects of feminism become precariously credible due to their treatment of the issue of authority.

This affects politics too. Outside of the Gospel's vision of things, the power structures of a society always tend to be pyramidal, in which the few at the top have almost complete power over the many at the bottom. In such societies it is difficult, even dangerous, to criticize the government or to satirize one's sovereign. Even in our democratic societies today, politicians try to make taboo the kind of criticism that touches their power. One poignant illustration of this occurred in the U.S. leading up to the 1996 Clinton-Dole presidential debate. The "character issue" had been in the media a good deal too much, it seems, for President Clinton, the target of the criticism. Perhaps knowing that his presidential power could be undermined by ongoing negative references to his character, he was frequently heard saying, "We must not criticize our leaders."

It affects male-female relations. This also affects the popular, and controversial, contemporary debate about male-female relations. Scripture asserts a particular kind of equivalence between men and women, and it regards a man's exploitation of his place in that relationship as a sinful outcome of the Fall. The description of Woman in Genesis 2:18 as a "helper suitable for him [Adam]" is quite clear in Hebrew. It is not about someone who irons the trousers and brews the coffee. There are other words for that. "Helper" is a term regularly used in connection with God Himself as a person's rescuer. It is help, then, in meeting Adam's otherwise hopeless inability to cope! The word "suitable" means something like "over against" or "counterpart." It is used fairly often in contexts of rivalry, and so a reasonable translation would be "a match for." Throughout Scripture, therefore, women appear doing jobs commonly attributed to men, and doing them effectively, even organizing strategies of war (Deborah, in Judges 4:4–16) and taking bold initiatives in commerce and management (Proverbs 31:16, 24). The "ideal wife" of Proverbs 31 is not tied to the kitchen sink and the nursery (much of the restricting effect of caring for small children that bedevils mothers today was overcome in ancient Israel by the support of the extended family; chapter 4). Jesus, of course, clearly resisted every custom that might diminish womankind. And Paul proclaimed that the difference between the sexes has no meaning at all when it is a matter of belonging to Jesus Christ (Galatians 5:6).

Nevertheless, within the family situation throughout Scripture there is no question that the husband is regularly thought of as exercising overall authority in the home. Authority is normally represented throughout Scripture by means of male and masculine symbols and metaphors. The evidence is so overwhelming that it demands that any explanation of the relationship between the sexes must take account of it. The issues involved here are extremely complex and beyond the scope of the present discussion. As exemplifying this, we might note that this does not imply that a woman has no power or no moral claims; she is at least "a match for" man when it comes to personal influence, as the Book of Esther shows, even within an extremely male chauvinist culture. Nor does it mean that there are no situations in which she might exercise authority over men, as the Book of Judges shows. Indeed, the peculiar way in which authority is understood in Scripture—as differentiated and distributed, so that no single person or group ought ever to have a total use of it—would resist such an idea. There may be valid arguments from the biblical evidence for a feminism contrary to the apparent drift of our arguments here, but if so, they must work with a logic different from that which identifies equality with authority.

As far as Scripture goes, then, the authority issue is quite different from the equality issue but not unrelated to it. The life-pattern of the Godhead demonstrates clearly that equality is not incompatible with subordination. Indeed, Jesus even said that being in authority meant being a servant (Mark 10:42–45). What is significant for our purpose here is that this idea is so peculiarly biblical that even Christians themselves have difficulty in accepting it, for their wisdom is only too often contaminated with that of the world, and they are weakened thereby.

The Doctrine of Creation and the Doctrine of God as Father, then, certainly have some possibilities that may not at first appear evident. They effect the very nature of reality and life itself, and they have immense practical implications reaching beyond religious issues and into our everyday lives from Monday through Saturday. And they can help us tremendously in our conversations and activities with today's world. More possibilities are explored in the following chapter.

~17~

Using Theology and Doctrine to Learn Wisdom, Part 2

In his writings, the apostle John makes a big thing out of the truth that Jesus Christ came to earth as a real human being. In his Gospel, he emphasizes that God became flesh, and in his first epistle he goes so far as to say that you could judge the spirit of a person, ministry, or movement by this test: if it did not believe that Jesus came "in the flesh" it could not be coming from God.

The Doctrine of the Incarnation helps heal the split between "the material" and "the spiritual."

Most Christians today would regard this as fuss over nothing. Yet there are a couple of current misunderstandings in our wisdom that the Doctrine of the Incarnation can help us to shake out. These surround our ideas about "spirituality" and "holiness." The problem is a manifestation of a wisdom that still suffers from that radical split between the world of our sense experience and the immaterial world. It was exemplified in a rather humorous way some years ago when a nine-year-old in a Sunday school class asked me[JP] a question that has stuck in my mind because of its initial shock and artless profundity. He said, "Sir, will there be lavatories in heaven?" I think I answered, "No, I don't think so." But I could not have given him a sound reason for that answer. The shock of the question was symptomatic of a common conflict in our wisdom: we find it desperately difficult to reconcile the seen world and the unseen world, what we often think of as "the material" and "the spiritual." If one of these two worlds engages our imagination vividly, then we will think that the other world is remote and relatively ineffective in the first world. The Doctrine of the Incarnation helps us tremendously to heal this split without losing the distinction, and this, as we shall see, will give us wisdom to be more consistently biblical in everyday life.

Christians are committed to the idea that the man Christ Jesus is Lord of all life—that He is God. This commits their minds to a special view of him. The problem is that present-day Western wisdom lies on the material side of the split between matter and spirit, and this has filled our christian minds and imaginations from childhood with the urgency of what can be seen, felt, heard, measured. This is what counts.

As a result, Christians today tend to live in two worlds that have become alien to each other, at least in their wisdom. One is the material world, the world of births and deaths, food and work, houses and mortgages, sex and war. The other is the immaterial world, which is largely understood in terms of ideas and ideals like faith, truth, beauty, thought, reason, and morality. And as a result of that kind of wisdom, it is hard indeed to conceive of heavenly lavatories. It may even disturb us to think of Jesus going to the lavatory, even though he himself refers to such matters at least twice within the brief compass of the Gospels (Matthew 15:17 and Luke 14:35, usually found somewhat delicately translated!). The really spiritual stuff that Jesus did, we tell ourselves, were things like praying, preaching, teaching, and healing. For we find it difficult to conceive how the more mundane activities of his life could be considered "spiritual." Thus, the influence of Western wisdom in this important area of christian thinking keeps us largely unaware of what the Incarnation, our special view of Jesus Christ, might mean for us in everyday issues and matters.

There are two meanings of "spiritual" in Scripture.
This split in our minds is most clearly seen when we speak of something as "spiritual." "Spiritual" has two possible meanings in the Bible. One is "that which belongs to the world of disembodied spirits." So we may speak of "spiritual warfare" when facing temptation, or we may speak of spiritistic (demonic) activity or miraculous signs and angelic visitations. This could be called a *descriptive* use of the term. The other biblical meaning of "spiritual" is "that which belongs to the Spirit of God, that which is owned by God, that which is used by Him." It is virtually a synonym for "holy." This is a use in which a value judgment, usually one of approval, is made about something. We could call this an *evaluative* use of the term. The biblical context normally makes clear which of the two meanings is at work. The split in our wisdom between the immaterial and the material worlds comes from a confusion of these two biblical ideas about "spiritual." But it can be healed by understanding these two ideas as we should.

Typically, we in the West tend to assume that things can only be "spiritual" in the evaluative sense when they symbolize moral and religious themes. Church activities we therefore consider spiritual, but our work in the world is only spiritual insofar as it supports good works, preferably religious ones. Art is only spiritual if it includes religious symbols or suggests obviously moral ideas. Music, to be spiritual, must be set to religious words and themes. In other words, physical activities and needs have to be specially "sanctified" in order to participate in "being spiritual." Let's take a few minutes here to challenge that common use and understanding of the word "spiritual."

The Incarnation spotlights the spiritual meaning of the material world. The Incarnation declares that matter and flesh and blood are, as they were created by God, naturally and normally spiritual in the evaluative sense; that is, they belong to God and are in themselves owned by God and used by Him. As Paul says, "I am convinced as a Christian that there is nothing unclean of itself." That is, nothing requires special treatment to make it acceptable and usable by God in itself (Romans 14:14). In a fallen world, of course, what God owns may be abused and misused for selfish or wicked ends, and treated as ends in themselves, as if "a person's life consisted in the abundance of his possessions." If so, this places what God owns in the service of "another god."

Our point is that the material world is spiritual in the evaluative sense because it is created and owned by God and sustained by Him. It is, as God Himself said many times, "Good." Thus in the life of the Christian, living and praying according to the message of the Gospel, what God owns is not only spiritual in the evaluative sense but also made holy (1 Timothy 4:3–5). This is so fundamental that even an unbelieving husband or wife is included in it (1 Corinthians 7:14).

Now this principle is spotlighted in the Incarnation. Jesus Christ was not born in church or under the auspices of some religious ceremony. Certainly his mother was a godly woman, but she was not a prophetess, or the wife of a priest, or without sin. Like the rest of us, she rejoiced in "God my Savior." Yes, Jesus was "conceived by the Holy Ghost," that is, by a miracle, but the resultant pregnancy and birth was natural enough. Further, to deny that the body of Jesus was not spiritual in the evaluative sense of "being holy" would be a heresy so long discredited as to be laughable.

The opposite of spiritual is not "material" or "physical." In its evaluative sense—as the word "spiritual" means "used by God for His purposes"—the contrast is not between "material" or "physical" and "spiritual," or between "secular" and "holy." The opposite of "spiritual" as a valuation is "carnal"; that is, thinking and living as if this material world were all there is worth living for. (Again, this would be to place it in the service of other gods.) And the opposite of "holy" is "profane," or simply, "unholy"; that is, alien to the will of the uniquely transcendent God. Speaking theoretically again, this means that there might easily be lavatories in heaven, and if so, their presence would be no more embarrassing to us than Christmas trees. It also means that our natural life here may be no less spiritual when we are watering the lawn than when we are having an ecstasy of prayer.

At the end of it all, the question in that day for Christians is not going to be, "How spiritual were you?" It is going to be, "What did you do with your spirituality?", if we could be allowed to put it like that. In whose service was it, God's or another god's? In other words, it involves issues of obedience. *That* is where the Bible draws the line, not between spiritual and unspiritual people.

This problem is most evident in our imaginations.

Of considerable importance in this matter is the problem of the imagination, for the imagination, in part, concerns the limits of what we can believe to be true. For instance, we must be wary of appeals to our imaginations as arguments against particular practices or institutions in our present age. I[JP] was once in a congregation where a preacher asked, as a plea against war, "Can you imagine Jesus Christ pressing a bomb-button in an airplane?" Of course we all replied no. But the argument is faulty. Neither can I imagine Jesus Christ driving a car, or getting trapped in an elevator, or wanting to make love, or working a computer, or running for Parliament. My mental picture of the human Jesus is of a man in first century Palestine, where there was little more lethal than a sword or sling and little more technological than scythed chariots. (I can, however, imagine the Jesus of the Book of Revelation unleashing the judgments of fire and famine on people who run concentration camps or torture chambers, or who feast while millions starve.)

The point is, our imaginations, just like the rest of what it means to be human in a sinful state, are disordered and unreliable. Our imaginations find it challenging to believe that the material world is spiritual in the evaluative sense, for our wisdom is infected with a kind of cultural schizophrenia in which what goes on in the immaterial world of meaning, value, motive, and vision so seldom becomes incarnated in the material world of fighting, food, and fun. If we could once attain a cure for this, then we might be able to sort out the problems of nuclear weapons and traffic control and computers more satisfactorily.

"And was made man . . . ." Let us begin seeking a cure by taking this clause of the Creed seriously.

Jesus' Godmanhood was utterly physical, but not unspiritual.

The Gospel story of Jesus presents us with other important facts that can help us revise our views about "spirituality." To begin with, Jesus was not disembodied, ever. He was born, in the first place, struggling for air, and he was so vulnerable as a baby that they had to get him away from Herod's soldiers, quick. As a teenager, he could be puzzled by his parents' protectiveness. He worked as a carpenter for most of his life, and he could be tired and hungry, pressured and relaxed, happy and sad. He could show amazement and anger, impatience and ignorance, depression and curiosity (Matthew 8:10; Mark 3:5; 9:19; 13:32; 14:33; Luke 2:46). If this is God becoming man, then this is God experiencing the richness and poverty of being human.

It is impossible to say, then, that work, anger, instinct, weariness, puzzlement, depression, and appetite—indeed, the whole business of blood and guts and emotions—are somehow in themselves "unspiritual." They may often be so *in us*, because we live so often as substandard (carnal) human beings. But that is not the point here. They are not *necessarily* unspiritual. In fact, when we are truly subject to Jesus, they may be the highest form of spirituality. By this we do not mean a spiritual pecking order. Rather, some moments in life seem to have more "spiritual" significance than others, for some choices involve greater self-denial and stronger faith and carry greater repercussions. St. Teresa of Avila once said, "Above all ecstasies I prefer the monotony of an obscure sacrifice." This surely challenges notions of spirituality characterized by unbroken peace, light, joy, and the "don't-rock-the-boat" attitudes about Christian fellowship, in which no forms of argument, criticism, or passion are tolerated.

And it was formed by a particular culture.

Another feature of this is one's cultural history. It is apparent that Jesus was a Jew. He was the Universal Man, so to speak, but paradoxically his universality was Jewish. He was heir to a cultural history whose wellspring is unfolded to us largely in the Old Testament. We would be shocked to discover how much of the New Testament would be lost to us if there were no Old Testament, or something like it. There are elements in Jesus' teaching that are only vaguely intelligible to us without some knowledge of the historical background, for example on "Corban" in Mark.7:11, or his admonition on going the second mile (Matthew 5:41).

To be human, therefore, means to have not only a personal but also a cultural identity, to be heir to a history. To hear some Christians talk, you would never imagine that being British, or South African, or American, or Indian was of any significance in one's discipleship to Christ. The result is that by default people of other cultures have often been persuaded that the only cultural expression open to a Christian was that of the missionary, or, still worse, that of the missionary's denomination.

All of this is to say that Jesus as a man was a being who made things, who calculated their prices, and sold them. He was a person who saved and spent money, and who knew the pleasure of a good story and was sensitive to its form and style. He was a citizen who made comments of political significance that endangered him. His humanity made him a being that sustained the great variety of personal relationships that go into making up social life, and it meant speaking a mother-tongue in a multilingual society, with the attendant needs of translation. It also meant living in a territory that posed occasional problems of obedience and faith, and making choices that involved him in sorting out priorities and in being clear in his mind about his calling. All of this is to say that by his incarnation Jesus legitimized the material world and human culture as belonging to God. Incidentally, this is not only a far cry from the traditional Western view but also from the gnostic view, which even some Christians today, in their uncaring and irresponsible attitude toward the environment, have fallen prey to in their ignorance of a spiritual view of nature in the evaluative sense.

Every aspect of human life is intended to be spiritual. The Incarnation means that Deity, and therefore spirituality and holiness, engages every conceivable aspect, religious and secular, of our created being. We therefore cannot speak of the religious activities of worship or evangelism or prayer as spiritual work and then speak of supporting a political candidate or writing poetry or driving a truck or having a party as inherently less spiritual or not spiritual. To do so, we would have to believe that when Jesus was making cabinets, or wine at a wedding party, he was less spiritual or less holy than when he preached or prayed. If that were so, it would also affect our reading of the Bible. The story of the Good Samaritan, for instance, would be less spiritual than the teaching about the Good Shepherd. And what would we do with stories such as those about the cursed fig tree or finding money to pay taxes? When we are faced with this, we are usually quite willing to agree, but in practice many of us seldom relate to life accordingly, for we find it difficult to let our imaginations be transformed enough to actually live as though it could possibly be true. A less than satisfactory notion of spirituality is so deeply ingrained that it takes great conscious effort, time and time again, to actually plan and live in the bread and butter of life more closely to the biblical view; that is, as if the bread and butter were spiritual.

This is Jesus' way of reasoning. In chapter 4 we highlighted an incident when Jesus told a "secular story" (about economics) to answer a "religious question" (about the appearance of the Kingdom). We noted there that *we* probably would not have responded that way because Jesus' way of thinking and reasoning about life was different from ours today. We also noted, in chapter 7, that one way to allow our wisdom to change is to let the "strangeness" of Scripture challenge and speak to us. Here we see clear examples of these two points. That is, in seeing the Incarnation's relevance to the material world, we may once again see how we can learn both from the strangeness of Scripture and from Jesus' way of responding to people. For both are rooted in a wisdom that life is all of a piece and not split into the material and the spiritual. For God owns it all.

We need keys to get us into this. Ideas like these are our keys for developing a wisdom for all of life today like Jesus and God's people in Scripture had. But the transformation takes time, effort, and discipline. Speaking as someone who has been taking this seriously for a long time, I[CS] still find it challenging, not to mention surprising at times. I remember once tackling a seemingly inconsequential one concerning the announcements made during church services. I used to despise the announcements because they interrupted "the flow," the really spiritual stuff of singing, praying, and listening to the message. Then one day it struck me that church announcements showed how the life of the Body was being fleshed out in service to God throughout the week. That simple insight completely transformed my view of "the announcements." It changed the way I *thought* about them. If serving God throughout the week was spiritual, surely any announcements were part of that spiritual service and therefore no less spiritual than the singing, praying, or preaching. But actually *living* as if I really believed it . . . , well, that took some time. Showing up at church with a favorable attitude toward the announcements, and talking with others about my changed view, and forgiving people who were terrible at making announcements(!), took practice. This may seem like a fairly insignificant illustration, but I can remember it producing quite a powerful shift in my wisdom. Giving our imaginations breathing space to believe something new to be true takes time and mental effort. Old and deeply buried assumptions die hard.

This kind of struggle is common to Western Christians. Think again of a point in chapter 13, that all the aspects, not just the religious one, are present during a church service. And now ask yourself, are the economic, the aesthetic, and the "lower" aspects not spiritual just because they deal with money, decorations, and aisle space? It may still be a struggle to believe that these aspects are no less spiritual than the religious aspect. For we were raised in a wisdom that spoke quite matter-of-factly of spirituality as meaning "devotedness to religious activities." So we tend to think of people as spiritual when they emphasize the need for prayer, Bible study, evangelism, and suchlike, as against someone who wants to debate questions like where the church gets the money from, or how the church persuades or trains someone to do a job, or who's going to paint the building and vacuum its floors. The doctrine that God became man cuts at the root of all this. Jesus is no less spiritual when he is arguing with an opponent or finding money to pay a tax than when he is at prayer or doing a miracle.

What about miraculous or supernatural channels?

Another tendency is to regard something as specially spiritual, or "of the Spirit," when it apparently reaches us through channels outside the "normal," "natural," ones. Illumination that comes into the mind "out of the blue" without the help of commentaries or hard thinking, or the embarrassment of making mistakes, is often assumed to be really spiritual and carrying a special authority for us. The Doctrine of the Incarnation challenges this too.

In no way are we suggesting that God does not give guidance, that God does not answer our prayers and speak to us. And it is true that the incarnate life of Jesus had its miraculous elements, and his continuous struggle with demons and their prince is unmistakable. That is, there were features of it that were spiritual in the *descriptive* sense, being concerned, as they were, with the world of realities that we think of as inaccessible to our natural senses, such as the world of disembodied spirits, or the world of ideals, values, and moral convictions, or the "gifts of the Holy Spirit." Yet though his was a miraculous conception, it was an uncomfortably natural birth. Though he could multiply loaves and fishes, Jesus still got thirsty and hungry. His stories bear all the marks of being finely crafted, which takes great discipline. And does anyone think that his woodwork was done by a wave of the hand? Further, Jesus said that he would be disowning some people who could miraculously cast out demons. What we are suggesting is that the "miraculous way" of getting guidance and help is not more spiritual than the "normal" ways, and that dealing with demons is not more spiritual than working with wood. It's just different.

To be spiritual simply means to...

All of this, admittedly, is rather complicated, so it will need patience and maybe discussion with a sympathetic friend. Keep in mind that it is complicated mainly because of the two different wisdoms (that of our cultures and that of

Scripture) whose conflicting ideas are informing the process of transformation. And throughout this lifelong process, we will continually be facing various nuances of the evaluative and descriptive senses of "spiritual" that may be quite challenging indeed. For instance, a tendency exists to think of the "gifts of the Spirit" as the really spiritual gifts. Yet the whole thrust of 1 Corinthians 12–14 is that you can use "spiritual" gifts in an "unspiritual" manner!

Whatever *spirituality* means to the Christian, it must always be understood in relation to Jesus Christ and judged by him. If we go back to Jesus' incarnate life and ask ourselves what it could be that, as a man, made his carpentry as spiritual as his crucifixion, it seems to us that the common denomination is obedience of faith. Here we come full circle to the opening remarks of this section. Because the temptation to become overly involved in things that are seen besets us so continually, prayer, meditation, and mystical experience of the unseen world has a special place in counteracting this world's pressures on our hearts and minds. The real issue of spirituality in the evaluative sense, however, is not whether something is spiritual in the descriptive sense but whether we are living by obedient faith in Jesus Christ. So, to be spiritual simply means to "trust and obey."

The Doctrines of Sin and Redemption make the practice of realistic self-criticism feasible. Everybody would agree that the power of self-criticism is a vital part of wisdom. But in the biblical Gospel this power is built in. The Bible teaches that we are a "fallen," or sin-infected, race; that is, that even when we are at our best we are nothing near what we ought to be and might be. This view has produced profound cultural attitudes. For instance, the attitude expressed in the words "do not put your trust in princes" (Psalm 146:3) has had a powerful political effect.

After all, hardly any of the heroes of The Biblical Story are portrayed without fault; they are often portrayed with serious fault. Think of the life of David, the man "after God's own heart"! This view has meant, in particular, that in Protestant countries, especially those whose constitutions are most affected by biblical (rather than, say, even Roman) law, there have always been political structures designed to prevent any individual or group from having absolute or unchallengeable political power. The British notion of a "governmental opposition" owes much to this mindset, as does the "separation of powers" in the U.S.

The Doctrines of Sin and Redemption, therefore, open a society to possibilities of change in a unique way. For instance, it is a characteristic of biblical Christianity that it repeatedly mounts a critique of the social status quo, even when that has been professedly Christian. Outside of the influence of biblical Christianity, the social structures of civilizations have often survived unchanged through centuries and even millennia, altered only by war or natural disasters, or occasionally collapsing under the pressures of their own growth. However, the wisdom that is based on regard for the Lord is always aware that human beings, including rulers, are subject to criticism. Interestingly, even rulers of almost totalitarian power have been unable to resist this indefinitely. We could call the power of this kind of social and political critique "dissenting Christianity," which has done much, in the nations where it is found, to bring about redemptive cultural change in ways that, for instance, were not possible in the status quo even of early Greek democracy, nor in Muslim lands.

They save us from expecting too much from even the best people and projects. This places a special kind of realism on christian ideals. We may contrast such ideals with those of communism to make the point clear. The communist vision is of a classless age on this earth in which wealth will be so distributed that greed and oppression will no longer have any point. This will be seen as untenable by the christian ideal of a society that acknowledges the effects of sin in its structures.

As far as this world is concerned, christian wisdom has no such "perfect" vision, and its policies are not aimed at eventually producing one. That is, its policies are not aimed at producing an ideal state of affairs; rather, they aim to restrain sin so that goodness may have a fair chance to flourish. So in Romans 13, Paul sees government not as an agency for social engineering but as a divine instrument for dealing with the excesses of sin and for maintaining a certain moral order in the nation. One of the exciting things about Old Testament law is that its provisions do not presuppose a populace that will be enthusiastically law abiding. It recognizes that among them will be thieves, rapists, murderers, and perjurers, as well as people who have such a poor moral sense that compromises might have to be made for their sake. The provision for divorce (Deuteronomy 24), the revocation of oaths (Numbers 30), and the regulation rather than the call for abolition of slavery (Exodus 21; Leviticus 25) are cases in point.

They have a bearing on racism and multiculturalism. But alongside this sense of human fallibility is an attitude that finds its fullest expression in the Gospel of Jesus Christ. Its message is that God took the initiative in becoming man. Jesus identified himself with us so fully that he died on a cross to bear the penalty consequent upon our sins. When we become united to him by faith, we are made right with God and His Law, and we receive God's Spirit. This bare bones outline of the Gospel has deep implications for our purposes in everyday life. Let's take one hot area today: race.

In the Gospel's message, certain ideas have been taken for granted in order for it to make sense. One idea is that as a race we are a unity. We belong to each other. Thus, if one of us is perfect we may all get the benefit of it. A significant case in point today would be the profound implications for racism. For instance, you cannot regard Jews as a lesser breed without calling into question your own standing as a person made in the image of a God who became a Jew; or if you are a believer, your standing as a Christian, since you belong by faith to a Jew. Since people of all types belong to Christ, no race may be regarded with contempt. This has momentous affects, for instance, on how social policy takes shape. And when the unity breaks down in the extreme, you can have a holocaust. This was the situation in fascist Germany in the 1930s and early 1940s. In answer to the basic question "What does it mean to be human?", the Nazi Party answered, "You're human if you're a member of the Aryan race. If you're a Jew, you're not." Violà! Social policy takes shape.

Its implications also have a bearing on multiculturalism, which is quite complex and can get downright nasty. A common methodology today for trying to create civil multicultural societies is enlightening. That is, in order for diverse "people groups" to live together with equanimity, each group must first be dead sure of its own beliefs and conventions. The assumption seems to be that a clear knowledge of one's own beliefs and conventions coupled with human goodwill and a clear acceptance of another group's beliefs and conventions is enough to build civil multicultural societies. We see the first step in this process going on repeatedly in our day, as individual groups take great pains to define themselves. But this is where the process breaks down and gets stuck, and will continue to get stuck. We are seeing the first fruits of this. As the gap of dissimilarities between groups becomes clearer, further alienation among the groups results because the process tends not to include what we might call "the redemptive element" of the Gospel. Conventional wisdom therefore serves to further alienate the groups—rather than unite them in their distinctions, as the Gospel would do. All races certainly do belong to each other, but only in the Gospel of Jesus Christ is the redemptive clout to heal our divisions in a fallen world, divisions not just between individuals but also among groups. No amount of defining ourselves and accepting others' definitions of themselves can take the place of that. Until the redemptive element is incorporated into the process, attempts at civil multiculturalism will inevitably fail, and the rise of tribalism and ultra-nationalism will continue.

*They influence views
of punishment and justice.*

Another assumption of the Doctrines of Sin and Redemption is that there is a moral order in creation that sin upsets and that punishment does something to restore it. The Christian is therefore committed to something like a "retributive" theory of justice. In this view, punishment is not about protecting society from criminals or giving them treatment till they give up their criminality, or even putting off other would-be criminals. It is not even about a combination of all these.

There is a fundamental quality about punishment that is absolutely essential for the biblical intentions of justice to have a validity: when we do wrong we have violated a Law that is above and beyond all of us, and therefore some corresponding loss or pain is morally necessary to compensate that Law for our wrong. Simply put, we deserve it. Justice, therefore, is about restoring the moral order that governs creation. The Law in itself is not redemption in the Gospel sense of bringing forgiveness, but neither is it vengeance, which is a distortion of the principle by using it in the interests of private and self-centered satisfaction—the avenger makes up his own scale of justice and carries out his own sentence. The kind of retributive process we are talking about sees life as subject to a higher law whose claims must be recognized beyond the desires of personal satisfaction.

*Justice maintains the
moral integrity of the universe.*

Let's think about forgiveness for a minute and then come back to justice and law. For the Christian, God's forgiveness cannot be the arbitrary act of a merciful God who might equally rightly refuse mercy if He felt like it. Gospel forgiveness includes the remission of sins and the removal of their penalty, but on a consistent, righteous basis. It is something special: it is (to use the technical term from Scripture) "justification"—God's acceptance of us because the penalty of our wrongdoing has already been adequately met in Christ's death for our sakes.

The idea of one person being punished for another is perhaps naturally thought of as immoral. This is because we think of such an action under the "normal" conditions of our fallen human experience. At the back of our minds somewhere, we assume either that the sufferer is doing so unwillingly (and therefore unfairly) or that he is attempting to distort the course of justice as it is properly administered. (Perhaps the most readable effective treatment of this is found in C. S. Lewis's *The Abolition of Man*.) In Christ's case, however, not only is the substitutionary suffering being accepted willingly, but the purpose of the action is different in a fundamental way. Certainly it is intended to uphold the course of justice, but more than that it aims at maintaining the integrity of the very moral structure of the universe, upon which the idea of justice itself depends. We doubt if our imaginations can absorb this reality enough for it to support the teaching of it in our minds. So we may simply have to bow to the mystery of it.

The Gospel's view of punishment breeds a peculiar kind of lawmaking.

We are not dealing here with sinners passing or waiving judgment on other sinners, or even with a righteousness in judgment upon sinners. This is about an *ultimate judgment*, even, so Scripture suggests, in which the very character of God is involved: "that you [O God] are... justified when you judge" (Psalm 51:4). Or as Paul says, "So as to be just and the one who justifies those who have faith in Jesus" (Romans 3:26). A mercy that does not come to grips with the fact of sin's deserts will always become uncertain in that remote center of operations where the moral structure of all existence is maintained. In its outworking, it will never sustain the ineradicable distinction between the gloating torturer and the innocent victim. People who reject the biblical idea of the retributive process because, they say, it is merciless and unloving, insist that the wrongdoer ought to be pitied rather than punished. If any society acted consistently on such a principle, then the unrepentant criminal who has enjoyed inflicting misery on someone else would go unpunished and untroubled. But in that case, what would we pity him for? Such logic is so outrageously ridiculous that those who accept its premises tend to argue that this shows the fallibility of reason rather than the falsity of their premises!

The biblical idea of justice would criticize such ideas in another way too. For it is the justice of a saving God (compare Exodus 20:2). That is, it is specially concerned to protect and restore the innocent who are helpless. This has special significance for the poor person who has been robbed, for the foreigner who has been swindled, or for the small shopkeeper run out of business by unfair trading of a big company. It is concerned especially, therefore, for the victim.

The wisdom of the Cross affects our way of framing legislation.

Further, an understanding of life that includes the Gospel-view of punishment breeds a particular kind of lawmaking. For instance, it fixes sanctions for a broken law first and foremost in relation to one penetrating question: "What does this action deserve?" Other questions, like "How shall we make people feel differently about this wrongdoing?" or "How shall we prevent this person from doing it again?", will have their place, but they will only be additional considerations, refining details. Such lawmaking would not produce perfect justice (which relates to the inner motives and psychological mechanisms of our nature, and is the prerogative of God), but it would make outright perversion of justice unlikely if not impossible, especially when considered with other biblical ideas.

Recently in English law, two cases illustrate how distortions can happen. In one case a man murdered his wife in anger (there was no plea of insanity), and a mere three years later he was out of prison, incidentally having had enviable opportunities of further education while in prison. It is true that he suffered in other respects, of course, such as in his business affairs and emotionally. But these things happen to anybody. In the second case, a landlord was imprisoned for a similar period because tenants were keeping illegal drugs on her premises without her permission or even her knowledge; indeed, she had actually been trying to get them out! The law may be an ass, but it does not have to be a rogue elephant.

Incidentally, one of the curious effects of policies of legislation based on non-retributive views of justice is that they seem gradually to develop greater sanctions for crimes against property than for crimes against the person. Historically, I[JP] am told, theft has been regarded as a form of murder because it deprived a person of his or her means of survival. Such reasoning might apply to theft from the poor, but that is not, of course, the way that the law takes effect in practice, since wealthy wrongdoers don't commit theft or burglary but use fraud and oppression. I'm not quite sure why that is, but I have my suspicions that such a notion of theft is held in the interests of the rich rather than the poor.

The Doctrine of Grace also applies beyond religious matters.

Another element in the Gospel's way of thinking is known in theology as the Doctrine of Grace, and this can also helps us tremendously in developing a wisdom for secular life. Grace has been defined as God's love in action where it is most needed and least deserved. We usually associate this, of course, with the things of religious experience. But it applies in other aspects of life, too. For instance, we all have the gift, the grace, of being alive. In the normal course of things, every function essential to human life—eating, drinking, sex, sleep, company—is pleasurable. This is part of what is meant in Genesis 1:28: "God blessed them" (that is, declared His intention that they should enjoy life).

Grace is about not only finding God but also being alive.

This, too, is about grace. For as far as we know, we have done nothing to deserve this. We may, through folly or wickedness, lose life and its pleasures, but we did not earn them to begin with. We do not earn our parents or our brothers and sisters, and for the first years of our lives none of us earn our food, clothing, shelter, or training, and we regard it as cruel that poverty drives some children to start earning early in life. Although there is a sense in which we need to earn the love of a good man or woman to be our spouse, it is fatal to love that we should actually think that we merit it. So, too, when we become parents, with the pleasures and heavy responsibilities attached to that status, we can hardly say that we earned that position or were properly qualified for it. In parenthood—the most serious of human responsibilities—everyone begins as a learner and indeed remains so, however many children they have.

So we take it for granted that we should all start life with a place in society that we did not earn, even though later in life we may seek to earn another one. A christian wisdom in society will be powerfully aware of this element of "givenness"; that is, that we have to live as those whose being and well-being is *given*. This does not negate a sense of the need for proper qualifications and fair dealing; indeed, these are the appropriate responses to the sense that when we are given something we have an obligation to develop it faithfully. (This principle applied to "salvation" might help Christians struggling with the "faith-works" paradox.)

The awareness that life is fundamentally a gift will be a suspicious concept, for instance, to the "self-made man." There is a famous example of Dr. Samuel Johnson's wit in the story of one prosperous gentleman who, taking some umbrage at the Doctor's manner, said, "Sir, I will have you know that I am a self-made man." To which the Doctor rejoined, "Sir, you have relieved the Almighty of a great responsibility!" In a community where wisdom is dominated by the idea of personal merit such a remark begins to lose its humorous appeal.

It can influence employment policy and educational theory. One area where Christians can employ this is in the business world. For instance, the wisdom of God's grace is open to the possibility that office and privilege are not always best filled by people who have clawed their way up to it and expect to fill it by right. Many people are actually made by their responsibilities: they rise to what is expected of them. Merit is not the only criterion for giving people power. Think of two kinds of employer, each with a different approach to the task of filling an opening. One approach is dominated by qualifications; the one with the best, other things being equal, gets the job. The other approach is exemplified in the experience of a man who applied for a job in computer maintenance at one of the giant firms of the chemical industry. He mentioned to his prospective employers that he had no qualifications in that area, but they quickly brushed his doubts aside, saying, "If you're the right kind of person, you'll learn." They hired him and were proved right.

There are great advantages in hiring people like that. For one thing, they are more likely to realize that they don't know anything! Now it is quite possible that someone with qualifications might have been equally teachable.

Presumably the job could have gone to that person, but even so, in this case that person would not have earned the position due to his or her qualifications, for the employer was working with the principle of grace: if a person's attitude is receptive, he or she can grow into a job. Such wisdom endeavors to foster the expectation that people will grow into the responsibility that is given them. This is grace. Indeed, they may take the new-found position more seriously than a "qualified" person would.

A disturbing example of the reverse trend is growing today in school teaching. Formerly it was assumed that children were to treat a teacher with respect because of his or her position. Whether a teacher was a good or a bad disciplinarian, or whether the lessons were interesting or boring, was immaterial. In other words, teachers did not have to earn that respect; it was theirs anyway, a gift, if you will. As a result, a substantial number of teachers survived tough initial problems and are doing better work today because of the experience. They were given better treatment than their achievements or abilities deserved at the time. (Applied to the nurturing of new Christians, this principle might help them understand just how forgiving God is!)

Today there is an increasing tendency for teachers only to be able to teach if they are *qualified;* that is, if they have been through formal teacher training. This is not to deny the value of teacher training. But teaching is rather like some aspects of marriage, and trial marriages never tell you the facts about the real thing, and the best teachers learn by doing it. Even more serious is an attitude fostered in the minds of the children by the prevailing mental climate. Namely, that if a teacher does not qualify by the *children's* standards, he or she does not merit their respect. (A little reflection will bring to mind examples of this in politics and social action.)

It is not always easy to use the principle of grace properly, because there is also a proper principle of reward for merit that should operate in any society as well. Yet the principle of grace, or givenness, is nevertheless built into creation and manifests itself in some unlikely situations for those able to see and use it. Christian wisdom will be open to perceive where such a principle is appropriate and be ready for it.

Grace makes creative change possible in society. One important effect of the Doctrine of Grace is to make creative change more possible in society. The life of Jesus and his followers is itself an example. After all, their chief opponents were those who had earned their qualifications to lead the people. The Jews wondered how Jesus could be so knowledgeable when he had not been properly trained (John 7:15). The authorities were astonished at the articulate frankness of Peter and John, observing that they were ordinary and uneducated people (Acts 4:13). Another example is the history of the arts, which is strewn with famous people who were never qualified to produce masterpieces (though not quite as many as some radicals would have us believe). The Greenbelt Christian Arts Festival (see footnote 2, chapter 2) was started by completely unqualified people. How could they be qualified? It was a new concept! Yet Greenbelt has grown to become home to, and to provide opportunities for, many creative and professional persons.

The same is true in the sciences. Even today it is possible for a small boy with a telescope to discover a heavenly body. Just recently (1997), two amateur astronomers discovered the powerfully bright Hale-Bopp comet. The young Einstein worked full-time in a patent office while he was grappling with radical questions about space and time. Thomas Kuhn, in his book *The Structure of Scientific Revolutions,* remarks that the introduction of new ways of thinking about a particular scientific discipline are almost always brought about by persons who are quite young or new to the field of study. That is, in respect of that particular discipline, their insights and influences were not earned from the scientific community. People who will not see this invariably resist changes on principle and eventually fall by the wayside.

A truly godly wisdom continually refers to Scripture.

In the kind of reflecting we are doing here and in the previous chapter, we are considering how christian doctrine actually affects, and should much more affect, the way we think about the world about us. And we have only noted a fraction of the possibilities. The christian Doctrine of Scripture has profound significance for our view of the nature and the function of words and language. The Doctrines of the Spirit and the Church are important for understanding individual and social decision making. Doctrines of Eschatology affect our view of history and current world affairs. Covenant theology is a desperately neglected and needed doctrine for its significance in personal and commercial relationships. These and many other areas can be studied to great effect for our activities in secular life.

This is not just a matter of how as individual Christians we respond to life, but of how christian thinking will develop properly in the christian community. We are not suggesting that doctrine is a substitute for Scripture. It is a useful way of organizing and controlling our thoughts about what Scripture teaches. When we see it like this, and when we learn to see beyond the purely religious implications, we can use it in our task of developing a truly godly wisdom that continually refers to Scripture but does not rely on culling texts and stringing them together in the interests of proving some isolated proposition. Its understanding of life will be all of a piece with its understanding of the Bible and the teachings derived from it.

~18~

The Wisdom of Words, Part 1

We have been considering the effects of a godly wisdom by way of illustrations from various aspects of culture and Scripture. In this chapter and the next one, we want to develop more fully a theme of chapters 14-15, that of a culture's chief means of communicating values and insights: language. This will give us yet another means of driving in the secular lanes for the glory of God.

The wisdom of Scripture profoundly affects the way Scripture uses quite basic words, which makes this kind of study especially important because we use these basic words regularly today and yet our contemporary understanding of them tends to ignore key biblical ideas surrounding them. The way that Scripture means these words has implications that may surprise us in their relevance even for our complex Western societies.

Words are pivotal in any culture. The Bible gives special meanings to some common words, and we hardly imagine that they could have significant variations of meaning from the ones we are accustomed to from our cultures' use of the words. Not that their biblical meanings are completely different from our usual understanding of them, for then we would use different words altogether. It is rather that, although the original Bible words have cores of meaning in common with ours, the kinds of associations that go with the Bible words in their ordinary usages may be different. To use the technical language, their denotations are the same as ours but their connotations may be significantly different.

If for a moment we think of words as being like tools, the difference is like the variations in the kind of plows used in different parts of the world. Because words are so fundamental to human life, they affect the meaning of things wherever they are used, in much the same way that different kinds of plows produce different kinds of furrows in soil. In turn, this might give rise to different methods of cultivation, which may result in different kinds of crops being raised, leading to different levels and meanings of prosperity and different types of societies. Therefore, the same words differently understood produce different nuances of thought, different directions of the mind, different priorities in decision making.

There is a religious, devotional, way of reading the Bible.

It is important to be aware of and to overcome a recurring difficulty here, first referred to in chapter 2 as the "stained glass window effect." Enter a church that has stained glass and you will experience a distinctive lighting effect that invests everything with a special religious quality. At times this may be a valuable aid to devotion, but we would not want to try to write a book by its light. For that, a different kind of light is needed, and it is no less a gift from God!

The same effect is often at work in our minds surrounding our approach to the words of Scripture as we read and study them. And, quite properly, as we use them in our prayers and meditations, the words take on special value, gathering round them strong religious sentiments. (This is one reason why people often resist new translations—even when they offer other, different, reasons for their resistance.) Nothing is wrong with that quality of language. Devotion is an activity much like enjoying the beauty of a flower; that is not the time for pulling it to pieces to see what it's like inside. There is, however, a time for studying the botany of flowers, and it helps toward growing flowers that are even more healthy and beautiful. To appreciate the special meanings that the Bible gives to words, it is necessary to look at them in the light of day, as words used in everyday discourse, as words without having the stained glass effect.

But it has to be read as "ordinary" literature too.

We must not slide over any slight strangeness in the Bible's use of words by forever making special allowances for them as religious language only. It is true that the Bible is a religious book, even as Jesus, our great high priest, was and is a religious person. But as Jesus was also a person of the marketplace and the carpenter's shop (a secular person), so the Bible is also a book in the common language of everyday life, fashioned within the culture of its writers. It is, as we suggested at the beginning of this book, also a secular book. We have to take account of these two ways—the devotional and the everyday—in which language is used, for in the Bible they interact closely.

Below, we will do a bit of homework for you, looking at two words that claim the particular attention of Christians and noting some perhaps surprising differences between Western culture's and the Bible's use of them. We will do this keeping in mind the overall motivation of *Uncommon Sense*, which is to show how God's wisdom in Christ applies itself in the secular aspects, with a particular emphasis on how the Bible's understanding of the words would alter our contemporary understanding of them. This will be quite instructive for our work in the aspects using modal analysis. Of course, we're not going to do all your homework for you! We hope that these samples will encourage and show you how to get into your own way of studying like this, especially toward applying the findings to secular concerns. (It is something of a paradox in this kind of study that often one of the best translations for people to use not knowing Hebrew and Greek is not one of the newer translations but the Authorized, or King James, Version. That translation often keeps closely to a literal version and so preserves the strangeness of the original language. It is also generally more consistent in preserving within reason the same translations for words through the whole of Scripture. This policy has its own disadvantages, but it is helpful for our purpose here.)

"Truth" is a common illustration of the wisdom of words.

"Truth" is a basic word, if ever there was one. There is of course a core of meaning that people today have in common with the Bible's words for truth; so many occurrences of the word will seem quite natural and obvious to us. The word sits comfortably enough when, for instance, Jesus says to his opponents, "You are determined to kill me, a man who has told you the truth" (John 8:40). In his epistles to Timothy, Paul's references to having "knowledge of the truth" also seem straightforward. We have no problems when being admonished to "believe the truth" and "witness to the truth," and we do not have difficulty with popular ideas like *teaching* the truth, or *speaking* the truth, or *preaching* it, or *saying* it, or *believing* it, or *communicating* it, or *hearing* it, or *understanding* it. In other words, we are quite comfortable with truth as something to do with our mouths and heads.

The famous saying that "the truth shall make you free" is also clear enough, but we are so used to the phrase that it is easy to overlook that we regard it as a metaphor. That is, we don't normally think of truth as *doing* anything, like altering situations, like actually making something happen. After all, situations, we understand, are altered by people or earthquakes—things like that. The truth, we would say, has its effect because people believe it and act on it, or speak it and live by it. Still, it is not unnatural to think metaphorically of truth as a great liberator. Our point here is that there is a fundamental core of meaning that contrasts truth with falsehood and makes communication across the languages effective.

Some biblical phrases using the word sound rather strange to us.

But when we come to the phrase "obeying the truth" (Galatians 5:7), we are up against a more serious matter.

Obeying the truth is not quite natural for us, even as a metaphor. We know what it means, of course, but it is not a turn of phrase that comes instinctively to our lips in everyday life. Imagine a neighbor saying, "I've told you the truth, now *obey* it!" It would make sense, but it would also sound a little odd. For us, *obedience* is what we give to people who have a degree of authority, and therefore it is understood by us as essentially a personal activity that goes on within personal relationships. "Truth," however, is for us in the West an abstract concept. So in the phrase "I've told you the truth" or, "I'm telling you the truth," *truth* for us is about facts, and you don't obey facts like you would a personal authority. You act on them, or at most, give in to them. Thus for many of us, the phrase "obey the truth" is accepted not as a metaphor but as straightforward language about facts, data, statistics, and suchlike. Something very strange is happening here. We are accepting a form of language that turns an abstract idea into a ruler, a boss, something with authority.

Some phrases using the word "truth" sound even stranger. In 1 John 1:6, the NIV translators have the writer asserting that we lie and "do not live by the truth" if we claim to have fellowship with God yet walk in darkness. The NAS has "do not practice the truth." The RSV has "do not live according to the truth." A closer translation, however, is "do not the truth" (KJV). Now that really is peculiar. (Interestingly, the New English Bible comes close with "our lives are a lie.") However strange it might be to us, it was not strange to the original hearers. John gives no hint that his phrase might wrinkle his readers' brows when they heard it for the first time.

In Ephesians 4:15, another reference to truth takes us a step further. Here is an exhortation to resist false teachings and to become mature in Christ. English translations have problems with the language but seldom show it. They translate it as "speaking the truth in love." But the Greek phrase is literally "truthing it in love." The Living Bible suggests "follow the truth." The Amplified Bible offers "let our lives lovingly express the truth." J. B. Phillips has "hold firmly to the truth." However it is translated, "truth" in this verse is about character. And that too sounds a little odd to us today.

"Truth" in Scripture is a word about people.

Perhaps the most remarkable New Testament passage about "truth" is the most commonly known one, so it suffers most from the stained glass window effect. The verse, John 14:6, also drags in other words with it: "Jesus said, 'I am the way and the truth and the life. No one comes to the Father except through me.'" Any Middle Easterner even today would have no problems with the statement "I am the way." I[JP] have asked for directions in that part of the world, and someone—not knowing enough English, or maybe hoping for *baksheesh* (a tip)—once beckoned me to go with him, saying gutturally, "I am the way." But "I am the truth" is another matter. And it appears the more remarkable by being *the* truth. Greek Gentiles listening would tend to hear this as sounding philosophical, like we today might hear the word "Truth" (with a capital T). However, the notion of an abstract eternal principle, like Truth, being equated with a human being, who lived and died, and ate and drank, and got tired and had to blow his nose, would be so outrageous as to be nothing but a sick joke for Greek wisdom, which understood truth as something attained in the mind. Nevertheless, the phrase is put in conjunction with "the way" and "the life," and thus by "the truth" Jesus is unmistakably asserting something like: you want the Truth about life and death and the meaning of existence? I am It/He!

For New Testament writers, truth therefore is not just about words or ideas. It is a word about people. That includes what they say and how they reason, certainly. But it also includes their actions, their behavior, their character; in other words, what they are. This, we must admit, is a foreign concept to us. We want to make some further comments about truth, and the strangeness of "doing truth" and "truthing it," but before we go on, it is necessary to have some basic ideas about the kind of languages the Bible was written in, and especially the effect of Old Testament language on the New.

The New Testament was written in an ordinary language of the times.

The New Testament was written in an ordinary language of the time known as Common Greek, which was the language of ordinary Greek-speaking peoples in what had once been Alexander the Great's Greek empire. It was a simplified and greatly modified development from the Classical Greek of Plato's and Aristotle's writings centuries before. Naturally, regional variations of Common Greek sprang up, and one was found among Jews, particularly those of Palestine, who tended to be a fairly close-knit community and who read a Greek version of the Old Testament known as the Septuagint. This was a kind of Authorized Missionary Version to Jews in the diaspora who did not speak Hebrew. Besides its vital devotional use, it provided a Greek vocabulary of the Hebrew language, and its style had infiltrated Common Greek so much that the Jews tended to use the words of Common Greek in the sense in which they were used in the Septuagint. (The history of the word "truth" in Ephesians 4:15 follows this change; whereas the ancient Classical Greek writers, using the literary language of centuries before Paul's time, used the word to mean "to tell the truth." In this respect, our Western mindset resembles theirs, in contrast with the way the Jews of New Testament times understood it.)

But it was affected by the language of the Septuagint.

In the Septuagint, the verb "truth" is used regularly to mean something like "to deal faithfully" or "to be faithful," which points to the fact that the Old Testament had a subtly different mindset than that of the Classical Greek writers. We will develop this important point about "truth" and "faithfulness" shortly, but first something else must be said. When we are studying the meaning of New Testament words, it is absolutely vital to refer back to the Old Testament. This is not to ignore that New Testament language is the product of nearly four centuries' cultural development from the end of the Old Testament, through Persian, Greek, and Roman occupations, or that Jesus Christ himself is a force to be reckoned with in all this. Nevertheless, we have to take seriously the continuity of the tradition between the Old and New Testaments, for there was a strong element of conservatism among the Jews that resisted the inroads of other cultures, especially in Scripture translation. In many ways this resistance was accentuated in the early christian tradition. Jesus, for instance, emphatically claimed to fulfill, not to negate, the Old Testament. This was so evident that even a century later it could be said by Irenaeus that "Christ brought nothing that was new: he made all things new in himself." The Christians, too, saw themselves as heir to the Spirit of the Old Testament prophets (Acts 2:16–21). Also, many of the first Gentile converts had already had previous experience of synagogue life and teaching on the fringe of Judaism—instruction that would have come from rabbis, who did their studies in Hebrew.

And the Septuagint had meanings imposed on it by the Old Testament cultural tradition.

There is yet a further link with the past in all this. The Septuagint provided a style of Greek in current use whose vocabulary carried a significance bestowed upon it by the Old Testament Hebrew cultural context rather than by a Gentile one. This is vividly illustrated in the early chapters of Luke's Gospel, where the songs of the New Covenant are almost indistinguishable from Old Testament psalms. So to understand more exactly what New Testament writers meant by key words like "truth," we need to turn to the Old Testament usage. (Paradoxically, we are not suggesting that we can get at the truth of these key words in any "pure" way, as if we could study the Hebrew mind apart from the biases of our own wisdom. After all, we are a few years removed from that time! But we can, by at least acknowledging that we have our own assumptions, make important headway. It has been said, and rightly so, that the person most unaware of his or her assumptions is the one most bound to them.)

The words for "truth" in the Old Testament are connected in meaning with words and ideas that are especially illuminating. At this point we will need to do a little language study, but it will be worth it, because a little goes a long way.

Learning wisdom from the Hebrew use of words. To understand how Hebrew works, we can start with an example in English. Take a sentence like: "The mice began to attack the cheeses in the larders." You could find the meaning of any of the words in that sentence in a dictionary, but you would look up "mouse" not "mice," "cheese" not "cheeses," and "begin" not "began." This is because the changes in the words are not about their basic meanings but only about the way they are being used in the sentence, their grammatical function, whether they are singular or plural, past or present. English also depends heavily on word order for its grammar. "Dog bites man" is not news. "Man bites dog" is!

In the sentence about the mice there are two kinds of changes to the words. One kind adds sounds on, as in cheeses and larders. This method is the commonest one in most European languages. The other method changes the vowels, as mouse to mice and begin to began. Languages like Hebrew make infinitely more use of this method. That is, Hebrew uses consonants to give dictionary meanings, and then it uses vowels to show how the words are being used grammatically. Thus the dictionary meaning of a word tends to lie in a few basic consonants (usually three, and known as a "triliteral," or "three-lettered root"). Other sounds are added on, and there are the usual anomalies and exceptions that beset all languages, but generally the basic Hebrew method of expressing grammar and similar modifications is to change the vowels. This means that to find the dictionary meaning of a word like *shophetim* ("judges"), it is necessary to look up the three Hebrew consonants *sh-ph-t*. To make it pronounceable, this comes in one form of the verb (whether it is actually known to exist or not!), *shaphat*. It takes some getting used to, and there are pitfalls, but with care you may find that it gives quite helpful clues in reading Bible names even without knowing Hebrew (try, now, the name of Elisha's father in 1 Kings 19:16).

But back to truth. The basic consonants of the words for "truth" are *'-m-n* (the mark ' here stands for a light grunt, as a Cockney Londoner says the double t in butter). Our word "amen" comes from the same root and, strangely, so does the word *Amin*, as in Idi Amin! In Hebrew, underlying all the different forms for the word *'-m-n* is the notion of "stability." One of the best illustrations is Isaiah 7:9, where the prophet is trying to induce some consistency into the policy of the shifty king Ahaz. Isaiah makes a kind of pun that is difficult to render into English. Try saying the sounds of the Hebrew sentence out loud:

"Im lo ta'aminu, ki lo te'amenu." (Note the root for "truth" in two of the words.)
In English, a possible attempt at rendering it might be: "No faith, all fails" or,
"No trust, you go bust!" His point is that if Ahaz does not rest on God's
Word, he has no stability. Today we have pretty much lost the idea of
"stability" in "truth." As an example, in place of the word "Amen" today,
people sometimes say, "So be it." But the Hebrew person might say, "Let it
stand firm."

Another important feature is that almost all the Hebrew words for "truth"
are capable of a moral, as much as a rational, significance. Thus the word
'aman, "to confirm," "support," also has ideas of "being reliable" or
"trustworthy." The word *'emunah*, "firmness," is used for "steadfastness,"
"loyalty," and "faithfulness," and several times for "truth." The word *'amanah*
in Nehemiah 9:38 is used for pledging one's faith. Even the most common
Hebrew word for truth itself, *'emeth* (shortened from *'emen-th*), is a common
synonym for "faithfulness" or "reliability," especially applied to God. *Emeth*,
which derives from *'aman*, is applied as often to persons as it is to words and
ideas, which links up closely with what we have seen of the word "truth" in
the New Testament in its association with people and their characters.

___

**The Old Testament idea of "truth"
sounds odd to present-day thinking.**

This means that if we regard *our*
way of thinking about truth as
normal, the Old Testament person's
thinking about it is off-center. When we discuss what we mean by truth today,
our debate runs along different lines from how an Old Testament discussion
would run. We in the West instinctively apply the word "truth" to facts, data,
ideas, and teachings, rather in the Classical Greek style. Then North Americans
tend to assume that an idea must be true if those who use it are successful; if,
for example, its promulgators have many supporters and impressive
buildings. People in the U.K. would want prior evidence to support the idea
in the first place. On the continent of Europe, people tend to assume that
something can only be true if it is rationally consistent within a system of
thought. Of course, people everywhere are usually unconsciously applying
such standards. Everywhere, too, are ordinary people who just have to *feel*
that something is true in order for it to be true.

So far as we can judge, an Old Testament person would certainly apply
such criteria, but only as notions supporting something further, rather than
as the core meaning. That is, the determining notion in that person's mind
would be *how stable is it*, so, *how far can I rely upon it?* And there would be
other questions, such as, "Will committing myself to this result in a
relationship that would survive in crises like war, poverty, desertion by
friends, economic turmoil?"

We might think that such an approach is unsatisfactory. This is because people with that outlook would be at first instinctively relating truth *to who was saying it,* and not so much to the logical content of what was said or to facts and data. This does not mean that the Old Testament person could not imagine a bad man saying something that was formally correct, but the Old Testament person would be troubled about applying the word "true" to it. After all, he would think, how can you rely on a truth on the lips of a deceiver? So for the Old Testament person, "truth" was initially about character, about people. (We nearly capture it when we talk of someone as "being true to himself," but even this has a faintly old-fashioned sound to it nowadays.) In a large majority of cases, therefore, when the Old Testament mentions "truth" it is talking about "faithfulness" as well. (Note the above meanings associated with the words *'emunah, 'amanah,* and *'emeth.*) Again we are reminded of the "strangeness" of Scripture and our need to allow it to challenge and transform our contemporary wisdom.

The Bible, then, has a common way of understanding the term "truth" that in one quite significant fashion *does not* overlap ours. *It relates* truth *to people*, to their characters, and it is applied to people's words and thoughts with a concern for these as manifestations of what kind of people they really are. In this context, "doing truth" and "truthing it" may not seem so strange. To get a feel for the weight that this now gives to the discussion, if you have a Bible handy, try afresh Paul's teaching in Roman's 1 about the wicked who "suppress the truth," keeping in mind that, according to Scripture, truth is held by people.

"Knowledge" is another example with a strong personal force in Scripture.

Obviously there is a close connection between truth and knowledge. It is no surprise, therefore, that a study of the words expressing "knowledge" in Scripture reveals a usage that fits its words for "truth," including its personalness. This can be seen in Bible wordbooks as different as Rowley and Allmen's *Vocabulary of the Bible* and W. E. Vine's *Expository Dictionary.* Some of the more outstanding examples should be sufficient here.

A wide range of well-known texts use "know" words that sound slightly odd to us. At the end of Psalm 139, the psalmist asks God to "know" his heart and thoughts even though he has already confessed that God knows him through and through! In 2 Timothy 2:19, there is the assertion that "the Lord knows those who are his." But if God knows everything, that hardly needs saying! Psalm 37:18 says: "The days of the blameless are known to the Lord." Doesn't the Lord "know" the days of the wicked as well? Apparently not: of such Jesus said he will one day declare, "I never knew you." Now we know that Jesus was not saying that he was unaware of their existence and therefore had no knowledge of them. He meant that he did not *acknowledge* them; that is, he did not endorse their claim to be acceptable to him.

This meaning is far more common in the wisdom of Scripture than it is for us, and it is a good idea when you come across a "knowledge" word in Scripture to try that meaning on for size. It often sharpens up the meaning strikingly. For instance, it clarifies that powerful verse in Psalm 138:6: "Though the LORD is on high, he looks upon the lowly, but the proud he knows from afar." The picture is of a mighty king acknowledging one of his ministers who is out of favor, as we say "distant." Another is: "This is life eternal, [to] know . . . God" (John 17:3), not merely to have information or even an acquaintance but also acknowledgement. This active personal meaning to "knowing" words extends further. "To know" is a standard form of words in Scripture for sexual intercourse. Even allowing for it being a euphemism, its use is significant since Old Testament speech clearly felt it to be appropriate, as in: Adam knew Eve, his wife, and she conceived.

And it is not usually contrasted with "ignorance." One of the most remarkable occurrences of "knowing" is found in Proverbs 12:10, the first half of which is translated literally as: "A righteous man knows the life of his beast." In contrast to what follows that, we would expect the passage to close by calling the wicked "ignorant" about, or "negligent" of, his beast. Instead, the proverb ends with, "but the tender mercies of the wicked are cruel" (KJV). Instead of being a study in contrast between the smart and the ignorant, the verse is a study contrasting kinds of care bestowed upon animals. One kind of care is knowledge, the other is false compassion. Thus Keil and Delitzsch translate it: "The righteous knows how his cattle feels, and the compassion of the godless is cruel." Most English translations have something like, "The righteous man has regard for [cares for]..." This certainly captures a main idea, but the English misses the important link with "knowing." In fact, the word in Hebrew is *yada'*, which is by far the word most used in the Old Testament for "know." To get a feel for the weight that this personal dimension to "knowing" gives the discussion, check out Proverbs 27:23.

All this is expressed by Nelson's *Old Testament Dictionary* in the comment that "the knower has actual involvement with or in the object of the knowing." In that article in the *Dictionary*, Professor Leuba remarks, "The Old Testament writers are less concerned with grasping an object by means of the 'idea' of it than they are with allowing themselves to be encountered by a reality which invades the inner recesses of the subject himself."

The New Testament has an astonishingly wide range of words for "knowing" in all its aspects, but the ideas are still profoundly affected by what we have seen as their core in the Old Testament. We could, then, sum up the biblical circle of meaning for "to know" as "an experience of relationship with an object that has moral implications for the knower." Or, "'knowledge' is about a personal relationship with what you know, one that carries with it moral responsibility." Now this closely meshes with the biblical idea of truth, for if truth is predominantly a personal quality then knowledge will naturally participate in that same characteristic.

What about scientific knowledge? As the scholar Professor Leuba suggests, the biblical idea contrasts profoundly with traditional Western ideas of knowledge, which are largely inherited from a revived Classical Greek tradition. For us, knowledge, like truth, is largely a matter of ideas, of studying, of grasping facts in the mind. Further, we are still suffering from a powerful ideal of scientific knowledge, that it is the most authentic kind of knowledge because it seems detached from the observer. Thus it is thought of as especially "true" because it is said to be unaffected by the observer's personal interests.

To develop this kind of knowledge, the scientist, it is said, must be "objective"—virtually uninvolved except perhaps for conducting the tests and recording the "results." And one result is that the resultant body of information can then be assumed to be neutral, or unbiased. This powerful "scientific ideal" has functioned with the status of a god over our thinking, which shows itself in the reverence we have developed for statistical information, for example, because we assume that if it is obtained by techniques that preclude personal interests it will be absolutely reliable. Time and motion studies in factories are allowed the same kind of authority. At one period in the U.K., the same attitude was manifest in the willingness to allow IQ statistical tests to determine the future type of education for children at the age of eleven. Our family[JP] came head to head with this attitude once when one of our sons was still in school. The school counselor had absolutely no regard for our son's interests in playing the violin. She said, "It's not really that important, is it? He's got to get prepared for his career, perhaps for such and such." Long story short, our son has become quite an accomplished professional violinist!

Biblical wisdom would not deny a proper status to knowledge of a "detached" kind, but it would probably want to use it with a preposition, such as "knowing about" such and such. This would imply, and rightly so, that such knowledge was imprecise, like we might say, "About 1830 . . . ." Again, this comes as something of a surprise, because to us the great appeal of scientific knowledge is that we assume its exactitude.

Scientific knowledge is not exact knowledge.

But more and more nowadays it is becoming clear that scientific knowledge is not exact. First, it is inexact because it deals with *classes* of things and events, not with individual cases. Further, it can be inexact in other ways. For instance, in some scientific studies, one can even speak of a statistically average family that does not exist. In the U.S., for instance, one hears of 1.8 as the average number of children per family. Don't worry. It used to be 2.2! Also, and far more important, it is inexact because it never deals with objects of knowledge in their totality but only with a specifically chosen aspect, or aspects, of an object. In the biblical sense at least, claims for scientific knowledge (of a thing) to be full knowledge would be as silly as if a husband claimed to know his wife because he had a note of her vital statistics! By definition, the scientific method cannot tell the whole story of an object. (Recall how modal theory helped us to see this with the analysis of the wedding ring in chapter 13.) Also, scientific knowledge is inexact because it assumes that the universe is a closed system of cause and effect, so any effect with a cause outside the system is automatically excluded.

All of this is specially significant because the word "science" has become almost exclusively confined to what used to be called "natural science," the study of the non-human world. When that kind of science becomes identified with "knowledge," there is an overwhelming tendency to study human life by the techniques of natural science and to assume that if we achieve mastery in that realm that way, then we shall *really know* what a human being is. This shows the tremendous import that the secular world gives to the biblical question, "What is man?" But science cannot answer the question fully. It only makes contributions to the answer. Which ought to challenge some of our christian thinkers and philosophers to new heights.

This almost absolute linkage of the word "science" with studies of the non-human world has also over the years given rise to the great divide between "the sciences" and "the humanities" in most colleges and universities today. In his book, *Consilience: The Unity of Knowledge,* Pulitzer Prize-winning, Harvard Research Professor Edward O. Wilson wants to see this split mended. He is one of numerous people today who are seeking a "unity of knowledge" not just in the sciences or in the humanities but also between the two. Yet much of the thinking and theorizing, though exciting and not without benefit, still seems too caught by the tendencies of "knowledge" as they are understood by the Western world, and which we are critiquing here. Perhaps some of our more enterprising Christian thinkers and philosophers could find ways to bring the biblical core meaning of "knowledge" to this discussion.

*It leads to possessive
control and manipulation.*
A further contrast between biblical knowledge and the scientific approach to knowledge is in the underlying purpose. Scientific knowledge is aimed at achieving possessive control. Theory enables us to predict, and therefore to prevent. It also enables us to project, and therefore to bring into being. As we have seen (chapter 14), this is an essential means whereby we fulfill our cultural task of "subduing." But in the way that we use the word "know" for sexual intercourse (when we do so use it), there are connotations of strong possessive control that are only minimally suggested by the biblical use, and that, ironically (at least to some of us), in very obviously a man's world.

It is no accident that in our age tyranny is old-fashioned and its place at times taken by totalitarianism. Totalitarianism is scientific politics aimed not merely at government but also at total control. When religious knowledge and teaching takes the form of systems and techniques for living, it too has turned religion into a means of possessive control and manipulation and becomes closely affiliated to magic. When the scientific form of knowledge becomes the criterion of what is considered to be authentic knowledge, it becomes applied to man himself as a means of possessive control and manipulation, with disastrous results.

The biblical core meaning of true knowledge as involving a personal relationship with moral implications is clean counter to such a process. It means that even our control over nature has moral implications, and it suggests criticism of any use of science for exploitative purposes. The Old Testament person would certainly appreciate scientific knowledge (see Solomon the scientist described in 1 Kings 4:33), but that person would probably say that it only makes a contribution to what knowledge is all about. In this way it finds its proper place as contributing to the process of our caring involvement in the world. (We are reminded of Bacon's admonition to use scientific knowledge in a "holy" manner; chapter 14). In other words, biblical wisdom puts Western scientific knowledge in its place. However much this may distance us from nature in some respects, it can never cut us loose from our obligations under God toward nature and one another when we are doing our science. The Old Testament world, like ours, had its urgent temptations to power and profit, and against these the Law of Moses applied considerable legislation, for instance, of an ecological nature, such as the land-Sabbaths and the laws about nesting birds and hewing trees.

*It is never unbiased
or "objectively neutral."*
It is also becoming increasingly clear nowadays that scientific knowledge is nowhere close to unbiased. That is, "conducting the tests and

recording the results" is not in the least a neutral activity. Scientists are personally involved in their work, and research tends to develop in directions governed by the interests of individuals and groups. On the larger, historical scale, writers like Thomas Kuhn (*The Structure of Scientific Revolutions*) and Michael Polanyi (*Personal Knowledge*) have shown that even what seem to us to be the most obvious theories about the natural world have not gained credence because in some objective way the evidence demanded it. The powerful idea of "objectivity" that we in the west hold therefore needs rethinking.

More and more we are understanding that scientific knowledge in not unbiased and neutral. Interestingly, this is coming closer to the Bible's view of it. Research and experiments are not fashioned in the way they are simply because they can make objective testing possible. These activities are dependent on prejudgements in the mind of the scientist and the scientific community. Kuhn points out, for instance, that Copernicus's "revolutionary discovery," that the earth moved round the sun, had been anticipated by Aristarchus eighteen centuries earlier, but its acceptance then depended upon a certain climate of thought that aroused questions to which it offered an answer. And that had not arisen yet. To take a more current example, it cannot be accidental that Einstein's Theory of Relativity coincided with a shift in Western thinking whereby almost every other discipline is understood in relativistic form, even theology and ethics. However true Relativity Theory may be, it could not have gained any hold on the imagination of Newton's age, which had a different mindset. Theories, then, have their power because a certain climate of thought makes it possible for the imagination of some people, usually younger people from a different discipline, to visualize and respond to them.

Research and experimentation takes place within what Kuhn calls the "paradigm" of the scientists and the scientific community. The paradigm derives from the culture's wisdom (its assumptions, ideas, attitudes, priorities, and so on), and it controls: 1) the kinds of questions the science asked, 2) the kinds of answers given, and 3) the kinds of studies the science pursues. This, to go aside for a moment, helps explain why quite different cultures develop quite different kinds of science. Kuhn concludes that science is not really about "knowledge of the truth" at all, but about solving problems for which we have to assume a particular way of looking at the world in order to get going at all!

The place of truth and trust in godly science. By contrast, as we saw in the foregoing, the Bible's understanding of *knowledge of truth* is grounded in the idea of *trust*. The godly scientist does his task aware that the bases of his thought and research are convictions of faith, and he seeks to ensure that those convictions correspond with what he knows of God in Christ as the One through whom the world exists (see Appendix 1 diagram noting position of the *Logos*). Thus for the godly scientist regularity of the universe is guaranteed by a faithful Creator whose laws are consistent. This means that true knowledge for him is judged by its obedience to God's laws for human thinking, rather than by being judged as distanced from the subject. It is also judged by the truth of his assumptions about the nature of what he is studying, as well as by the evidence of his experiments, for the former may at times be no more than part of a probability structure built on error. Included in all this will be the honest acknowledgement that personal interest and bias are inescapable, with a readiness for them to be exposed and tested. The godly scientist knows no claim, however sincere, to objective neutrality.

He is also aware that he is answerable to God for the direction of his work in relation to man and nature. He abandons the myth of the scientist who is the impartial arbiter of truth, about which others must make their own moral judgments and leave him to his task of dispensing wonders for the benefit of the human race. The godly scientist's task is to ensure that theory, research, and experimentation are done in subjection to God's laws for thinking, analysis, and classification, and for testing, naming, and using (chapter 14). Above all, he is to love, care about, care for, and respect that realm of nature that is his field of study.

Anyone can know creation truly.

But what about us ordinary mortals? For those of us who are not scientists, the Bible's core meanings for truth and knowledge mean that you do not need to be a scientist in order to know creation truly. That is, science is the technical, differentiated knowledge of a thing, which, as we noted, we generally think of that as "true knowledge." In contrast to scientific knowledge, all human beings everyday have direct, nontechnical, nondifferentiated experiences of the things of creation and life. It's what we could call "naive knowledge." Now one of the implications of the Bible's core meanings of truth and knowledge is that "naive experience" of a thing is true and authentic knowledge in the sense that, though we may not know the thing as thoroughly or with as much precision as the scientist, our knowledge is no less valid. It is therefore not just the scientists, not just the experts, who "know." It is simply not true that naive experience of a thing is less near to its reality. The scientist, with his specialized disciplines and instruments, investigates a limited range of the experience of a thing. He studies the laws that appear to govern a particular aspect of the thing being analyzed. And to get this done he ignores a whole range of aspects of the thing, for these are not his concern (recall the different experts needed to fully analyze the wedding ring). The scientist therefore makes a contribution to true knowledge, but it is certainly a far cry from being what knowledge is all about. Our naive knowledge makes a contribution too, and is no less valid, no less true.

~19~

The Wisdom of Words, Part 2

This chapter continues the focus on language, which is a culture's chief means of communicating ideas, values, and insights, and of getting things done. We will explore several other common words in Scripture that are vital to the life of any community today.

The 19th century saw a great surge of emphasis on the place of emotion in human life. At the end of that century, the infant study of psychology, especially under Freud, extended that emphasis to the instinctual and unreflecting aspects of our lives. This in turn had a profound effect on our Western way of thinking. In particular, it focused our attention on features of life that are least obviously under our control, and one of the great casualties of this was the word "love."

"Love" is another vital word, but surrounded by the romantic ideal today.

Romantic love, the emotional longing between the sexes, has always been with us, and it has always been a strong claimant as a reason for getting married. In the Western world of our day, romantic love has been elevated to the position of final arbiter in relationships. "Being in love" is equated with "love" to a frightening degree, and its authority is such that it is now felt to justify defiance not only of social convention or parental direction but also of moral law itself. Not many years ago, what used to be called fornication and adultery are now felt to be tolerable if the two people are "really in love." Today, you don't even need to be "really in love." You just need "two consenting adults." Now there is an implication in phrases like "really in love" that some forms of love are not "real," but the distinction is rarely made plain. If it is, it tends to be based on a criterion of the intensity of passion. One of the favorite metaphors refers to the "chemistry between them," implying something quite beyond human choice or will. In fact, the divorce of sexual relations from *any* notion of love now seems to be complete in our time. For instance, in the conversation of many people, especially characters on television or in film, sex is no more of a big deal than deciding to go to McDonalds' or the pub. Even those set over us seem confused. "Whatever love is," Prince Charles once quipped to the media just before his marriage to Diana.

It is generally acknowledged that there are other forms of love, such as between friends, parents, and children, though it has to be faced that the current images of even these tend to become eroticized in some Freudian manner. In any case, these other forms of love also tend to be reduced to emotion, or even to a biological function like hormonal activity.

By contrast, the biblical words for "love" have quite different connotations. It is not that the meanings are completely different but that the halo of ideas surrounding the core meanings leads people's minds, especially their imaginations, in a different direction. (A full discussion of these words can be found in any good Bible dictionary, and a more extended treatment appears in C. S. Lewis's *The Four Loves*.) What must concern us here is that this difference of emphasis in the biblical use is largely due to the wisdom within which the words play their parts, for it is a wisdom wherein emotions and instincts play a less significant or authoritative part than they do in Western thinking. In biblical wisdom, other characteristics rise above emotions and instincts. One of these is "covenant."

The influence of "covenant" on love can help us in our relationships.

Surrounding the biblical words for "love" is the tremendous biblical idea of "covenant." In essence the word "covenant" means something like "agreement." It is such a pervasive biblical idea, however, that the word gets used in Scripture in many metaphorical senses (recall from the previous chapter that we today often use "truth" that way).

"Covenant" is used to describe the over-arching idea for Israel's moral, social, and political life. Thus oppression of the poor is seen as breaking covenant (Jeremiah 22:1–9). The power of this word is so extensive in the minds of God's Old Testament people that the promise of a new covenant in Jeremiah (31:31–34) and Ezekiel (34:25–31) becomes almost tantamount to the promise of a new religious system. Faithlessness is occasionally spoken of as "covenant breaking" (Ezekiel 17:18), and political scheming aimed at avoiding disaster without reference to the Word of the Lord is called a "covenant with death" (Isaiah 28:18). God's ordering of day and night is spoken of as His covenant (Jeremiah 33:20). And one of Job's counselors says that if Job repents he "will have a covenant with the stones of the field" (Job 5:23).

It is fair to say that in Scripture, especially the Old Testament, the word "covenant" could have been used in any situation involving a connection between persons or between a person and anything else. It was that common, without being less meaningful thereby. Think of it as having been used where in ordinary language today we use the word "relationship," at least before sex took hold of that word and ruined it. Further, think of it as having been a criterion in relationships as common as the way we today rely on "emotion."

Scripture refers to two types of covenant, one made by negotiation between equals, the other imposed by one party upon another. (British common law terms "contract" and "covenant" do not exactly cover these meanings.) So far as we can distinguish, the first idea is never found as applicable between God and man. Where agreements were in any sense formally made, the terms of the covenant were ratified by a solemn ritual involving sacrifice and the use of salt. In addition, pledges were laid down that were regarded as the sign, almost as our modern signature, of the covenant. The greatest example of this sign was the Ark in the great covenant between God and His people.

"Love" is a word about committed and disciplined caring action.

The covenant idea in Old Testament times was as all pervasive in people's thinking as our Western ideals of "freedom" or "progress" are to our minds. In particular, "love" was shot through with a covenantal slant. So the great Hebrew word *chesed*, often translated as "lovingkindness," referred to treating people as bound to one another by covenant bonds. Another word, *chen*, was defined as a love that went *beyond* the requirements of the covenant bond, especially towards those who had defaulted in it. So it is commonly translated "mercy." The greatest word of all, *ahabah*, which is applied to all kinds of love in the Old Testament, has a special use as applied to God. Those who translated the Old Testament into Greek used the quite common Greek verb *agapao*, which is related to the famous word *agape* (the noun *agape* may be a Septuagint coinage.) This special use gets particular emphasis in Deuteronomy 10–11, where it highlights its overall force as a love that seeks to bring the object of love into a covenant relationship.

In other words, the persistent associated idea to "love" in Scripture is not that of emotions or instincts, or even natural relationships. This is not to deny passion or a desire for family. It is to point out that predominately "love" in Scripture carries a strong idea of mutual or reciprocal commitments involving the exercise of the will in making a choice, even a difficult one. A striking example is Hosea 3:1, where God told the prophet, "Go, show your love to your wife again, though she is loved by another and is an adulteress." The word here almost certainly includes the idea of "making love." But for Hosea it is far more than that. Deliberately, even against the grain, he is to take her back into the covenant relationship of marriage and to treat her lovingly. The words for "love" in the Old Testament, therefore, are about committed and disciplined caring in action.

Two things follow from this. One is that love in this sense always has background thinking that relates to what we might call "law," but which might be better described in Old Testament thought-forms as the discipline imposed by a specific aim in life: toward the Lord. The second thing is that love is never thought of in exclusively emotional terms, or as feelings, or even attitudes. It is, basically, "acting in a loving (committed and caring) fashion."

For the Old Testament husband to say, "I still love my wife, but I cannot live with her," could mean only one thing: the covenant bond had become unworkable in one of a quite limited and clearly defined number of ways: the wife was dead, or had run away, or was living adulterously. Any other meaning was self-contradictory. In Western wisdom, however, something completely different is usually meant. For instance, on a recent television drama (TV is perfect for discerning dominant and widespread values; after all, that is what sells), a newly divorced couple were talking and the ex-wife said, rather mawkishly, "I still love you" to her former husband. Neither person had run away, or died (obviously), or was living adulterously. The storyline was that the woman had decided she couldn't "get on with her career" by being married to this particular guy, who was quite understanding and had therefore agreed to the divorce. For the Old Testament husband and wife, "loving" meant having one's spouse in the home, caring for that person, and working together toward a common direction: toward the Lord. It meant putting up with the other's idiosyncrasies and even struggling with jealousies (think of Abraham's domestic life!). This kind of loving finds its ultimate form in the New Testament word *agape*.

In the New Testament, **agape** *is love that creates value in the beloved.*

Love is always about values. The loves of family, friendship, and sex are all loves that respond to values—good looks, fine character, familiarity, emotional support, a sense of belonging—that are perceived in the object of the love. The noun *agape* reverses all that. It refers to a radical kind of love that does not depend on the beloved's value but actually creates value in the object of love. There is an inkling of this power in all loving, of course, but in *agape* it is the dominant characteristic, and as far as we know, the word is unique to the Bible in its day. So God commends His *agape* to us for no value that we have of our own, but while we were yet sinners, Christ valued us as beings for whom he had made an infinite sacrifice.

Correcting a pseudo-christian notion of love. We are not quite done with the word love yet, for the influence of today's world is not yet exhausted. There is a supposedly christian understanding of *agape* that acknowledges an "unconditional" determination to care for us but then imports a romantic element into it. This has a serious deficiency from the christian standpoint, for, as noted, romantic love today has no moral constraints beyond its own demands. The result is a logic which says that if *agape* makes no conditions—is "unconditional"—then it has no rules but simply responds always lovingly to the situational needs of the loved one. In this it is implied that christian love not only does not condemn but also does not make moral judgements or rules at all. And for not a few Christians, this has meant that God doesn't really care what we do because He loves us "unconditionally." We can follow our own desires, do what we want, regardless. Such a conclusion about love is only possible when it is seen apart from "covenant," which of course does have judgments and rules.

When *agape* is bestowed upon those outside the covenant, it seeks to draw them into it. And when that is seen as a way of acting so as to set a value on people and then treat them accordingly, and when it goes on to urge them to act according to the value set on them, then clearly love is no longer indifferent. It is going to think and act according to the Law of the Lord.

Yes, our Lord said, "Do not judge, or you too will be judged." But that does not prevent him from exhorting us to identify false prophets and reject them. Nor does it prevent Peter from saying to Ananias, "You have lied to the Holy Spirit." Neither does it stop Stephen from saying to the Sanhedrin, "You always resist the Holy Spirit!" *Agape* has standards and applies them. But as human beings, we are not to pass judgments on people as God applies them, such as judging their motives and thoughts and apportioning blame and penalties upon their inner moral character (1 Corinthians 4:5). Nor may we as private persons pass judgment on what others may do to us personally, or carry out such penalties as an offense against societal laws may require.

Agape is "unconditional," therefore, not because it does not care about wrongdoing but because it bears the impact of what is wrong with people without encouraging it. Some years ago, a Christian couple had a young woman living with them who was continually getting into trouble outside the home. After some months in their care, she said to them, "When people have found out what I'm like, they have either taken advantage of me or thrown me out. You are so strict, but you don't take advantage of me or throw me out." *Agape* means keeping close to the sinner without supporting the sin. In practice, this involves a special kind of continual faith in God, made possible because underlying it is a special kind of forgiveness, which the recipient cannot take for granted because it is based on the fact that on the Cross Jesus Christ has borne the judgment of God on the sin of this world. This is quite peculiarly Christian, and it is the archetype for all christian loving. We love because God first loved us. This is love: not that we loved God, but that he loved us and sent His Son as an atoning sacrifice for our sins. All of this is contained and implied in the one word *agape*. It is able to carry this weight of meaning because it draws on that total understanding of life dominated by the idea of covenant, which the New Testament writers had absorbed, mostly unconsciously, in their upbringing. Within this wisdom, it was then given new dimensions in the Cross.

"Justice" is another common word that means different things to different people.

Another common and basic keyword which has unexpected twists that will make a difference to our thinking, especially in politics, is the word "justice." We certainly hear enough about it! It is one of the great cheer-words of our age, along with "freedom" and "equality." It is such a common word that if you asked most people what we mean by "justice," they would probably reply, "Isn't that obvious!" If pressed, they might go so far as to say, "Everyone getting a fair share" or, "It's about fairness in the way everyone is treated."

If, however, we start asking what a fair share is, or what fairness is, or who we should be fair to, the discussion soon gets quite complicated. (Here we are back at our need to ask basic questions of things alongside Scripture.) Take the workplace. Should a woman holding the same job and seniority as her male counterpart receive the same wages as that man? If she works harder, should she get a bigger share? What if she does not work as hard but takes bigger risks? Or, suppose some relatively easy work is tremendously wealth-producing? What if people work hard and well but are paid menial wages? How about when people make mistakes but the mistakes help others to get on materially? Suppose workers fall sick? It is difficult to know what a fair share ought to be in such situations, and different persons will give different answers. Other problems arise with how work should be rewarded. Beyond a certain point, the wealth that can be fairly accumulated by work takes on a special quality of power. A person with wealth to spare has a special advantage over someone who has not, and this easily leads to exploitation and abuse of the latter by the former. Anti-monopoly laws try to prevent this. Yet how fair is it to penalize people who have been specially successful?

The question of crime and punishment complicates the subject. It may seem feasible to make a thief return what he has stolen, either in cash or in kind, but what if the theft is of something with little intrinsic but enormous sentimental value? Many years ago in England, a heart-rending appeal went out for the return of a stolen cassette tape, the only recording of the voice of a deceased father. It brought up the question of what do we do about the innocent dependents of a victim. Murder and rape raise further problems, for there is clearly no way of compensating the victims. Most people have a gut feeling that such wrongdoers should not only be punished but also forced to make some sort of restitution. Others would say that this is only a thinly disguised desire for revenge, and that surely all we should want to do is to teach the wrongdoer not to do it again and stop him from having the chance meanwhile. And then there is the question of what to do when criminal justice systems under the sway of behavioral psychologies contend that the criminals are also victims.

> **In the Old Testament, "justice" carried the idea of "rescue."**

The Bible's wisdom gives us clues even for complex contemporary areas like these. Two basic notions of the word "justice" are found in the Old Testament. One is a root we met in the previous chapter, *sh-ph-t*, which is the more legal term. As with the words we looked at in that chapter, the use of "justice" in Scripture most of the time is normal enough to us. But some slightly strange biblical usages may give us a much needed different slant. For instance, our words "judge" and "judgment," and even "justice," have a somewhat grim atmosphere about them today. When we sing or say "He shall come again in glory to be our Judge," it doesn't sound much like something to look forward to! This is because we look at the words largely from the point of view of the guilty party. The Old Testament writers, however, tended to see them from the point of view of the innocent. So one of their phrases, "The LORD judge," has a meaning rather like the cry today, "All I want is justice!"

Shaphat gave rise to many passages that carry the idea of vindication (Psalm 10:18; 26:1; 43:1; Proverbs 29:14; Isaiah 11:4; Jeremiah 5:28). This led to the idea of being vindicated by being rescued (2 Samuel 18:19, 31). It also gave rise to the use of the noun *mishpat* for "justice," which is sometimes almost equivalent to our word "rights," for example in Deuteronomy 18:3. We find in Scripture, therefore, an ideal of justice that is certainly impartial, but not in some abstract way, indifferent to the condition of the people involved. It seldom even denotes the specialized concepts of "fair play" and "legal equity" with which the term "justice" is often associated in our day. *It is chiefly aimed at supporting and rescuing the weak.* After all, the powerful are generally able to secure their share of the cake. So for the Bible, justice meant that the helpless could get a share as well, and who else could see to that but the powerful (Psalm 72:4, 12, 14). As a result, passages appear in which "justice" is almost an equivalent for "salvation." The Book of "Judges" (*shaphat*), for instance, is about leaders in Israel who delivered the people from defeat and conquest.

It was also about being rightly related to a source of authority, either a person or a law.

The second root for "justice" is *ts-d-q*. This is about the meaning of justice as applied to the idea of a "just person" (so commonly translated by the KJV). But the Old Testament has a subtly different way of using it. When we today talk about someone being "just," or "straight," with us, it is a reference to character. We mean that there is a consistency and fairness about the person's habits of thought and action, their general attitude and behavior. Now the idea of "character" is certainly found in *ts-d-q*, but the Old Testament words *tsadaq, tsedeq,* and *tsaddiyq* are more relationship-words, and in a very special way. They are about a person's relationship to a certain standard, normally a standard of law, whether governmental or moral. For instance, in Old Testament times one could speak of weights and measures used for buying and selling as "just" (if honest) or "unjust" (if dishonest; Deuteronomy 25:13–16; KJV). If they were "just," they had a proper relationship to the standard measure.

Isaiah helps us, in 5:23, to see this when he condemns a corrupt administration of the law by denouncing those who "justify the wicked for reward [a bribe], and take away the righteousness of the righteous from him!" In our present-day sense of the word "righteousness," this could not be done except by enticing someone into wrongdoing, and that of course is not done in a court of law. Isaiah's accusation is that a bad law, or a maladministration of law, has caused an innocent person to be condemned as guilty; that is, as no longer righteous because no longer in right relationship to, on the right side of, the law.

This idea is vital to the New Testament practice of referring to our salvation in Christ as "justification." To be "justified" or "made righteous" by God's grace is not in the first instance to change a person's character *but to alter a person's relationship to the Law of God*. It is basically a change of status: "in Christ" we are placed "on the right side of" the Law. So it is possible for a sinner, even a criminal, to be "just" or "righteous" in relationship to God's Holy Law, and so be accepted by Him. This would be immoral if it were not for the fact that God Himself paid our debt to the Law in the death of His Son, Jesus Christ. So instead of having to become upright in character *before* we can be accepted by God, God accepts us as "right"—places us on the right side of His Law—in belonging to His Son. On that basis God then sets about making us upright in character. This is all too often just the reverse of how we think about it. Nevertheless, though it may seem strange to us today, it fits perfectly with biblical wisdom. Incidentally, this may help us understand a paradox in Scripture in which people can be declared righteous even when their characters are not all that special. Think for a moment of Noah and Lot, both of whom the Bible calls righteous, yet both went on benders after their ordeals were over! Like ourselves, their weaknesses and imperfections are apparent, but, also like ourselves, the Judge of the whole universe had declared them to be "on the right side of" His Law.

Under normal conditions, a "just man" in law should be "law abiding" as well. But things are not always proper and normal. In most of the first three centuries of the Church's life, it was illegal to be a Christian in the Roman Empire. Christians then were, in the Bible sense, "just" before God but not "just" in the eyes of Roman law.

> **"Righteousness" (being just) also carries the idea of "rescue."**

There is yet another quirk about the Bible's use of these words for justice (if we pursued this line of study at any length we would expect something like it). Surrounding the word *sh-ph-t*, we saw the general idea of rescuing the weak or oppressed, who might otherwise be unable to get "fair" treatment. This meant that it could bear the general notion of "deliverance" in its meaning. A similar idea is found with *ts-d-q*.

In Scripture, a righteous judge was one whose mode of passing judgment protected the interests of the innocent weak against the strong. Insofar as the word "righteous," then, was used to describe character, it was quite naturally associated with mercy. The psalmist points out that "the righteous showeth mercy" (Psalm 37:21; KJV), and the proverb "the righteous care about justice for the poor" agrees (Proverb 29:7). The finest exposition of this idea is found in the Book of Job. Eliphaz accuses Job of exploitative use of his authority in chapter 22. In chapter 29, Job rebuts this charge (from verse 7 onwards): the help that he gave the helpless stems directly from his position as a magistrate "in the gate," as the Old Testament phrase put it.

By our Lord's time, "righteousness" had become a synonym for giving alms to the poor, similar to how we today would show mercy to the poor. An interesting illustration of this occurs in Matthew 6:1, where there are two versions of the Greek text. One version would be literally translated as "give your alms," the other as "do your righteousness." It doesn't matter which because, as the context shows, they were synonymous. (Maybe our idea of righteousness as a rather unattractive quality comes from its association with the Pharisees in the Gospels.) So the words for "righteousness" and "justice" in Scripture carry within them the associated ideas of rescue and mercy—to use a larger Bible term, redemption. Because of this strong sense of rescue and mercy, when justice or righteousness are used about God, they are continually associated with salvation. In Isaiah 62:1, the Lord says he will not rest "till [Zion's] righteousness shines out like the dawn, her salvation like a blazing torch," and the psalmist says that he waits for God's salvation and the word of His righteousness (Psalm 119:123). It is true that in this there is also the idea of God keeping His covenant. But this is so continually connected with salvation that the two ideas go in parallel and cannot be separated. For instance, when we read in the New Testament that Jesus, the righteous (just) one, came to save sinners, and that he is faithful and just to forgive us our sins, and that God is just and the justifier of them that believe in Jesus, we should hardly be surprised.

Many texts take on a new slant with this understanding of the words. On occasions when the words "just" or "righteous" appear in the New Testament, it is worth re-reading them as "mercifully righteous" or "mercifully just." For instance, when Joseph learned of Mary's pregnancy (Matthew 1:19), he considered breaking the engagement *quietly* because he was a just (righteous; KJV) person. As it stands, it should sound a little odd to English readers. It does not mean that Joseph was divorcing her because he was a just man, and then, for reasons not explicitly stated (say, being also kind, he felt sorry for her; hardly that he believed her innocent!), he wanted to keep the matter quiet. It would be taken for granted that the arrangement was at an end, for that would be more a matter of inviolable custom than justice. No, it means that because he was righteous he mercifully wanted to spare her unnecessary publicity with its attendant disgrace.

The flavor of the Bible's words must penetrate our societies.

The words we have been trying out in this chapter are common and basic in the life of any community. We could examine many others in the same way—peace, hope, work, life, faith, honor, and suchlike—and find similar subtle differences between biblical wisdom and Western wisdom. These differences would not be obvious in the large majority of occurrences but would show up in unexpected usages or contexts. In many of these differences, some characteristic biblical ideas would stick out and keep recurring. One would be the importance of moral responsibility, especially within a covenant. Another would be the idea of rescue or salvation. A third would be the notion of personal relationship.

These ideas flavor the Bible's way of thinking and reasoning not just about religious and devotional life but about secular life too, just as individual freedom, personal identity, equality, liberty, and progress flavor ours. They are the taste of a special kind of wisdom, the wisdom of a personal, morally demanding, saving God.

~20~

Journeying Deeper into the Process

The world pooh-poohs the wisdom of a personal, morally demanding, saving God. Nevertheless, despite the general resistance to God's wisdom, we must find ways to apply this special understanding of life to its ills. And we must find ways today. We cannot put off doing anything until some imaginary date in the future when there may be more Christians or more sophistication in our approaches. Or more openness. We cannot give the sick child of culture over to death simply because she refuses to take the pills that taste bad in her mouth. We may not have sophisticated medicine for her yet, but what cures we have, if they are cures, must be articulated and applied whenever and wherever possible. And in the process, we must develop better ones as we go along.

In this chapter we will take some contemporary issues and work them up by pulling together ideas from previous chapters. We are unlikely to find decisive answers at this stage, but we should be able to find new avenues of approach, and this should help us immensely in the long haul. In this process also, we should see ways in which ideas that are floating about in the world generally may find a home in some consistent policies. In a world that has largely run out of convincing ideas for its social and political problems, that in itself could be a blessing.

God's wisdom can instruct our educational systems.

In Britain and America, widespread dissatisfaction with the present educational system is seen by many as the worst ill. Class discipline is under stress, functional illiteracy seems to be increasing, and children emerge from their schools cynical and unreflective. Even training in the natural sciences, so important for national prosperity today, can seem to be less than satisfactory for many employers, who often feel the need to re-educate their job applicants. And in areas like computer technology, some employers are suggesting that the present secondary education is often counterproductive, since students come into the workforce thinking that they know computers when in fact computer activity in the real world is different again. Teachers themselves are suffering serious loss of morale that shows itself in a decline in applicants for teacher training and increased numbers seeking early retirement. School systems can get caught so much in a negative downward spiral that any hope of breaking the fall has been replaced with teacher preoccupation with pay and conditions. Can biblical wisdom offer any practical comment on such situations?

Learning about one's God is to discover what governs one's conscience in secular life.

One thing inevitably comes to mind: the fear of the Lord is the foundation principle of wisdom. Thus education in the Bible had as its core subject: directing children to understand their God. Unfortunately we today have equated "understanding God" with religious instruction only, the narrow sense of what goes on in our churches, or when teaching theological, devotional, and moral material. But as far as the Bible is concerned, the fear of the Lord must not be confined to purely religious matters (in our common sense of the word). As we have noted throughout this book, the fear of the Lord relates to matters that we hardly even count "spiritual." So, for example, it is obvious from the Book of Proverbs, which was among other things an educational manual for instructing a king's son, that the fear of the Lord is foundational also for every matter of secular life. This is also true of the basic teaching literature in the Law of Moses and the prophets.

When the People of God in the Old Testament made assertions about the Lord their God, which they did continually, they often used that "secular" word *elohim* for "God" (chapter 3). This is because for them the word "god" in any religious context meant that which bore ultimate power and authority *also in the secular life of the community*. A "god" was whatever gave that life its meaning, its values, its purpose, and its sense of consistency, and this controlled the way things were done in that life. A biblical secular education, then, would major on encouraging children to reflect on questions like: "What is man?" "How did we come into being?" "What is the most important thing in life?" "What is our life?" "What makes us think and feel the way we do?" "Why is Israel different from all other peoples?" "What is wrong with us?" "What are we in the world for?" And so on. Christians, then, ought to plead that whatever religious convictions people may have whereby they answer ultimate questions, children ought to be taught to ask and reflect on such questions, for it will help them understand why their cultures have turned out the way they have.

Some people will complain that this is too abstract, too demanding for children. But the fact is that children naturally ask these questions, and only too often their elders and betters put them off, often because they are not used to facing them themselves. Yet the prophet Haggai stresses the need for people to "consider" (KJV), to "give careful thought to" (NIV), their lives. This favorite phrase of his means to "apply your heart," which implies more than merely "think about" it. It means "in the very core of your being, face up to life." Unless that childish instinct for facing up to radical questions is fostered, adult life becomes unreflective and undiscriminating. Children naturally want to know about ultimate questions—unless we educate them not to.

A biblical teaching method is centered on asking and raising ultimate questions.

Naturally Christians will want to give christian answers to such questions in a christian educational program. And, again, the style of instruction referred to in Scripture gives us hints. For instance, one of its remarkable features is the way God often deals with people: by facing them continually with questions. After the Fall, God's first approach to Adam was not with accusation but with questioning. So, too, in the story of Abel and Cain and God's approach to the latter. And when everyone had exhausted their theological resources against Job's challenge, the Lord deluges Job with what? Answers? No, with questions. Nearly a hundred of them! In Deuteronomy, an account of the Passover Feast includes instruction to the children as to its meaning, and at the heart of it is a dialogue in which the eldest son asks "What is the meaning of this?" and receives a reply. The ceremony is constructed so as to make one cry out for explanation. It is no different in the New Testament. Jesus' experience as a boy in the Temple is not described in Luke's Gospel as a process of receiving instruction and being tested on it but of hearing, questioning, and answering questions. And our Lord's way of using parables as the basis for questioning in response to the queries of others is also illuminating.

Only too often our style of instruction, even overtly religious instruction, scratches where it does not itch. Because it is not question-orientated, the teaching skills required for stimulating questioning about the serious things of life are neglected, the children do not expect to be puzzled, and they react with impatience rather than with persistent inquiry.

There are teachers, certainly, who wholeheartedly subscribe to this approach, but then only too often there is a tendency among them to allow the student's *own* questions to set the agenda of learning. The biblical method was clearly more subtle than that. The questions had particular aims in mind, as can be seen when each of the foregoing examples are examined. Educationally speaking, the biblical method stimulated questions that proceeded naturally in the direction of a particular curriculum. In that process, the parable, for instance, posing as a kind of riddle to which there could be only one sort of answer, had a crucial place.

This contrasts painfully with mainstream educational policy today. This is surely in strong and painful contrast with the mainstream of educational policy today. Under pressure of economic difficulty, a powerful tendency exists to shift emphasis from the humanities (where the possibility of facing the radical questions of meaning and value is much greater) to the natural sciences (which offer expectations of more efficient production). The prophet Haggai calls for a complete reversal of policy. "Do you have inflation and a stagnant economy?" he asks. "Then stop and consider... consider... consider..." (Haggai 1:5–7; 2:15–18; KJV). Give careful thought to it, in the context of Ultimate Reality. (A related study might be conducted by some enterprising educators regarding how the entire Western educational system is driven by an economic determinism that influences even the way Christians run their schools and develop curriculum.)

Substantial evidence indicates that one of the most serious problems among today's schoolchildren and students is a sense of hopelessness and meaninglessness, a loss of direction, and a loss of purpose. Goals important to their parents are not satisfying them. They are not ultimate enough in the face of possible global annihilation, for instance, and the children know it instinctively. Parents who had to struggle to get where they are tend to regard such attitudes as luxuries indulged in by a spoiled and ungrateful generation that has too much leisure for its own good. There is some justification for this view, but the fact remains that children and students need to know what life is about in order to live effectively as adults when the issues of sheer survival are settled. Nothing will excuse our inability to supply a training to meet that need.

A christian wisdom also affects curriculum and classroom methodology. Such a framework of thought also affects the rest of the curriculum. Many evangelicals are sensitive to the effects of a nonchristian way of thinking, for instance, when it comes to teaching evolution in biology, and they often protest vocally and insistently. In practice, however, their approach has been quite limited in results. Seldom is any distinction made between the use of the evolutionary theory, on the one hand, as a provisional framework of thought whereby scientific thinking and investigation can proceed at all and, on the other hand, its use as a philosophy of life (chapter 16); that is, as an attempt to answer those fundamental and all-embracing questions about life that were noted above. Further, it is often not realized that every subject in the curriculum, without exception, is ultimately affected in its form by the kind of mindset that is brought to it and that the resultant form in turn appears to validate the mindset. Geography as a school subject may serve as an example.

Geography is a case in point. For most people geography is, well, geography. But several revolutions in teaching methods the past several decades have changed classroom approaches to geography. Most of us have been taught in terms of one of these revolutions, and it may not have occurred to us how different they are. My[JP] memory of geography is in terms of brightly colored maps and lists of towns, rivers, mountains, and imports and exports. But younger people have learned it somewhat differently, such as in terms of doing experiments or fieldwork. Or they might look into where people have congregated and what sort of culture they have developed, or how topography affects what people do. Other students find themselves involved in a stringent program of statistical analysis in which the interaction between various factors in any geographical situation is carefully quantified. These students work as much with graphs and tables as with maps and lists. Such different styles of teaching are often fierce rivals for the allegiance of the educational profession. But the point here is that behind the differing styles lie different notions of what geography is about and, indeed, what life is about.

Christian educators, aware of the many-dimensioned wisdom of God in creation, will want to insist that these are not rivals but styles that need to be integrated. At the same time, this integration must not be a potpourri. Different approaches cannot necessarily be thrown together indiscriminately as if they all had the same function and the same kind of value. You cannot bake a cake as if it did not matter how many eggs are used and how little flour.

Modal thinking can help us greatly here. A Christian must believe that the Ultimate Reality which underlies the existence of our earth and its peoples is a Person. This means that there will be a certain scale of meaning and value in the Christian's mind, so that in the educational mixture the subject could never be dominated, for instance, by statistics or economics. But neither would these aspects be neglected. They would be understood to contribute to the subject by giving insight into the conditions under which people have to fashion their particular way of life in these aspects, which, therefore, would be given due weight and not dismissed as of marginal importance. The framework of dimensional plurality offered in modal theory serves us well here. Using the visual aid of modal analysis, a teacher could do, albeit in a more complex manner, the same sort of analysis performed in a simple way on the wedding ring (chapter 13). As far as the big picture, one would ask basic questions about "education," such as what is it, what is its purpose, how does knowledge from all the aspects inform it? And so on. Think again of the island approach, in which wisdom from many different aspects (approaches) of the subject are added up to make a fuller picture. As far as features within the big picture, a teacher could use modal theory as an aid in answering basic questions about, say, curriculum.

An educational style called "whole language learning" has classroom applications that have possibilities in this direction. The basis of numerous educational programs, this style presents many aspects of a subject. It has become especially beneficial in the early grades where one teacher is responsible for all the subjects, and it has been well liked by teachers who want different ways ahead. Take the unit "Egypt" for instance. History, of course, comes readily to mind as an obvious aspect. But with modal thinking, other possibilities immediately arise. Maths can be taught using the pyramids (triangles, geometry). Social and religious customs are easily taught from the mummies and the temples. The pharaohs can be sources for reports on politics and government. The desert and the Nile supply facts and information for reports on the land itself and the ecology. Further, the subject of English could easily be tied in to the stories the children write. Because this educational style tends to excite the students to research and creativity, it is a style in which the children are more apt to become responsible for their own learning, rather than just sitting back and saying, "Teach me." Rather than just being a dispenser of facts and data which are then merely tested, the teacher acts more like a coach helping the children to gain insight.

Teachers using this style say that a good thematic unit transforms the entire atmosphere of classroom. One teacher told me[CS] that the Rain Forest unit was his favorite because it transforms the classroom into a miniature rain forest, with leafy tree branches and hanging vines, pictures of exotic birds and weird bugs, and cutouts of endangered animals and jungle scenes. Thus even the aesthetic aspect comes into the picture. "The children get excited," the teacher said. "They're not just studying Egypt, or a rain forest, or a pueblo; not just maths or geography or English. They're studying consistent to the way life is, as a whole with many aspects, and in that way life opens up to them." This approach may be used in other settings. For instance, a home-schooling mom regularly starts every unit with what she calls a "Blitz," which she describes as a simple brainstorming session where her children try to come up with as many concrete examples of modal (aspect) analogies for the given topic. She has been doing this for a number of years, and her children have a good grasp of the unity and diversity of God's creation, which will equip them with a powerful wisdom to discern and resist the reductionist philosophies and practices of Western society as they enter mainstream life.

It brings students back to the creation of God and the God of creation.

In addition to this, the Christian teacher is also concerned with instilling into children an attitude towards the earth and its peoples that would include awe, wonder, respect, and a sense that the world is not a closed system: its geography can actually be altered by a people in terms of the values that determine that people's lifestyle. This would lead to considering that this is a spoiled planet. It is then that the geography teacher would be leading students to face those radical questions, which eventually demand answers of a religious kind. How the school offers answers to the questions posed at this point will depend on what sort of school it is.

There are, of course, teachers that teach geography in roughly this way. They are not all that common, however. Those that do are frequently teaching in schools where the general trend of the educational program does not support such a style. And it is rare to find a teacher who is aware that such an approach has the support of a christian framework of thought. Some who are not Christians, however, would indignantly repudiate the idea.

God's wisdom can also instruct politics and government.

In chapters 16 and 17, we looked at the way religious doctrines working through a biblical wisdom will affect our thinking about political issues. Here we want to draw several other threads through that thinking and build up a fuller christian understanding of politics and government.

Set alongside the way Scripture speaks of it, a study of government as it functions in the world at large enables us to characterize it fairly clearly. The two basic elements required for a government to function as such are: 1) law backed by 2) force. Where there is no law there is anarchy, in which the strongest have the rest at their mercy. Where law is not sanctioned by force it is either ineffective or unnecessary. The combination of these two factors is clearly spelled out in Romans 13, in which government is understood to exist for the purpose of restraining and penalizing evil, in the last resort by wielding the sword.

A number of implications immediately arise from this. For instance, it means that Christians cannot acknowledge any aspiration to political power which assumes that it can succeed by appealing to people's better nature! It also makes Christians resist modes of government that attempt to control people through economic manipulation. Further, Christians cannot recognize a government as valid which cannot draw upon enough resources to enforce its laws, however acceptable those laws might be. Thus there is a godly wisdom at work in the biblical view of government that takes the facts of our material life seriously: it takes into account the fact of human sin and recognizes the necessary use of law enforcement when necessary.

All government is under law and subject to criticism.

Another implication of a biblical view of government is that its function is not to change the spiritual and moral problems of a city or nation. It is about keeping law and order so that the citizens can get on with their lives. This does not mean that Christians will support the status quo uncritically, but they will acknowledge that the juridical aspect does not function in the way that the religious and ethical-moral aspects do. Again, its purpose is about keeping law and order, not about changing hearts. Further, the Christian sees those who wield governmental power as subject to its laws like everyone else. This is clearly in opposition to totalitarian kinds of government, and it has to be taken into account when certain basic principles of law are suspended indefinitely for the sake of "national interest" or "national security." It also means that an officer of government, even a sovereign, can be indited as a lawbreaker.

It was on such grounds that Charles I of England was condemned for treason by due process of law in Parliament and executed in 1649. Charles' own view of the divine right of kings made it impossible for him to recognize such a court as valid. He could not see himself as responsible to any human law system, though he sincerely felt himself responsible to God. A not too distant American example would be President Nixon's resignation under mounting pressure that he had placed himself above the law. An even more recent example was the impeachment process of President Clinton, which, incidentally, showed how many people elevated the economic aspect above the moral one (see Appendix 1)—if the many polls at the time were to be believed. Indeed, because the love of the gods of silver and gold is so prevalent in America, if the national economy had not been so strong that year, it is probable that many of those same people would have found Clinton's moral behavior a handy excuse to support the impeachment process instead of to decry it.

The issue of sovereignty depends on assumptions about ultimate authority.

People tend to equate sovereignty with government, but these are not the same. Sovereignty is about the authority on which a government operates. In most modern forms of government in the West, the principles of "the sovereignty of the people" generally lies at the bottom, although often concealed. At any rate, sovereignty is always expressed somewhere in the whole structure of national law. In governments that carry the notion of a divine kingship (whether of the Charles Stuart version or of the ancient Middle East), no point of reference exists beyond the king himself, even though he may have an instructed conscience. Thus any control over him would need to rest in a balance of power within his kingdom. Modern democracies usually have a written Constitution, and that, for practical purposes, indicates where sovereignty lies. In the United States that sovereignty is expressed as certain ideals and principles, which govern and justify government. They are most famously expressed in the words:

We hold these truths to be self-evident, that all
men are created equal, that they are endowed
by their Creator with certain inalienable Rights,
that among these are Life, Liberty, and the pursuit
of Happiness . . . . That whenever any Form of
Government becomes destructive of these ends, it
is the right of the people to alter or abolish it...

The key in this statement is the word "self-evident." There can be no authority beyond a self-evident principle. It justifies and authorizes itself. Note that "the people" are not authorized to alter such a principle but to act in accordance with it. If the government, however, ever becomes "destructive of these ends," then "the people" may alter something, or abolish it: the government. These "truths," then, are the ultimate authority (what the Old Testament would call the "the gods") of U.S. law. This is what makes it the powerful medicine that it is, because it follows that if the U.S. government fails to guarantee these "truths," a revolution is not only justifiable but also in a sense mandatory.

The U.K. does not have a formal, written Constitution; it is more a body of law, precedent, and custom. The hereditary monarchy is the symbol and bearer of sovereignty. The monarch, however, is not ultimately the sovereign authority of the nation. The British monarch has a status roughly equivalent to the U.S. Constitution. Further, something else stands above that as equivalent to the self-evident truths in the States. It may seem difficult to believe it today, but that "something else" is the Bible. The ultimate sovereignty of the U.K. is vested in the Bible. At every coronation service the new monarch is solemnly presented with a Bible with the words, "These are the lively oracles of God..." The Coronation Oath likewise declares the intention to uphold the laws of God.

A biblical vision distributes governmental authority and makes laws according to moral standards.

Views of government derived from a biblical vision will tend to produce constitutions that have one particular family likeness: the exercise of authority in the state becomes distributed among different institutions; whether between priest, king, or prophet-counselor (as in ancient Israel), or in elected parliaments with an independent judiciary and civil administration (as in the U.K.), or among "estates" (as in Scotland's history), or among legislative, executive, and judicial branches (as in the U.S.). In a biblical vision, therefore, governmental structures will always exist to prevent any arm of government from exercising unlimited control. Since force is an essential resource of government, this tends to be specially reflected in the way the armed forces are accountable.

When we were considering the relationship between law and moral standards (chapter 8), certain principles stood out quite clearly. For instance, biblical politics, though it is about compromise of a kind, is not concerned to legislate for the lowest common denominator of a people's desires. For the Christian, lawmaking will involve compromise, certainly, but, using the example of Mosaic Law in the Old Testament, it will always think in terms of accommodating the law as nearly to the moral standard for social behavior as possible. Thus it is not demagogic, simply legislating for the majority's wishes.

What about the government as educator?

The state is not understood in Scripture to be an educative institution. Education, as the Christian sees it, is necessarily not inculcated by the use of force except insofar as it may relate to behavior against lawful authority. Christian wisdom, however, always takes into account that legislation tends to have an educative effect on people, at least in our present social climate. One significant problem here is seen at the present time and has special relevance to the issues of divorce, abortion, and homosexuality. Quite simply, idolatrous views of governmental law have led people to think that what has been made legal is therefore also morally allowable. A striking illustration of this was the immediate change in the attitude of many Americans toward abortion after the *Roe v. Wade* decision by the Supreme Court (1973). Without any higher authority that the Court, Americans let the Court "legislate" their morality for them, and abortion suddenly became okay. In Old Testament terms, the Supreme Court had the status of a "god" over their thinking in this area.

This is a version of a confusion that constantly bedevils mankind. Even Jesus faced it in the leaders of Judaism in his day. It is the confusion between morality, which is chiefly concerned with the highest that people ought to be, and legislation, which is chiefly concerned with the minimum that people must be restrained from doing. Morality is about personal character and motivation; legislation deals with the problems of social disorder. The Jews of Jesus' day had confused the two functions, as people today tend to do, and thought of morality as functioning like legality. That is, they thought of morality as concentrating on actions and what may or must be forbidden. Citizens of this age tend to think of morality as defined by legislation, thinking that what is not illegal is therefore not immoral. Christians have to be realistic about this, and they naturally enough wish to resist any relaxation of good laws, but they should be seeking ways in which this confusion may be overcome.

What about government and economics?

One of the knottiest problems today is the increasing tendency of government to be involved in controlling national economics. Biblical wisdom has its own approach to this. Economics, like art or social relationships, is an aspect of life that has its own laws of operation under God. Governmental attempts to ignore, violate, or manipulate such laws can only be disastrous. For example, legislation that attempts to fix prices arbitrarily or to manipulate the value of coinage is as useless in the long run as legislating about artistic styles—as any free-market economist can prove to you. (One special problem here is that once government embarks on a course of intervention, it becomes "hooked" into it so that even the refusal to intervene then becomes a kind of intervention. This is true not only for economics but also for any area in which the government focuses its legislative prowess.)

Nevertheless, biblical legislation had an economic character about it. It has been pointed out that the jubilee system in the Old Testament, whereby every family regained its landed inheritance, is a clear witness to the fallen character of a "free" market and the failure of any economics built upon it. Unregulated, a free market eventually moves towards monopolies (this has been occurring more and more through massive, global corporate mergers since the 1980s). The economic power of monopolies is as threatening to human well-being as uncontrolled political power. An early account of a monopoly and its effect is given in Genesis. When Pharaoh had secured a monopoly of food, the people said, "Buy us and our land in exchange for food, and we with our land will be in bondage to Pharaoh" (Genesis 47:19).

Probably Psalm 73 has as clear a vision as anywhere in Scripture of the purpose of government as securing the conditions needed for *shalom* (peace). If, as is expressed there, the ingredients of this *shalom* are prosperity, social order, and national security, then certain curbs on economic freedom will be as necessary as on any other kind of freedom. In addition to this we must acknowledge that biblical law was not merely restrictive but also redemptive. Its provisions for the poor, especially in the Jubilee, actually restored the poor to a foothold in the welfare of the community. The great difference between that system and today's welfare programs is that it did not destroy the independence and sense of responsibility of those who were rescued by it. It was not a dole or a system of compulsory public work to qualify for the benefits.

It is of course impossible to develop a thoroughgoing educational or political theory in these pages. In any case, developing such sophisticated theories is work for minds trained to do so in those fields. But it may hint at what is possible, and it may indicate a way in which we may all as Christians discuss the educational and political issues of our day with reasonable intelligence and imagination.

This kind of wisdom also has an evangelistic value. The basic ideas of the Bible in this respect are not only for the intelligentsia, and they do not count only for politics and education either. Much earlier in the book, in chapter 4, we noted that the secular ideas of Scripture can work in today's complex age because they share the same basic logic as the Gospel, which is for all peoples at all times. Because this framework of thought is the backdrop to the kinds of thinking and analysis we are doing here, contemporary issues when presented within this milieu lend themselves naturally to the Gospel.

Some time ago I[JP] gave a ride to a truck driver who had left his load in London and wanted to get home for a few hours. Inevitably we got talking about the state the world is in, and in particular we got round to the threatened dismantling of the present system of social care. Rather hesitantly I said that in the course of reading some ancient political writings, I had come across some astonishing provisions in, of all places, the Old Testament. He was interested, at first I think from sheer curiosity. But in response to his questions, I found myself referring to this curious redemptive, rescuing quality about biblical law (chapter 19). I'm not sure how it came about, but we then found ourselves talking about redemption through Christ Jesus. This is not an isolated example. And it has meant for me that the old evangelistic idea of maneuvering the conversation to "get in a word for Jesus" now seems slightly ridiculous, for there's no way Jesus can be kept out! It is noticeable in such conversations that Jesus is not merely the Savior of the individual soul. He is also *Lord*, not in an alien, mystical or ceremonial world but in familiar, everyday life, in its politics, its economics, its work, and everything else.

~21~

A Special Case: Art, the Necessary Luxury

A young couple brought their new baby, a boy, home from the hospital. He was their second child; the other was a 4-year-old girl. After the new baby had been home for a couple of weeks, the 4-year-old told her parents that she wanted to see the baby alone.

"Okay," said the mother, "I'll take you to see him."

"No," said the little girl. "I want to see him alone."

The parents looked at one another. They had been warned of this. The older child gets jealous of the attention being paid to the baby and finds a way to strike back.

"I'll take you in to see him," said the father.

"Nooo. I want to see him alone!"

"Well, maybe later," the mother said.

The next day, the mother started to take her daughter to see the baby, but the child pulled back, refusing, saying she would only see the baby alone. This went on for two weeks. Finally one evening, the parents made the momentous decision. They did not tell their daughter, but they would listen closely on the intercom while she was in the room with the baby, and they would be ready to act immediately if necessary.

"Promise you won't come in," the daughter said.

"We promise," said the parents.

The little girl stepped cautiously into the baby's room, looking back at her parents, who watched attentively from the hall. They quietly shut the door and quickly retreated to their bedroom, where they fixed their ears on the intercom. They heard nothing for a few seconds. Then there was the soft noise of their daughter making her way toward the baby in the crib. Then silence. There was a small chair in the baby's room, and the parents heard what they took to be the sound of their daughter moving the chair to the side of the crib. And then silence.

The parents didn't see their daughter sit down in that chair next to the crib. But they did hear her say to the baby, "Tell me about God. I'm forgetting." The artist is like the baby.[1]

In everyday life, is art beside the point?

It may seem as if art is beside the point of both a book like this and the christian life. After all, people often think, art is that highly specialized and ephemeral discipline. Like a satellite orbiting the earth, it's "out there," but so what? It seems to have little, if any, connection with the bread and butter of life. Never mind that the bread and butter come packaged in advertising art. And aesthetic theory? Crumbs, man, now you're really going to make me work for it. Thinking about business, education, and political theories was bad enough!

Keep in mind that this is a book about bringing into obedience to Christ all the aspects of our lives, the social, the economic, the political, the religious, and so on. Just because we live in a time when the aesthetic aspect of our lives gets neglected, this does not mean that it ought to continue to escape the demands of christian discipleship. On a hopeful note, people who have played with the kind of ideas that this chapter presents find the experiences refreshing and pleasing. Even surprising, such as when it is discovered that aesthetics affects quite common things such as the atmosphere of our homes and church services, or that contemporary christian aesthetics often hamstring our efforts at evangelism. So let's see if we may, as Calvin Seerveld has put it, "shake some blessings from our Almighty Father's hand here."

Art is a necessary luxury.

It is difficult to define art. Most of us can recognize it though, at least when it is pointed out to us. It is about meanings and values, not survival or efficient production. It is not propaganda. Nor does it inform or seek to convince. It is essentially a relaxant, a kind of necessary luxury. The artist has had an experience, a vision that is significant enough for her to want to share it. It may be trivial and ephemeral or immense and world-shattering (it's not always easy to tell which). But the artist is not content to describe it to you and outline some technique for you to follow. She wants you to enter the experience yourself. Her method is a complex one, but she has no alternative method. "Stop working," she says first of all. "I'm offering you a moment of relaxation. So stop, look, listen, feel." Here is the enticement of pleasure or the arousal of curiosity, interest. Then she creates a little "world" within the world (the frame of a picture, a stage, a rhythm, an arrangement of colors). It is a world

---

[1] Sean Penn told this story to Charlie Rose on the "The Charlie Rose Show" (PBS-TV). They were talking about acting and the subject had turned to art in general.

in which one can engage in make-believe. (Drama shows this most clearly, but it is present in any art, even in the singing of a tune or the telling of a joke.) Then in that world, she creates the barest outline of a situation, the experience, the vision; just enough clues for you, almost unconsciously, to work out the rest for yourself. (One sees the process clearly in biblical parables. See below.)

This is the special power of art. It comes like the Gibeonite embassy, as if from far away, in disguise. This is why artistic activity does not appear to offer a "clear message." If it does, its cover is blown, its power gone.

Scripture is filled with verbal art forms.

It does not take long to realize that a vast proportion of God's word to us in Scripture is by means of works of art. Its poetry is a case in point, and the Psalms are another obvious illustration, as are the Song of Songs and many other Old Testament passages. An art that may not immediately occur to us as such is storytelling, which is a fundamental art, the basis for drama, opera, ballet, and film. It is to those arts what a tune is to music; you can do without it for a while but not for long. The Bible came to us through a cultural tradition that even to this day has its professionals who address a public that is used to a high standard of artistic skill in the fashioning of stories. It should be no surprise, therefore, that storytelling reaches a high degree of sophistication in Scripture. Examples are many and varied. The parables, not only of our Lord but also of Nathan (2 Samuel 12) and of Jotham (Judges 9), are gold nuggets. The books of Judges, Samuel, and Kings are rich in stories that contribute to longer historical narratives. Gideon's call and victory in Judges 6–8 is a work of art in its own right, and David receiving the news of Absalom's death (2 Samuel 18) is heart-wrenching. The books of Ruth and Jonah are especially captivating in the way their biographies are told.

Hesitancy toward discussing the art of Scripture.

There is also an artistic skill about the Gospels that makes me want to include them in the list, but for various reasons I[JP] am hesitant to see them as works of art. They obviously have their own aesthetic value, and as accounts of the Messiah's ministry told in narrative in a milieu so dedicated to the art of storytelling, this is to be expected. But they seem to me to be so taken up with the task of faithful instruction in the facts of the faith, so theologically committed, that the artistic qualities recede into the background. In my earlier christian life I was extremely hesitant to speak of Scripture in this way at all. To treat revelation as art at all seemed irreverent. When God is calling a sinner from death into life it seemed to me appalling to respond by saying something like, "What a beautiful story!" After all, that is exactly how Ezekiel was treated by his "cultured despisers" (Ezekiel 33:32).

I still believe this to be a real danger. But my general attitude has changed for a number of reasons. In the first place, I had not understood what art is all about. I had thought it was no more than frivolous entertainment. I had not realized that it could be about experiencing the very meaning of life. In the second place, I had not seen what the Scripture is about as much as I do now. I had imagined that it was only about saving two aspects of life: the religious and the moral. The only way in which the Lord applied his Gospel to life, I thought, was through ensuring that I could pray, worship, witness, and behave in a generally loving way. These are, of course, the fundamental and essential aspects. But that's not the whole highway through the Kingdom. Politicians must learn from the politics of Scripture, economists from its economics, scientists from its understanding of the created order, and artists from its art. And they must learn in ways that appreciate how these aspects relate in the whole of life.

A third hesitancy I had was about speaking of Scripture as if it were an ordinary book. It is, after all—emphatically—not just "another" book. And that must never be forgotten. Yet it is a book, or a collection of books. That is, if Scripture were completely unlike all other books, we could not speak of it as a book at all. The uniqueness that marks Scripture off from other literature does not lie particularly in its form but in its authority. When it comes to the ultimacies of life—its ultimate law, truth, cause, value, meaning, purpose, energy, unity, authority, identity; in religious terms, life's true God—then in whatever aspect we are moving the Bible's authority is final, and in this life there is no appeal beyond it. In this respect the Bible shares the characteristics of the One to whom it refers. As Jesus is truly God and truly man, and as the denial of one aspect damages understanding the other, so Scripture is a truly human as well as a truly divine book.

Further, I felt a hesitancy about calling the Bible "superb literature" or "great art" because it sounded condescending, as if I were a reviewer complimenting God on having written a masterpiece. It seems that we are all short of a suitable vocabulary at this point. I do not know how to overcome this problem, except to say that any comments of this kind that I do make nowadays about Scripture are expressions of continual wonder and amazement, not to mention awe, rather than mere commendation of its art.

Art in the Bible is done by individuals but never in isolation.

Certain characteristics of art in Scripture are significant for this present age and can help us immensely in fulfilling our obediences to God in this aspect. One is that as far as the Bible is concerned art is never an isolated, solitary activity. It is inspired by a Triune God who is a community of Persons and who, though He sets the solitary in families, ordains that only in community with others can we normally develop our identities satisfactorily, even as artists. Unfortunately, in many of our churches, the artist is seen as a kind of extra person or accessory, or as someone who ought to get a job. When the churches cop this attitude, the artists experience deep rejection and stop coming around. This "christian" attitude hinders our artists in developing their art, which in turn deprives the churches of much grace. On the other hand, because art is a way in which people communicate (cause something to be shared), we have to abandon the arrogant elitism of the artist who says, in effect, "I'm an artist. I must express what is within me. That is my task. I cannot do more without compromising my art. If you cannot understand me, that's too bad. It's your problem, not mine." Art by Christians will care about communication, understanding, and a sharing of experience. Of course, it will be communication done in ways appropriate to art and not the sort that relates to, say, a preached message, an algebraic equation, or a piece of abstract logic.

Art by Christians has distinct implications. Art by Christians is of course infinitely more exacting than propaganda. In particular, it is not enough for it to be intensely religious. One's view of creation—from stars to bathrooms, from families to parliaments—has to be colored by an awareness that God is active in the whole thing, in every aspect. The artist must also be sensitive to the implications of shape, form, style.[2] Otherwise the art may give the lie to what the artist wishes to say. As some of us used to say in England, "You can't use punk to go with words like, 'Let go, and let God take over.'"

Art also imposes on the artist an awkward conscience. He knows that to regard art as a minnow to catch trout violates his integrity, as well as being silly. And he knows, or should know, that while many insights tend to separate him from other Christians, he is still committed to the same beliefs about God, the same moral disciplines, the same need to share in corporate worship. Art in Scripture also gives some indications of what kind of understanding is appropriate. The parables are probably the most obvious examples. Jesus often talked about "understanding" in relation to his parabolic teaching, and it is clear that he was not simply talking about understanding his vocabulary or being able to enjoy a story. It was much more than that, as the Scribes and Pharisees knew full well!

Art takes us into a "let's pretend" world, where we can make discoveries. As storytelling, a parable works by taking the hearer into a hypothetical world where the

---

[2] Calvin Seerveld's excellent book *A Christian Critique of Art and Literature* will help many readers here.

outward appearances are different but the rules for making the decisions or judgments are the same as in the "real" world. So, you listen to the story of a wounded man lying by the roadside and only one person out of three bothers to look after him. You're surprised at that, and you are drawn into the situation and begin to make relatively unbiased judgments about it because you are not the person directly involved. You don't have to do anything about it in your own "real" world. The storyteller has for a time set you free in your imagination, free not just to understand some abstract idea about life but to enter into a situation and make fearless, cost-free decisions in it, the sort you know you ought to make in "real life" if your heart were not confused by other interests. As a Jew you find yourself admitting the previously unthinkable: a Samaritan can be a neighbor.

Art can initiate people into experiences of life under God.

Storytelling makes clear how all forms of art can take us into a "let's pretend" world without it being a lie. Parables and proverbs are particularly effective in this because they can reach us when our guards are down. Their nature is to allow us to make discoveries that our normal prejudices would make impossible. After all, who wants to be preached at, that the "disgusting Samaritans" can be just as much our neighbors as anyone else? Art, therefore, can be the means whereby the outsiders can, for themselves, taste something of what life under God in Christ is like. They can enter into it precisely because they are not being cornered into a self-commitment, so they do not have to be on their guard. They can be tempted to enter into it because a work of art offers a possible pleasure, and they can feel free to enter it because the artist is simply inviting them to look, listen, whatever. They are not having ideas imposed on them, and they are left free to make the discovery in their own way.

Of course, we still have to decide whether we are going to take on board the discoveries as we return to our real world. When the Jewish authorities heard Jesus' Parable of the Wicked Husbandmen, the Gospel writer tells us that they understood it well enough. They knew that it was about much more than people not paying their rent and killing the landlord's son and getting into big trouble over it. They had been made to feel that they themselves were under judgment. Nevertheless, they rejected the insight that the parable had granted them for a moment and they set about to get rid of Jesus.

It can free us from our hang-ups and enlarge our sympathies.

Not all stories initiate their hearers into crises of decision, however. Stories have different roles. David getting news of Absalom's death, for instance, thrusts us into the switchback of his hopes and anxieties and his final heart-rending grief. We may share almost unbearably. It is a different kind of experience from the Parable of the Wicked Husbandman or the Parable of the Good Samaritan, but the same process is at work. Nathan's compelling story before the throne of David powerfully illustrates what being taken into a world created in our imaginations can do, as we live it out for ourselves for a while. Its power gives us enlarged sympathies and insights, remote from the restrictions and responsibilities of our ordinary life. It is, in fact, liberating, potentially redemptive. We are meant, not necessarily in a trivial or superficial way (though not all art is world-shaking) to be moved by the experience, or to enjoy it, or to be renewed and refreshed by it. But sooner or later we may, and sometimes must, assess for ourselves how we are going to be affected by it.

All this is not only true about arts that use words but also about arts like dance, instrumental music, painting, and sculpture. It is true even of the arts that use the senses of smell and taste, though it would take too long to explain this here.

It involves us, by offering the pleasure of a rest from life's demands and restrictions.

How is it that art has this power to engage our interests? Quite simply, it is most likely the artist's offer of pleasure. It is an invitation to another world, to a kind of daydream, to an escape from the hard realities of life in this fallen world, where our experiences are always tied to an inexorable chain reaction of causes and effects. Art offers us participation in a game and being a spectator at the same time. Like so many other features of our creaturely existence, it is a pleasure that comes because God blessed the creation and the human beings that He had made. Of course, as with our other creaturely features, obvious dangers lurk therein. For instance, we may use the escape as escapism, as an evasion from responsibilities instead of as a resource for meeting them. Amos, for example, rejects outright the art of a culture that does not care about the poor and about injustice:

> *Away with the noise of your songs!*
>   *I will not listen to the music of your harps...*
> *You strum away on your harps like David*
>   *And improvise on musical instruments...*
> *But you do not grieve over the ruin of Joseph.*
>   *Therefore you will be among the first to go into exile...*
> Amos 5:23–6:7

Now Amos is not averse to using art himself. In a certain sense he was a performer. Much of his work is poetry, and the first two chapters of Amos are highly stylized art. What concerns him is an art that bears no relation to the realities of life. So we do not hear Amos complaining because their art is purely secular, for his first condemnations are of how art is being used in worship. Nor is Amos disapproving of art about pleasurable experiences, else the Song of Songs would be ruled out. He is condemning art that is wickedly lopsided because it encourages a view of life that is callously selfish and pleasure seeking and offers neither strength, nor vision, nor motivation to serve the needs of the poor.

Art always betrays a vision of life and is a powerful clue to a culture's wisdom. Art of any kind carries in its bosom a particular way of seeing life, with particular priorities and a particular scale of values. That is, it derives from a certain wisdom. For this reason art always betrays the true values of the culture from within which it arises, at least to those who know how to read its clues. It makes no difference if our art is good or bad, great or trivial; it will still give us away. In its commitment to geometrical symmetry, harmony, and balance, the great art of the Renaissance, in part, betrays its preoccupation with abstractions and ideals. The historical progression of American art is also enlightening. "Before the West was won," landscape art was a national theme, much of it carrying images clearly analogous to Moses with his throng off to the Promised Land, as you might expect from countless numbers excitedly heading West into a vast uncharted territory with the vision of America as God's new chosen nation. The art of people such as Thomas Cole, who inspired the Hudson River school, symbolized America's immensity and seemingly inexhaustible resources. The closing of the American frontier ended that state of mind, and with the new myth that arose—that of the God-like power of science and industry to rival the hand of God in re-ordering the world—the metaphors of art for the power of the city, the machine, technology, and medicine symbolized the age. Landscapes became, well, like ancient history.

A culture's wisdom also influences what we might call our common, generally unnoticed, background art. Today, for instance, the decorative art that makes a Formica tabletop look like wood displays the conflict in our culture between the longing to find personal identity in nature and the desire to master it scientifically and technologically. Or, the Formica that looks like abstract art can be a symbol of the hunger of our culture for "spirituality." And speaking of our technological age, its wisdom comes through to a large degree in the command of technique that is found in advertising art, such as in magazine layout and graphics design. All of this, of course, is a complex discussion. Here we are merely trying to indicate that works of art of all kinds reflect a much bigger picture, the cultural wisdom behind them.

It is true that some art is innovative and challenging, prophetic even. Yet it can only thrive as such when it has some foothold either in the thinking of the people or in the tradition of the community. I[CS] remember the first time I saw Henry Miller's play *The Crucible*. I was so affected by it that immediately afterward I could barely enter into conversation with the actors who were milling around after the performance waiting to talk with us. I spoke briefly with one actor and promptly left in turmoil. A play about the Salem Witch Trials? Not just! Something much more historical than that was in the air.

As far as any art that claims to be christian, it has to initiate people into experiences of life under God, in which Jesus is the one whose kingdom makes claims upon this world with priorities beyond it. If there is to be any worthwhile amount of such art, then there must be christian communities who really do experience life in that way, and who in their sharing provide resources and stimulus for the artist's imagination to do its work. It will be an expression of true biblical wisdom and not simply of christian religious beliefs. Again, we can only glance at the subject here. It is an enormous matter and of critical importance.

We must develop Gospel-shaped principles of taste and judgment in our art.

We remarked earlier that we need to decide how to deal with the experiences that art grants to us. The mere fact that it needs to be said indicates that most people are not so discriminating. This means that good, effectively produced art has immense power for good or evil, and thus we need frontier checks for our minds and hearts. Most nations have a system of frontier checks on people wanting to come in, and it is normal, if visitors stay any length of time, to require them to report periodically to officials, such as the police. Our minds need to work in the same way. Good art finds ways to get past the border-posts of our minds. Fair enough. After all, most of us have prejudices and bigotries the size of the Great Wall of China that would keep us cruelly narrow-minded. But, as the Chinese themselves would say, it is one thing for the birds to fly overhead and quite another to let them nest in your hair. We need to cultivate and use our critical sense to check on the significance of those artworks that we particularly enjoy. If we do not, then our imaginations might be infiltrated by the assumptions and values of a wisdom that does not come from God. When this occurs, what we believe as Christians dedicated to our Lord can become less real to us than the significance of the images that we have accepted into our minds.

Confining ourselves to religious art won't be enough to protect us from this, either. For one thing, we cannot shut our eyes and ears to the artwork that surrounds us and imposes itself on our attention from every side, such as television commercials and advertising jingles. For another, as Amos' condemnations demonstrate, religious art can also be ungodly. It can lack a perspective on life as a whole which is truly wise in the Bible sense. It can also subtly persuade us that the great immensities of our faith and worship can be understood in the world's terms: its wealth, status, numbers, success, or power-structures; or alternatively: its revolutionaries, elitism, violence, disorder, destruction, or contempt. Religious art can even trivialize the great immensities of our faith. I[CS] remember the morning I phoned a christian business and got stuck waiting on hold for several minutes, listening to the piece "How Great Thou Art" playing in the background while I waited. What an aesthetic shock it was! This tremendous song about God's grandeur had been reduced by a computer to a sequence of tinny notes played one at a time like a bad music box.

A biblical wisdom helps us see and appreciate the strengths of art by non-Christians.

Too often we Christians have viewed good, effectively produced art by non-Christians as deserving only our contempt simply because it is done by non-Christians, or because it carries a rather raw in-your-face moral approach to life. Here we are reminded again of the split view of life in which the religious and moral aspects alone become the lens for christian analysis. Some of the more revealing indications of this attitude, and its downside, pop up continually in our comments about television viewing. Frankly, this makes us look pretty silly to non-Christians, and it undermines our credibility as cultural observers. It will take a few minutes to develop this, and some readers may take issue with it, but the effort should prove worthwhile for all of us. We want to use television to do this, not to discuss whether television entertainment is art but because it is so popular and uses principles of art (see storytelling, above).

There is a critically acclaimed weekly police drama in which solving crimes seems incidental to the show's realistic treatment of hardworking cops trying to keep it together. Detective and recovering alcoholic Andy Sipowicz, who is one of television's most compelling and layered characters, is usually at the center of the action. The series began with Sipowicz being given a last opportunity to turn his career around at the precinct, and viewers were invited to enter the world of an alcoholic and enlarge their sympathies. Andy's struggles, failures, and victories have been depicted with candor, tears, and exhilaration. Over the years, the detective has regained the respect of his colleagues, remarried with quite marked success, and restored the terribly alienated relationship with his oldest son, who had been grossly neglected during the detective's years of drinking. It would not be missing the mark to see these as redemptive threads running through this storyline.

Another hot cultural theme, racism, often crops up. In one stunning episode, Sipowicz, he's white, gets accused of being a racist by a black suspect who is enduring a particularly grueling interrogation from the detective. Eventually the man is no longer a suspect, but by then the *tête-à-tête* has reached near-violence in the squad room as the character rages at Sipowicz for being racist. Andy's boss, Lieutenant Fancy, intervenes and throws the guy out of the precinct. Sipowicz can't understand the guy's attitude. But Fancy can. He's black. "You busy after work?" Fancy suddenly asks Sipowicz. "Not particularly," Sipowitz replies, wondering what that was all about. At the end of the shift, Fancy, in an unusual move, takes Sipowicz out to eat.

You watch them being seated in a large, busy all-black restaurant. Soon, being the only white there grates deeply on Andy's nerves. Fancy pokes around. Why the angst, Andy? Are you being discriminated against? Were you kept out of the restaurant? Is anyone bothering you? Are the people unfriendly? Wouldn't they serve you? Is the food bad? Is the service lousy? No, Andy responds, the food's great. So's the service. And no one's bothering me.

"So why aren't you enjoying yourself?" Fancy presses. "Is it the atmosphere?"

"Oh, that's possible," Andy tosses out with his inimitable sarcasm. "Something about me being the only white guy here."

"Now why is that a problem? Is it because you feel this isn't your place, and maybe some of these people think so too? Maybe some of them just don't like you?"

"Look, I'm entitled to my feelings, just like everyone else. What's your point, Lieutenant?"

"Well, you're being served, aren't you, Andy? They cooked those ribs for you. Maybe they wanted to spit in your plate, but they didn't. They served your white ass just like they would anyone else who came in here. Even though some of them hate your guts."

The penny drops. Sipowicz stops chewing. So this is what it feels like to be surrounded by an "alien" culture.

"Now," Fancy concludes, "what if they had guns and badges?"

People can recognize themselves in the "pretend world."

The stunning end to the episode leaves Sipowicz caught in the valley of decision, not unlike "the expert in the law" after hearing Jesus talk one afternoon about good neighborliness. And viewers watching from a majority perspective get a world created in their imaginations in which it becomes possible to appreciate, at least to some degree, what minorities may feel. A strong case can be made, therefore, that this police drama captures the popular imagination because viewers get invited into the true-to-life ways in which the main characters engage reality and square off against their own personal demons, demons at times tamed or even exorcized. Viewers recognize themselves, perhaps get a little insight, hope, sympathy. A case in point is Sipowicz's ongoing battle with recovery vis-a-vis the slow attitude adjustments of his fellow detectives toward him. It's possible to reconstruct yourself around fellow employees who retain grave doubts about your character. It won't be easy, but it is possible. Redemptive threads like these can be found throughout the long run of this award-winning series.

Now, if you will forgive us a little literary playfulness, we have withheld the name of this police drama, but not capriciously. For even before its first episode aired, hundreds of thousands of American Christians received mailings or heard from friends who told them, in so many words, that *NYPD Blue* was strictly *verboten* viewing. The repulsiveness which that generated toward the series remains so strong today in the minds of many Christians, that we believed some readers would not have given our critique a chance had we immediately stated that it was *NYPD Blue*. The power of our prejudices can be quite strong. Those with such a strong bias against the show never give the drama a look see, and so they remain oblivious to the show's potential as cultural narrative in a good sense.

Modal theory can help us to appreciate and to influence cultural art. One reason for the strong anti-*NYPD Blue* sentiment is because we Christians tend to analyze television, and cultural art in general, through the religious and moral aspects only, which does not give us any criteria for appreciating what may be good in television or film outside those two aspects. So with *NYPD Blue,* Christian moralists called for advertiser boycotts and raged about the pilot's full-length, flesh-toned bedroom segment, the freshly bloodied bodies at the crime scenes, and the "adult" language. Certainly we should critique promiscuity cut loose from moral and social consequences, or the irony of "adult" language that indicates, at least in part, how immature at communication a person is. But that is not what the moralists were doing. They were reacting as if the whole show were evil. For them it was unimaginable, unthinkable, that the pilot for *NYPD Blue* could be setting the stage for some redemptive threads to be pulled through the storylines.

Clearly, *NYPD Blue* is hard-hitting in many ways, and some of it is admittedly controversial, if not catering to the low tastes of some.

Nevertheless, it has won over viewers with its solid storytelling, strong cast, and creative consistency. The problem for us is that we cannot assess this with a religious and moral lens only, and so our analysis falls far short. The baby gets thrown out with the bath water, and no bridge is built for christian artistic dialogue with people like Steven Bochco and David Milch, who created *NYPD Blue*.

When we begin to understand what art is for, and when we bring a full view of Scripture—its dimensional plurality—to our subject, any value that even a television program might have becomes imaginable. This we tried to show by bringing some secular aspects of modal analysis, such as history, aesthetics, and social relations, into our brief assessment of *NYPD Blue*. Occasionally, one of the aspects is specially prominent. Some years ago, for instance, one of the show's then main characters, police office Janice Licalsi, literally got away with murder. Bochco and Milch then drew Licalsi's[3] tremendous crisis of conscience out over numerous episodes and resolved it in a way that would please even the moralists. Well, maybe. Here we could mount a critique from the moral-ethical aspect, perhaps commenting on the differences between a cop's sense of right and wrong and the legal standards of justice versus moral ideals. Overtly religious characters also appear on the show from time to time (the Greek Orthodox priest, the Catholic priest, the black pastor). So we could include principles and ideas from that aspect in our critique. (Bochco and Milch show these religious figures in an intelligent manner.)

Modal analysis, therefore, assists us in building up a truer picture (recall "the island approach"). We gain a fuller critique by getting past the blood and the language. Four hundred years ago, Christians had to get past them in Shakespeare too! We would critique the "adult" language, violence, and nudity, but we would not be limited to those.

This kind of analysis also exposes two other faults in our thinking. One is an assumption that if people watch shows like *NYPD Blue* it must be due only to the sex and violence. For the program may appeal to people for quite different reasons. The other thing is this. Modal analysis gives the lie to the widespread assumption that "if we can just get rid of sex and violence on TV, we'll be okay." No. Things are presented on television that may be just as damaging to "family values," if not more so, than the overt violence and immoralities shown without consequences. The unclosed sluice of sexual jokes and innuendos that runs uninterrupted during the "harmless" sitcoms, and

---

[3] Andy Sipowicz is played by Dennis Franz; Lieutenant Fancy, by James McDaniel; Janice Licalsi was played by Amy Brenneman.

the perennial undermining of parental authority that dominates virtually every program—themes at home even on the "family" networks—may be more damaging to the development of our children's christian character in the long run, because at least the children see the sex and violence coming. With modal theory we have a way to mount criticism of these less noticed, yet subtly more powerful, influences.

Our artistic sense has to become largely instinctive.

The multi-dimensional wisdom of Scripture as applied to art can help us identify, address, and influence things in culture that may at first appear to be surprising to us. Some insightful Christian once wrote: "Ascetic Christianity called the world evil and left it. Humanity is waiting for a revolutionary Christianity that will call the world evil and change it."

People may argue that we just don't have time to stop and consider every bit of art that comes our way. Of course not. Yet when we are playing a game, say tennis, we don't have to "stop and consider" how we are going to hit the ball every time either. We act instinctively, governed by a complex set of impulses about where our opponent's weak spots are, whether we can reach them, whether we can get back in position in time to return the ball, and so on. From time to time we may have to stop and consider to a certain extent, by slowing the game up or pausing for the service. Those same instinctive impulses give us a sense of when that, too, is necessary. Some impulses appear to be built in, but many are learned, often, if we take the game seriously, by effort, practice, coaching, and thought. Altogether, they constitute a kind of wisdom in playing tennis. It improves with practice, and how well we play the game is also very much decided by whether we do some "considering" after each game is over. Now we do not develop such wisdom, either in tennis or in life, on our own but in playing or living with others, preferably with some who are better at it than we are. A godly artistic wisdom works in the same way, although much of it may, at the outset, have to be painfully learned and awkwardly practiced before then. Anyone who has to teach it or think it through for new situations has a big task and not much time.

The connection between art and evangelism.

Just as we noted in the previous chapter that the Bible's social, economic, and political wisdom has evangelistic value, there are clear connections between art and evangelism. Marshall McLuhan's "the medium is the message" is at least partly true. A message is not only carried by the words spoken but also by the medium through which they are conveyed. The way in which a medium is used to carry a message is the technique of the artist, and it works therefore as all art does, by providing clues, suggestions, and associations. It may never occur to our evangelists that they are *ipso facto* artists to some degree when conveying the Gospel message. To use a simple illustration, hand out a dirty, wrinkled tract and there is a strong implication that the Gospel itself is tatty. Make the context too glossy and it looks to the poor as if the Gospel is not for them. Make it too entertaining and it comes across as nothing much too serious. Make it only about words, or ideas, or techniques of decision and it may have no sensitivity or be unaware of life's mystery. Evangelism cannot do without art. Unless Christians have some artistic expertise, their evangelism is going to suffer. In fact, it is suffering. Much of our "clear message" is communicating too many conflicting things to its thoughtful hearers.

Part Four

Building the Future

~22~

New Discoveries Can Be Intoxicating

Quite rapid changes are overtaking us, not only in the world we live in but also in the way we respond to the challenge of its gods. In the process, we are making some new discoveries, and they are at times overwhelming. When the Spirit starts something new, it isn't only the world at large that thinks Christians are drunk. Often their fellow Christians feel the same about them, sometimes with justification! Conflicts between the past and the contemporary in periods of change are notoriously bitter. But there are surely lessons that a christian wisdom can learn from history. Maybe we can't make omelettes without breaking the eggs, but we don't have to spread them all over somebody's face.

Ever since evangelicals were called to be concerned with the world's problems, there has been a considerable reaction against the older style of evangelicalism. We rebel against the obvious folly of having prayer meetings to prepare for prayer meetings about prayer meetings. We throw off the petty restrictions that were supposed to mark off Christians as holy people. In terms of God's will, we scorn explanations of life that leave us with no way of facing our mistakes or of seeking for remedies in the midst of them. We see old wineskins bursting under the pressure of new wine in ferment, with threats of bitter crippling conflicts within christian communities. We forget that there is old wine still left in the bottles, and that old wine is notoriously worth prizing.

Don't discard the past:
personal reliability and self-discipline.

One of the most serious of these conflicts is the tendency of those of us with a social concern to play down the traditional demands for personal christian integrity. For instance, we are now aware that human beings are caught within social structures that often frustrate their high ideals. In a world of high unemployment, how can we say to someone, "If a man will not work, neither shall he eat!"? In a world of inflation and wildly negotiable prices, people committed to the command "owe no man anything" find themselves unintentionally in debt. And when so many people let you down, how do you fulfill promises that depend on such people keeping *their* promises? Do you even need to, when nobody seems to feel strongly about promise keeping any more (Promise Keepers aside)?

To those of us who were reared in that older tradition of individual responsibility, the change of climate is painful, not least to our own conscience. We evangelicals used to insist that smoking was bad stewardship and ruinous to our bodies, which we understood to be the temples of the Holy Spirit. We used to plead for temperance against the "demon drink," and we were extremely fussy about behavior between the sexes. Now, just when our society in its own pathetically clumsy fashion is beginning to admit that the old evangelicals had a point, just when society is introducing non-smoking areas, drink rehabilitation programs, and setting up instruction in schools to head off indiscriminate sex, the new evangelicals don't seem to care any more. Must we always be different from the world, even when the world has come round to agreeing with us? It is, frankly, puzzling. And distressing. Because wherever the sense of moral principle has weakened, thousands of young Christians have become cruelly vulnerable to the worldly drive for self-liberation. The result is heartbreaking pain in confused and uncontrollable relationships, and in addictions with their consequent loss of self-respect and purposeful commitment. There is, only too often, a stark contrast between them and those who have managed to stick to the values of the "old-time religion."

I[JP] for one do not believe that traditional personal moral training was completely wrongheaded. The Gospel has always attacked the world with the integrity of individual believers. The Christians of those first few centuries, for all their faults, could still be said to have "out-loved, out-thought, and out-died" the world around them. It was the courage of the individual Christians in the face of arbitrary tyrannies that saved Europe from sheer barbarism after the fall of Rome. Christians of the puritan sort gained influence because people knew that you could get your money's worth from them. The Evangelical Awakening changed England not because a vast number of converts was made but because they became thrifty and responsible. To build a social challenge to our age on the basis of undisciplined and easygoing moral character is to build on sand.

It is not uncommon for Christians who get a long way down the road in social critique to become unconcerned for the older moral disciplines. This is because models like the one being articulated in this book give them a way past single issues to a more comprehensive critique. Emphasis on social structure can lead to a view in which sexual license, for instance, is okay, because the individual action doesn't count as much as the broader critique. This attitude is easily absorbed by the children of those Christians.

Don't discard the past: personal devotion and respecting the text of Scripture.

Another conflict exists in devotional life. I[JP] remember the sense of shock I felt in the 1950s when an older minister frankly confessed to a group of us that he didn't pray any more. I am now more shocked to find that such confessions don't disturb me now to anything like the same extent! Let's face it, the old devotionalism, with its wordy harangues to God, its shopping lists of intercessions, its mindless appeal to inner spiritual impressions, and its use of public prayer to manipulate sensitive souls has made the whole exercise stink in our nostrils. So we have this prejudice against "religion and devotion." But the human spirit abhors a vacuum. So in our search for reality and integrity we find ourselves praying like teenagers who only phone home when they're short of money, or we find ourselves desperately taking on some prayer discipline that looks like a catholic version of the discredited protestant one. Nevertheless, Christ pledges to be present among those who combine their petitions in his name, and the biblical life of faith is punctuated with both prayerfulness and set times of prayer. George Herbert still speaks true: "If thou art not a praying man, thou art not a Christian."

The way I have been arguing for prayer in those last sentences is symptomatic of another conflict. Forty years ago, we would have been bombarded with texts on the matter. Now we refer to something much vaguer: "the biblical attitude," the "thrust of Scripture," and so on. I believe in this approach, for we cannot go back to using texts as ammunition. Nevertheless, if our understanding of individual texts about particular issues adds up to something compatible with a biblical outlook on life, it will become heretical and sectarian. I am afraid we are going to take on board a third generation scholasticism that has lost touch with the text of Scripture. It will not do just to extrapolate ideas from a biblical philosophy and promulgate them as *ipso facto* "biblical," for those ideas may be being unwittingly used (just as isolated texts themselves can be) within contexts that are markedly unbiblical. The Bible's meaning of the idea or text thus gets rearranged so that it comes into the service of another set of values, or gods.

A biblical philosophy (chapter 23) is an inference from, and an approximation to, Scripture. Ideas developed from that will be second order approximations and inferences. It is disturbing to see that so many of our new generation know the theoretical inferences so much better than they know the text of the Word itself, except as it relates to their special interests! We need those theoretical inferences. We'll need more of them, and better, and in greater variety. But they must be seen for what they are. Because they are vulnerable and susceptible to distortion, there must be a continual dialogue with the whole of the biblical text, and that will be only fully effective if our brain cells are soaked in it from Genesis to Revelation.

Don't discard other Christians: have space for both reasoning and miracles.

The need for good theoretical thinking leads on to another tension: between commitment to responsible reasoning and faith in the miraculous. For instance, it seems difficult to be both charismatic and engaged in in-depth social concerns without suffering some sort of schizophrenia. To people wrestling with economic principles, the charismatic who cites a miraculous financial deliverance sounds slickly superficial. To the charismatic, christian economists seem like dry rationalists leaving God out of the account. Yet it must be at least generally obvious from Scripture that Christ's ministry and promises of healing miracles were never meant to do Luke out of a job!

The difficulty is that if you are dealing in miracles, then the need for reasoning about symptoms and causes and effects seems to be irrelevant, and the reverse is also true (note closing paragraphs of Appendix 1 text). This must surely be a matter of mindset, and there are certain aspects of our mindset that are largely formed by our calling. The effect is to present some elements of God's reality more vividly to our imaginations (therefore more easily drawn on) than others. We need to acknowledge this and to accept and respect the witness of those whose callings give them a different mental orientation. Surely our reasoning ought to be able to show where only a miracle will do anything! Failure to see this produces divisive polemics in the body of Christ. One only has to experience christian television or radio in the U.S. to see the frighteningly judgmental form this conflict can take. One orientation gets characterized as obscurantist or New Age, the other an arid rationalism or liberal compromise. Neither orientation has the slightest interest in learning from each other.

Don't discard the present: let's learn from one another.

We are back to the need for a discipleship that learns of Christ from those against whom we react as much as from those with whom we share a common vision. Everybody nowadays seems to be talking about discipleship and worldview, but one might be forgiven for wondering how much we are actually learning in the sense that we have had to unlearn something that we had got wrong. We are in a world designed for our probation. All that we say and do is provisional, subject to judgment, either here or hereafter. Unless we keep our hearts open, unless we take the unnerving risks of taking fresh ideas seriously by giving them time to make sense to us, and then go back to Scripture to see whether in fact they fit into its special vision of life, we shall once more display to the world a Church that can do nothing without tearing itself apart. Like that, we shall not need to carry Christ's cross, for we shall have one of our own making. But it will do little for a hurting world.

Don't discard the future: philosophy is not dogma or wisdom.

Finally, to those whose calling means working with theories and ideas, to those involved in the war of competing philosophies of life, there is a special danger of misusing philosophy. It easily becomes a dogma or a hallmark of intelligence. Philosophy is not in itself wisdom. It is a description, a grammar, of a wisdom (chapter 23). It only has authority insofar as it approximates to the testimony of Scripture. Like all else in the Church it is *semper reformanda*. I[JP] want to remind my friends who belong to the Reformed and Reformational movements (to whom I owe unpayable debts) that those terms mean "being *continually* subject to reform by Scripture."

Philosophy is not even the rules for wisdom. It is a means for disciplining the intellectual content of our wisdom. It is only a means. Whether it actually disciplines our thinking properly will depend on how faithfully we think, and whether we do so with the heart of a disciple, that is to say, a learner. There must be humility of mind. The philosopher is a servant to the servants of God, providing them with resources prepared for their tasks. Unfortunately, the dualism in our thinking between the religious and the secular precludes letting ourselves be served by our christian philosophers. We are often completely oblivious to our need of them.

Yet even the best of philosophies is not a cause to be espoused and defended at all costs. It is a tool for thought with a view to obedient living, now and in the future. Insofar as it is a good tool, we recommend it today with all the enthusiasm we have for anything that furthers our service to the Lord. When it fails us, we must either sharpen or modify it for the future as best we can till we find something better; that is, till we develop a more faithful scriptural understanding of God's creation. That we may live a life worthy of the calling we have received. That we may know how to answer the issues of our cultures with a wisdom based on the fear of the Lord and redeeming grace. That we may fulfill our everyday obediences to God more consistently for His glory.

The great composer Johann Sebastian Bach is quoted as saying, "All music should have no other end and aim than the glory of God and the soul's refreshment; where this is not remembered, there is no real music but only a devilish hubbub." It appears that this was not just a fanciful theory or ideal for Bach. He headed his compositions with the letters "J.J." (*Jesus Juva*, for "Jesus help me"), and he ended them with the initial "S.D.G." (*Soli Dei Gratia*, for "To God alone the praise"). Let us make a commitment to engrave the initials J.J and S.D.G. upon the start and end of each of our days, and to mean it, whether we're going to be running the home or heading out the door to sell insurance, defend a client, run a business, or meet with the board of directors. We may not be as consistent or influential at this as Bach was, but through prayer, study, and like-minded fellowship we can at least commit ourselves to the process and make some progress. Any other end and aim leaves the devilish hubbub secure.

~23~

Toward a Biblical Philosophy of Life

Part 1

Philosophy as the Grammar of a Wisdom

We would all like to hide somewhere from the strain of christian obedience, and perhaps especially from the kind of discipleship of mind that is the challenge of this book. We may bury ourselves in our families or work and have to be dragged out to give a plain confession of the faith. We may take refuge in religious observance as an escape from caring service. We may use evangelistic zeal to evade the long haul of enlarging our vision of God into everyday life. Anything can be used as a dodge from exacting duties. Nevertheless, we must give our lives and energies to the vision of God's glory as infiltrating all of life—a process of wisdom development that we have been considering throughout *Uncommon Sense* as a means to respond to problems that this age presents to us. The world, though it will say otherwise, is longing for truly prophetic responses and affirmations in the name of Jesus.

Because much of this is still new to Christians, as it was to the authors not many years ago, we have included this chapter in six-parts for readers who want to use the Bible to make more concerted efforts. Mind you, you may need to be ready to work through this material if you don't want to miss a lot of it. It's a curious thing, this. For instance, it's interesting how many Christian college students lug around massive tomes on law, science, or economics, but if you ask them to apply that sort of interest to another tome, the Book of books, "Oh, dear." Nevertheless, as wisdom herself tells us, our discipleship is not just about gaining insight. It's also about applying insight. And that is going to take working with the Book. At the very least, if it turns out that this chapter is not your scene, you may still wish to read it and pick up what you can.

We think that you will find significant clues for everyday life along the way, and in the present crisis of Western culture, this is particularly important. And to assist all readers, this chapter is presented in a way that makes its use alongside Appendix 1 especially insightful. (We have indicated jumping off places for ideas linked to Appendix 1.)

We don't have the time simply to wait to absorb biblical wisdom naturally today.

Let's begin by stating the obvious. We're adults not children, and time is short. So what can we aging Christians possibly do, having lost the ability to speak the word of the Lord to and in the world in biblical categories? That is, we do not have the time or the cultural context to absorb a godly wisdom naturally (chapter 6). But what we can do is learn it like adults learn a new language. Our language is a kind of transcript (chapters 14–15; 18–19) of our wisdom, of our way of understanding life and coping with it. In fact, we learn the two together; we learn the language while we are learning to cope with life. Throughout this book we have maintained that the wisdom we absorbed and received from childhood is not as biblical as we may have thought and that we can't go back and absorb one as we should. This means that for adults to acquire a biblical wisdom the process must proceed like adults learning a foreign language, deliberately.

It must be deliberately learned.

I[JP] once new a French girl who had a fair working knowledge of English, but since she was about to marry an English man and live in England, she decided to learn the language "properly." And she managed to do it in an amazingly short period of time. How did she do that? Of course, she learned it at a school, where it was set out systematically in a grammar and vocabulary. Naturally she lacked the fluency, flexibility, and freedom of someone reared in the language—characteristics that would take years of living in the midst of it to acquire, using it continually with others. But through systematic study she was on her way. Incidentally, it also gave her a command of the language in certain respects, such as for translating and teaching, quite beyond many ordinary English people. Through deliberate study, she gained a quick mastery of the rules, the patterns, the outlines, and the principles of the language by means of a systematic presentation and explanation of it. If we want to learn a different way of understanding the world from the wisdom in which we have been raised, especially if we are called to teach, then we will probably have to learn it the same way, systematically. Even this is not unusual, for we learn much of the accumulated wisdom of our cultures by the same method, by learning its basic rules and principles from books and from planned courses of teaching.

A philosophy as the "grammar" of a wisdom.

It is possible to set out the wisdom of a community or a culture systematically, to produce a grammar of it, so to speak. The ideas will be arranged in some kind of order, such as showing their priorities, seeking to explain their inner logic, and setting out the principles. This process appears within the New Testament itself in regard to the Gospel. For example, the Gospels and Acts tell the basic story of Christ's redemption. Then Romans sets out the themes of the Gospel, applying them first to the Jew-Gentile situation, then to the individual, then to human history, and finally to the Church. Within that schema, the Gospel is expounded in terms of basic principles such as love, faith, grace, human solidarity, and so on. Here, then, is the first theology: a systematized grammar of christian faith, and within it, too, is a special view of cultural history, a special way of understanding life and coping with it—a special wisdom.

Now this language-learning process, this grammar we are suggesting for deliberately developing a biblical wisdom, comes out as a kind of philosophy. For some years in my christian life, I[JP] was put off from the whole subject of philosophy. The philosophies that I had encountered all seemed to undermine the Gospel in one way or another, and my attitude was reinforced by my interpretation of Paul's exhortation in Colossians 2:8: "Beware lest any man spoil you through philosophy and vain deceit." This was in the Authorized, or King James, Version, which I had been enjoying those years, and it reads as if any kind of philosophy is *verboten*. Several years later, I realized that I had not grasped the meaning of the whole verse, which is: "Beware lest any man spoil you through" a philosophy that is "vain deceit" because it is formed "after the tradition of men, after the rudiments of the [fallen] world"; that is, a philosophy not based on Christ. What we badly needed, I then understood, was a philosophy based on Christ, a philosophy that could expose and attack the ungodly systems of thought that so persuasively lead people today. The NIV comes closer by saying: "See to it that no one takes you captive through hollow and deceptive philosophy, which depends on human tradition and the basic principles of this world rather than on Christ." It is a "hollow and deceptive" philosophy, not a philosophy based on Christ, that is the apostle's concern. When I saw that you could have a philosophy based on Jesus Christ, this was a turning point for me.

The need and power of being systematic. Systematizing the thinking-structure of the Bible's wisdom—showing how different elements in it fit together in a consistent whole—is roughly what we may mean by "philosophy." In fact, one early Greek meaning for "philosophy" was "love of wisdom." Trouble is, most philosophies tend to concentrate on a culture's abstract thinking; that is, they produce edifices of thought that seem remote from everyday life. This is because of their idolatrous nature. (In fact they are not remote. For instance, Einstein's Theory of Relativity brought us our non-stick saucepans. The technology for them was developed from the needs of space travel, and it was Einsteinian maths that made that possible.) Besides misunderstanding Colossians 2:8, evangelical Christians are nervous of philosophy in general because it often suggests arid intellectualism, a rationalistic undermining of our faith, a loss of the miraculous, or the reduction of our life to a mental exercise. Only too often the nervousness has been justified, for that has been its use and effect. The trouble is, we cannot afford to do without philosophy in some form or other any longer. But we need a different kind, that's for sure.

In describing the foregoing, we do not mean "philosophy" as understood as the subject Philosophy, which universities deal with, which is often a study of the systematic philosophies that great thinkers have produced, and the methods and reasoning involved in making them. Surprisingly, some people (scholars) can do this work efficiently and yet live by a personal philosophy that is quite pathetic. The individual philosophies studied are usually the efforts of individual people and rarely biblical—most institutions of learning would not consider the latter project "wise." Its initial value is really in enabling people to penetrate to the hidden presuppositions of a line of thought and identify the kind of thinking it leads to. This way of doing philosophy addresses questions that it hardly occurs to most of us to ask, but it is only by such studies that we can come to understand the outlook of an ancient culture like that of classical Greece or medieval Hinduism. (The great thinkers seem to have been able to catch the flow of a society's corporate thinking and show which way it must logically develop, but the relationship between any systematic philosophy and the culture within which it appears is not a straightforward affair, and the philosophy often confirms, even produces, as many attitudes as it expounds.)

Everyone has a personal "philosophy of life."

In this chapter we are not talking about studying the subject Philosophy or philosophy as an arid intellectualism. We are suggesting the development of a personal and down-to-earth biblical philosophy, for that would give us a grammar of a wisdom that would let us speak sensibly and forcibly in the public square. Employers speak of their "business philosophy" and pastors of their "ministry philosophy," and it is not unusual to hear someone refer to his or her "philosophy of life." If asked, the person may not be able to articulate that philosophy, or at least not very easily or quickly, and probably not fully. But that is not our point here. At least the person acknowledges a "philosophy" of life. This is really the big theory of life whereby people cope with the demands that life places on one's ingenuity and fortitude, and whereby, when questions are asked, people can feel reasonably consistent explaining what they do. Our task as Christians having a philosophy of life is to develop a systematized thinking-structure, a grammar, of a biblical wisdom—to deliberately learn the "foreign" language.

Just before we start to look more fully at this in Part 2 (below), we want to note several more key features about the kind of philosophy we mean. For one thing, one's philosophy of life has characteristics similar to those of one's wisdom. For instance, it enables us to cope with demands on our integrity and fortitude, and whereby when questions are asked, we can feel that we are reasonably consistent in what we do. It is what one draws on when asked, "Why do you say that?" Or, "What's the point in doing that?" This working theory is therefore important for maintaining one's sanity. Further, it controls not only one's responses (what is said at such times) but also the kind of arguments the person chooses to offer, the kind of values appealed to, and the style in which they are acted out. If there is no truly biblical philosophy available to us, then ungodly ones take command in our lives and cultures by default. This has been especially true in our colleges and universities, even those which purport to have christian origins. Since we Christians are so far behind culture, if we could encourage ourselves to develop a grammar of a biblical wisdom, we might be able to catch up on the curve a bit, if not someday get ahead of it. At the very least, we can do it for our children's sake, that they may be raised much more intuitively in it (as they absorb it from childhood) than would otherwise be possible. Perhaps they will be the ones, then, who will be able to show culture how the Gospel is not merely for "souls" but for all of life. Philosophy may not be able to make a Juliet, as Romeo knew, but it can tell both how to get on with life under God.

Developing a biblical philosophy is a gift from God, giving wise direction.

Another thing, as you will have noticed, is that we're back to theories again (chapter 7). This power to form theories, even when the theories are philosophies of life, is a gift from God that should not be underestimated, for it enables us to expand our effectiveness for God in the world and give *direction* to the way that effectiveness is going to take. In the example of the coca leaves given in chapter 7, obviously the extracted cocaine can be used either medically as a pain reliever or illegally as an addictive drug or even as a poison. Or in the example of the game bowls, think of the direction those large black balls would take if shot from cannon! To take a different area, many mass-produced objects of our time appear to us to have been made to last forever. Why not automobile bodies? It seems fairly certain that by now technology could make car bodies that would almost never rust, not to mention razor blades and light bulbs that would last almost indefinitely. But that's not the direction that Western research theory, funded largely by industry, is encouraged to go!

We all, therefore, work with some sort of theory that governs our thinking *and* the direction our effectiveness in culture is going to take. This theory helps us determine what life is for, how it is supposed to go on (the direction we take it), and what is important in it. Again, we must not assume that just because we have been raised in a christian environment, such as through our churches and seminaries, that the direction we are going is as wise as it ought to be. This is shockingly clear from Galileo's time, for biblical and theological "evidence" produced against the helio-centric theory was not the reason for holding to the medieval belief in the geo-centric theory. It was part of the supporting "evidence" *for* the geo-centric theory! (Galileo's science was headed in the right direction; the church's wisdom on this point was not!)

A good philosophy is a theory for effective living.

A life theory, therefore, where the meaning is one's "philosophy of life," is the mental, rational framework for our wisdom. It is the logic behind the way we see life and cope with it. It makes certain things important or unimportant to us, it makes us effective or ineffective in certain areas, and it provides wise or other-wise direction. A person with a muddled and incoherent life theory tends to have a muddled and incoherent life. No Christian escapes being controlled by this principle; it is simply a principle of life. For instance, if a Christian's life theory assumes that the intellect is the all important factor, then that person's faith will tend to take the form of an intellectual exercise. If one's life theory assumes that spiritual experience is the all important factor, then that person's faith with take on a highly subjective character. You can work out for yourself the direction that people's faith would go when held within life theories that make, say, works, or decisions, or miracles, or intensity of emotion, the dominant factor.

Here, too, is where the nature of philosophy is similar to wisdom. If our philosophy has faulty values and distorted priorities, then wherever in our lives these values and priorities apply, our behavior will be affected accordingly and not bring glory to God in those aspects. Whenever this happens, we are following a way that seems right (not merely attractive, for it can be painful), "but in the end it leads to death" (Proverbs 14:12). And since birds of a feather flock together, we shall naturally gravitate toward others who share our particular philosophy. These will be the folk that we feel we can communicate best with, and even when they disagree with us, they still make some sense to us. We are thus part of a group, community, subculture, and culture that endorses such a philosophy of life and therefore strengthens its authority in our minds. On such a basis we build our relationships, our supporting ideas, our institutions, our customs. This in turn confirms particular viewpoints of that life theory still further in the community, and it makes further creative activity in terms of that theory possible and "successful." (We build what are sometimes called "probability structures," which become self-authenticating to those who live within them.)

Insofar as we try to act consistently and reasonably, our total philosophy of life determines the range of our choices and our courses of action (whether, as individuals, we understand it with any thoroughness or not). It also affects our devotional life, our understanding of church life, and even the limits within which we may listen to and be ready to recognize and obey the voice of God. So then everybody, without exception, has some kind of philosophy of life, which enables them to cope with life in what seems to be a rationally consistent manner.

The hidden roots of any philosophy are always accepted by faith.

One's philosophy of life, therefore, is the reasoning aspect of one's wisdom; thus coherence and consistency are its special concerns. But, and this is quite significant, every philosophy of life includes more that its intellectual dimension. It is organized in the mind around certain basic convictions or assumptions that are matters of faith rather than of reason, whether they appear to be religious or not. To a determined skeptic, for instance, it is impossible to prove rationally that you exist or that what you see around you is the same reality as what everybody else sees, or that reason is a reliable guide to truth. That is the skeptic's ultimate assumption. (Thoroughgoing skepticism is logically untenable, for in denying the possibility of any truth, the skeptic denies the truth of his statement. It's like the person who holds to the assumption "there are no absolutes" but does not see that the very statement, being an absolute one, undermines the assumption.) Our point is that everyone, but everyone, even an atheist, has assumptions about life that they take on trust and faith in just the same way as a Christian takes the reality of Jesus Christ on trust and faith. The rest of this chapter will attempt to outline the kind of philosophy of life that such a study based on faith in Christ Jesus as Lord might involve.

Part 2

Begin by Asking Basic Questions

We want to disclose more fully now a way of reasoning that has been used throughout this book: breaking down the complexities of Western life into their fundamentals by asking basic questions about them alongside Scripture. Early in the book we noted that Scripture can seem non-germane to secular life today because our specialized societies produce technical jargon such as geo-political structures, complementary medicine, fiscal control of inflation, market-based economy, outcome-based education, and such like— you can't look those up in your *Strong's Concordance!* We also mentioned that even when the subjects are more familiar, like environmental stewardship, early childhood education, university campuses, judicial decisions, artistic expression, or family values, that their complexity can bewilder us when it comes to using the Bible as a guide for instruction. But we also noted something else. When we break down the complexities of contemporary life into their fundamental parts, we may be able to find ways in which the Bible, especially its secular wisdom, instructs us about those fundamentals, and that we may then be able to apply that instruction to today's complex issues. We developed this approach, albeit in an introductory fashion, when topics like education, the family, politics, business, and art came up, as well as when we thought about high ideals like love, truth, knowledge, and justice. We were trying to identify basic elements of the thing under consideration, but without losing the whole. In fact, this process would help us to see what the whole is really all about.

Breaking down life's complexities alongside Scripture helps us identify faulty assumptions.

This approach is key because we tend to take for granted (assume) what the aspects are all about, at least their more familiar-sounding features, such as relationships, knowledge, education, or love (see Appendix 1 for aspect names and characteristics). When we examine an aspect in its basic elements, however, and ask questions of them *vis a vis* Scripture, it is not unusual to find places where our assumptions are mistaken, even about areas that we are familiar and conversant with. Such an approach goes beyond mere self-instruction. It gives us ways to engage our cultures biblically, for in all probability the cultures hold to some quite fundamentally wrongheaded assumptions about these aspect meanings and relationships. Indeed, cultures are built on many mistaken notions. When Scripture instructs us about how God's understanding and laws act as correctives here, well, the possibilities for engaging the public square with sensible and forcible christian ideas increase steadily.

This approach may take some getting used to, but people are doing it all the time anyway, albeit perhaps not as consciously and deliberately as we are suggesting here. For instance, people always do it when something new enters their experience, something they don't recognize or understand. When that happens to them, they always ask the same kind of questions, like, "What is it?" Or, "Where did it come from?" Another is, "How does it work?" Which is usually asked alongside a related question, "What is it for?" Supporting questions also get asked, like, "What is it made of?" "What kind of object is it?" "What's its name?" And perhaps, "Is anything missing or broken?" Or, "What's it supposed to be like?" Or, if the new experience is one in which people find themselves being ordered about, they often ask, "Who gave them the right to . . . ?" If the answer includes new and unexpected information, then people are likely to ask, "How do we know that's true?" So the process is not foreign to us in the least.

People also do this when an unexpected change takes place. If the computer breaks down, someone has to know how it works. If the repairman finds something that to him is peculiar about the problem, he is likely to ask another expert for information, or perhaps where you got the computer from. If you want an unusual modification, he is likely to ask, "What do you want it for?" Serious changes of any kind always give rise to questions of that sort, and we cannot cope properly without finding answers for them.

For anyone wishing to become more conversant with modal theory, working like this with the aspects is a good place to begin. For one thing, you can see how the unity and diversity in life begins to unfold as basic questions are asked of the aspects. Take the religious aspect. What is religion? What is its purpose? How is it expressed? Answers would lead immediately to related questions, such as about the worship in our churches and the direction of one's faith. And when answering questions such as those, we would notice that this led us, quite naturally, to consider features of other aspects. So questions about *worship* in *churches* means gathering ideas from the societal and aesthetic aspects, since a church is about people acting as a group and since worship involves the use of symbols. As the process went on, it would lead you into building up a biblical wisdom about features of many other aspects. Further, you can begin the process by jumping in with a basic question about any aspect, and carry on from there. Start with an aspect that particularly interests you, and then play around with the process.

Now, we can ask questions like that not only about anything but also about everything; that is, "everything" thought of as one big whole. When we deal with such questions on that scale in any serious and methodical fashion, we are really doing philosophy on the grand scale, though normally we don't stop to do it at any length. Our own answers are part of our mental bloodstream, and we leave it to the experts to make any further investigations, and good luck to them! We can also concentrate on particular subjects while we are doing our philosophy, and produce a philosophy of religion or science or politics. When profound changes take place in a culture or civilization, inevitably such large-scale questions come to the surface. That's why we are confronted with them (the so-called culture wars) in this present generation.

We are not asking questions as skeptics. It might be helpful to say that we are not asking these questions as skeptics ask such questions. I[CS] was once caught up short here by some people during a conversation about "the faith movement." We were not getting anywhere and so I asked, "What do you mean by *faith*?" They immediately replied, "Well, *believing*." So I asked, "What is *believing*?" Answering became difficult for them at that point, but finally they said, "Having a conviction about what the Bible says." That was close to what I was fishing around for, so I asked, "Why have a conviction about that?" And they said, "Because God wrote it." So I responded, "Why believe it because God wrote it?" This evoked, "Brother, what's wrong with *you*? You sound like a skeptic. Why are you asking all these questions?" "Because," I said, "you're asking me to take some things by faith but you're having difficulty explaining what *faith* is."

These Christians were taking a vital area of life very much for granted, yet when pressed they were not quite sure what it was. I then explained that my questions were not the random queries of a child or those of a skeptic, but that they were a process directed toward a certain end, which would help people like us, who were mis-communicating, to get on the same page in order to get the discussion about faith really going. Using basic questions, I was driving for the Old Testament notion of faith as stability, perseverance, and firmness, which they came close to with their word "conviction." Then I was going to set that Old Testament understanding alongside current christian and cultural notions of faith.

Such a process can help all of us to see more clearly where we are at. So we are not skeptics. We know in whom we have believed. We are asking with a direction in mind.

Learning how the Bible's wisdom instructs about ultimate issues. To deliberately learn a biblical wisdom, we must ask the basic questions about both everything, the whole, and its parts. Above, we suggested asking basic questions as a good way to build up our wisdom about the aspects, the parts, more fully, and throughout the book so far, we have pretty much stuck to basic questions about the aspects. For the rest of this chapter, however, we want to spend time with the big picture, chiefly asking basic questions about "everything" and about the God behind everything. If we are going to develop a philosophy of life based on Jesus Christ, and learn the grammar of a biblical wisdom, this is essential. For biblical answers to basic questions about "everything" give us the foundation for a godly philosophy of life as it applies to the aspects, which in turn gives wise direction to the practical matters of everyday life. This foundation has been implied in our discussions throughout this book.

They are our (the authors') assumptions. Here you'll see what some of those are, and why for all of us, this is no mere academic exercise.

Asking basic questions about the big picture is key. Regarding "everything," for instance, were we to ask "How does it all work?", Scripture instructs that all aspects of creation can only be explained as a unity in God, and that to explain them as a unity otherwise is to make an idol of one or more aspects. This is the thought behind numerous passages, such as Romans 11:36: "From him and through him and to him are all things." This unity in God is represented on the visual aid of modal theory (Appendix 1), where God the LORD is seen as the Source of Ultimate Authority. If any other Ultimate Authority is found to be located there, such as Mind, Matter, Rationality, or Intuition (see below), then you have an idolatry, because some area of creation is being used in place of God as the ultimate source, authority, and explanation of "everything." This is what the Old Testament would call a false god. (If you turn to the Appendix 1 and place any aspect, or aspects, where you see the words Source of Ultimate Authority or *Logos*, you will begin to get a feel for how this works. When an aspect, or aspects, usurps the place of God, it becomes an idol, giving people direction in the other aspects according to its characteristics.)

St. Paul's declaration in Romans 11:36 answers three basic question about everything: "Where does it come from?" "How does it work?" "Where is it headed?" Now he ends that great doxology by exclaiming, in so many words, "It came from God, it functions and is sustained through God, and its goal is God." Notice that this is a statement not only about everything but also about God. Everything finds its source, and its goal, and the way it gets from one to the other (is sustained), in God. Note, too, that Paul is exclaiming this as an act of worship, for worship is interested in similar concerns to those of philosophy—whatever is ultimately important in life. Here is Paul the worshiper using the language of Paul the thinker, for his faith was all of a piece with his philosophy of life.

The Bible's answer is greater than 42![1] Paul's answer to these three fundamental questions about everything, then, is "God." Now when we were considering the effects of theology on wisdom (chapters 16–17), we saw how a christian belief in God affects our understanding of subjects like physics, biology, politics, anthropology, and so on. That is, God is, to use Paul's idea, at the beginning and in the process and at the end of whatever subjects we're talking about, because all subjects are included in

---

[1] The number 42 is given by a vast computer as the Ultimate Answer to "Life, the Universe, and Everything" in Douglas Adams' cult classic *The Hitchhiker's Guide to the Galaxy.*

"everything." At least we know this to be the christian answer, and we also know pretty much what we mean by "God." But how do we know what is "god" for our culture's wisdom?

One enlightening way is to begin with a part. Ask basic questions of an issue or subject, and repeatedly ask them until there is no way of answering further. This is not unlike what happened in the foregoing illustration that was asking questions about "faith." But here we mean reaching a place not where it becomes difficult to ask any more questions about a subject but where in principle it is impossible to ask any more, where it appears foolish or pointless to press the matter any further because either the answer is self-evident or it goes round in a circle.

A chain of questions can take us to the "god" of a system of thought.

For example, while attending a seminar, a young woman was asked by the instructor what she had been thinking about lately. She replied, "Getting married," to which the instructor simply asked, "Why do you want to get married?" "Because I'd like to settle down and have a family," she said. "Why do you want to do that?" She thought and then said, "To be happy." When the instructor asked her why she wanted to be happy, she had no further reply. In her way of thinking about marriage at the time, "happiness" was the "god" of the way of thinking about it.

Ultimate concerns can be approached the same way. Imagine a conversation between two friends, Christopher and Quizzical. Christopher has been asked what he means by "God," and has replied, "Well, He is my Heavenly Father."

Quiz: "Father, eh? You mean like my father? Used to come home drunk three nights a week and…"

Chris (in horror): "No, not that sort of father! A kind one, a good one."

Quiz: "Oh, you mean like Kenny's. Used to get him anything he wanted, soon as he said, 'Dad, I want ____.' Was always forking out."

Chris: "Well, no, not that. God wouldn't spoil anyone like that. But He does give us things, according to His will."

Quiz: "You mean like my dad, again? Never let me have what I wanted. Always some excuse or another. Only got what he wanted me to get, which wasn't much, I'll tell you."

Chris: "No, not that either."

Of course, Quizzical could respond in all sorts of ways to any of Christopher's statements, and vice versa. Christopher could say that if it was God doing anything, you could hardly accuse Him of being stingy, surely. Or Quizzical could go on offering all kinds of unsatisfactory models. And so on. Eventually Christopher would get round to his ideal of a father. Now if Christopher were speaking as a Christian, his ideal would certainly be different from that of a Hindu, a Moslem, or a Marxist. And when Quizzical discovered that about Christopher's ideal, he would probably ask, "What makes you so sure your ideal is the right one?" And possibly, "Where have you got it from?" Of course, we don't know how Christopher might reply. He might say, "Well, I just feel that's how an ideal father would be." Or, "That's what my own father was like." Or, "You know what I mean. Anybody who wasn't being either cussed or daft would know."

Now Quizzical's responses are betraying what he means by "God" too. These could be effectively challenged, of course, and the questioning could go on until they reached a dead end. When we got to that stopping point, we would have arrived at Quizzical's ultimate answer to the initial question. We would have uncovered whatever it is that has ultimate power and authority in his philosophy of life. It is what makes sense of that way of thinking; it is what gives direction to that way of life. We would have exposed its god. And that would give us an important clue to a culture's wisdom. Now we can't cheat here, especially when we are asking these chains of questions about our own views as Christians, for different gods generate different ways of thinking about a subject. They produce different kinds of art, science, politics, educational theories, family environments, business management styles, and so on for bettering the human race. And if we have got it wrong...

People justify their gods in different ways. In the long run, the nature of the final answer, the ultimate authority ("god"), has determined the direction in which the thinking and the behavior has developed. Again, the bite of this is felt in everyday life. For instance, the power of the god "happiness" to break up a marriage, if one spouse is not "happy enough," is only too common. It is in ways like this that a particular god alters one's attitudes and directs one's life.

Now people justify their final answers in different ways. For some it is felt to be intuitive (a typically "Romantic" or "New Age" attitude—make the psychic aspect the *Logos* on the modal theory chart in Appendix 1). These folk may refuse to think in terms of an articulated justification at all. "That's just how it is," they might say. For others, their final answer is regarded as supported by accumulated evidence (typically empiricist; make the rational aspect the *Logos*). For others, it is justified by its practical effectiveness (typically pragmatist, a very American *Logos*). The point is that justifications can always be demolished by another chain of questions. This means that ultimate answers cannot be justified rationally. They are accepted by faith. They are beyond proof, and indeed all proofs depend on their being true. So one gets responses like: "It's obvious." Or, "You can't ask the question. It's foolish." Or, "If you question that, you've got nothing left." This is why religious people often answer "God" when they can't think of any other kind of answer to the last link in a chain of questions.

Again, this process helps identify the real gods that govern people's thinking and behavior in the society to which they feel they belong. These are their fundamental principles. You may be thinking that different chains of questions might lead back to quite different ultimate answers. So many gods? Precisely. This appears to be what Paul is referring to in the Letter to the Colossians when he talks about "basic principles" in 2:8 and 2:20, which can also be translated "elemental spirits," which we will look at shortly.

Here are some examples readers may wish to try. In law: who or what gives the policeman the right to stop and question you? Or, where does the authority of a policeman come from? You may say, the police chief. But who gives the police chief this right? And so on. In education: where does the authority of the teacher come from? Or, who authorizes the teacher? You may say, the principal. But who authorizes the principal? And so on. In anthropology: where did you come from? My parents. And where did they come from? And so on. In physics: where does the power of the wind come from? In biology: what is the origin of animals? When you get to the final answer, you have revealed the ultimate authority, the god, of the system of thought. In fundamentally different cultures, you end up with different final answers.

Part 3

The Significance of a Wisdom's Logos

On to another feature. There is a deep human craving to see life (everything) as a single whole. And people throughout history, today too, have often asked that succession of basic questions in a search for a single source, channel, goal, and meaning of the whole creation. One answer that has been and still is enormously influential in the entire history of Western culture came from the thinkers of Classical Greece, stimulated probably by the vast cultural change from agrarian to city life. Their answer, in a biblical context, can be a great help to our thinking here.

The ancient Greeks developed a whole body of thought and language about the question of what gives meaning, coherence, and consistency, even reality, to our lives. They sometimes spoke of it as a Principle functioning like the life-force of a seed, which produces and controls the form of the unified yet complex plant-growth. Eventually, they took up the conviction that something like an Ultimate Thought—a cosmic Mind, or Intellect, or

Rationality—was the Ultimate Reality behind all of life and everything experienced. As our thoughts are expressed by and hardly divisible from our words, so the Ultimate Thought was the Ultimate Word. Thus Reason, Word, and Principle, as descriptions of whatever it was that made coherent sense of the whole universe, became so closely identified that one term in Greek came to bear all three ideas together. It was the famous term *Logos*.

*A **Logos** gives people a way to say what and who "God" is.*

Popular at the time of Christ, the term appears in John 1:1–14 with great emphasis: In the beginning was the *Logos*, and the *Logos* was intimately with God, and the *Logos* was God. . . . The *Logos* was made flesh and dwelt among us." The passage would remind Jewish readers inescapably of that first "beginning" in Genesis 1, where creation gained form and coherence by the repeated, "And God said . . . ." They would hear John saying that the world had gained its form and coherence through the operation of Jesus Christ as God speaking his mind. This, no doubt, would be a stretch in their thinking because the Jews would be recalling Yahweh not Jesus.

But Greek consternation would be much greater. John's Greek-speaking audience would equally naturally hear John through the filter of their wisdom, which was different from that of the Jews. At first, the Greeks would be with John. Yes, they would say, we agree with you that the *Logos* made all things. But when John gets to verse 14, he comes to what is unthinkable to the ancient Greeks: that what all their great thinkers had discussed as the Ultimate Thought, the Great Principle, or Mind, that which penetrated all existence and held everything together by its Word, was that flesh and blood man Jesus Christ! This would be utter foolishness to the Greeks, for their word *Logos* meant pure intellect, the pure non-material power of the mind that could handle abstractions independently of time and matter. Thus it could never be "contaminated" with a material body. No way. To them, the idea of *Logos* becoming flesh, let alone being crucified, was outrageous, ludicrous, nonsensical. This is why Paul could say that the wisdom of the Cross was "foolishness" to the Greeks.

The apostle John is giving people a way to say what and who God is. For it is not enough merely to have the answer "God" at the end of our chain of questions. It has been said, and rightly so, that "God" is the most ambiguous word around because it can be made to mean just about anything. People using the word in conversation may think that they are on the same page when in fact they may be miles apart, in different worlds even, as to the meaning of "God."

**It gives authority and
meaning to communal thought.**

So we must know what others mean by "God," as well as what we mean by it, and clues to that are found in the kinds of *Logos* behind different philosophies of life. The *Logos* is one aspect of deity. It is the godhead operating in our human cultural thinking. Whatever gives authority and meaning to people's thinking in a particular area of communal thought, that is its *Logos*. In the foregoing example, the two types of *Logos* produce different social atmospheres of thought. The Greek *Logos* gives authority to the experts in abstract reasoning. John's gives authority to those whose lives are most redolent of the life, work, and character of the Lord Jesus Christ. The Church has been constantly bedeviled by the first, and the rest of the world has been haunted by the second.

When Paul declares his doxology in Romans as an act of worship, everybody would feel sure of what he means because he is talking among Christians and has just been expounding the Gospel of God in Christ. But when that statement is made about "Life, the Universe, and Everything" (see footnote 1, this chapter) as Paul makes it, and when it is made to politicians or scientists or artists who might be Moslems, Hindus, Marxists, humanists, or agnostics, then it needs explanation. For somebody is going to say eventually, "What do you mean by God?"

One sort of christian answer might be from the way the Bible uses the term *elohim* (chapter 3) in religious contexts as "whatever bears ultimate and absolute power and authority." This is certainly important as a description of what we mean by the word "God," but it does nothing to help others toward knowing what our God is like. For example, Moslems thinking about "whatever bears ultimate and absolute power and authority" would have in mind something rather different from Christians; animists and pantheists would have in mind something different again. And if we asked those who would not claim to be religious (in the common use of the word), then we would get different sets of answers still, some of which might surprise the people themselves.

**Picture language helps
us "see" a particular Logos.**

There is another feature to this. That is, one needs an Image of God. Try the following exercise. Describe how you understand God without using any kind of picture language—no metaphors, similes, comparisons, or images of any kind. No words like Father, Mind, Power, or Love, because your hearers are going to accept these as pictures drawn from human fatherhood, human thinking, human power, human love. (Recall Quizzical's notions of God as Father.) "Spirit" won't do, either, for the word originally meant "breath."

Of course, it is impossible to say anything of any significance at all without picture language. There is no way in which the idea, the concept, "God" can work for us, be anything at all for us, except through imagery. No way. And the problem is the same for everybody, but everybody, Christians and pagans alike. People's minds cannot get an intelligent, workable access to any "god" without at the very least some sort of mental image of that god. To say it another way, everyone reaches an understanding of the term "God" for practical purposes through an image, maybe several images. Human beings find these images in nature, or they make them up using elements of this created order to do it, for there is nowhere else to look. In many cultures they make them out of wood, stone, or metal. In today's Western world they are "hidden," and so one finds them, for instance, in ideologies such as "equality," "liberty," "happiness," "freedom," "science," "love," and so on. Some images are more significant than others, and there is always one image through which people feel that any particular god is most fully known, and which therefore gives them special access to that god. This would be their Image of God.

A related point is this. One's Image of God becomes the standard by which the person judges all suggestions about God. Think of Quizzical's responses to Christopher. Quizzical is using an Image of God constructed in his own mind, his own imagination, and it is the standard whereby he assesses Christopher's suggestions about God as Father. So besides a *Logos*, in which all things are unified, there has to be an Image by which all other images are judged, and which itself is beyond question.

In practice, therefore, the Image becomes very special, much more than a mere mental picture. It becomes so important that to have the Image is tantamount to having access to the God being imaged. When the Image is from some part of nature, for instance, the worshiper seeks to manipulate the "God" through it. Yet at the same time, the person has given it divine authority and must obey it. The Christian, however, responds in the words of Colossians 1:15, "He [Jesus Christ] is the image of the invisible God" (see also 2 Corinthians 4:4)—Someone through who we find God but who is moved not by manipulation but by loving obedience. As John quotes Jesus' claim, "Anyone who has seen me has seen the Father."

In using the term *Logos*, the apostle John is saying that the Principle through which all things are unified is a Person, Jesus Christ. In using the term Image, the apostle Paul is saying that this *Logos* is also the Image of the invisible God through whom we gain access to God. Further, since Jesus Christ is the "place" where we are to get our mental picture of God, through the study of Scripture, over time, we develop accordingly in our understanding of "everything" and the direction it is going as expressed in daily life. So our philosophy of life must have Jesus Christ as our Image and Principle because, at the least, the non-Christians around us are constantly constructing their own Images and Principles. They use their imaginations to do this, and they will be terribly distorted if not idolatrous.

To sum up, the ideas (principles, forces, determining concepts, or whatever) at the end of any chain of questioning that leads to the fundamentals (the *Logos* or the Image) are (a) beyond question or challenge, (b) not provable but taken on trust, by faith, (c) necessary assumptions felt to make reasonable and consistent behavior possible, and (d) assumptions that determine the kind of thinking and behavior we and those around us find acceptable. Now that is at the very least—a very significant part—of what sincerely religious believers would say God should be in their lives: beyond debate or question, the source and criterion of all sanity and right behavior, the starting-point for living. How does Paul put it? The Source, Channel, and Goal of all things. Surely this is what we mean by "God."

Now we have two clues for applying our knowledge of God for understanding the world.

We now have two ways in which for the practical purposes of life the word "God" gets a workable meaning. One is by means of an Image, using something in this universe as picture language for a "model" of God. The other is by means of some starting point for our thinking, some Idea, Principle, Assumption, or *Logos* (this becomes in practice the "spirit" or "power" of the Image). We have, then, 1) an Ultimate Principle to govern our reasoning and 2) a Supreme Image to govern our imagination. Again, this is why two characterizations of Jesus Christ in the New Testament are so essential, as the Word, *Logos*, of God and as the Image of God (John 1:1–3; Colossians 1:15).

(Some readers may be wondering how what we've written can apply to Old Testament religion, with no image, or to Islam, which rejects all images in its art. A large part of the message of the Book of Hebrews argues that Old Testament religion was incomplete. Thus it used image language of Jesus and said that before him the Jews only had partial and fragmentary knowledge, dispersed across their history. No wonder they found idolatry so attractive! The Old Testament represents Israel's faith as one awaiting its consummation, as the Letter to the Hebrews demonstrates. And the case of Islam demonstrates that you don't need graven images. For practical purposes, the Koran functions as Islam's "image," the holy means of God's self-revelation. It does not describe any other Image as the Bible does; indeed, it is believed to be beyond translation. It is believed to be a transcript of letters of fire in heaven of Allah's nature.)

People submit to many kinds of Images and Logos, which then take on an authority over them.

There have been many kinds of Images and *Logos* at large in history. In the ancient world most of these were the powers of nature, such as the sun, the storm, sex (Canaanite Baal-Asherah), or the cohesive power of the clan. Often they were connected with the means of survival. The Philistines, for example, were a sea people who worshiped the god Dagon, whose image was half-fish, half-man.[2] Such gods and their images were often understood in an intimately personal way and were more easily objects of prayer and ritual than of abstractions. And, of course, they are easier to identify as "gods" than many Western equivalents, which are "hidden"—you don't see them adorning the hearth! After all, it is difficult to imagine praying to Science, Humanity, Nature, or Reason! Some folk may think we are joking, here. We're not. There is no difference in principle between submitting to the old gods and giving ultimate meaning and authority to human reason or to scientific laws.

The vision of life governed by the notion that Art is the ultimate clue to Reality, which was common in 19th century Europe, still has its devotees. Closely connected has been the idea that a "Life-Force" or "Nature" holds the key to ultimate reality, with its special concerns for spontaneity and freedom from ethical restraints. This also has its devotees today. And the vision of life as governed by the notion that Reason is the ultimate clue to Reality, which became strong during the Enlightenment, still holds people's allegiance.

Throughout history people have submitted to many kinds of *Logos*. Some have been personal; most in the West are impersonal. And you can have a combination of these, each for different purposes in life. One example of that has been indicated in the artwork on a cereal box. Polytheism is just as rife in Western society as it has been anywhere. The way polytheism works is that a different *Logos* explains a different area of life: Reason for one area, Intuition for another, Emotion for another, and so on (compare our analysis of the cereal box in chapter 6). In ancient Greece and Rome, for example, one went to the god Aries or Mars about matters of war, or to Bacchus for a blessing on feasts and celebrations, or to Aphrodite for matters of affection, sexuality, and marriage.

In every such case, people are subjecting their lives to gods that are no gods (1 Corinthians 8:4), and they are, in the totality of life, in everything,

---

[2] Some scholarship offers other explanations for the name Dagon, such as that it is a vegetation or grain god. The authors, however, question this.

worshiping the creature instead of the Creator (Romans 1:22–25). Now, and this is important, when they are doing this they are allowing their thinking and consequent behavior to be ruled (directed) in practical matters (life in the aspects) by the kind of qualities and principles attributed to such "gods." A strange thing happens in consequence: these gods take on an authority over people's lives that is virtually supernatural, a kind of power over and above the power that human beings intended to bestow upon them. They become "demonic," "elemental spirits" (Colossians 2:8, 20), so that people are unable to break loose from the masters they have adopted for themselves. As Paul said, "To whom you yield yourselves servants to obey, his servants you are." It does not take bowing down in a temple for this to occur. Non-religious professing people today are no exception to this rule.

Christians can get burned here. Most serious for the People of God is the possibility, repeatedly pictured and condemned in Scripture, that those who are committed to the Lord may in some areas of their lives have their thinking governed by gods unthinkingly accepted from the pagan world outside. One only has to read the stories of Israel's ancient kings to see this. Many of them worshiped Yahweh in the Temple but were committed to "other gods" in other aspects of life. Our point is that a Christian's thinking has to be subject to one particular *Logos* and Image, Jesus Christ, for everything. (Of course Jesus Christ is infinitely more than those.) That is, the Christian has to "keep [himself or herself] from idols" (1 John 5:21), not only religiously and morally but also intellectually, politically, economically, aesthetically, and so on, right the way through all the aspects.

Can there be any truth in a pagan religion? This is not to say that there can be no truth in pagan religion or in the world. Truth can be found there because idolatry depends on a true Creation; that is, the lie derives its power from the truth. It is not the other way round. Mark Twain once said, "Get your facts first, and then you can distort them as much as you want." It's that sort of thing.

The relationship between the Christian mind and that of the world's is not a simple one. We have seen that it is impossible for human beings to live without gods, and that these gods' images are found somewhere in creation, for there is no place else to get the images from. Now since it is God's creation, and is therefore "true" (that is, it doesn't let you down; you can depend on it), every idolatry will at least have elements of truth derived from that part of creation which is idolized. Distortion thus always begins with the truth, for lies and deceptions do not exist in vacuums. Distortion leading to idolization takes place because: a) some parts of creation receive the status of deity, and b) idolatry changes the pattern of priorities by altering the relationship of each part to the rest.

Modal analysis helps identify idolatries. You can play around with the Appendix 1 illustration here. For instance, place Matter or Reason in the area of *Logos* and try to work out what, say, the direction of the religious, the economic, or the social aspects might look like. Hints to get you started: Reason directing religion would make faith an intellectual affair, while Matter directing economics would give an extremely high value to material possessions. You can play around with this in other ways too. For instance, the Matter *Logos* is formed by making chiefly the four lower aspects as Ultimate. The Reason *Logos* is formed largely by making the rational aspect as Ultimate. You can also discover the Ultimacies of people's "spiritual" beliefs. Take the occult numerologist, for instance. Looking at the Appendix illustration, can you venture a guess as to which aspect is Ultimate for that person? That's right, the numerologist uses "number" as the secret of life. Others, as we have noted, have Self, of Mind, or Intuition, or Energy, and so on. In this respect, the Gospel seems to have driven idolatry underground in cultures and societies where it has had wide-ranging influence. Everyone in the West knows you can't worship visible things like rivers, stars, or the sun. Instead, divine authority is given to ideas, like humanity, life-force, or whatever.

One's **Logos** *determines the shape (direction and meaning) of the aspects.* We need to understand this because one's *Logos* determines the "shape" in which one thinks about the nature and meaning of the aspects and the direction they should take in everyday affairs. Imagine a tray on which iron filings and tiny metal scraps are scattered. For the purpose of the analogy, think of each filing and scrap as a "unit" of human knowledge and experience. If we put a magnet underneath the tray, the filings and scraps will arrange themselves in a pattern determined by the magnet's magnetic field. But if the magnet is pushed away, and if one of the scraps is heavily magnetized, then the pattern of all the pieces on the tray is altered: it will tend to orientate towards the newly magnetized object.

You can press this analogy further, though it has its limits, of course. Nevertheless, this is analogous to how Science, Reason, Intuition, Self, or Whatever can become, for all practical purposes, God for people (in place of the true God). And it gives us a way to see how the nature, meaning, pattern, function, and direction of the aspects changes in people's wisdom with different kinds of *Logos*. This is indicative of Romans 1:18–23, where the apostle to the Gentiles speaks of people who "hold [suppress; NIV] the truth in unrighteousness" (KJV); claiming "to be wise, they became fools and exchanged the glory of the immortal God for images made to look like mortal man" (NIV).

So the Christian's task is not to ignore or reject completely what human beings think and discover in their history. (Recall that one source for wisdom is "culture"; chapter 14.) Our task is to recapture the pattern of priorities and relationships that appears under the "magnetic" influence of Jesus Christ and then to restore the idolatrously disoriented human understandings to their proper and meaningful place in the pattern. Since the pattern is only in Christ, Christians are the only people who can learn from anybody anywhere, and the only people who can unsuppress and undistort the truth; that is, redeem, renew, save—bring the Gospel into everything, the whole of life.

Part 4
Creation, Fall, Redemption

We go about our task in a fallen situation.

So, we have the Creation by God, and we know what we mean by "God." Now it is a good creation (Genesis 1), but something has gone terribly wrong (Genesis 3). This has not, however, completely wiped out the goodness and truth of it all, but we need to find ways of communicating that pattern and its Secret effectively in this predicament. It's quite exciting to think about the possibilities and what God has on offer to the world through it. After all, a new earth as well as a new heaven is coming, and somehow with it the healing of nations (Revelation 22:2). The earth will be released from its bondage to decay and come into great liberty (Romans 8:21). But in all the excitement and potential, we must keep conscious of the fact that our task for goodness and truth goes on in our fallen world. In this situation, there are special characteristics of our tasks that we must take to heart. (See chapter 14, where we covered several key ideas and principles about life before things went wrong, especially as they relate to "conserving," "cultivating," and "naming." These God-givens were never withdrawn after the Eden incident. They remain, but have become terribly distorted. We pick up here with "the Fall" to note some of the key consequences as they affect life today and how this must influence any philosophy of life that is called "Christian.")

Judgment on sin results in types of alienation.

So we have sinned. And the judgment that comes is revealing (Genesis 3). It produces various kinds of alienation. One is the barrier that arises between God and man. Man hides from God, and in the end God becomes an enigma to man, hidden even. This is the primary effect of the Fall, and it ought to produce humility in us as we go about our task of learning from Scripture as we seek to develop a philosophy of life, for it means that we can only approximate the goodness and truth of it all.

Secondary results follow, such as the alienation between the husband and his wife. He blames her; she eventually becomes dependent on him; he abuses that dominion. This particular alienation affects his understanding of his wife. Before the Fall, she was "woman," a kind of alter ego, or alternate version of himself. A colleague—not a hint of "sex" in Genesis 2! After the Fall, she becomes "Eve" (Hebrew: life-maker), defined as the bearer of his children, the means whereby the race would be perpetuated. In short, a mother. He's looking at her pretty much only biologically now, which a woman might resent very much! A third result of the Fall is the alienation that develops between people and the world they live in, the total environment. Creation, which we were commanded to cultivate and to care for, is no longer properly under our control.

The full judgment is tragic. It affects not only our relationship with God and other people but also the universe we live in. We've got to be part of it, and we've got to cultivate and conserve it (the command has never been rescinded), but we've lost proper control, which is why things in the aspects get so balled up.

Sin is never merely a human problem. Another key point is that man is not the originator of sin. Sin has, as it were, penetrated the human family from the outside, and we have welcomed it. Though we are certainly responsible before God for our sin, nevertheless we are not its ultimate originator. This means that sin is never merely a human problem *and* that we are not in ultimate control of it. That is, supernatural, or spiritual (in the "descriptive" sense; chapter 17), forces in the world must be taken into account. Sin, therefore, can initiate things outside of human control.

An analogy can be taken from planning events like a wedding or a family reunion. Though all the planners eventually come round to agree on what it should be like, the final result may easily look quite different from anyone's, or everyone's, ideas at the beginning. What happened was, the event took on a sort of life of its own. Sin is like this. But on a much more profound level. It creates structures and influences decisions that are outside of human control. If these are outside of the will and intention of God, then they become idolatrous. And if that goes on without check, then they become demonic. This seems to be the thinking, in part, behind the biblical passages about principalities and powers.

On a simple level like planning weddings and family reunions, it doesn't matter much (well, on second thoughts . . . !). But what if we raise the stakes to the level of business corporations, social structures, or educational facilities?

The potential for idolatrous use of the aspects is only too real, because sin is a structural as well as a personal problem.

This creates an ambiguous situation. "Ambiguity" may be the best word to now describe the situation, both personally and structurally. And it is a peculiar one. We are not people who are completely bad or utterly isolated. It is not that the image of God in us has been thoroughly obliterated and beyond recognition or remedy. It is not that we have lost complete control of creation. It is that there is nowhere for us where the perfect will of God can be identified in a situation. Further, it is not that we are now stupid. It's not that we cannot now create a paradise. It's that when we try to make one, it always gets spoiled. What we do may be good, but it can still go haywire. The products always get spoiled. Or when we "exercise dominion," it becomes oppressive, possibly degenerating to totalitarianism or worse. Or the good things we create sometimes just plain fail, or they have a downside to them and get used for dubious or evil purposes.

The ambiguity can be seen in all the aspects and in all their ingredients. Take medicine. In an age in which we've got almost miraculous mastery over medicine, we still get sick, still worry over our health—perhaps more than ever before! In agriculture and farming, we produce amazing results with crops or certain kinds of livestock, and yet concurrently we produce all kinds of dangers, such as from pesticides that get into the food chain, or from nasties like "Mad Cow Disease," or from grain "terminator seeds." Not to mention that certain vegetables, like carrots and tomatoes, start looking the same and tasting, well, rather tasteless. Then there is science. Through its technology, we produce amazing benefits, such as from nuclear power, but then that produces the threat of a nuclear disaster and the horrible dilemma of nuclear waste disposal.

The ambiguity also affects psychiatry and psychology. How do therapists proceed to get "a healthy mind?" What do they mean by "a healthy mind?" Such questions are vital when you are saying that your discipline heals people's minds. What is the model for a healthy mind? Is it a fully balanced, fully integrated individual within society? Sound good? But what is meant by those terms? And, if that's what it is, what do you do with people like Ezekiel or John the Baptist, or even Jesus, whom people today might call "marginalized"? What about "progressive" thinkers like Freud and Jung? And what about people who are "fully integrated" and, well, bad? They have a good family, good parents, a good job, a good husband or wife. Some of the commanders of Nazi death camps were highly cultured family men. All seems well. It all seems to be working out smoothly. Then suddenly things go sour.

There's the ambiguity. The two disciplines of psychiatry and psychology are beset at their roots by the problem that they do not know for certain what kind of effect they are supposed to produce.

And what about the squealing child of genetics? Here the ambiguity comes romping home with real seriousness. The discipline holds out some exciting possibilities. If you can alter biological structure to alleviate disease, you've got a good thing going, something quite valuable. But when you are talking about altering the structure of the *human* seed . . . . What kind of race do you then want to produce? Who is going to decide? An individual? A group? Most sci-fi books portray that people want geniuses. But what kind of geniuses? Extra-good scientists? An elite body of earth-rulers? Pulitzer Prize winning intellectuals? And who is going to decide what is "the best" kind of genetic experimentation and development? Someone's got to decide. After all, it's here, and it's not going away. Someone's got to give "direction"— aim, goal, purpose. But those who decide such things have their own hangups! And this is true for everyone of us.

> *Without the Fall there is no way to mount a critique of what's really wrong.*

So all the way through, throughout all of life, everything, we are beset by the ambiguity as a result of the Fall, not only personally but also structurally, corporately. This accounts for one of the peculiarities of human society, that it is never quite fully satisfied. Things are never quite right, not even in the eyes of those who belong to it (the business, the family, the church, the political party). Yet we rarely want to admit this too clearly or forcefully. After all, this is when prophets get stoned and messiahs get crucified. Nevertheless, these are the folk we must listen to because they turn our complaining into a possible critique and a way ahead.

Outside of the truth of the Fall in our wisdom, there is no way to mount a critique of what is really wrong. Outside of the Fall, there is no way that philosophy, or science, or psychology, or any other discipline, even theology, can provide an explanation of human society or community that does more than authenticate what is already existing, the status quo. Evolution, for instance, tells us that things are progressing, evolving, getting better and better. Yet all that says is: the way things are going is the way they should be going. Which is not saying anything at all.

If the wisdom of your discipline does not include the Fall, then you have no way to mount a biblical critique of things as they are. If you do not have the Doctrine of the Fall in your discipline, you will have a doctrine of self-justification and self-authentication. And if you and your discipline are self-justified, they are not justified by Christ. (The first reaction to sin is to pass the buck. Which is what happens when people do not allow a place for the Fall within their discipline. They have passed the buck to another reason.)

This is not just theoretical. The inception and rise of Buddhism is an outstanding illustration. Buddhism carries a deep practicality and earthiness in it. Thus, you would have thought that it would have mounted a dramatic change to people's nature, or at least to the priestly system of Hinduism. But no. After a couple of hundred years, Buddha had merely risen to the status of a god and it was back to the status quo. We wish to stress again that unless you have an understanding of the Fall, you simply do not have a foothold to mount a real critique of the way things are. That—the Fall—is *the* insight that makes possible real radical change for the better. For it helps us understand what "good" might be done in the world.

We have two activities for "good." And so Christians find themselves immersed in two activities for "good." One is "preservation." This is the process of holding the ropes, of putting one's finger in the dike. Having a fence at the edge of the precipice is better than having an ambulance at the bottom of the cliff. Government is the biblically classic example of this. The biblical notion of government is that you cannot have a perfect society. So the juridical aspect is about keeping sinners in control enough so that other things can get accomplished. In a fallen world, it's a kind of first aid. With some governments, there is a notion (it's idolatrous) that if you could have perfect laws you could have a perfect society. Not so, says Scripture. Government is merely about stopping the patient from dying so you can get on with other things. Another biblical picture of "preservation" is found in Jesus' teaching about salt, for one of its functions is to stop things from going rotten.

"Redemption" is the other activity for "good." This is not quite the same as re-creation. And it is different from "revolution," which destroys to rebuild. Redemption is not about obliterating the old that the completely new can exist in its place. Even in the Flood there is that thin line of humanity and animals saved. In redemption, things go through a transformation in which the past gets incorporated into a new kind of present. "Behold, I make all things new," says our Lord, not, "all new things." And so my past, my history, lives in my present in a way much different from how I would now be living if I were not a Christian. This is true, too, when we work redemptively in our disciplines and in the aspects. Redemption, therefore, is an injection of new creative powers, so that things function in a new way. And this will apply to our notions of education, industry, family, politics, business, science, art, law, and every other thing that has to do with both our religious and secular selves.

Part 5

An Adventure in Analysis

"Intelligent amateurs" mount some critique of Western science!

The following pages are for readers who would like to travel a little further to see how implications of Creation and the Fall might affect a christian philosophy of life in a particular discipline. We want to use science for our experiment here and a methodology that we hope will be useful in a number of ways. One is as an illustration of how Christians might mount some basic critique of Western science in particular. Another is how this means of analysis can act as a pattern for critiques of other disciplines. Also, we (the authors) are not scientists. We mention this to show that it is possible for the "intelligent amateurs" (chapter 15) among us to have important things to say to the experts. This ought to give most of us some hope! With a little study and effort, we too can make our contributions. (Remember that it may be helpful to find your way around by using Appendix 1.)

Let's begin by saying that one of the most exciting areas of Western science in our time is its exploration of the history of the universe. Remember, it is the creation of God, and it is being explored by beings made in God's image. Thus the possibilities of such an exercise are almost limitless, and not infrequently unbelievable. Indeed, science's way of exploring the universe is at present fascinating, for we are, apparently, witnessing its past! So you never know what's ahead, or is that behind? Or… Anyway, you never know what's possible!

It is too easy for the natural sciences to claim to explain everything.

Yet it is precisely the vast possibilities of the exercise that make it so easy for the natural sciences to step beyond their bounds and claim a privileged method of attaining the truth about our total existence, rather than be content to be *a contribution* to the totality of knowledge as a personal rather than a merely manipulative relationship with nature (chapter 18). There is, for instance, a serious ongoing temptation to succumb to the idea that the astro-physicists' efforts will give the world a satisfactory answer to the question: "Where did the universe come from?" Physics, however, is the study of the properties of inanimate things. It is not concerned with the nature of love or faith or beauty or honesty or our psychological hangups, though human beings (who do experience such things as love and beauty) do nevertheless occupy physical space and function in obedience to physical laws. Physics, therefore, can provide insight into the physical conditions under which other aspects of human life operate, but no more.

Each science has only a limited field and range of answers.

This means that physics can never give an answer to the question of the origin of the universe except in terms of its own interest. If a physicist were studying, say, some interesting and as yet inexplicable phenomenon on an oscilloscope, and you said that you knew what caused it, he might get excited. If you then said that a joke caused it—a lab assistant was laughing so much that she accidentally slapped a set of buttons and switches—his excitement would probably be replaced by annoyance. Not just because of the joke. For he is studying only one system of causes, and that does not include considering things from outside that system, such as how people react to jokes. He has no way to assess in his study anything that may have a bearing on his study but is outside of his scientific system. (A principle somewhat analogous is found in another discipline, law. In courtrooms there are times when "evidence" is withheld from a jury as "immaterial" or "irrelevant,"so it cannot be brought in, cannot have any bearing on the case.)

In the wisdom of the West, the natural sciences have gained such a high status in our communal thinking that this simple fact of the discipline's limits easily gets forgotten, and the result is serious. For example, the prevailing theory of how the universe began is that of an initial explosion, the Big Bang. In principle scientists work with the belief that the distribution of matter-energy throughout the universe can be accounted for by rigid laws of mechanical causes and effects. In practice such a belief is almost meaningless. There is no way of proving it, for the calculations involved in trying would take computers longer than the lifetime of the human race. Likewise, there is no way of using it comprehensively, for none of us actually live as if we and our brother and sister human beings were only highly sophisticated machines. This means that if the Big Bang is accepted as the comprehensive explanation (*Logos*) of the universe, the only way in which we could understand it would be to see the beginning of the universe in terms of explosions as we know them: as events the results of which are for practical purposes entirely random. We are what we are because, well, that's how the explosion happened. The incredibility of this has been described as being like a tornado hurtling through a junkyard and leaving behind in its wake a fully assembled 747 ready to fly. Might as well call it a miracle and be done with it!

Science can idolatrously use unprovable ideas by faith.

Such an ultimate understanding of the universe (remember, it is taken by faith and is therefore unprovable) has tremendous power to shape or change one's perception of life. And it has and does. (If you place "Big Bang" or "Explosion" as "the Source of Ultimate Authority" on the Appendix 1 diagram, you'll get the picture. Try to work out what that does to upper aspects like the religious and the ethical. Clue: they will take on a direction and meaning completely without reference to Christ as *Logos*.) This power to shape and change even a society's perception of life is also clear when considering a parallel ultimate understanding: the current evolutionary account that life began as basic molecular formations developed as the result of uncountable millions of transformations in a primordial cosmic soup. The odds against such an event, including subsequent events producing human beings, have been reckoned as one in a number greater than all the calculated atoms in the universe. Now put the pilots and crew in the 747! Yet all that can be said about it is that it happened, that humanity is the result of an incredible jackpot in a cosmic slot machine. When ultimate ideas like these are combined with similar notions in other natural sciences, any significance to human life is eliminated. No ultimate reason any longer exists for human beings to direct their lives in one way rather than another, or another, or another. If family or society does not work for us, then something new can only be created by another explosion, a bloody revolution, a schoolyard massacre, a mindless risk.

Christian vision opposes that. It does not deny the validity of a scientific explanation. It denies that a scientific explanation can ever be an ultimate or comprehensive explanation. It maintains that such an attitude is idolatry, with machinery as the Image of a mechanistic *Logos* received by faith. This is because whatever formulae may be found to express our perception of how things are what they are, the Christian insists that behind that is a Person with a will and a purpose, Someone who relates to us knowably on a personal level, not as a machine or an animal or some natural phenomenon or physical law but as Jesus Christ the Lord. This means that even the randomness of some experiences of life have an ultimate meaning for us that is not entirely alien to our human personalities.

The **Logos** *of an idolatry of physics is an impersonal Force.*

An intractable problem exists in the physics of origins that precludes it from ever being a comprehensive or ultimate explanation of the universe. It is this: how can some initial entity (with nothing in any one part of it that can be distinguished from any other part of it) in an explosion proceeding by rigidly consistent mechanical laws, laws whereby any given cause can only have one effect, produce such a mind-boggling conglomeration of phenomena with such an uneven variety of mass, position, color, energy, direction, and velocity? Not to mention personality. If the beginning of the universe is seen as a mechanical Force, so the beginning of personality has to be seen.

The christian understanding of the Ultimate Cause as a Person has its own explanation: the universe exists by a Person expressing His will through an infinitely creative imagination. Such a view accounts for the mind-boggling variety that the universe is, as well as its unity, and it gives dignity, meaning, and purpose to the creative imagination of human beings. It explains and supports the human respect for art, vision, experiment, exploration, discovery, and inventiveness. It sets one free from the enslaving commitment to mathematical symmetry that seeks to make a "true" environment for life on the one hand while longing for freedom in random behavior on the other. It would also drive physicists back to the drawing board to take a fresh look at their mathematics as expressive of purpose and meaning at work, and to discover what Thomas Kuhn (*The Structure of Scientific Revolutions*) would call fresh paradigms (theoretical models) for their work.

Part 6
The Source, Channel, and Goal of Everything

God in Christ as the Source and Goal of all things.

Both the secular physicist's and the Christian's *Logos* are received by faith. But only one offers value and meaning to life. A christian philosophy of life, then, has God in Christ—because Creator—as the Source of all things.

And also as the Goal of all things. It is not surprising that nonchristian notions of how the universe began do not produce inspiring visions of the future. Again, the dominance of the natural sciences has produced an idolatrous spirit in our culture that offers vast pictures of the universe but pathetically short-term goals. The prevailing myth is of a curious life-form having its life-cycle on a minor satellite of a fairly average star that will one day collapse as its contribution to the death of a universe. Such a perception makes an individual life virtually meaningless in the long run; so goals become short-term. (Scientistic idolatry is shortsighted; earlier ages were less impatient.) If we are unhappy, let's not waste time. Let's get happy quick, by any available means—drugs, laws, theft, marriage, divorce, violence, breast implants, facial cosmetic surgery, anything. Our Christian forebears often endured, even willingly embraced, long years of unhappiness in marriage or in pain, poverty, frustration, deprivation. They did not enjoy it, yet they contrived to make something of it, and to die no less contented, at least, than the best of us now. They did so because they thought in terms of an eternal life span where the inequities of life here might be amply rectified. (It is a matter for debate whether our own generation as a whole experiences more or less misery than past ones. We certainly seem less happy and more impatient about life than they were, and we tend to view them with mingled contempt, resentment, and envy.)

Christ gives meaning to history, culture, and persons.

The Christian conception of life and existence as finding its goal in Jesus Christ transforms one's thinking. It gives value and meaning even to the fall of a sparrow. It changes human history from a meaningless succession of events to a process in which human cultures make choices in relation to values that are embodied in Jesus Christ, and by those choices they flourish or perish.

The fact that the goal of existence (everything) is in the God of our Lord Jesus Christ is even more significant. It means that the goal is a unifying one with possibilities in new dimensions of existence. The goal is not one in which everything is finally a cold, black, entropic fog, or an endlessly swinging seesaw, or a battle of forces no one knows who the winner will be.

Further, in our human experience, the preciousness, the value, and the meaning of life does not reside in things themselves. Things receive value only as they are related to persons and to the kind of persons they are. People who love wealth value gold; power has value for people who want to rule. The Christian vision of the universe, whose goal is Jesus the Lord, results in a special scale of values being placed on the things of the universe and life. The universe, then, and everything in it, receives meaning, special meaning, in relation to him.

Though Jesus did not condemn wealth and power, his earthly possessions were few and he was not overly concerned about them. This means that wealth and power have little future. Jesus did, however, die to save his fellow men. This means that sacrificial love is among the most precious things that there are in this world, not just for individuals but also for peoples and civilizations. Consider why it is that on the throne of the universe Jesus is described as "the Lamb" (Revelation 5, 7, 21–22). At the very least, this shows why even a christian philosophy and value system is ruled by the Cross.

God in Christ as the Channel of all things.

So it all comes from God and is going to God, which places a special meaning on everything. But how does it all work? What are the processes by which the changes in the universe and the world take place? What are the laws governing the way it functions? Some of them are "natural" laws, such as gravity, entropy, and magnetism. We never seem to arrive at a final expression of these laws, but they are there, nonetheless. But is that all there is to how the universe works? Clearly not. As we have seen, the scientist can only make a contribution to the discussion. Because the Source of creation is a Trinity of Persons, we also have moral laws, aesthetic principles, and laws of production and exchange, of logic and government, of society and communication, and so on.

Laws can be seen as descriptions of how things work effectively. Now if everything operates only through the laws of mechanical causation, then moral laws become less significant. If human life works only through rules that human beings make for themselves, then all that matters for our art or our reasoning is to have a supporting peer group, regardless of whether we are "right." But if we see "all things" as existing "through him"—God in Christ—then in the long run even the so-called laws of nature are not merely mechanical or sheerly impersonal. They are the will of a personal God. If you will allow us the image, the laws of nature become a means whereby we touch the hem of God's garment. The Christian therefore sees the laws of nature as expressions of a personal Sovereign Will. This is the force of passages such as Romans 11:36; 1 Corinthians 8:6; Colossians 1:17; Hebrews 1:3.

We are bound to a life within an inescapable personal relationship that necessarily involves value judgements, commitments, and choices that require us to justify or to explain ourselves so as to be acceptable to those around and above us. Human life, whether humans believe it or not, becomes an experience of responsible choices and a relationship with at least one Person at all times, and this, one wants to shout, is an experience that overrides all isolation, even death. There really is Someone at home in the universe, Someone sustaining all things.

There are no "neutral" areas. This means that origins, processes, and ends are all related to God in Christ. It also means that there is nothing, but nothing, that we ever do or have, no aspect of our existence whatever, which is not subject to that Person's will. Thus there is no area of life within which we must not seek to be acceptable to that Person. There is no neutral ground. There are no aspects of human art, science, or custom of which we can safely say that they are not significant, or that they do not make any meaningful contribution either for or against the interests of that Person "through whom are all things." As Abraham Kuyper said, "There is not one square inch in the universe of which Jesus Christ does not say, 'It is Mine'." At any point at which neutrality or indifference is declared, the first seeds of idolatry are sown in a territory that is denied Christ's rule and care. Again, we are back to the obediences we must fulfill to God's glory in everyday life, not just in religious life.

Our conclusions must rest on Scripture, and on Christ as he is known from Scripture. Of course, there are many other basic questions that we will need to address in building a christian philosophy of life, like where does evil come from and where is it going, or how do we know anything? And we would consider issues like: how is Jesus the Ultimate Authority in the state, the Ultimate Value in economics, the Ultimate Pattern for social relationships, the Ultimate Meaning in art and language? And so on. Many of these will require thinking that forces us to ask more questions about Jesus Christ himself, since he is the *Logos* of the philosophy of life we are seeking to develop and communicate in our cultures. Knowing what he is like will give us clues for meaning and direction in the aspects. So we would ask questions like: what kind of economics did he acknowledge? What was his political, cultural, or social history? How did he use language?

This brings us back to the necessity of Scripture and the approaches to it that we have been experimenting with throughout *Uncommon Sense*. The brute fact is that without Scripture we have no possible source of information about Jesus that could have any comparable claim to reliability. All legends and histories about him are manifestly filtered through the alien mindsets of other cultures and ages. To believe in Jesus Christ commits us inevitably to believing in a biblical Christ. Any other commitment would involve the belief in a Person who commanded our ultimate trust and had at the same time told us nothing trustworthy about himself on which we could exercise it.

The arguments involved in this are discussed in other books and will no doubt go on. All we would point out here is that whatever alternative to Scripture is offered, in practice it will involve some other criterion for judging and explaining what Jesus Christ was and is like, and this will lead to a philosophy different from what is attempted here, which is seeking to think within Scripture itself. Objections to this are based on philosophies that do not reflect the peculiar viewpoint of Scripture, that do not have as their *Logos* a Person whose historicity could only be transmitted through eyewitness records. They are inevitably at odds with it, and their attractiveness rests in the fact that they have much in common with the prevailing wisdoms of this age.

Keep in mind, too, that the *Logos* of the Christian functions and is known just as any other *Logos:* through things bound up in some necessarily intimate association with it. The Science *Logos* has the body of scientific tradition. The Matter *Logos* has sense experience. The Reason *Logos* has the human mental processes. Such associated ideas have, for practical purposes, and only in association with their *Logos*, an authority that is virtually identical to the *Logos* itself. It follows that we Christians have to subject ourselves to Scripture in what it says about Jesus, and in that one respect Scripture has unquestioned authority. We do not submit to Scripture apart from Jesus, for that would be an idolatry of Scripture and lead to a legalistic enslavement. Scripture is not an unquestioned authority on nuclear physics, biology, geography, or art, though that does not imply that it is ever at fault where it might speak on such subjects (I[JP] personally would argue that this was "christologically impossible"). In such matters it simply supplies reliable evidence to a larger body of information. But it is the fundamental authority about Jesus.

Without a Christ-centered philosophy...

Of course, knowing Jesus is more than knowing "about" him, but it surely includes that. To know Jesus is to trust him, to converse with him, to think our thoughts in company with him, to permit our moral, economic, social, and other senses to be ruled by him. And this can go on amid often desperately confused ideas of what he is really like. Those ideas only get instructed as his Spirit is allowed to speak the words of Scripture to us, renewing our minds, correcting our fallen and faulty wisdom.

As we saw earlier in the book, human culture proceeds by naming things; that is, by classifying them and identifying them accordingly. How this is done depends on how life is understood, and that depends on the community's gods. Apart from God in Christ conveyed to us through Scripture, human beings give the wrong names to things. The sun, moon, stars, seas, and trees they call gods. Human beings they call highly developed apes. The human mind they call a sophisticated computer. Shame and guilt for sin they call morbid self-denigration. Mass producing consumerism they call economic progress. And they act accordingly.

Make no mistake. Philosophy counts because it both transcribes and reinforces how people are thinking. It also dictates the kind of wisdom people should follow to cope with change. Without a Christ-centered philosophy, we inevitably use a pagan one.

Remember, too, that godly wisdom itself, as we have been indicating throughout this book, is emphatically not a predominantly intellectual affair, for it involves character, relationships, devotion, confession, caring, and much else that has to do with practical, everyday life and decision making. So remember this too. As C. S. Lewis once said, "It is not a matter of 'be good sweet maid, and let who will be clever,' but of 'be good sweet maid, and remember that means being as clever as you can.'"

~Appendix 1~

Modal Theory and Analysis[1]

This Appendix and the diagram that goes with it (see next page) provide more ideas for working with the way of reasoning developed in *Uncommon Sense*, in particular to assist people to build up a biblical wisdom more fully. In brief, the diagram shows that life is all of a piece under God in Christ. Also evident is the unity, variety, and distinction in creation and between Creator and creation, not monism or pantheism, and one *Logos*, not polytheism. In particular, the diagram and this Appendix should be used alongside chapters 13 and 23 (the latter references this Appendix frequently.) Some aspect characteristics and brief explanatory notes appear on the diagram itself. Others are given relevant to each aspect category delineated below. There are also illustrations and questions in each aspect category that are pertinent to doing modal analysis in that aspect or in relationship with other aspects.

The authors would like to state that the diagram must not be thought of as the Law of the Medes and the Persians—unalterable. Rather, it is provisional, merely a device to assist one's thinking, subject to debate, change, improvement. It is simply the best way of looking at and reasoning about "everything" that we have found so far. We are certainly open to discussing ways that might be more true. Play around with it, and let us know what you come up with.

Essential Points of Modal Theory

• Everybody works with some kind of theory about how life works—a philosophy of life—which is absorbed along with the wisdom of the cultural community.

---

[1] This way of reasoning comes from a tradition of Dutch Christian philosophy most clearly developed and articulated by Abraham Kuyper and Herman Dooyeweerd.

• A theory of life can be, and often is, articulated systematically as a philosophy, addressing basic questions about origins, goals, and the course and meaning of our existence.

• Every coherent life theory or philosophy is shaped by at least one basic principle, which is its *Logos*.

• Such a basic principle normally has the unquestioned power and authority and status of a "God" in a person's reasoning processes, making that person feel that he or she is acting consistently and meaningfully in life, and with integrity.

• For the Christian, there is only one basic principle, or *Logos* (John 1:1-3): the God-Man, the Lord Jesus Christ, who is the Word made flesh (John 1:14), in whom all things hold together (Colossians 1:17), and who is the Ultimate Image (Colossians 1:15), through whom we can reach God in thought, prayer, or action.

• A Christian will not be without a philosophy of life, although it may often be an unconscious one, and one of the goals of discipleship is to continue developing a more consistently biblical one.

• A christian philosophy will recognize the truth of the creation, the ambiguity of life after the Fall, and the Gospel calling in which all of the christian life is to proceed. It will seek to learn from all people, as well as to instruct them in terms of a christian vision in Christ Jesus the Lord.

Essential Principles about the Aspects

1) Everything is subject to the laws that govern its particular kind of existence or being.

2) It is possible to explain anything in the most basic terms, but that will be unsatisfactory.

3) The aspects, or modes, range from "lower" to "higher."

4) In this ascending scale, the lower can get "taken up" into the higher, and the higher can give new meaning and significance to the lower.

5) Things in the higher aspects are subject to their own, additional, laws for their existence.

6) Human beings are specially subject to the higher aspects.

(Except for number 6, this is the list from chapter 13. Number 6 was a subhead point following the original list.)

Modal Theory
Plan of Law Structure

Upper aspects give *meaning and value* to lower aspects.
Lower aspects give *conditions of existence* to those above.

The common structure of all law-aspects enables the functioning of
those on the lower end to provide illuminating analogies for higher ones.

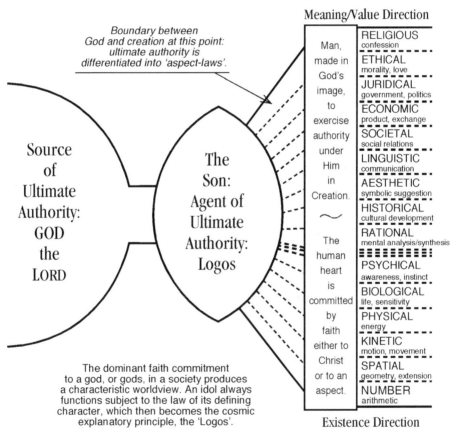

Meaning/Value Direction

*Boundary between
God and creation at this point:
ultimate authority is
differentiated into 'aspect-laws'.*

Source
of
Ultimate
Authority:
GOD
the
LORD

The
Son:
Agent of
Ultimate
Authority:
Logos

Man,
made in
God's
image,
to
exercise
authority
under
Him
in
Creation.

~

The
human
heart
is
committed
by
faith
either to
Christ
or to an
aspect.

RELIGIOUS
confession

ETHICAL
morality, love

JURIDICAL
government, politics

ECONOMIC
product, exchange

SOCIETAL
social relations

LINGUISTIC
communication

AESTHETIC
symbolic suggestion

HISTORICAL
cultural development

RATIONAL
mental analysis/synthesis

PSYCHICAL
awareness, instinct

BIOLOGICAL
life, sensitivity

PHYSICAL
energy

KINETIC
motion, movement

SPATIAL
geometry, extension

NUMBER
arithmetic

The dominant faith commitment
to a god, or gods, in a society produces
a characteristic worldview. An idol always
functions subject to the law of its defining
character, which then becomes the cosmic
explanatory principle, the 'Logos'.

Existence Direction

About Aspect Characteristics, Illustrations, and Questions

The following is a survey of each identifiable aspect of our experience, with brief comments on aspect relations. This, of course, is not a comprehensive look at our life and work in the aspects. It is meant to help readers think and work up ideas for themselves, and this can be especially productive by getting small groups together to brainstorm. Further, since working with modal analysis is new to many people, to bring the aspects alive, anecdotes and comments have been included from numerous College House seminars on business management. Due to space constraints, with some exceptions, we have been limited here to that one field, yet this should show how one may adopt modal analysis in any other discipline or aspect. Questions at the end of each aspect survey are offered to stimulate further thinking in an aspect or discipline.

RELIGIOUS/FAITH—what people regard as life's ultimate concern

This is about the fact that all individuals and communities are committed to certain basic notions about what gives life its meaning and purpose. This is the faith that forms the starting point of the explanations we give to each other for acting the way we do. (This aspect is sometimes referred to as the faith aspect.)

Common examples of such faith commitments are: wealth, progress, power, sport, a scientific interest, or a cause such as national independence, a clan, or religion. Such things are usually taken for granted in the background of life. Indeed, they are usually absorbed from the ethos of the community in which the people were reared. They may express themselves in ceremonial acts, such as saluting the flag, singing corporate songs, displaying symbolic things (aesthetic aspect) such as status symbols, or in more obviously religious behavior. Such faith commitments also determine what people feel is the (morally) "right" thing to do (ethical aspect), and in ways that are not always obvious, such ultimate concerns also direct our reasoning process and the things about which we feel good or bad. They are what Paul Tillich calls our "Ultimate Concern," and what the Old Testament calls people's "gods."

People may not be very consistent about this. For instance, people may profess and understand themselves quite sincerely to be Christian. But these same people can be committed to quite different "gods" in some aspects of their lives. It is not uncommon for a business to make an overt claim to a christian ethos but to let economic-aspect considerations in the last analysis override all else in business matters. And there are people who, after working hard all their lives, turn listless and die shortly after retirement without any apparent alteration in general health. Such people live for their work; without it, life has no meaning. When paid work is regarded in this light, and when no alternative meaning is offered, the resultant demoralization is traumatic.

Some companies, especially in the U.S., have a recruitment policy that involves investigating not merely the candidates' competencies but also where they live, their leisure interests, their friendships, the social status and talents of the spouse, the school the children attend, and so on. Some companies have comprehensive provisions for their employees, which include not only health care but also home purchases, banking, sports, and other leisure activities, not to mention social and cultural interests. In such cases there is an assumption that the company is to encompass the whole of the employee's life, to be the object of faith for the person's meaning and purpose.

Note: there are many Christians who have a lot of trouble with this upper aspect. One of the most common expressions of this in our time are those who bristle at any notion that Christianity should be "religious." They will say of themselves in no uncertain terms, "We're not religious," or that they like their church because "it's not religious." We, the authors, can appreciate what is behind this attitude, which is a kind of prophetic statement against worship and devotion that has become static, ritualistic, legalistic, hypocritical, and so on. It is therefore not uncommon to hear Christians arguing for non-religious Christianity. And we can appreciate what is behind that too, a seeking after ways to become dynamic, spontaneous, grace-filled fellowships serving each other. The way ahead, however, is not to hammer the religious aspect to pieces. What people are thoroughly frustrated about is the abuse and distortion of the features that constitute overtly religious life: worship, devotion, confession, prayer, witness, the preaching and teaching, and so on. The way to address this is not to wipe out the religious dimension of life (can't do that anyway, because it's ordained by God) but to work within it to renew what's gone wrong. The irony is that many of the "non-religious" Christians are doing this; they just don't recognize their work of renewal as life within the religious aspect.

Trouble is, if we neglect renewal of this aspect of life, we shall eventually lose that whole aspect to the enemy. The first step here, then, for many Christians, will be to accept the religious aspect as a fact of life, as they accept the other aspects, and then to understand that a church functions primarily in that aspect, otherwise it is not a church. This means that churches, all of them, are religious. And this is okay. This is no different in principle than what we have been saying throughout this book about life in the secular aspects, such as that government functions primarily in the juridical aspect, or that business functions primarily in the economic aspect. Once this is understood, we can then move on to discover the purpose and meaning of this aspect and how our churches ought to be functioning in it under God and how we ought to be fulfilling our obediences to God there. Again, this is similar to what we have been saying is the work we have to accomplish in the secular aspects. Just because it is the overtly religious aspect does not mean that it is no less established by God. Many Christians are in jeopardy of losing this aspect like many others have lost the aesthetic or the political aspect. If we ever hope to have vital contemporary churches, we must obey God also in this aspect of His creation.

Questions

What superordinate goals determine the values? What are the implied or confessed notions of Ultimate Authority, Concern, Value, Power? Any formal religious appeals? What kind of myths, religious texts? Any notions of transcendence, conversion, salvation, divine providence, judgment? What explanations are given for coherence, moral conviction, unpredictable things, unjust things, unexpected failures? Are there any modes of worship: individual, collective, corporate, vicarious, external? What things lift or create the personal or corporate morale?

———————————————————

ETHICAL/MORAL—what people ought to do

This aspect is about the basic need for people to trust one another voluntarily and to be trusted. An ex-pupil at Rugby school when Matthew Arnold was headmaster said, "You just couldn't lie to him; he put such trust in you telling the truth." In other aspects of life the basic need for people to trust one another voluntarily and to be trusted extends to caring for others' needs, feelings, and aspirations.

Moral ideals do not exist in a vacuum, and they are not nearly so obviously agreed upon as people might think. They are always formed by the kind of faith assumptions to which a community is committed. A christian ethic, for instance, always has a special obligation to the helpless. This aspect is especially significant in rearing children. Education and instruction are always given in the context of family relationships, in which trust and mutual care are communicated either badly or well. This aspect of life depends on a prior concern, that of justice (juridical aspect).

Hewlett Packard has a policy of keeping open cupboards and shelves for taking things you need, trusting that you will only take what you need for work. (David Packard once, on principle, cut through a padlock he found on a store cupboard door.) IBM's guidelines on business conduct lay down the principle "honesty is integral to ethical behavior and trustworthiness is essential for good, lasting relationships." This is expounded with considerable subtlety through some 50 pages: from not using IBM's size to gain unfair advantage, to avoiding facial expressions that might suggest criticism of a competitor's products.

Questions

What kind of moral values are appealed to? What notions of right and wrong, good and evil, "spiritual" and "unspiritual"? What are the notions of faithfulness, love, courage, honesty, chastity, both personal and social? How far is ethics significant?

— — — — — — — — — — — — — — — —

JURIDICAL / LAW—the just way for people to treat each other

This aspect is about the fact that our social relationships have to be ordered to make it possible for all creatures to functions as God intends. It involves a responsible use of power.

Justice is especially significant for organizing communities. The biblical notion of authority involves overlapping hierarchies in which people at the top of one will have lower, even bottom, places in others. The rule of law most clearly demonstrates this in balancing the conflicting interests of national life. This is the special task of politics and government. Biblical justice is less concerned with "fair" distribution of goods and more concerned with persons, protecting the weak from the ungodly powerful.

So companies have rules about time-keeping, complaints procedures, departmental priorities, and so on. Justice issues can become acute during periods of unemployment or a recession. "Last on, first off" may not acknowledge the commitment a new recruit has made in joining the firm. Hewlett Packard has a policy of cross-company pay cuts when possible rather than laying people off. IBM has been known to turn its production staff into salespeople during a recession when possible, and it has a policy of redeployment and retraining for such eventualities. It is unjust to demand that an employee perform a task for which essential resources were not made available (Pharaoh demanding that the Israelites make bricks without straw), or to require working conditions that would undermine family life.

Questions

What are the types of rules, and where do they come from? What are the ideas of justice? What are the methods of discipline and government? What are the concepts of law and punishment? What legal procedures or political theory are at work? What type of law: criminal, civil, mercantile? What are the notions of overall legal authority and the authority structures, within groups and between them?

— — — — — — — — — — — — — —

ECONOMIC—the values in producing, saving, and exchanging things

All the resources of creation are limited, and this aspect is concerned with the choices that have to be made to take account of this.

Economics is founded on other aspects. It assumes that people are interrelated in a society, sharing its resources. Currency value is about symbols whereby we can measure the stewardship of goods, products, and services. Emotional disorders such as obsession, driven-ness, or clinging-ness prevent people from making free economic decisions. "Economic growth" is an analogy from the biological aspect. Economic theories are applications of the rational-analytical aspect. A biblical economics would judge a community's wealth not by growth of production but by the standard of living of its poor.

The special calling of a business enterprise is to facilitate the process of exchange between services and products, so it is "focused" in this aspect. John Laing, founder of Laing Construction, used to attribute his success to faith in God and accurate costing. In the economic aspect, from our perspective, these are one and the same thing.

Questions

How do people exchange, share—coinage, barter, credit? What types of credit are operative—interest, credit rates? Is there a use of gold, silver, paper, credit cards, or notional accounting? What types of economic arrangements are found? How is manpower balanced with energy, materials, time, space, resources, talents, goodwill, effort? In a family, what are the children taught about money; are they taught anything about it?

— — — — — — — — — — — — — —

SOCIAL—how people relate to each other

This aspect is about the fact that human beings are not made to function in isolation. Societal relations function in recognizable patterns that have to be understood and utilized.

Social relations develop in certain ways: large groups tend to depersonalize and function differently from small ones. Single-sex groups differ from mixed-sexed ones. And groups tend to relate to each other differently. The growth of business necessitates management decisions that take account of such things. All social acts are founded on other aspects. For instance, people communicate respect, care, and foster well-being through symbolic actions such as handshakes, hellos, hugs, and kisses. Social acts also arise from our need to cooperate together in the historical (cultural-formative) tasks, and in our sharing of common space on earth. Note also how an emotionally insecure person finds it difficult to foster social relationships.

One hospital suffered a continual turnover of its cleaning staff. The situation was transformed by setting up teams of cleaners with no more than 14 in each team. A sense of personal solidarity then became possible. Many corporations spend considerable sums to provide facilities for their employees' social lives. Every expense account makes provision for the business lunch, and the power of a game of golf is legendary!

Questions

Why are certain types of groupings evident—classes, guilds, unions, clubs, family-types, clans, tribes, business communities, and so on? What bonding interests are at work—power, wealth, birth, connections, pressures, interest groups? Is it oligarchy, meritocracy, or gerontocracy? Is anything known about the group dynamics? What phases of group growth are current? What kinds of mutual understandings and agreements exist within a group or between groups? How do these affect any common activity?

— — — — — — — — — — — — — — —

LINGUISTIC/LANGUAGE—how people communicate ideas

This aspect is, of course, about communication and is sometimes referred to by that word. It is concerned with the human activity of giving information, instructions, directions, explanations, ideas, projections, plans.

Language takes richer forms in the aspects above it. Coinage is symbolic of exchange-values (economic aspect). A scepter is a juridical symbol. A handshake in ethical life is a sign of mutual agreement. Bread, wine, and water used by Christians in the sacraments are symbols of an ultimate commitment. A christian understanding of communication would involve the responsibility to rescue people from ignorance and misunderstanding, and it would carry a willingness to become vulnerable by listening.

Increasingly, management is required to ensure that communication "upward," "downward," and "sideways" is clear and unequivocal. M.B.W.A. (management by wandering around) is partly to aid the communication process. (At least one management theory sees the whole task in terms of communication: "Organizations exist as networks of directives and commissives . . ."; Winograd and Flores, *Understanding Computers and Cognition*, Apex, Norwood, NJ, p. 157.) Communication also provides the resources for intersocial bonding; hence the development of language systems and of group jargon. Learning the language of a European or an Asian customer may be crucial to American or English business, and vice versa. The influence of information technology in this area is still to be fully appreciated.

This aspect "opens up" the rational-analytic aspect of our experience.

Giving signs or names to things enables us to manipulate highly complex ideas, even chains of reasoning. In the business world, this is most clearly exemplified in the formal presentation of ideas or projects.

·   *Questions*

What kind of vocabulary is found—technical, clichéd, undefined, esoteric, popular? What kind of literature, or is there lack of it? Are there loan-words from other languages or nonverbal languages—drums, ideographs, hieroglyphs, body-language, uniform-language, status-language? How effective, extensive, comprehensive, consistent, accurate, relevant, and significant is it?

— — — — — — — — — — — — — —

AESTHETIC—how people produce meaningful images of life

At the heart of this aspect of life is the free exercise of the imagination. It is essentially not geared directly to utilitarian values of survival and progress. For this reason it is easily undervalued.

The aesthetic task is to provide material resources for people to "have a holiday" at least first in their imaginations and then maybe to share it with others. This is true recreation, a kind of Sabbath. Hence a well designed workplace aesthetically refreshes those who work in it.

The aesthetic aspect is about celebration, taste and style, adventure, experiment, brainstorming, wit, expressivity, playfulness, fun, entertainment, fantasy, jokes. A christian view of art will include this function, but it will also be aware of the underlying values implicit in the styles and motifs, which will give clues to the operative faith values. All of us are called to respond to God, to our world, and to each other aesthetically, all of the time. Some of us are called to deepen this aspect and become artists, musicians, authors, playwrights, or actors.

Innovation depends heavily on this aspect. The ability to imagine impossible things (not necessarily before breakfast!) is often the key to solving an otherwise intractable problem. We've all heard about a troubleshooter who changed a business with some crazy punch line. In one large company's department, in response to complaints of dullness, a budget presentation was transformed by showing the projections as like the flight of a airplane, soaring, stalling, diving, and so on. An in-house joke can be a powerful bonding agent for a team. Blessed is the manager who can use a joker in his pack.

Questions

What kinds of images are current? What kinds of suggestive symbolism are popular? What is a work of art thought to do? How are values, goals, standards, and ideals imaged? What kinds of connotations cluster around words, actions, artefacts? Consider forms, styles, processes of selection, analogies, and non-natural portrayals. What is the significance of accents? How are problems and solutions visualized? What kinds of humor, decor, design, logos, games, or entertainment are present?

— — — — — — — — — — — — — — —

HISTORICAL (formative-cultural)—how people work with Earth's raw materials

Sometimes called the techno-formative, or techno-historical, aspect, it is about formative power, developing the values latent in creation's raw materials. For this purpose, tools and institutions are created and the environment is shaped. A classic example is the change from keeping records and creating pro forma documents by hand to computer. Troubles often arise, however, such as in one firm that wanted to retire a little old lady but had to keep her on to check for errors that the computer bookkeeping method, which was to "replace" her, kept making!

Factories, workshops, artefacts, techniques, and institutions are particularly characterized by this aspect. Psychotherapy relates to our psycho-sensitive life in this aspect, as do various tasks and offices in other aspects. Because our activity in this aspect is creative, and leaves visible traces over long periods of time, and initiates changes in our relationships and environment, it is especially connected with human history. Obedience results in development that poses new challenges about how we develop our artefacts, technology, and artistic styles; about how we cope with the altered meanings of words and symbols; about how we create new institutions, modify legislation, face new moral dilemmas, and see our ultimate concern in a new light.

In *The Practice of Management,* Drucker identifies business management in techno-formative terms as the product of modern technology. It exists, he says, "to make a productive enterprise out of human and material resources." The rapidity of change has given rise to management programs that especially relate to this aspect of life.

Questions

How are the earth's resources being controlled and developed? What stage of cultural development is under consideration? How far are the various aspects of life individually embodied in the institutions and practices of the culture (art galleries, churches, banks, law courts)? What kinds of tools, machines, furniture, buildings, synthetic materials are there (wood, concrete, plastic)? Historically: stone age, iron age, nuclear age, information age? Or tribal, mercantile, agricultural, industrial? Is anything out of date, ahead of its time?

—————————————————

RATIONAL/ANALYTICAL—how people organize ideas

Sometimes called the analytic aspect, it relates to the human practice of reasoning, manipulating abstract ideas, analyzing, constructing chains of logic, and making inferences and deductions. Probably the simplest example of this in industry would be the job description. But it is fundamental to budgeting, systems analysis, marketing strategies, and to most other areas of business. The models so beloved by management theorists are the products of various analyses of the tasks. Analysis is not confined to intellectuals. Everyone understands abstractions like: "color," "good grain," or "texture" in a piece of wood; "profit" and "loss"; 2 +2 = 4.

The analytic mode is inseparably bound with all the other modes (aspects) as basic to our powers of "dominion" in them. In particular, reason depends for its direction on its presuppositions, and these are in turn generated by our ultimate commitments and concerns. Christian reasoning always takes account of the plurality and unity of our world as reflecting the tri-unity of God. In a subtle way, this can be expected to affect any distinctive approach to the natural sciences. The multiplicity of management theories demonstrates how faith assumptions determine what evidence, what purposes, are significant for study. The university is the institution typically characterized by this dimension.

The rational-analytic aspect has been specially subject to idolatry in our culture. Under pagan, Hellenistic influence, reason has been elevated to a transcendent, timeless position, from which it is seen as the arbiter of all truth about the mere physical world. (This is at the heart of the tension between blue collar and white collar workers.) A backlash to this has been the Romantic Movement, in which art, poetry, and imagination are thought to get at the real essence of things. Much New Age thinking, so-called, rides on this wave, with its stress of the irrational and its overmuch emphasis on the intuitive. Such movements at least recognize that people are not machines or computers. Their rational processes arise out of the way they are aware of the world around them and how they respond emotionally and aesthetically to it.

Intellectualism and anti-intellectualism are twin products of idolatry of the intellect. Hence the ambivalent attitudes toward a book like this! For some it becomes a dogmatic formula, and for that very reason others reject it outright. Rationality is not in itself knowledge; it is but one aspect of our whole multifaceted experience of life.

Questions

What type of reasoning is present? What assumptions? What's the logic? What philosophy of life is there? Any scientific processes? What about processes of abstraction, methods of analysis—monistic, dualistic, pluralistic? Any theory of knowledge and truth? What theories of each modal aspect are implied or expounded? How important is reasoning?

———————————————————

PSYCHICAL (psycho-sensitive)—instincts, feelings, emotions

Sometimes called the psycho-sensitive aspect, it is about awareness, instinct. We have this in common with animals but in a vastly expanded fashion. Our whole being is aware of, and responds emotionally and instinctively to, our environment.

Emotions are immediate, intense, and bodily aware of being totally moved through the whole range of our experience. People *feel* that an argument is right more often than they are persuaded by its strict logic. In this process, our instinctual makeup plays a considerable part. In many cases, such as our experiences of other people's personalities and characters, we do not have enough evidence to make logical judgments, especially as people tend to react unpredictably if they sense that we are attempting to deal with them by strict rationality.

Human emotions always belong to a specific context: the joy of building something, of caring and being cared for, sorrow at loss, anger at injustice, fear of danger. As such, emotions are appropriate, inappropriate, exaggerated, distorted, or misused in terms of the larger human context and the mode of life to which they are directed. In this respect, the emotional life of Jesus provides important insights.

When we function properly in this aspect, responsive action can be rapid and efficient. Most sports rely heavily on this, because in such situations focusing on the analytic process is inhibiting. These characteristics often commend this aspect as an alternative idol to the analytical.

Robert Haas, talking about Levi's business policies, remarks, "It used to be that what happened to your employees when they went home at the end of the day was their business. But today that worker's sick child is your business, because if that worker is worrying about her child or calling in sick when she isn't—and probably feeling resentful because she's had to lie—she isn't going to be productive." He wants workers to feel supported not just financially but "psychically."

This aspect often affects teamwork, which can become dangerously explosive when emotions are suppressed. Emotions underpin our thinking, judging, loving, socializing, economizing, and our faith. Hence the common practice of banning emotional expression from the office or the boardroom. But "die rather than cry" is unrealistic. Actually, the "male" emotion of anger is often accepted but the "female" emotions of pity and helplessness are to be suppressed. In other words, the powerful persona of vulnerability is an unused resource.

Questions

What instincts or appetites are manifest or operative—hunger, sex or reproduction, herd-instinct, aggression, self-defense, rest, satisfaction, excitement, ecstasy, weakness, curiosity, fear, freedom, pain, sensations, insecurity? Everything distinctively to do with animal life is included in this aspect of human life.

— — — — — — — — — — — — — — —

BIOLOGICAL (biotic-organic)—people's conscious animal nature; its needs and functions

Sometimes called the biotic mode, this is about our biological life, growth, health, reproduction, metabolism, and aging.

Health is often affected by unexpected causes. Emotionally stress-related illnesses are not unusual today. Poverty is another. Other aspects heighten the meaning of this aspect, such as with indiscriminate sexual behavior (moral aspect). Since WW2, "music while you work" is an aesthetic factor now taken for granted for its role in the biological aspect. Medical professionals heighten this aspect especially in the rational and the social aspects.

A century ago, Marks (of the Marks & Spencer stores), selling goods in the open markets, led the way in this aspect, putting wooden platforms behind the vendors' stalls to keep their feet warm. An increasing number of companies implement ways to provide comfort for employees who are pregnant. Time off for illness each year, when added up among a company's numerous employees, can mean much work lost each year. Its unpredictability is particularly disruptive. Thus most businesses are concerned with provisions such as canteens, sports facilities, and healthy work environments especially in relation to new technologies.

On a global scale, problems of environmental pollution are becoming increasingly pressing. The possibility that scientific development may have taken some wrong turns in this respect may have serious consequences for management.

Questions

What kind of life-forms and biological processes are involved? What about growth and decay (vegetation), or the appearance of germs, viruses, or mutations? What are the issues surrounding food, rest, health, survival (fertility), temperature, air control, seating?

_____

PHYSICAL & KINETIC—nonconscious growth and adaption; energy; movement

Note: on the diagram, these are shown as two aspects (some schools of thought work with two, others with one).The physical dimension is characterized by energy and movement, including lack of movement and seemingly little or no energy.

Malcolm Wheatley, when discussing Japanese management techniques, cites Hyogo Railways' solution to the strain on workers who were reaching up to install wiring and control components in the carriages' roofs. "Each carriage is simply placed in an enormous jig and turned upside down." Gravitational energy is thus made to work *for* workers instead of against them.

Access to sources of energy and means of transport are vital in locating a factory. The ecological (biotic) aspect of this is increasingly important in the use of fuels. Use of mechanical energy has often equalized the relation between the sexes in some types of work. Time and motion studies, though often overused and abused, yet bear witness to the importance of this aspect. And as with all lower aspects, its value is heightened as it is "taken up" into the higher aspects.

Questions

What sources or resources of energy are available—wind, tides, rivers, sun, fuels, geothermal, animal, human (hence the climatic and environmental conditions)? Where are things and people moving, being transported? What direction, what speed (hence geographical and geological terrain)?

_____

SPATIAL—geometry, extension

This is about the fact that everything exists "apart from" but "related to" everything else. It is technically called "continuous extension." Geometry and geography are typical sciences of this dimension of life.

In one apparently ideal new office plan, the staff manifested an ongoing tendency to irritability. The problem was eventually traced to not quite enough room for two people to pass comfortably between desks and cubicles. When space was increased, the problem disappeared. Consideration for the disabled often focuses on this aspect especially within the social.

Questions

What significant areas, localities, distances, elevations, and dimensions are involved (hence geometrical calculations)?

——————————————————

NUMERICAL—number, arithmetic

Numbers are about the countability of things. By counting, we can, and do, identify things simply as mere isolated items having some common characteristic. Numbering is the foundation for all the others. There is nothing in which it does not play a part. (Many other aspects, however, have things about them that cannot be quantified, such as the arts, or loyalty, or a faith commitment.) This aspect when taken as a comprehensive explanation for all of life, as it is done by occult numerologists, becomes a gross idolatry.

A company accountant's insistence on accurate costing "down to the last nail" illustrates the significance of this aspect in budgeting. Though selling stocked items will involve many other aspects, working out a commitment figure for stocking a commodity in the first place is directed here. A car parts department is a good case in point. Many of the upper aspects (social, rational, economic) come into play when a customer becomes upset because "the car dealership ought to have that part in stock" but does not. That customer, whose car is now tied up, doesn't want to hear that "it was an odd part that's not worth stocking because we only stock what sells." That customer expected better service than the stocking inventory permitted.

The fact that numbers are fundamental means that there is a temptation to idolatry that gives statistics a special authority. Peter Drucker talks about an apparently thriving business having all the right statistics, yet the CEO felt that something was wrong. It's not hard to guess that complacency—an unquantifiable factor—was threatening future profitability.

Questions

What numbers are involved? What proportions? Any fractions? Any particular methods of counting or calculation? What kinds of comparisons of figures are made? What are the figures supposed to tell us?

A Final Word

We hope you have benefited from your visit to the aspect survey, and that it has opened you to more of the possibilities available through modal theory and analysis. Keep in mind that the aspects (modes) are all interdependent yet relational. As a building needs foundations, walls, floors, and a roof, so each of these builds on the other. For example, you cannot have law without a community, but law is meaningless if not morally directed. Also, the central ideas in each aspect have analogies that contribute to the way the others work. Economic growth, for instance, takes a cue from the biotic aspect. Yet each aspect also has its own mode of functioning: no amount of religion will free people from the laws of gravity; beautiful pictures are no good to a starving person. Further, and importantly, only in Jesus Christ do all these aspects and their "laws" find authority and unity. Only *in Christ* are they all resolved, not in any one, or even in all, of them.

This way of seeing things:

1) enables us to see more clearly different kinds of idolatry: making the laws governing one aspect govern all the others (e.g., Marxism; the Theory of Evolution);

2) enables us to develop distinctively christian theories about things—if Jesus Christ is Lord, then God's way of doing things must be (a) consistent (a "faithful" creation) and (b) rescuing (God is Savior of all aspects);

3) enables us to allow the Bible to feed our imaginations, for we can sample God's way of doing things;

4) enables us to "locate" particular activities in the total scheme of things; a game may be in the aesthetic, an exercise in the economic, and so on.

A Postscript? No Way!

At times, the significant question comes up: where is the Holy Spirit in all this? It is tempting to say, "The Holy Spirit is implied in all this," and let it go at that. But the question deserves a fuller answer.

The first thing that may be said is that all models break down at some point. They have their limitations, and this one is no exception. Perhaps the greatest limitation of this model is that it is not much help for looking at the supernatural world. Having said that, it is somewhat useful here, because it does helps one to see how idolatries arise, such as when Mind, or Life-Force, or Matter, or Self, or Feelings, or Intuition, or Whatever usurp Jesus Christ's place as *Logos*. And when idolatries reach a certain pitch, they become demonic, which in turn affects aspect understanding and the kind of life that goes on within the aspects. Modal theory helps us see that.

Another thing is this. All Christians will probably agree, in so many words, that our obedience works through the Holy Spirit. With that as a starting point, we can all probably also agree that modal theory shows a way in which the Holy Spirit can help us to think about how we can fulfill our obediences to God more broadly. Modal theory is therefore an activity focused on the rational-analytical aspect, seeking to reason obediently about the wisdom of Scripture, with a view to clarifying the meaning-value of things in the aspects, with a view to effective living. Yet following on the heels of that comes the question, "Why don't we immediately comprehend modal theory this way?"

The discussion here is subtle but quite significant. It is also a good exercise in "worldview analysis," revealing how assumptions of Western culture can become so deeply imbedded in our wisdom, even as Christians, that we become oblivious to the Bible's instincts on life. That is, when we in the West look out at creation and the world, we generally visualize it as a mechanistic system, even as a machine maybe. Again, this is a deeply buried assumption, not something we ever think about. In this kind of wisdom, if you introduce something "from the outside," you're going to mess up the works, like tossing a screwdriver into a running machine. It stops the machine, or at the least, the cause and effect processes are going to get damaged. Try to bring the supernatural into this mechanistic picture and it appears as very alien, perhaps an impossibility. So people see miracles and divine intervention as incredible. To Western Christians, even the Holy Spirit may appear kind of alien, something from the outside that comes and goes, or that we try to add, like oil, to situations in the mechanistic picture. It's all quite puzzling, because we're trying to see how the Spirit can function in the machine.

However, if we see modal theory as a way of understanding what the Bible teaches, that all of life is "in Christ," then we see that creation is more of an organism than a mechanism. And if we believe that Christ works through the Holy Spirit, creating and sustaining all things, then, as with an organism, you can introduce something from outside without messing up the cause and effect processes or grinding things to a halt. So it becomes more like medicine going into the system, rather than parts replacement engineering. Even miracles become possible, then.

Further, according to Scripture, but unlike our Western wisdom, you have this "outside something," the Spirit, on the inside, meaning that the Spirit is always at work in the organism anyway, always. Scripture affirms this numerous times. By this we do not mean only the Spirit's work in miracles or in people's conversions to Christ. We mean the way the whole thing runs, the way it is sustained and holds together, the way it is renewed. True, evangelical theology has been weak at this point, especially when it comes to the work of the Spirit in secular matters, but that does not mean we cannot learn from Scripture here. Scripture continually associates the Spirit with great power in creation and with helping God's people in their daily lives, not to mention that the Holy Spirit is many times called the Spirit of Christ, such as in 2 Corinthians 3:17, Philippians 1:9, and 1 Peter 1:11.

The irony in all this turns out to be the question itself. "Where's the Holy Spirit in all this?" "There's no way He can be kept out!"

~Appendix 2~

Conversation with John Peck

Charles Strohmer interviewed John Peck for the inaugural issue of the quarterly magazine Openings *(Autumn, 1998). They spoke about John's "conversion" to modal thinking, and then the conversation surrounded its use as a biblical way to examine issues of everyday life both within and without Christendom. As it may fill in some blanks, or say things in a different way, or reveal some helpful practical critique, the conversation, minus its original introduction, is reprinted here in its entirety.*

Charles Strohmer: **John, you haven't always thought like a Christian as you do now, have you? How did you arrive at this new attitude of mind that gave you an appreciation for God's activity in so-called secular life?**

John Peck: Well, the sort of nursery, if I can put it like that, in which I was cared for and taught as a new Christian was strong on christian separation from the world. So we didn't drink, smoke, dance, play cards. That sort of thing. I didn't go to a movie theater for ten years. Actually, I'm rather glad that was my first christian discipline because it left me with a lot of freedom to get to know the Word, to learn how to pray and witness, and so on. But over the years it left me in conflict. Part of me was certainly committed to what you could call the devotional life, and I would not for a moment want to deny or detract from my christian obligations here. Trouble was, I couldn't match that with things in the world that I recognized to be of value. For instance, having done my degree, I was teaching non-Christian religions at Glasgow Bible Institute, and I could not deny what seemed to me the considerable spiritual power of the exordium in the first chapter of the Koran. I also found a lot of the spiritual psychology of Buddhism teaching me quite unconsciously about different aspects of my christian devotional life. But I couldn't match what was going on here with the way I'd been taught as a Christian to see life.

CS: **Something quite fundamental wasn't right?**

JP: Yes. And it came to a head in a particular way with literature. My two great loves were the metaphysical poets and Elizabethan drama. I could not deny the value in these, but I had no way to say that I could appreciate that value because there was this complete separation of the religious and the secular going on in my mind. Secular things were not on; they were bad. Of course, I'd try to pick out bits and spiritualize them, but that wasn't a satisfactory process. I simply did not have a way to appreciate what was of value in literature (or culture, for that matter) or to criticize what wasn't. There was nothing I seemed to be able to do about this, and all sorts of uncertainties arose in me as a result. I knew this left me vulnerable, but there was nothing I could do. Then something happened that changed everything. I had to teach Ethics at G.B.I., and in pursuance of that a friend lent me a book called *The Christian Philosophy of Law, Politics, and the State,* by Hebden Taylor. That book introduced me to "modal theory," and that theory unlocked so many doors that enabled me to see the validity of the "secular" areas of life.

CS: **So that turning point opened you to a new way of seeing life and being a Christian in it. Sounds like a kind of conversion.**

JP: Well, I nearly had a nervous breakdown! There were so many things I wanted to explore all at once. And then I gravitated toward others who had already learned this stuff and began to explore a christian perspective of things like politics, business, science, and the arts. In fact, it was in looking at science from the point of view of the Bible that I began to recognize that all science is religiously driven, and it was then that I began to learn what idolatry was. Before that, I thought idolatry was the heathen in his blindness bowing down to wood and stone. It hadn't occurred to me that you could be a scientist and make an idol of your science.

CS: **Or of your politics, or your business, or your art, or your family...**

JP: That's right. These can be disguised idolatries. Another key was that I began to understand that life was no longer divided into two unrelated bits, the religious and the secular. This revolutionized my understanding of spirituality. I saw quite clearly that spirituality is about obedience to God's order for the universe that we live in, and that God is just as involved in economics, or politics, or science, or art as He is in our church-related (religious) activities. The thing is, once you realize that "secular" life has laws that are ordained by God, then you're obeying God in obeying them.

CS: **Sounds like a whole new world opened up to you. You must have felt like you'd come home.**

JP: I remember sitting back from my desk one day and saying about this, "Nothing can be that good!" Although, mind you, I've always held it subject to criticism. For example, as a theory, modal analysis doesn't cope much with the supernatural dimension. But okay. I wasn't expecting it to be perfect. In fact, I'm quite glad I'm aware of its limitations, because I know folk who've made a kind of orthodoxy out of it, which has brought them all sorts of headaches.

CS: **What is modal thinking, modal analysis, and how can we put it to work for us?**

JP: It will be difficult to summarize here, but I'll have a go. It's a theory that looks at the "whole" of life as being made up of different aspects, or modes, of life and existence under God, aspects such as art, law, religion, economics, social matters, and so on. Modal theory sees each of these aspects as functioning by its own God-ordained laws or principles. It therefore helps us get to grips with the way God has ordained that the different aspects of everyday life should be conducted. It gives us a way to do distinctly Christian studies of the arts, business, politics, economics, sociology, and so on. It shows that our obediences to God cannot be limited to the religious and moral modes of our being. And it has unexpected benefits too. It enables us to deal with the paradoxes of Scripture, for instance, and to understand the disguised idolatries of our modern cultures more clearly.

CS: **How does Jesus fit into all this?**

JP: Well, there's no way he can be kept out! It's his creation. For instance, modal thinking gives us a way out of one of our age's most fundamental problems when thinking about life. For example, non-christian theories of life fasten on one or two of the aspects as *the key* for understanding the universe and human nature. For example, humanists fasten on reason, communists fasten on technology and economics, Buddhists tend to fasten on psychology. And they do this as a way for understanding and judging *all* of life. This gets them into trouble in the long run because everything can't be explained only economically or only psychologically, and so on.

Now Christians have their equivalent to this. They often judge the value of everything only in terms of religion and morals. And this gets them into trouble in the long run for the same reason. Modal theory helps you steer clear of this because it shows that no aspect is capable of fully explaining all of life, for each aspect is but a part of life. Further, it helps you to see the aspects as having their unity and "explanation" in Jesus Christ alone. The Bible can help us understand this, as well as to see where we may be violating God's laws in the aspects and therefore in need of making changes in our wisdom.

CS: **Isn't there a problem here that is as subtle as it is profound? I mean, many Christians think they are already applying this way of reasoning, but in actual fact they are arguing only with the Bible's religious and moral** ideas as the remedy for ills within the "secular" aspects of life, such as in art, politics, economics, and social issues.

JP: Yes. Our obedience to God cannot be limited to *or defined by* our religious and moral obediences. When Christians do this, they violate God's laws for the other aspects of life without even knowing it. What's needed is instruction from Scripture for fulfilling our political, economic, and social obediences, and so on.

CS: **It's difficult to get this across. Why is that?**

JP: Because people have an *assumption* that they're doing it biblically, and assumptions are difficult to discuss with most people. You can be getting it quite wrong without realizing it. I remember running across a christian business some years ago. It claimed to be Christian, anyway. But its advertising sounded just like the world's, and I knew folk who worked there who told me that the employers were extremely hard to work for. Now, if you haven't got a truly christian theory, or vision, of business as, among other things, a rescue operation—if it isn't a saving, a liberating, vision—God's laws for that aspect get violated, things go wrong, and people suffer.

CS: **Are you suggesting that the employers assume they're working out of a christian view of business just because they're Christians?**

JP: That's why it's so hard to discuss it with them at times. You're dealing with assumptions. Further, should you get going in a good discussion with these folk, it can get quite complicated. One thing I try to point out is that we don't do anything in life without a theory, or vision, of how a thing works. And if Christ is Lord, then he has to be Lord even of our theories, our visions, which means that, fundamentally, they have got to have a Gospel-shaped character. That's why I talk about it as being saving, rescuing, and liberating. But it's difficult to get this over. Most people tend to think that good business is not telling lies, not breaking contracts, not flirting with the secretaries. Well, okay, we need to be good moral people. But that's not enough of a theory for business. So you find, for instance, that when you talk to a person in business about making contracts that are generous in nature, there's the rub, because the person is not thinking of business as being a liberating process, for business has been reduced, even for the Christian, to making as much profit as you can. Full stop. And because it's an assumption, it's not known.

CS: **I was recently burned by this attitude in my field, Christian publishing, and it left me thinking that the enterprise is evolving to become driven strictly by making money. Should publishers like this even refer to themselves as Christian anymore?**

JP: The problem here is partly economic, certainly, but it's not just in that aspect that God's laws are being violated. For instance, the publishers are part of an entire industry in a culture that fails to ask some quite radical questions, such as about the sorts of books that are published—those that sell so well only because they appeal to the prejudices and preoccupations of the worldly Christians, and feeding it. Why, just recently, I happened to be looking through a christian book catalog and came across things that were out of this world. Well, out of God's world, anyway!

There was a title in the personal growth section indicating that the book's contents, which were going to tell us about love, had all the trappings of romanticism. But love isn't an emotion you can hope to cultivate lastingly, as the catalog blurb suggested. Love is a decision. This book is certainly not talking that way. Another I saw claimed to be about gaining emotional freedom. The jacket blurb promised readers a well-balanced emotional life, and I wondered what the author would do with Jeremiah, Ezekiel, or John the Baptist! Others that I saw were filled with "how to" formulas to help readers with their marriages. *Methods* are how to do it. Well, my wife and I have been married for a long time, through some pretty rough patches, too, but we've never read books on marriage about how to keep each other interested. At the beginning we made an assumption that we belonged to each other and that we had to care for each other no matter what. That's what it's all about.

CS: **So the publishers must do more than examine the economic aspect.**

JP: One of the radical questions the industry is not asking about these books is that they're all concentrating on getting yourself right. To me, the christian life is about forgetting yourself. It's about saving, rescuing, liberating others, about getting to know the needs of those around you and doing something about them. Now that I think about it, one of the things that has helped move our marriage along is that we've always been involved in other people's troubles. My question to christian publishers is: are we always going to spend our time concentrating on examining ourselves? It's a kind of perpetual childhood, isn't it? I mean, it's kids that are absorbed with themselves, who are the center of their universes. And then there's all the family stuff, which assumes the nuclear family. I defy anyone to find a nuclear family in the Bible. Certainly the family of God is not a nuclear family; thank God.

CS: **Although we try to live like we are one.**

JP: And that can produce churches that live like that. It's a shame, really. I can appreciate the occasional book like this, because you've got to have something for children—I mean children in the faith. But this is a whole industry dedicated to giving middle aged adult Christians children's material.

CS: **Modal thinking and analysis sounds quite different from what we're accustomed to.**

JP: Yes. And when you start to try to cope with the questions it raises, then the complexities begin to arise. It's like I often say about the Gospel: it's like a daisy; any child can pick one, but if you want to understand it, to study it biologically and so on, it takes a lifetime.

CS: **And you use the Bible for this study about secular life?**

JP: Yes. For me it meant that I was able to stop reading Scripture through what I call the "stained glass window effect." That is, I was able to start understanding Scripture other than religiously and morally and I began to see the Bible's "secular" wisdom. For example, when I was first involved in the arts with Greenbelt, I was obviously confronted with the need to be able to articulate what art was about and what God's design for art was—rules for how art works. I'd read a lot of books about it and looked at different theories, some of which were helpful, but when I went back to the Scripture and looked at its art, in particular the parables and the Psalms, then I had living examples, if you will, of works of art that were authorized by God. And that gave me a point from which I could see the positive values of some people's theories as well as the negative ones. In that process, working as a Christian believing in the Gospel of salvation, I came to develop an aesthetic theory. At first I was a bit schizophrenic about the whole thing because I couldn't see how I could relate to the arts as a Christian. Now I can.

CS: **Are you saying that Christians can develop theories like this for business management, economics, education, psychology, politics, the family, and so on?**

JP: Absolutely. And now there are christian writers who can contribute to this. Whereas twenty-five years ago there wasn't much available.

CS: **In your own calling, you and some colleagues, such as at College House, have tackled such areas.**

JP: That's right. Take business. We dug around not just for some vaguely christian moral view of business and management but for something that had the Gospel as its heart and how the patterns of the Gospel would influence biblical themes of management. We were looking for a distinctly christian mode of management. So, first, we started with the Gospel, which meant that we looked for ways of doing management that are saving, rescuing, and liberating. We also looked into Scripture to see how people were managed and how people in authority managed the managers. Moses, for instance, is classic here. He lost his temper and it cost him dearly; he learned to delegate authority, and so on.

CS: **You're talking about much more than the kind of rescuing that makes non-Christians Christian.**

JP: That's right. It's equipping people to do what God wants them to do in their work. Human beings, you see, are more than just religious and moral beings. They are also citizens, which means they live politically (even to not vote is to make a political statement). They are also social, which means they relate to one another in groups of various kinds. They use language and aesthetics. They are economic beings. And so on. No one escapes this stuff. We have obediences to fulfill before God in these aspects, to make rescues there, if I could put it like that. If you think you can do politics simply by using morality, then you will end up violating God's authority in the political realm. The same is true for any of the other aspects. God has His own way of ordering them, and if we're going to have a wisdom based on the fear of the Lord, we've got to bring more than the Bible's religious and moral values to bear on them.

CS: **But surely religion and morality have a bearing on politics and on all the other aspects?**

JP: Yes, indeed. To put it simply, one's faith gives direction not only to one's morals and ethics but also to one's politics and economics and art, and so on. And so these too are part of a Christian's obedience. The problem is that you cannot pass laws, for instance, telling people that they must love one another *or else*. What you can do is pass laws that *liberate* people to be loving. For example, laws that make medical professionals nervous or afraid about helping an injured person they may come across on the street, or in a serious accident, are not liberating laws.

CS: **But the Bible doesn't give us fully developed theories of business management, economics, politics, or art. So how may we depend on Scripture in these aspects then?**

JP: The Bible provides samples, not exhaustive treatments. It's St. Paul, for instance, stating that "these things happen for our example." Now the samples from Scripture are different from samples found elsewhere in that they are authoritative for the Christian. After all, outside of Scripture, you don't know what you're getting. I would say that God's purpose in the Old Testament was to create a sample of how He would order a culture and its history in a fallen world. The glory of this is that it does this by taking sin and sinners seriously. Most "good advice" assumes that you haven't sinned. And this is one of the problems of nonbiblical theories about life. If there's no sin, there's no redemption, no true liberty. So something quite fundamental gets left out of the picture. Christian theories of the aspects wouldn't do that.

CS: **Can you give us an example?**

JP: How about, instead of looking at the Story of Naboth's Vineyard as a purely moral lesson, we see it also as instructing us politically. This could help us to see, for instance, how the fear of the god you serve (your faith, even if you're an atheist) influences your politics in quite practical ways. So you've got Jezebel, whose wisdom is based on the fear of a Baal, which gives her a certain politics regarding the land, which has drastic consequence for Naboth. Elijah then comes along with a wisdom based on the fear of the Lord, which gives him a different view of politics with regard to the land *and* a way to mount a critique of Jezebel's political theory. This story, then, can help us to see that different gods rule different ways of thinking about politics. So, if you've got a nation whose politics is based on dialectical materialism, or on life, liberty, and the pursuit of happiness . . . . Samples from the lives of Joseph and Daniel are also quite illuminating.

CS: **This is fascinating, isn't it, because folk like Joseph and Daniel held high political offices, were highly respected, and known for doing a good job. Yet in fulfilling their secular obediences before God here, they obviously had quite a different way of looking at life than we do, and God seemed okay with it.**

JP: Yes. This is bristling with all sorts of issues, like what one writer calls "responsible compromise." So, Daniel, for example, is prepared to receive instruction in spiritistic areas and he's willing to carry the name of a Baal, which must have been a constant thorn in the side, but he's not willing to compromise in the matter of food. That was his sticking point.

SC: **His sticking point?**

JP: Yes. We all must have them. When you know what yours are—they're a matter of conscience under the fear of the Lord—then you can do responsible compromise. It will be different for different Christians. You can have areas of responsible compromise only if you first know where you'll say, "This far, no farther."

CS: **You're saying that Christians can use this principle under God?**

JP: Yes, as God's people have always done. And alongside it is the vital thing, for instance, for Old Testament politics. That is, it was not so much the structure of the politics that mattered as it was the tacit agreement between the people and the rulers that they were going to obey the word of the Lord. That's the key to biblical kinds of politics. The problem with a modern democracy, I would say, is that it is more a demagoguery. Candidates tend to appeal not to people's consciences but to their desires. There should be a common assumption between the candidate and his constituency that his business in politics is to obey the Law of the Lord.

CS: **Sounds like you're calling us to get to know the Bible as a "secular book."**

JP: You could put it like that. One of the beauties of the thing is that this kind of thinking lets you talk about your family, your business, your politics, your art, and so on from many points of view *under God*. You are not limited to the religious and moral ways of seeing, as important as these are. We must be obedient to God in the way we live our public lives. And the Book can show us how.

Note:

Openings is a 12-page quarterly magazine published by The Living Wisdom Center, which was founded by Charles Strohmer to promote a biblical wisdom that appreciates the unity, diversity, and complexity of life under God in Christ. *Openings* seeks to provide alternative christian perspective to issues important to all of us. This is done through interviews, short articles, lists of organizations, and other culturally relevant pieces. *Openings* is sent free-of-charge to people in any nation. To subscribe, contact *Openings* at:

PO Box 4325, Sevierville, TN, U.S.A., 37864. Or e-mail livewise@esper.com. (Back issues available.)

Bibliography

The following titles come from a number of outlooks, including the Reformational school of thought, a broad Evangelical footing, and Roman Catholic. Some titles may be still emerging from individualistic pietism and spiritual-material dualism, some may still be a bit too issue-oriented or suspicious of philosophy, some may be merely catalogues of worldviews, and many may be focused on theory or the mind without much emphasis on practical everyday life. Nevertheless, in their dialogue with Scripture, these titles often produce valuable insights and creative possibilities. Some titles from outside christian traditions are also listed because they provide fruitful ideas and material for the development of wisdom as it is being proposed in *Uncommon Sense*.

It is recommended that readers peruse all the titles, not just those in a particular category of interest. This is because a title is listed only once, even though it may have a bearing in more than one area, e.g., Lewis' *Discarded Image* could be listed under "culture & society" as well as "toward a christian wisdom," and Owens's *And the Trees of the Field* could be listed under "science & technology" as well as "creation." Some titles may be relevant primarily for the U.K. or for the U.S. If you can't find a book through your usual means, try these contacts:

Christian Studies Unit Booklist, 65 Prior Park Road, Widcombe, Bath, Somerset, BA2 4NL, England, email: 113135.2944@compuserve.com

Institute for Christian Studies Booklist, 229 College Street, Toronto, Ontario, M5T 1R4, Canada, email: ics@icscanada.edu. Tel: (416) 979-2331; Toll Free (888) 326-5347; Fax: (416) 979-2332

Book Resources: Gerry Williams, 6043 Babeley Road, Knoxville, TN, USA, Tel: (865) 689-8326

Codes used below: np = publisher's name not available; nd = publishing date not available

Toward a Christian Wisdom (Worldview)

Baillie, Donald, *God Was In Christ*, Macmillan, 1981
Blamires, Harry, *The Christian Mind: How Should a Christian Think?*, Servant, 1978
Clark, G., *A Christian View of Men and Things*, Presbyterian & Reformed, 1952
Clouser, Roy A., *Knowing with the Heart*, IVP, 1999
_____, *The Myth of Religious Neutrality: An Essay on the Hidden Role of Religious Belief in Theories*, Univ. of Notre Dame Press, 1991
Colson, Charles, and Nancy Pearcey, *How Now Shall We Live?*, Tyndale House, 1999
Dooyeweerd, Herman, *New Critique of Theoretical Thought: The General Theory of Modal Spheres*, Edwin Mellen, 1997
_____, *New Critique of Theoretical Thought: The Necessary Presuppositions of Philosophy*, Edwin Mellen, 1997
_____, *New Critique of Theoretical Thought: The Structures of Individuality of Temporal Reality*, Edwin Mellen, 1997
_____, *In the Twilight of Western Thought: Studies in the Pretended Autonomy of Philosophical Thought*, Craig Press, 1968
Frey, Bradshaw, William Ingram, et. al., *All of Life Redeemed*, Paideia Press, Ontario, nd
Hart, Hendrik, *Understanding Our World: An Integral Ontology*, Univ. Press of America, 1984
Hasker, William, *Metaphysics: Constructing a Worldview*, IVP, 1983
Heslam, Peter S., *Creating a Christian Worldview: Kuyper's Lectures of Calvinism*, Eerdmans, 1998
Holmes, Arthur, *All Truth Is God's Truth*, IVP, 1983
_____, *Contours of a Worldview*, Eerdmans, 1983
Karlsbeek, L.,*Contours of a Christian Philosophy: An Introduction to Herman Dooyeweerd's Thought*, Wedge, Toronto, 1985
Kok, John H., *Patterns of the Western Mind: A Reformed Christian Perspective*, Dordt College Press, 1996
Kuyper, Abraham, *Lectures on Calvinism*, Eerdmans, 1983
_____, *Christianity: A Total World and Life System*, Plymouth Rock Foundation, 1996
Lewis, C.S., *The Discarded Image*, Cambridge Univ. Press, 1995.
Middleton, Richard, and Brian Walsh, *Truth is Stranger That It Used To Be: Biblical Faith in a Postmodern Age*, IVP, 1995
Nobel, David A., *Understanding the Times: The Religious Worldviews of Our Day and the Search for Truth*, Harvest House, 1994
Peck, John, and Charles Strohmer, *Uncommon Sense: God's Wisdom for Our Complex and Changing World*, The Wise Press, 2000
Schaeffer, Francis, *Collected Works*, Crossway, 1985
_____, *Escape from Reason*, IVP, 1991
_____, *The God Who Is There*, IVP, 1998
_____, *He Is There and He is Not Silent*, Tyndale House, 1998
_____, *The Francis A. Schaeffer Trilogy*, Crossway, 1990 *(The God Who Is There; He Is There and He Is Not Silent; Escape from Reason)*
Shaw, Steve, *No Splits: Can You Trust God with the Whole of Your Life?*, Marshall Pickering, 1989
Sire, James, *Discipleship of the Mind: Learning to Love God in the Ways We Think*, IVP, 1990
_____, *The Universe Next Door: A Basic Worldview Catalog*, IVP, 1990
_____, *Why Should Anyone Believe Anything At All?*, IVP, 1994
Spier, J.M., *An Introduction to Christian Philosophy*, Craig Press, 1973
Stott, John, *Your Mind Matters*, IVP, 1973
Walsh, Brian, *Subversive Christianity*, Alta Vista College Press, 1994
Walsh, Brian, and Richard Middleton, *The Transforming Vision: Shaping a Christian Worldview*, IVP, 1984
Weeks, Stuart, *Early Israelite Wisdom*, Oxford Theological Monographs, 2000
Wilson, Marvin R., *Our Father Abraham*, Eerdmans, 1989 (explores Hebrew mindset)

Wolters, Albert, *Creation Regained: Biblical Basics for a Reformational Worldview*, Eerdmans, 1985
_____, *Our Place in the Philosophic Tradition*, Institute for Christian Studies, 1975
Wolterstorff, Nicholas, *Reason Within the Bounds of Religion* (second ed.), Eerdmans, 1984
Vroom, Hendrik M., *Religions and Truth: Philosophical Reflections and Perspectives*, Eerdmans/
Rodopi, 1989

AESTHETICS, THE ARTS, THE IMAGINATION

Begbie, Jeremy, *Voicing Creation's Praise*, T&T Clark, Edinburgh, 1991
Brueggemann, Walter, *The Prophetic Imagination*, Fortress Press, 1978
Chaplin, Adrienne, and Hilary Brand, *Art & Soul: Signposts for Christian Artists*, Solway/Paternoster, 1999
The Earl of Listowel, *Modern Aesthetics: An Historical Introduction*, Allen & Unwin, 1967
Finney, Paul C. (ed.), *Seeing Beyond the Word: Visual Arts in the Calvinist Tradition*, Eerdmans, 1999
Forbes, Cheryl, *Imagination: Embracing a Theology of Wonder*, Multnomah, 1986
Goodwin, Nigel, *Arts and Minds*, Hodder Headline, 1994
Harries, Richard, *Art and the Beauty of God: A Christian Understanding*, Mowbray, London, 1993
Jeffries, David, *Christianity and Literature*, Eerdmans, nd
Lewis, C.S., *Studies in Words*, Cambridge Univ. Press, 1974
McIntyre, John, *Faith, Theology and Imagination*, Handsel Press, 1987
O'Connor, Flannery, *Mystery and Manners*, Farrar, Straus & Giroux, 1969
Pieper, Josef, *Only the Lover Sings: Art & Contemplation*, Ignatius Press, 1990
Rookmaaker, H.R., *Art Needs No Justification*, IVP, 1978
_____, *The Creative Gift: Essays on Art and Christian Life*, Good News, 1981
_____, H.R., *Modern Art and the Death of Culture*, Crossway, 1994
Ryken, Leland (ed.), *The Christian Imagination*, np, nd
Ryken, Leland, *The Liberated Imagination: Thinking Christianly about the Arts*, Harold Shaw, 1989
_____, *Triumphs of the Imagination*, IVP, 1979
_____, *Windows to the World: Literature in Christian Perspective*, Zondervan, 1985
Sayers, Dorothy, *The Mind of the Maker: An Examination of God the Creator Reflected in the Artistic Imagination*, Harper & Row, 1979
Scott, Steve, *Crying For A Vision*, Stride, Exeter, 1991
_____, *Like a House on Fire: Renewal of the Arts in a Post-modern Culture*, Cornerstone Press, 1997
Seerveld, Calvin, *Bearing Fresh Olive Leaves: Alternative Steps in Understanding Art*, Solway/
Paternoster, 1999
Seerveld, Calvin, *A Christian Critique of Art and Literature*, Wedge, 1995
_____, *On Being Human: Imaging God in the Modern World*, np, 1988
_____, *Rainbows for a Fallen World*, Radix Books, 1980
_____, *Take Hold of God and Pull*, Paternoster, 1999
Schaeffer, Francis, *Art & the Bible*, IVP, 1973
Schaeffer, Franky, *Addicted to Mediocrity*, Crossway, 1981
Thistlethwaite, David, *The Art of God and the Religion of Art*, Solway/Paternoster, 1998
Van der Leeuw, Geradus, *Sacred and Profane Beauty: The Holy in Art*, Abingdon/Hopper, Rinehart & Winston, NY, 1963
Wolterstorff, Nicholas, *Art in Action*, Eerdmans, 1980
_____, *Christianity and Art*, Eerdmans, nd
Zylstra, H., *Testament of Vision*, Eerdmans, 1973

APOLOGETICS

Bahnsen, Greg, *Van Til's Apologetics: Readings and Analysis*, Presbyterian & Reformed, 1998
Burnett, David, *Dawning of the Pagan Moon: Understanding the Roots, Characteristics, and Influences of Western Paganism*, Thomas Nelson, 1992

Clark, David K, and Norman L. Geisler, *Apologetics in the New Age: A Christian Critique of Pantheism*, Baker, 1990

Drane, John, *What Is the New Age Still Saying to the Church?* Harper Collins, 1999

Groothuis, Douglas, *Revealing the New Age Jesus: Challenges to Orthodox Views of Christ*, IVP, 1990
_____, *Unmasking the New Age*, IVP, 1984

Hagopian, David, et. al. (eds.), *Back to Basics: Rediscovering the Richness of the Reformed Faith*, Presbyterian & Reformed, 1996

Mangalwadi, Vishal, *In Search of Self: Beyond the New Age*, Spire, 1992
_____, *The World of Gurus: A Critical Look at the Philosophies of India's Influential Gurus and Mystics*, Cornerstone, 1996

Miller, Elliot, *A Crash Course on the New Age Movement*, Baker, 1989

Osborn, Lawrence, *Angels of Light?: The Challenge of the New Age Spirituality*, Daybreak, 1992

Rhodes, Ron, *The Counterfeit Christ of the New Age Movement*, Baker, 1990

Strohmer, Charles, *America's Fascination with Astrology: Is It Healthy?*, Emerald House (U.S.), 1998
_____, *What Your Horoscope Doesn't Tell You*, Word Books (U.K.), 1991

Van Til, Cornelius, *Works of Cornelius Van Til*, Presbyterian & Reformed, 1996

Zacharias, Ravi, *A Shattered Visage: The Real Face of Atheism*, Baker, 1990
_____, *Can Man Live Without God?*, Word Books, 1994

THE CHURCH, CHRISTIANITY, MISSIONS

Barr, James, *Fundamentalism*, SCM Press, 1981

Boer, Jan, H (ed.), *Missions: Heralds of Capitalism or Christ?*, np, 1984

Bosch, David, *Transforming Mission: Paradigm Shifts in Theology of Mission*, Orbis Books, 1991

Bradshaw, Bruce, *Bridging the Gap: Evangelism, Development and Shalom*, Marc/World Vision, 1993

Carry, Ellen, *By the Renewing of Your Minds: The Pastoral Function of Christian Doctrine*, Oxford, 1997

Cheyne, John R., *Incarnational Agents: A Guide to Developmental Ministry*, Marc/World Vision, nd

Clapp, Rodney, *A Peculiar People: The Church as Culture in a Post-Christian Society*, IVP, 1996

Drane, John, *Cultural Change, Biblical Faith and the Future of the Church*, Paternoster, 2000

Harris, Harriet A., *Fundamentalism and Evangelicals*, Clarendon Press, 1998 (chapters on the Dutch influence in Evangelicalism)

Hays, Richard, *The Moral Vision of the New Testament: A Contemporary Introduction to New Testament Ethics*, Harper San Francisco, 1996

Hiebert, Paul C., and Eloise Hiebert Menses, *Incarnational Ministry: Planting Churches in Band, Tribal, Peasant, and Urban Societies*, Baker, 1995

Lewis, C.S., *Mere Christianity*, Macmillan, 1981

Macaulay, Ranald, and Jerram Barrs, *Being Human: The Nature of Spiritual Experience*, IVP, 1978

Mangalwadi, Vishal, *Missionary Conspiracy: Letters to a Post-Modern Hindu*, Nivedit Good Books, 1996

Marsden, George, *Reforming Fundamentalism: Fuller Seminary and the New Evangelicalism*, Eerdmans, 1987
_____, *Understanding Fundamentalism and Evangelicalism*, Eerdmans, 1991

Newbigin, Lesslie, *Foolishness to the Greeks: The Gospel and Western Culture*, SPCK, 1986
_____, *The Gospel in a Pluralist Society*, Eerdmans, 1989

Newbigin, Lesslie, Lamin Sanneh, and Jenny Taylor, *Faith and Power: Christianity and Islam in 'Secular' Britain*, np, nd

Noll, Mark A., *The Scandal of the Evangelical Mind*, Eerdmans, 1994

Peck, John, *What the Bible Teaches about the Holy Spirit*, Tyndale House, 1979

Schaeffer, Edith, *L'Abri*, Crossway, 1992 (autobiographical)

Snyder, Robert A., *Models of the Kingdom*, Abingdon, 1991

Strohmer, Charles, *Building Bridges to the New Age World*, CPAS, 1996
_____, *Explaining the Grace of God*, Sovereign World, 1993
_____, *The Gospel and the New Spirituality: Communicating the Truth in a World of Spiritual Seekers*,

Thomas Nelson, 1996, U.S. only
_____, *Wise as a Serpent, Harmless as a Dove: Understanding and Communication in the New Age World*, Word Books, 1994, U.K. only
Webber, Robert, *The Church in the World: Opposition, Tension, or Transformation?*, Zondervan, 1986
Wells, David F., *No Place for Truth: Or What Ever Happened to Evangelical Theology?* Eerdmans, 1993
_____, *God in the Wasteland: The Reality of Truth in a World of Fading Dreams*, Eerdmans, 1994
Vandervelde, George (ed.), *The Holy Spirit: Renewing and Empowering Presence*, np, 1989
Vanhoozer, Kevin, *Is There Meaning in This Text?: The Bible, The Reader, and the Morality of Literary Knowledge*, Zondervan, 1998
Volf, Miroslav, *The Church as the Image of the Trinity*, Eerdmans, 1998
Wright, N.T., *Jesus and the Victory of God*, Fortress, 1993
_____, *The Meaning of Jesus, Two Visions* (with Marcus Borg), Harper San Francisco, 1999
_____, *The New Testament and the People of God*, Fortress, 1992
Wright, Tom, *New Tasks for a Renewed Church*, Hodder, 1992

CREATION

Cooper, Tim, *Green Christianity*, Hodder, 1990
Craig, William Lane, and Quentin Smith, *Theism, Atheism, and Big Bang Cosmology*, Oxford Univ. Press, 1993
David, Percival, and Dean H. Kenyon, *Of Pandas and People: The Central Question of Biological Origins*, (Thaxton, Charles B., ed.), Haughton, 1993
Dembski, William A., *Intelligent Design: The Bridge Between Science and Theology*, IVP, 1999
Dembski, William A. (ed.), *Mere Creation: Science, Faith, and Intelligent Design*, IVP, 1998
DeWitt, *Caring for Creation: Responsible Stewardship of God's Handiwork*, Baker, 1998
Johnson, Philip E., *Defeating Darwinism by Opening Minds*, IVP, 1999
_____, *Objections Sustained: Subversive Essays on Evolution, Law, and Culture*, IVP, 1998
Kaiser, Christopher, *Creation and the History of Science*, Eerdmans, 1991
Marshall, Paul, *Heaven Is Not My Home: Learning to Live in God's Creation* (with Lela Gilbert), Word, 1999
Moreland, J.P. (ed.), *The Creation Hypothesis: Scientific Evidence for Intelligent Design*, IVP, 1994
Owens, Virginia Stem, *And the Trees of the Field Will Clap Their Hands: Faith, Perception and the New Physics*, Eerdmans, 1983
Rifkin, Jeremy, *The Biotech Century: Harnessing the Gene and Remaking the World*, J.P. Tarcher, 1999
Van Dyke, Fred, David C. Mahan, et. al., *Redeeming Creation: The Biblical Basis for Environmental Stewardship*, IVP, 1996
Van Till, Howard J., et. al., *Portraits of Creation: Biblical and Scientific Perspectives of the World's Formation*, Eerdmans, 1990
Walsh, Brian, J., Hendrik Hart, and Robert E. VanderVennen (eds.), *An Ethos of Compassion and the Integrity of Creation*, Univ. Press of America, 1995
Wilkinson, Loren (ed.), *Earthkeeping: Christian Stewardship of Natural Resources*, Eerdmans, 1980

CULTURE, THE MEDIA (INCLUDING ENTERTAINMENT),
SOCIAL ASPECT OF LIFE (INCLUDING FAMILY AND RELATED),
SOCIETY, SOCIAL STUDIES (INCLUDING PSYCHOLOGY)

Adams, Douglas, *Hitchhiker's Guide to the Galaxy*, Random House, 1995
Bellah, Robert, *Habits of the Heart: Individualism and Commitment in American Life*, Univ. of California Press, 1985
Blamires, Harry, *The Post-Christian Mind: Exposing Its Destructive Agenda*, Servant/Vine, 1999
Blaswick & Morland, *Social Problems: A Christian Understanding and Response*, Baker, 1990
Bloom, Alan, *The Closing of the American Mind*, Simon & Schuster, 1987

Bloom, Harold, *The American Religion: The Emergence of the Post-Christian Nation*, Simon & Schuster, 1992

Burtchaell, James, *Rachael Weeping and Other Essays on Abortion*, Life Cycle Books, 1990

Clapp, Rodney, *Families at the Crossroads: Beyond Traditional and Modern Options*, IVP, 1993

Cook, David, *The Moral Maze, A Way of Exploring Christian Ethics*, SPCK, 1994

Daniélou, Jean, *The Lord of History*, Longmans, 1958

Dawson, Christopher, *Religion and the Rise of Western Culture*, Doubleday, 1991

De Santo, C., et. al., *A Reader in Sociology: Christian Perspectives*, Herald Press, 1980

DeGraaf, Arnold (ed.), *Views of Man and Psychology: Readings in Psychology and Christianity*, Institute for Christian Studies, nd

Dengerink, Jan, *The Idea of Justice in Christian Perspective*, Wedge, 1978

Dooyeweerd, Herman, *Roots of Western Culture: Pagan, Secular, and Christian Options*, Wedge, 1979

Ellul, Jacques, *The Betrayal of the West*, Seabury, 1978

_____, *The New Demons*, Mowbrays, 1975

_____, *The Technological Society*, Random House, 1967

Evans, Stephen C., *Preserving the Person*, IVP, 1977

Gay, Craig, *The Way of the Modern World*, Eerdmans, 1997

Gladwin, John, *God's People in God's World: Biblical Motives for Social Involvement*, IVP, 1980

Goudzwaard, Bob (trans.), *Idols of Our Time*, IVP, 1984

Grenz, Stanley J., *A Primer on Postmodernism*, Eerdmans, 1996

Hart, Hendrik, *The Challenge of Our Age*, Wedge, 1974

Huntington, Samuel P., *The Clash of Civilizations and the Remaking of World Order*, Simon & Schuster, 1996

Kennedy, Paul, *Preparing for the Twenty-first Century*, Random House, 1994

Leech, Kenneth, *The Eye of the Storm: Living Spiritually in the Real World*, Harper Collins, 1992

Lewis, C.S., *The Abolition of Man*, Macmillan, 1977

_____, *The Four Loves*, HBJ, 1960

Mangalwadi, Vishal, *India: The Grand Experiment*, Rann (Pippa) Books, 1997 (clear implications for Britain)

Marsden, George, *Fundamentalism and American Culture: The Shaping of Twentieth-Century Evangelism, 1870-1925*, Oxford Univ. Press, 1980

Marshall, Paul A., and Robert VanderVennen (eds.), *Social Science in Christian Perspective*, Univ. Press of America, 1988

Marshall, Paul A., Sander Griffioen, and Richard J. Mouw (eds.), *Stained Glass: Worldviews and Social Science*, Univ. Press of America, 1989

Matthews-Green, Frederica, *Real Choices: Offering Practical, Life-Affirming Alternative to Abortion*, Multnomah, 1994

McCarthy, Rockne, et. al., *Society, State, and Schools: A Case for Structural and Confessional Pluralism*, Eerdmans, 1981

Meyers, David, *The Human Puzzle: Psychological Research and Christian Belief*, Harper & Row, 1978

Meyers, Ken, *All God's Children and Blue Suede Shoes: Christians and Popular Culture*, Crossway, 1989

Moseley, Romney M., *Becoming a Self Before God: Critical Transformations*, Abingdon, 1992

Neuhaus, Richard, *America Against Itself: Moral Vision and Public Order*, Univ. of Notre Dame Press, 1992

_____, *The Naked Public Square: Religion and Democracy in America*, Eerdmans, 1986

Niebuhr, H. Richard, *Christ and Culture*, Harper & Row, 1983

Olthuis, James, *I Pledge You My Troth: A Christian View of Marriage, Family, and Friendship*, np, 1989

_____, *Keeping Our Troth: Staying in Love through the First Five Stages of Marriage*, np, 1986

Packard, Vance, *The Hidden Persuaders*, Longmans/Pelican, 1957

Postman, Neil, *Amusing Ourselves to Death: Public Discourse in the Age of Show Business*, Penguin, 1985

_____, *Conscientious Objections: Stirring Up Trouble about Language, Technology, and Education*, Knopf, 1988

Rahner, Hugo, *Did You Ever Practise Eutrapelia*, Quaestiones Disputatae, Burns, Oates, nd, c. 1970
Rifkin, Jeremy (with Ted Howard), *The Emerging Order: God in the Age of Scarcity*, Ballantine, 1979
Rolheiser, Ronald, *The Shattered Lantern: Rediscovering a Felt Presence of God*, Crossroad, 1995
Schaeffer, Edith, *The Hidden Art of Homemaking*, Tyndale House, 1985
_____, *What Is a Family?*, Baker, 1993
Schlossberg, Herbert, *Idols for Destruction: Christian Faith and Its Confrontation with American Society*, Thomas Nelson, 1983
Schluter, Michael, and David Lee, *The R Factor*, Hodder, 1993 (how Western society undermines relationships)
Schuurman, Egbert (trans.), *The Future: Our Choice or God's Gift?*, np, 1991 ("Christians in exile" approach)
_____ (trans.), *Reflections on the Technological Society*, Wedge, 1977
Shalet, Wendy, *A Return to Modesty*, Simon & Schuster, 1999
Sider, Ron, *Just Generosity: A new Vision for Overcoming Poverty in America*, Baker, 1999
Sine, Tom, *Cease Fire: Searching for Sanity in America's Culture Wars*, Eerdmans, 1995
_____, *Mustard Seed vs McWorld: Reinventing Life and Faith for the Future*, Baker, 1999
Storkey, Alan, *A Christian Social Perspective*, IVP, 1979
_____, *Marriage and Its Modern Crisis*, Hodder, 1996
Storkey, Elaine, *Created or Constructed?: The Great Gender Debate*, Paternoster, U.K.; Univ. New South Wales, Australia, 1999
_____, *The Search for Intimacy*, Eerdmans, 1995
_____, *What's Right with Feminism?*, Eerdmans, nd
Tenner, Edward, *Why Things Bite Back: Predicting the Problems of Progress*, Fourth Estate, 1996
Tournier, Paul, *The Meaning of Persons*, Harper & Row, 1982
_____, *The Whole Person in a Broken World*, Harper & Row, 1981
Van Leeuwan, Mary Stewart, *The Person in Psychology: A Contemporary Christian Appraisal*, Eerdmans, 1985
Volf, Miroslav, *Exclusion and Embrace: A Theological Exploration of Identity, Otherness, and Reconciliation*, Abingdon, 1996
Wink, Walter, *Engaging the Powers*, Fortress, 1992
Winter, Richard, *The Roots of Sorrow: Reflections on Depression and Hope*, Crossway, 1986
Zuidema, *Communication and Confrontation*, Wedge, 1972

ECONOMICS, MONEY

Beisner, Calvin E., *Prosperity and Poverty: The Compassionate Use of Resources in a World of Scarcity*, Crossway, nd
Cramp, *Notes Towards a Christian Critique of Secular Economic Theory*, Wedge, 1975
Ellul, Jacques, *Money and Power*, IVP, 1984
Goudzwaard, Bob (trans.), *Capitalism and Progress: A Diagnosis of Western Society*, Eerdmans, 1979
Kuyper, Abraham, *The Problem of Poverty*, Baker, 1991
Nash, Ronald, *Poverty and Wealth: The Christian Debate Over Capitalism*, Crossway, 1986
Neuhaus, Richard, *Doing Well and Doing Good: The Challenge to the Christian Capitalist*, Doubleday, 1992
Rifkin, Jeremy, *The Age of Access: How the Shift from Ownership to Access is Transforming Capitalism*, J.P. Tarcher, 2000
Sider, Ronald J., *Rich Christians in an Age of Hunger*, IVP, 1977
Storkey, Alan, *Transforming Economics*, SPCK, 1986
Schumacher, E.F., *Small is Beautiful: Economics As If People Mattered*, Harper & Row, 1976

EDUCATION

Aay, Heny, and Sander Grifioen (eds.), *Geography and Worldview: A Christian Reconnaissance*, Univ.

Press of America, 1998

Badley, Ken, *Worldviews: The Challenge of Choice*, 1996 (high school textbook, contact ICS Booklist, see above)

Bolt, John, *The Christian School and the Christian Story*, Christian Schools International, 1993

Blomberg, Doug, and Ian Lamber (eds.), *Reminding: Renewing the Mind in Learning*, Centre for the Study of Australian Christianity, 1998

Burtchaell, James, *The Dying of the Light: The Disengagement of Colleges and Universities from Their Christian Churches*, Eerdmans, nd

De Boer, Van Brummelen, et. al., *Educating Christian Teachers for Responsive Discipleship*, Univ. of America Press, 1993

Garber, Steven, *The Fabric of Faithfulness: Weaving Together Belief and Behavior During the University Years*, IVP, 1996

Greene, Albert E., *Reclaiming the Future of Christian Education: A Transforming Vision*, Assoc. of Christian Schools International, 1998

Heie, Harold, and David L. Wolfe (eds.), *The Reality of Christian Learning*, Eerdmans, 1987

Holmes, Arthur, *The Idea of a Christian College*, Eerdmans, 1975

Jones, Arthur, *Science in Faith: A Christian Perspective on Teaching Science*, np, nd

Lambert, Ian, and Suzanne Mitchell (eds.), *The Crumbling Walls of Certainty: Towards a Christian Critique of Postmodernity and Education*, Centre for the Study of Australian Christianity, 1997

Leeper, John, *The Brothers of the Sled*, Emerald House, 1996 (for children 7-13, several unique modern day fables, superbly illustrated in pen and ink by the author, with faith building lessons to help children face the "wilderness of the unbelieving world.")

_____, *The Riddle of the Outlaw Bear*, Emerald House, 1996 (same concept as above title.)

Lockerbie, Bruce, *A Passion for Learning: The History of Christian Thought on Education*, Moody Press, 1994

MacKenzie, Pamela, with Alison Farnell, Ann Holt, and David Smith, *Entry Points for Christian Reflection Within Education*, Care for Education (53 Romney St., London, SW1P 3RF), 1997

Marsden, George, *The Outrageous Idea of Christian Scholarship*, Oxford Univ. Press, 1997

_____, *The Soul of the American University*, Oxford Univ. Press, 1994

McCarthy, Rockne M., James Skillen, et. al., *Disestablishment a Second Time: Genuine Pluralism for America's Schools*, Books on Demand, nd

Melchert, Charles, *Wise teaching: Biblical Wisdom and Educational Ministry*, Trinity Press International, 1998

Oppewal, Donald (ed.), *Voices from the Past*, np, 1997 (20th century essays giving Reformed vision for Christian schooling at all levels)

Perks, Stephen C., *The Christian Philosophy of Education Explained*, Avant Books, 1992

Roques, Mark, *Curriculum Unmasked: Towards a Christian Understanding of Education*, np, 1989

_____, *The Good, The Bad and the Misled: True Stories Reflecting Different Worldviews for Use in Secondary Education*, Monarch, 1994

Schwehn, Mark, *Exiles from Eden: Religion and the Academic Vocation in America*, Oxford Univ. Press, 1993

Shortt, John, and Trevor Cooling, *Agenda for Educational Change*, Apollos, 1997

Smith, David, *The Gift of the Stranger: Faith, Hospitality, and Foreign Language Learning*, Eerdmans, 2000

Taylor, Jerome (trans.), *The Didascalicon of Hugh of St. Victor*, Columbia University Press, 1991 (medieval, but recommended by one person as the best book ever written on education from a christian worldview)

Runner, H. Evan, *The Relation of the Bible to Learning*, np, 1982

Sire, James W., *Chris Chrisman Goes to College: And Faces the Challenges of Relativism, Individualism and Pluralism*, IVP, 1993

Steensma, Geraldine, and Harro Van Brummelen (eds), *Shaping School Curriculum: A Biblical View*,

Signal Press, 1977

Van Brummelen, Harrow W., *Steppingstones to Curriculum: A Biblical Path*, Alta Vista College Press, 1994

_____, *Walking with God in the Classroom: Christian Approaches to Learning and Teaching*, Alta Vista College Press, 1990

Weaver, Richard, *Ideas Have Consequences*, Univ. of Chicago Press, 1948

Wilson, Douglas, *Recovering the Lost Tools of Learning: An Approach to Distinctively Christian Education*, Crossway, 1991

Wilson, Douglas (ed.), *Repairing the Ruins: The Classical and Christian Challenge to Modern Education*, Canon Press, 1996

Wilson, Edmond O., *Consilience: The Unity of Knowledge*, Random House, 1999

POLITICS, THE STATE

Budziszewski, J., *The Revenge of Conscience: Politics and the Fall of Man*, Spence, nd

Cromartie, Michael, *Caesar's Coin Revisited: Christians and the Limits of Government*, Eerdmans, 1996

Dooyeweerd, Herman, *The Christian Idea of the State*, Presbyterian & Reformed, 1967

Ellul, Jacques, *The Political Illusion*, Vintage, 1972

_____, *The Politics of God and the Politics of Man*, Eerdmans, 1972

Gedraitis, *Worship and Politics*, Wedge, 1972

Goudzwaard, Bob, *A Christian Political Option*, Wedge, 1972

Marshall, Paul, *Thine Is the Kingdom: A Biblical Perspective on Government and Politics Today*, Regent College, 1993

Mouw, R. J., *Politics and the Biblical Drama*, Baker, 1983

Nash, Ronald H., *Social Justice and the Christian Church*, Mott Media, 1983

Neuhaus, Richard, *The Naked Public Square: Religion and Democracy in America*, Eerdmans, 1984

Noll, Mark, *One Nation Under God? Christian Faith and Political Action In America*, Harper San Francisco, 1988

Noll, Mark, Nathan Hatch, and George Marsden, *The Search for Christian America*, (expanded edition), Helmers & Howard, 1989

Runner, Evan, *Scriptural Religion and Political Task*, Wedge, 1974

Skillen, James, *Recharging the American Experiment: Principled Pluralism for Genuine Civic Community*, Baker, 1994

_____, *The Scattered Voice: Christians at Odds in the Public Square*, Zondervan, 1991, or Center for Public Justice, 1996

Skillen, James, and Rockne McCarthy (eds.), *Political Order and the Plural Structure of Society*, Scholars Press (Atlanta), 1991

Taylor, Hebden, *The Christian Philosophy of Law, Politics, and the State*, np, nd, (hard to find)

Wolterstorff, Nicholas, *Until Justice and Peace Embrace*, Eerdmans, 1984

Yoder, John H., *The Politics of Jesus*, Eerdmans 1994

SCIENCE (INCLUDING PHYSICS), TECHNOLOGY

Barbour, Ian, *Issues in Science and Religion*, Harper & Row, 1971

Dooyeweerd, Herman, *Secularization of Science*, Christian Studies Center, 1954

Groothuis, Douglas, *The Soul in Cyber-Space*, Baker, 1997

Henry (ed.), *Horizons of Science*, Harper & Row, nd

Hooykaas, R., *Religion and the Rise of Modern Science*, Eerdmans, 1972

Kuhn, Thomas, *The Structure of Scientific Revolutions*, Univ. of Chicago, 1970

Lucas, Ernest, *Genesis Today: Genesis and the Questions of Science*, Scripture Union, 1989

MacKay, Donald, *The Clockwork Image: A Christian Perspective in Science*, IVP, 1974

Mitcham (ed.), *Theology and Technology: Essays*, Lanham, 1984

Pearcey, Nancy R., with Charles B. Thaxton, *The Soul of Science: Christian Faith and Natural*

Philosophy, Crossway, 1994

Polanyi, Michael, *Science, Faith and Society*, Univ. of Chicago Press, 1964

_____, *Personal Knowledge: Towards a Post-critical Philosophy*, Routledge & Kegan Paul, 1958

Schumacher, E.F., *Guide for the Perplexed*, Harper Collins, 1978

Schuurman, Egbert, *Technology and the Future*, Wedge, 1980

Schuurman, P., *Perspectives and Technology and Culture*, Dordt College Press, 1995

Stafleu, M.D., *Theories at Work: On the Structure and Functioning of Theories in Science, in Particular During the Copernican Revolution*, np, 1987

Stevens, *Patterns in Nature*, Little, Brown, & Co., 1974

Work & Play

Berryman, *Godly Play: A Religious Way of Education*, Harper San Francisco, 1991

Buber, Martin, *I and Thou*, Collier, 1987

Chesterton, G.K., *The Romance of Faith*, Doubleday, 1990

Chewing, Eby, & Roels, *Business Through the Eyes of Faith*, Harper San Francisco, 1990

Cox, Harvey, *The Feast of Fools: A Theological Essay on Feast and Festivity*, Harper & Row, SF, 1970

Diehl, William E., *The Monday Connection: A Spirituality of Competence, Affirmation, and Support in the Workplace*, Harper San Francisco, 1991

Frey, Bradshaw L., William Ingram, et. al, *At Work and Play*, Paideia Press, Ontario, 1986

Hays, Edward, *Holy Fools & Mad Hatters: A Handbook for Hobbyhorse Holiness*, Forest of Peace Books, Leavenworth, 1993

Heintzman, Paul, et. al. (eds.), *Christianity and Leisure: Issues in a Pluralistic Society*, Dordt, 1994

Huizinga, Johan, *Homo Ludens: A Study of the Play Element in Culture*, Routledge & Kegan Paul, 1908

Johnson, Paul, *The Christian at Play*, Eerdmans, 1983

Merton, Thomas, *New Seeds of Contemplation*, New Directions Books, NY, 1972

Midgley, Mary, *Science and Play*, Routledge, 2000

Miller, David, *Gods and Games: Toward a Theology of Play*, World Publishing, Cleveland, 1970

Novak, Michael, *Business as a Calling: Work and the Examined Life*, Free Press, 1996

Ryken, Leland, *Redeeming the Time: A Christian Approach to Work and Leisure*, Baker, 1995

Samra, Cal, *The Joyful Christ: The Healing Power of Humor*, Harper & Row, 1986

Saward, John, *Perfect Fools: Folly for Christ's Sake in Catholic and Orthodox Spirituality*, Oxford Univ. Press, 1980

Turner, Victor, *From Ritual to Theater: The Human Seriousness of Play*, PAJ Publications, NY, 1982

Subject & Name Index

A

abortion 5, 15, 16, 23, 85, 95, 96, 97, 242
Abraham 30, 87, 226, 300
absorbing wisdom 42, 50, 56, 63-68, 76, 174, 228, 265, 270, 273, 303, 306
accounting 14, 33, 39, 310
actions, relation to ideas 9, 50, 54-64, 211, 310, 313
activism 5, 6, 70, 169
actors 50, 253, 312
administrator 60
adultery 90, 97, 114, 115, 223, 225, 226
advertising 44, 64, 65, 66, 78, 246, 252, 254
aesthetics 26, 31, 44, 64, 134, 140, 146, 155, 157, 195, 238, 246, 247, 254, 257, 277, 288, 299, 305, 306, 308, 312, 314, 316, 319
Africa 69, 134
African medicine 63
agape 225-228
Age of Aquarius 17
agnostics 284
agriculture 93, 292, 313
Ahab 59, 60, 67, 79, 126
aims (see also, goals) 154, 200, 235
Alexander the Great 211
alienation 199, 290, 291
allegory 29, 30, 32, 33, 34, 39
Amalekites 128
amateur (see also, expert) 81, 170, 171, 182, 205, 295
amen 213
America 3, 10, 12, 15, 66, 111, 180, 233, 240, 252
American Family Association 86
Americans 57, 71, 79, 172, 242
amusement 64
analysis 42, 51, 74, 103, 104, 108, 123, 136, 148, 150, 156, 158, 160, 166, 167,

169, 171, 209, 218, 221, 237, 244, 254, 257, 287, 295, 303, 306, 311, 314, 315, 318, 319
Anglican 108
animal 69, 85, 103, 106, 113, 129, 137, 141, 143, 144, 146, 156, 158, 180, 185, 216, 238, 282, 294, 297, 315, 316, 317
animism 74, 105, 284
anomaly 183, 213
anthropology 279, 282
Aphraates 183
Aphrodite 287
Apocrypha 28
archetype 182, 184, 185, 186, 228
architect 77
architecture 64, 103, 125
Aries 287
Aristarchus 220
Aristotle 80, 155, 211
arithmetic 77, 305, 318
armament 125, 128
armed forces 242
armies 127
Arnold, Matthew 308
art 4, 8, 9, 11, 14-23, 28, 42, 45, 64, 127, 134-140, 150, 153, 162, 173, 174, 180, 191, 205, 243-258, 265, 276, 281, 286, 287, 294, 298, 300-302, 312-314, 318
artefacts 313
artificial insemination 160
artist 134, 135, 140, 246, 249, 250, 251, 253, 258
ascetic 258
Ashtoreth 27
Asia 79, 311
aspect (see also, dimensions, mode, secular lanes,) 7, 11, 18, 19, 23, 25, 31, 33, 37, 38, 44, 45, 59, 65, 97, 104, 117, 125, 130, 134-150, 155, 157, 167, 168, 170, 178, 186, 194, 195, 202, 204, 207, 209, 217, 218, 221, 223, 237, 238, 240, 243, 246, 248, 249, 254, 256, 257, 266, 274-281, 284, 288-297, 300, 301, 303-319
assumptions (see also, presuppositions) 6, 16, 38, 42, 49, 53-61, 64, 67-73, 76, 78, 88, 168, 169, 174, 195, 212, 220, 221, 253, 275, 276, 279, 286, 308, 314, 319
astro-physicists 295

astronomers 205
AT&T 70
atheists 18
atoms 297
attitudes 5, 10, 12, 39, 42, 54, 57, 61, 66-68, 75-78, 98, 153, 160, 193, 197, 220, 226, 236, 272, 281, 314
Augustine 8, 39
authority 21, 24, 25, 27, 30, 31, 34, 35, 40, 58, 63, 66, 87, 88, 101, 102, 105, 113, 114, 158, 167, 170, 179, 180, 185-187, 196, 210, 217, 223, 231, 234, 240-242, 248, 267, 274, 279, 281-289, 301, 304, 309, 318, 319
authors 4, 5, 8, 9, 18, 130, 141, 153, 269, 279, 295, 303, 307, 312
auto mechanics 14
automotive 57

B

baal 59, 60, 80, 81, 128, 287
Baal-Asherah 287
Babylon 27, 30, 35
Bacchus 287
Bach 15, 267
Bacon, Francis 155
bad language 92
ballet 247
Bangladesh 6
bankruptcy 68, 107
banks 16, 307, 313
baptism 39
basic elements 24, 77, 165, 239, 276
basic ingredients 24, 77, 165-167
basic principles 40, 240, 271, 282
basic questions (see also, radical questions) 159, 166, 168, 181, 228, 237, 275-282, 300, 304
Beatles, the 15
Beats, the 16
beauty 28, 51, 55, 75, 155, 184, 190, 208, 295
Beckett 15
behavior, relation to beliefs, ideas (see also, actions) 18, 50, 51, 52, 56, 58, 61, 64, 86, 97, 106, 163, 173, 184, 211, 230, 242, 264, 274, 281, 282, 286, 288, 298, 306, 308, 316

Scripture References Index

Wherever a parenthetical number, e.g. (2), appears after a verse below, it indicates that the verse appeared that number of times, e.g. twice, in that book chapter. Note also that some references appear in more than one chapter. A number in the list that appears without a verse, or verses, listed after it is a reference to the entire chapter of a particular Bible book, e.g., Lev. 13.

Chapter 3
Lev. 13
Deut. 6:4; 7:22; 10; 11; 15:18; 16:19; 17:13; 17:17;
19:3-7; 20:19; 22:6; 22:9; 23:1-14
Esther 4:4; 4:11; 4:14-16; 6:1; 6:13; 8:17; 9:16-26
1 Sam. 28:13
1 Kings 11:33; 20:28
Job 1:1; 4:27
Psalms 8:5; 82:6
Prov. 16:24; 17:8; 17:15; 19:3; 19:5; 19:9; 19:12;
19:17; 20:14; 20:15; 21:13; 23:1-3; 24:11-12;
24:33-34; 25:6-10; 25:11; 25:25
Heb. 9:23; 12; 13

Chapter 4
Exod. 6:3
Deut. 19:15; 25:4
I Kings 3:28; 4:22
Psalms 49
Prov. 1–8; 1:7; 22:20-21
Eccl. 12:13
Luke 19:11
Acts 6; 15; 15:15; 15:29; 21:25
Rom. 13
1 Cor. 1:24; 9:9; 10:6
2 Cor. 13:1
Gal. 1:6-9
Phil. 2:1-8
1 Tim. 5; 5:19
James 3:15-17
Col. 2:8; 3:2
2 Peter 3:15-16

Chapter 5
1 Kings 21
Psalms 104:24
Prov. 8:22-36
Jer. 10:12
Acts 26:9
1 Cor. 1:18; 1:20-21; 1:23-24; 1:24(2); 30; 2:1;
2:4-5; 2:6-8; 13
Phil. 2:1-11

Chapter 7
Gen. 1:26; 2:15
Dan. 2:28; 3:2
Rom. 12:1-2
1 Cor. 3:1-3
Gal. 3:1-3
Col. 2:20–3:2

Chapter 8
Gen. 9:5
Lev. 20:10
Deut. 22:22
Eccl. 5:5
Amos 1:6-10; 1:11; 2:1-3; 2:6
Mal. 2
Matt. 5:17; 5:33
Mark 2:23-27; 10:9-11
John 20:19
Acts 20:17
Rom. 13:9
Heb. 3; 4; 4:8-9
James 5:12

About the Authors

John Peck is a philosopher, theologian, author, pastor, and itinerant teacher. He is a co-founder and Head of Staff for College House (Cambridge, England), which offers courses leading to the Cambridge Diploma in Religious Studies and conducts seminars on ways to make christian philosophy relevant to every area of life. He is also a co-founder and past Executive Director of the influential Greenbelt Arts Festivals (England). He is an advisor and lecturer for christian organizations in several nations, including: Trinity House Theatre and Arts (Livonia, Michigan), where he was scholar-in-residence for a year (Staley Lecturer); "The Christian Arts Seminar" (Rotterdam, The Netherlands); "The Kuyper Foundation" (U.K.). He was senior lecturer for many years at the Bible Training Institute (Glasgow, Scotland; now "International Christian College"); first chairman of Open Bible College; and itinerant lecturer to the Institute for Christian Studies (Toronto). Peck has also served as a consultant for the Cambridge-area National Health Service. He teaches Hebrew and Greek and is a contributor to numerous magazines, periodicals, and radio programs. He travels in the U.S. and Europe lecturing and conducting seminars and working with churches and organizations in various contexts that explore ways to apply biblical wisdom in every area of life. His previous books are *What the Bible Teaches about the Holy Spirt* (Tyndale House) and *Wisdom in the Marketplace* (Greenbelt Files). He and his late wife, Hanna, raised five biological and forty foster children. He lives in Suffolk, England. Email: John.R.Peck@care4free.net

Charles Strohmer is the author of several books and numerous magazine articles. He is also a minister, itinerant lecturer, freelance editor, and founder of The Living Wisdom Center, The Thursday Club, and the quarterly magazine *Openings: Alternative Christian Approaches*. He has a special interest in the type of communication that takes the reach of biblical wisdom into all areas of everyday life. When he is not writing or editing books, he travels in the U.S. and the U.K. running seminars and workshops. In the late 1970s, he studied the works of Francis Schaeffer and other L'Abri writers. He met John Peck in 1983 and soon came under Peck's informal but significant tutoring. Raised in the American Midwest, he lived in Scotland for a number of years where his wife, Linda, was a missionary who helped to establish the Wee Friends christian pre-school in Paisley. Strohmer's previous books are: *What Your Horoscope Doesn't Tell You* (Tyndale House, U.S.; Word Books, U.K.); *Explaining the Grace of God* (Sovereign World); *Wise as a Serpent, Harmless as a Dove* (Word Books, U.K. only); *The Gospel and the New Spirituality* (Thomas Nelson, U.S. only); *Building Bridges to the New Age World* (CPAS, U.K. only); *America's Fascination with Astrology* (Emerald House). He and his wife now live near the Great Smoky Mountains, Tennessee. Email: livewise@esper.com